CONFRONTING PE[

This monograph considers the correlation between the relative success of retributive penal policies in English-speaking liberal democracies since the 1970s, and the practical evidence of increasingly excessive reliance on the penal State in those jurisdictions.

It sets out three key arguments. First, that increasingly excessive conditions in England and Wales over the last three decades represent a failure of retributive theory. Second, that the penal minimalist cause cannot do without retributive proportionality, at least in comparison to the limiting principles espoused by rehabilitation, restorative justice and penal abolitionism. Third, that another retributivism is therefore necessary if we are to confront penal excess. The monograph offers a sketch of this new approach, 'late retributivism', as both a theory of punishment and of minimalist political action, within a democratic society.

Centrally, criminal punishment is approached as both a political act and a policy choice. Consequently, penal theorists must take account of contemporary political contexts in designing and advocating for their theories. Although this inquiry focuses primarily on England and Wales, its models of retributivism and of academic contribution to democratic penal policy-making are relevant to other jurisdictions, too.

Confronting Penal Excess

Retribution and the Politics of Penal Minimalism

David Hayes

•HART•
OXFORD • LONDON • NEW YORK • NEW DELHI • SYDNEY

HART PUBLISHING
Bloomsbury Publishing Plc
Kemp House, Chawley Park, Cumnor Hill, Oxford, OX2 9PH, UK
1385 Broadway, New York, NY 10018, USA
29 Earlsfort Terrace, Dublin 2, Ireland

HART PUBLISHING, the Hart/Stag logo, BLOOMSBURY and the Diana logo are
trademarks of Bloomsbury Publishing Plc
First published in Great Britain 2019

First published in hardback, 2019
Paperback edition, 2021

A catalogue record for this book is available from the British Library.

ISBN: HB: 978-1-50991-797-6
PB: 978-1-50995-213-7
ePDF: 978-1-50991-799-0
ePub: 978-1-50991-798-3

Typeset by Compuscript Ltd, Shannon

ACKNOWLEDGEMENTS

This book has had a simultaneously very long and very short genesis. Very long because I have been thinking about the ideas that it contains, in one form or another, since my PhD studies at the University of Nottingham. Very short because virtually all of the words that follow were written between 1 May 2018 and 31 March 2019, as a lecturer at the University of Sheffield. For those of you thinking of working on long writing projects of your own, this is a terrible idea and I don't recommend it. But as a result, I have a great many people to thank for the contributions they have made to this project, which have substantially enriched it.

In particular, Christopher Bennett, Fergus McNeill, and Gwen Robinson provided incisive critiques of individual chapters, helping to improve the clarity and quality of the argument throughout. Gwen Robinson, Mark Brown, and Rob Canton also looked at the overall argument of the book and helped to ensure the chapters hung together cohesively.

At Hart, Bill Asquith supported my initial proposal and helped me to refine this book's title into something a bit more meaningful to the prospective reader. Rosamund Jubber and Kate Whetter supported publication through to completion, and organised its cover design. All three were extremely supportive and accommodating to a first-time monograph author. I don't think I could have asked for better support throughout the process.

More generally, I owe a many number of people thanks for acting as sounding-boards, helping me to work through structural issues, and generally assisting in an informal manner with the intellectual process of putting this tangled mess of theory into some sort of order. I am particularly grateful to: Beatrice Anderson; Cormac Behan; Russell Buchan; Cerys Gibson; Nicholas, Megan, and Sam Hayes; Richard Kirkham; Yin Harn Lee; Tara Lai Quinlan; Paul Roberts; Christy and Marc Shucksmith-Wesley; Ruth Smart; Oisín Suttle; David Thompson; Philippa Tomczak; Joseph Tomlinson; and Dimitrios Tsarapatsanis. All errors and failings – of intellect, skill, conscience, and nerve – remain my own.

TABLE OF CONTENTS

PART II
PURSUING PENAL MINIMALISM

PART III
CONFRONTING PENAL EXCESS

LIST OF TABLES AND FIGURES

Introduction: The Politics of Penal Minimalism

I. The Pursuit of the Minimal Penal State in an Age of Excess

The ideal of penal minimalism, that criminal punishment should be applied to as few people as possible, as harmlessly as possible, is entrenched in both criminal and penal theory. Criminal punishment is both a politically popular institution and a morally intuitive response to criminal wrongdoing.[1] However, it also involves the imposition of both an extreme formal condemnation and of the delivery of (psychological, emotional, and indeed sometimes physical) pain to its subjects.[2] There are a number of reasons why penal minimalism might be preferred: in the defence of individual freedoms from a potentially authoritarian State;[3] out of humane concern for the subjects of punishment; or because overly harsh treatment reduces the effectiveness of punishment at achieving its aims.[4]

In short, the pursuit of penal minimalism enjoys widespread academic support. However, the academic literature is equally unified in observing that modern penal systems are anything but minimalist in the actual imposition of punishment.[5]

[1] See, eg, Paul Robinson, *Intuitions of Justice and the Utility of Desert* (2013, Oxford University Press); Rob Canton, 'Crime, Punishment and the Moral Emotions: Righteous Minds and their Attitudes towards Punishment' (2015) 17 *Punishment and Society* 54.

[2] On the concept of pain delivery, see Nils Christie, *Limits to Pain: The Role of Punishment in Penal Policy* (1982, Martin Robinson), especially pp 9–11 and 19.

[3] Throughout this book I capitalise the word "State" when referring to a central political organisation responsible for criminal justice, to underline the essential power imbalance between State and citizen in even a liberal political community, and thereby, the tensions at the heart of the 'problem of punishment'.

[4] See, eg, Stanley Cohen, *Visions of Social Control: Crime, Punishment, and Classification* (1985, Polity), pp 127–139; Michael Tonry, 'Proportionality, Parsimony, and the Interchangeability of Punishments', in: RA Duff, Sandra Marshall, Rebecca Dobash, and Russell Dobash (eds), *Penal Theory and Practice: Tradition and Innovation in Criminal Justice* (1994, Manchester University Press); Doug Husak, *Overcriminalization: The Limits of the Criminal Law* (2008, Oxford University Press); Ian Loader, 'For Penal Moderation: Notes towards a Public Philosophy of Punishment' (2010) 14 *Theoretical Criminology* 349; AP Simester and Andreas von Hirsch, *Crimes, Harms, and Wrongs: On the Principles of Criminalisation* (2014, Hart), pp 19–32; and Nicola Lacey and Hanna Pickard, 'The Chimera of Proportionality: Institutionalising Limits on Punishment in Contemporary Social and Political Systems' (2015) 78 *MLR* 216.

[5] See generally ch 2, below.

In other words, although scholars generally agree in theory that penal minimalism is worth defending as a principle in the arrangement of criminal justice, that theory has not translated into practice. This book examines why this is the case, from the perspective of penal theory and philosophy, and considers what penal theorists who value penal minimalism should do to try to remedy contemporary penal excess, in the specific context of England and Wales. It argues that retributive theories, in particular, have failed to deliver on the political promise that they can restrain the penal State.[6] Although it ultimately defends retributivism as a potential tool for penal minimalists, this book concludes that a substantially altered, 'late' retributivism is needed if we are to make penal restraint a core feature of our theoretical approach. In this, it attempts to seriously consider, in political terms, a foundational issue in penal theory: the 'problem of punishment'.

II. The 'Problem of Punishment'

Societies have punished criminal offences (or their analogues) for millennia, and some of our oldest ideas about what punishment is and why it might be an acceptable State practice predate almost every tenet of modern political philosophy. For instance, the retributive ideal of proportionate punishment comes to England and Wales via the Judeo-Christian *lex talionis*, which in turn draws upon the ancient Babylonian Code of Hammurabi.[7] Moreover, the criminal justice system of a jurisdiction such as England and Wales substantially predates the modern, post-Enlightenment modes of thought that condition current thinking about what the State may and may not do to its citizens, and what the State should allow its citizens to do to themselves and one another. I do not think it problematic to assume that the average citizen of England and Wales supports the existence of the criminal justice system, but also opposes the sort of authoritarian, intrusive government that characterised its imperial and feudal past. Anglo-Welsh history is one of slow reform towards democratic self-governance, rather than wholesale revolution. As a result, its institutions are a hodgepodge of new innovations, reformed (or reforming) vestiges of bygone eras, and old wine surviving in new bottles.[8]

The pre-modern origin of at least some contemporary penal theories and practices helps to explain the significance of 'the problem of punishment'.[9] This issue reflects a central tension at the heart of post-Enlightenment Western societies. These polities tend to view themselves in broadly *liberal* terms: that is, they share

[6] On the 'penal State', see David Garland, 'Penality and the Penal State' (2013) 51 *Criminology* 475.

[7] Michael Fish, 'An Eye for an Eye? Proportionality as a Moral Principle of Punishment' (2008) 28 *OJLS* 57, 58–62.

[8] For a critical view of glacial British reformism, see Thomas Paine, *Rights of Man, Common Sense, and Other Political Writings* (1995, Mark Philp (ed), Oxford University Press).

[9] See generally David Boonin, *The Problem of Punishment: A Critical Introduction* (2008, Cambridge University Press), ch 1.

a commitment to protecting and enabling the freedoms of the citizen to at least some extent.[10] On a liberal account, respect for individuals' moral autonomy – their capacity to make up their own mind and pursue their own desires – is central to what State governance ought to pursue.[11] The many strains of liberal theory are therefore united by a belief in the maxim that 'the best government is that which governs least'.[12] The State should, wherever possible, let citizens decide how to live their lives, and only intervene where necessary to preserve the ability of *all* citizens to pursue their own autonomous wishes.[13]

In a liberal political community (or 'polity'), then, the problem of punishment is that criminal justice stands in apparent tension with liberal values. The problem is twofold. Firstly, we allow the systematic imposition of coercive, harmful, and painful non-freedom on our fellow-citizens, to whose liberty and autonomy we owe a duty of respect. Secondly, it is a particular problem that we allow the State, as an immensely powerful socio-political actor claiming a monopoly on the legitimate use of force, and as an institution with an historical track record of authoritarian brutality, to impose those conditions. In short, it means allowing the State to do what it otherwise should not be able to do, on the basis of a breach of the criminal law (designed, mind you, by that State).[14] Thus the problem of punishment tells us that if we want to continue punishing offenders, in fidelity with the values of our liberal polity, then we must maintain a level of scepticism and discomfort about the infliction of pain even on those whose conduct is clearly morally reprehensible.[15] We must also have a *justification* for acting in a way that seems at first blush to be in tension with our shared socio-political aims.

A. The Problem of Punishment in Penal Theory

The justification of criminal punishment as a moral and social practice might seem intuitively obvious, given that the offender has done something wrongful and blameworthy. However, it is the task of penal philosophers to look beyond this intuition – to challenge ourselves to answer why, whether, and to what extent we can justify harming those who have committed (harmful) wrongs against others. Broadly speaking, (Western) penal philosophers have advanced three broad families

[10] See generally Nicola Lacey, 'Punishment, (Neo)Liberalism, and Social Democracy', in Jonathan Simon and Richard Sparks (eds), *The SAGE Handbook of Punishment and Society* (2013, SAGE), pp 264–267.

[11] See generally Joseph Raz, *The Morality of Freedom* (1986, Oxford University Press).

[12] John O'Sullivan, 'Introduction' (1837) 1 *The United States Magazine and Democratic Review* 1, 6.

[13] See, eg, Dan Markel, 'Are Shaming Punishments Beautifully Retributive? Retributivism and the Implications for the Alternative Sanctions Debate' (2001) 54 *Vanderbilt Law Review* 2157, 2194–2196.

[14] See Victor Tadros, *The Ends of Harm: The Moral Foundations of Criminal Law* (2011, Oxford University Press), p 1; Boonin, *The Problem of Punishment*, above n 9, p 1.

[15] Compare Barbara Hudson, *Justice in the Risk Society: Challenging and Re-Affirming Justice in Late Modernity* (2003, SAGE), pp 3–39.

of responses to these questions: *intrinsic-value* justifications, *consequentialist* justifications, and more *radical* reactions.

Intrinsic-value approaches, as the name suggests, seek to justify criminal punishment on the grounds that the act of punishment is *valuable in itself*.[16] In other words, we can (and on some accounts must) punish crimes because doing so is morally good in its own right. The most common cluster of intrinsic-value theories is *retributivism*. Retributivists assert that punishment is good because criminal wrongdoing *deserves* some sort of punitive response. Although there are many variations on this basic theme, retributive theories are united by the principle of *proportionality*, that is, by the idea that the severity of the punishment deserved (and therefore imposed) ought to reflect the wrong done. In short, punishment is good, but only if it fits the crime.[17]

By contrast, from a consequentialist perspective punishment is inherently wrongful, but is nevertheless defensible so long as the end justifies the means by achieving a greater overall public good. The three most significant consequentialist justifications are: *deterrence*, which views punishment as justified if it prevents future offending through the threat of unpleasant consequences for law-breakers; *incapacitation*, which justifies punishment if it physically prevents offenders from committing further offences; and *rehabilitation*, which (usually) argues that punishment is justified if (and only if) it reduces reoffending by addressing the factors that cause the offender to commit crimes.[18] Consequentialist justifications treat punishment as an instrument of social policy, rather than an especially important site of moral activity.[19] While they vary widely in their approach to crime and how to deal with it, consequentialist theories are united by a tendency to treat the problem of punishment as a necessary evil, and to produce instrumental and empirically testable grounds for justifying penal interventions in actual practice.

The third family of penal philosophies in response to the problem of punishment are more radical, rejecting the status quo to at least some extent. This broad church includes, firstly, *penal abolitionism*, which argues that punishment is straightforwardly indefensible. Abolitionists vary in terms of what sort of punishment they wish to abolish: the punishment of certain groups of offenders;[20] certain forms of punishment;[21] or indeed, altogether, in any of its forms and contexts.[22]

[16] See generally Leo Zaibert, *Rethinking Punishment* (2016, Oxford University Press), ch 2.

[17] See generally Andrew von Hirsch and Andrew Ashworth, *Proportionate Sentencing: Exploring the Principles* (2005, Oxford University Press).

[18] See generally Michael Cavadino, James Dignan, and George Mair, *The Penal System: An Introduction*, Fifth edn (2013, SAGE), pp 33–41. See also ch 4, below.

[19] Compare Barbara Hudson, *Penal Policy and Social Justice* (1993, Macmillan).

[20] See, eg, Edwin Schur, *Radical Non-Intervention: Rethinking the Delinquency Problem* (1973, Prentice-Hall).

[21] See, eg, Mick Ryan and Tony Ward, 'Prison Abolitionism in the UK: They Dare Not Speak its Name?' (2015) 41 *Social Justice* 107; David Garland, *Peculiar Institution: America's Death Penalty in an Age of Abolition* (2011, Harvard University Press).

[22] See generally Vincenzo Ruggiero, *Penal Abolitionism* (2010, Oxford University Press).

A second radical response to the problem of punishment is the *restorative justice* movement, which rejects conventional criminal justice in favour of processes centred on resolving the conflict represented by the crime instead of confecting a dispute between offender and State.[23] On this account, crimes ought to be handled by some coming together of victims and offenders (and potentially, other stakeholders) to find a mutually agreeable solution. The extent to which restorative justice is compatible with the conventional mode of State prosecution, conviction and punishment is controversial,[24] but even if those ideals were incorporated into a 'conventional' system of criminal justice, it would require profound institutional change.[25]

This list is not intended to be exhaustive of actual or possible solutions to the problem of punishment, or to suggest that these positions are mutually exclusive of one another. Indeed, in practice sentencing and penal enforcement regimes tend to pursue multiple purposes in tandem.[26] Instead it shows the diversity of possible philosophical responses. Which of these approaches we favour, overall or in particular circumstances, will depend upon a variety of factors, not least our views of society, human nature, and ethics. In other words, the problem of punishment is not only philosophical, but also inherently *political.*

B. The Politics of the Problem of Punishment

Our choice of penal theoretical perspective, and the extent to which we put those theories into penal practice, is intimately political. But the problem of punishment is also political in a broader sense, in that the nature of the problem of punishment is to at least some extent defined by the kind of political organisation in which criminal punishments are imposed. The problem of punishment would exist in twenty-first century England and Wales, Ming China,[27] and in a futuristic utopia.[28] However, the solutions that would make sense in each of these places and times would differ considerably, since each system imposes different expectations upon the State. Given, as we shall see, that England and Wales (and the wider UK) at least claims to be a liberal democracy, the precise problem of punishment it faces

[23] Nils Christie, 'Conflicts as Property' (1977) 17 *British Journal of Criminology* 1; see also Daniela Bolívar, Inge Vanfraechem, and Ivo Aertsen, 'General Introduction', in: Inge Vanfraechem, Daniela Bolívar, and Ivo Aertsen (eds), *Victims and Restorative Justice* (2015, Routledge).

[24] See generally Andrew von Hirsch et al (eds), *Restorative Justice and Criminal Justice: Competing or Reconcilable Paradigms?* (2003, Hart).

[25] See, eg, RA Duff, 'Probation, Punishment and Restorative Justice: Should Altruism Be Engaged in Punishment?' (2003) 42 *Howard Journal of Criminal Justice* 181, especially pp 183–189.

[26] See, eg, the Criminal Justice Act 2003, ss 142–142A.

[27] See, eg, Jiang Yonglin (trans), *The Great Ming Code: Da Ming Lü* (2005, University of Washington Press).

[28] Assuming that such a utopia even imposed criminal punishments: see Vincenzo Ruggiero, 'Crime and Punishment in Classical and Libertarian Utopias' (2013) 52 *Howard Journal of Crime and Justice* 414.

is that it treats liberal subjects, whose freedoms are of principal importance within a liberal penal order, in illiberal-seeming ways.

Indeed, concern with limiting the penal State's ability to interfere with individual autonomy has been a major feature of recent Anglo-Welsh penal policy. For much of the twentieth century there was broad political and academic agreement about how to structure the criminal justice system, on both sides of the Atlantic. This orthodoxy favoured a 'treatment' paradigm based around psycho-medical rehabilitation. At the same time, broad statutory maximum sentences, combined with flexible judicial discretion was broadly trusted to come up with individual sentences that were relatively fair and achieved the prospective purposes of sentence. This consensus was shattered over the course of the 1970s and 1980s, during the so-called 'decline of the rehabilitative ideal'.[29] This phase was partly motivated by waning faith in the ability of existing rehabilitative methods to show empirically that they were reducing reoffending (and therefore achieving the consequential aim that justified their existence).[30] However, it was also driven by a general concern that treatment-based rehabilitation produced undesirable consequences, including: a tendency to perceive crime from the mostly middle-class perspective of policy-makers and experts, which tended to encourage an over-simplistic account of crime that treated it as being caused exclusively by 'deficiencies of the individual and his upbringing'; and, significantly, a concern that rehabilitative values tended to produce disproportionate sentences in policy and practice.[31]

This latter point about (dis)proportionality is a common defence of retributivism.[32] Although retribution appears to rest on a misanthropic claim that human suffering is (sometimes) intrinsically desirable, in practice retributivists impose upper limits on penal suffering though the principle of proportionality. By contrast, in a purely reductivist system, the success of the penal system is measured only by its ability to reduce crime, and that end justifies any means. Rehabilitation came to be associated (especially in the United States) with lengthy, indeterminate sentences where the duration of punishment depended not upon the nature of one's wrongdoing, but on how long it took to 'fix' you. The decline of the rehabilitative ideal was therefore partly driven by a desire for penal minimalism. Constraint was needed to avoid the excesses of both purely vengeful and purely treatment-focussed approaches.[33] As a result, in England and Wales, penal rehabilitation

[29] See, eg, AE Bottoms, 'An Introduction to "The Coming Crisis"', in: AE Bottoms and RH Preston (eds), *The Coming Penal Crisis: A Criminological and Theological Exploration* (1980, Scottish Academic Press), pp 1–2; Peter Raynor and Maurice Vanstone, 'Towards a Correctional Service', in Loraine Gelsthorpe and Rod Morgan (eds), *Handbook on Probation* (2007, Willan), pp 62–68.

[30] See, eg, George Mair, 'The Origins of What Works in England and Wales: A House Built on Sand?', in: George Mair (ed), *What Matters in Probation?* (2004, Willan), pp 14–15.

[31] See, eg, American Friends Service Committee, *Struggle for Justice* (1971, Hill and Wang), p 12; Bottoms, above n 29, pp 2–4.

[32] See, eg, Cavadino, Dignan and Mair, above n 18, pp 41–42.

[33] Compare Cohen, above n 4, pp 127–139.

was increasingly marginalised in the 1980s and early 1990s, although it was never completely abandoned.[34] During this period, retributive ideals (particularly as expressed in the censure-based 'desert model') were an obvious alternative: they professed to achieve minimal, proportionate sentences, and to provide moral justifications for penal institutions without overly ambitious prospective aims. The desert model's rise culminated in the Criminal Justice Act 1991, which cemented the Anglo-Welsh system's move away from the rehabilitative ideal towards a more limited, rights-focussed 'Justice Model'.[35]

The political success of (desert-based) retributivism is particularly interesting because of the broad support that the desert model drew from across the political spectrum.[36] Penal minimalism was attractive across traditional political divides, uniting liberals and conservatives who were drawn in by the promise of proportionality as a means of constraining (but still ultimately justifying) the penal State. By radically reducing the ambitions of the penal State, the desert model seemed to offer a way to redirect political focus (and budgets) away from criminal justice, towards less coercive and stigmatising systems for preserving social order, such as education, social welfare, and job creation.[37] However, even on the most sympathetic reading of subsequent history, penal minimalists' hopes for the Justice Model were badly let down. Offender populations have skyrocketed, both in probation offices and in prisons, and especially after the War on Terror, criminal law and justice are ever more prominent features of everyday life in a securitised State. Moreover, criminal justice continues to disproportionately target the socially marginalised, in terms of race, class, and mental health. So something seems to have gone wrong in the three decades since the Criminal Justice Act 1991 adopted a strong commitment to proportionality. Far from achieving penal minimalism, the current era is characterised by penal *excess*.

Given the correlation between this excess and the rise of (desert-based) retributivism, a fairly common charge has been that retributive penal policies have *caused* penal growth over the last three decades. In effect, the claim is that the retributivism of the Justice Model *could not prevent*, and perhaps even *actively encouraged*, penal expansion.[38] These failures might have been political, in that retributivism was unable to entrench itself deeply enough into penal politics, and

[34] See generally Fergus McNeill, 'A Desistance Paradigm for Offender Management' (2006) 6 *Criminology and Criminal Justice* 39; Gwen Robinson, 'Late-Modern Rehabilitation: The Evolution of a Penal Strategy' (2008) 10 *Punishment and Society* 429.

[35] See generally Andrew von Hirsch, *Doing Justice: The Choice of Punishments* (1976, Hill and Wang); Barbara Hudson, *Justice through Punishment: A Critique of the 'Justice' Model of Corrections* (1987, Macmillan Education).

[36] See Cohen, above n 4, pp 128–130.

[37] Compare Cohen, above n 4, pp 116–155; David Garland, *The Culture of Control: Crime and Social Order in Contemporary Society* (2001, Oxford University Press), pp 55–63.

[38] See especially Hudson, *Justice through Punishment*, above n 35, pp 162–170; Cohen, above n 4, pp 245–254; Garland, *The Culture of Control*, above n 37, pp 75–102; Lacey and Pickard, above n 4; and Nicola Lacey, 'The Metaphor of Proportionality' (2016) 43 *Journal of Law and Society* 27.

was discarded in favour of the policies that drove increasing penal excess. They might also have been theoretical – an inbuilt and far more fundamental problem in the reasoning that suggested that retribution could constrain the penal State.[39] This book explores and responds to these charges – arguing, in brief, that retributivism *did* fail to prevent penal excess, but that it is a necessary feature of the pursuit of penal minimalism in contemporary English criminal law and justice, although it requires substantial reform before it can meaningfully confront penal excess. While previous accounts of retributivism's link to penal minimalism have seen this as a side-benefit of deserved, proportionate punishments, justified in the abstract, this book turns that association on its head, arguing for a retributivism that *actively pursues* penal minimalism and constitutes merely a theory of political action in pursuit of that end. It therefore takes retributivism in a new direction, dismissing its contemporary defenders but also ultimately rejecting those who decry retribution as an insufficient sop to mere vengeance.

III. The Structure of this Book

This book is divided into three parts. Part I considers the allegation that contemporary penal excess represents a failure of retributivism, over three chapters. Chapter 1 considers the concept of 'penal excess', outlining the key features of what it would mean for a liberal-democratic State to rely on criminal punishment too much. In particular, it argues that a liberal democracy should pursue a strong conception of penal *minimalism* as a public good in its own right.

This discussion yields two spatial metaphors to map out the concept of penal excess in a liberal democracy: the *size* and *shape* of the penal State. Chapter 2 uses these dimensions to explore academic critique across various fields and disciplines, establishing connections between them to identify the extent to which penal excess *is* prevalent in contemporary England and Wales. It concludes that there is evidence that penal excess has been prevalent over the last three decades, and indeed, has become worse, in terms of both the size and shape of the penal State.

Chapter 3 then considers the extent to which this penal excess indicates a *failure* of retributive penal theory in general, and the desert model in particular. The retributive claim that proportionality limits penal excess is explored, and three major critiques of that claim are evaluated. While none of these critiques indicates a fundamental *theoretical* failure of the claim that (retributive) proportionality constrains the penal State, they correctly identify a range of *political* failures of retributive theory in practice. Retributivism *has* therefore at least played a role in worsening Anglo-Welsh penal excess, if only because it could not resist its political rise.

[39] Compare Michael Tonry, 'Can Twenty-First Century Punishment Policies Be Justified in Practice?' in Michael Tonry (ed), *Retributivism has a Past: Has it a Future?* (2011, Oxford University Press).

In the light of that failure, we ought to consider whether it is worth giving retributivism another chance. That is the purpose of Part II, which consists of two chapters. Chapter 4 considers three competing theories, to which disenchanted penal minimalists appear to have turned since the 1990s: a resurgent *rehabilitation*; *restorative justice*; and *penal abolitionism*. Although there are good reasons to think that the latter two could produce less excessive penal States, both can only do so to the extent that they are accompanied by more-or-less radical social change, which raises the question of what to do in the meantime to pursue penal minimalism.

In the absence of any clear, short-term alternative, Chapter 5 then considers proportionality as a limiting principle in its own right, in comparison to four other limiting factors proposed by penal theorists: parsimony; mercy; respect for human dignity; and solidarity. It concludes that each limiting principle offers something for the penal minimalist, but that proportionality is particularly well-placed as a guiding principle around which to deploy the others. Accordingly, there must be some role for retributive (or at least proportionality-based) theories in the short- and medium-term pursuit of penal minimalism. It is worth giving retributivism another chance at confronting penal excess – provided we learn from its earlier failures.

Reconfiguring retributivism in the light of those failures is the task of the three chapters in Part III. Chapter 6 lays down the groundwork of this 'late' retributivism (so-called because of the need to see it as a temporary compromise position that has its own irrelevance as its ultimate aim), and in particular, argues for a 'thrown' approach to penal theory as a rationale for principled political action under imperfect penal conditions, rather than for abstract institutional justifications.

From this base, Chapter 7 then proposes four essential features that this 'late' retributivism would need to possess: social awareness; political outspokenness; basis on an intersubjective measurement of penal severity; and, fundamentally, *self-deprecation*. Each of these characteristics distinguishes late retributivism from more orthodox approaches to retributive theory, and highlight ways in which a late retributivist theorist should interact with theorists from other traditions and with other policy agendas in the pursuit of penal minimalism.

The book ends, in Chapter 8, with an overall summary of its themes, arguing against the punitiveness and managerialism of recent penal policy, and for a radical reimagining of what we want the penal State to be. Ultimately, the critics of retributivism are right that proportionate sentencing alone is not enough to resist penal excess. It, and the underlying socio-political and cultural factors that drive it, require active political confrontation. But by the same token, retributivism can contribute something unique, and uniquely valuable, to that confrontation, which other penal theories fail to deliver. In drawing out the best features of orthodox retributive thinking and re-evaluating retributive theory's weaknesses, the late retributive approach offers at least better odds of defending penal minimalism as a liberal and democratic public good.

PART I

Defining Penal Excess

1

Penal Excess and Penal Minimalism

If the criminological literature on punishment over the last few decades is united by one theme, it is that things have gone badly wrong in the criminal justice system, in a number of ways.[1] In this book I argue that a number of the problems identified in the literature can be understood as part of a wider complaint about 'penal excess' – that the State is somehow using the penal system too much. To parse the concept of 'too much' punishment, however, we need to start with some groundwork, and that is the task of this chapter. Specifically, we must start with a *conceptual* grounding of the concept of penal excess, compared against the related concepts of penal *moderation* and penal *minimalism*. However, conceptual definition can only take us part of the way to a label that is helpful or applicable in the context of actual practices. We must also therefore develop a *political* grounding for our enquiry. Given the political nature of England and Wales as a (purported) liberal democracy, I argue that we should commit to a rather robust conception of penal minimalism as a public good, on the basis of fundamental liberal and democratic principles. This will imply an equally strict and demanding definition of penal excess. In particular, I advance two spatial metaphors about the penal State (*size* and *shape*) which we can then apply to specific phenomena in contemporary Anglo-Welsh criminal justice, in the next chapter.

I. Conceptual Foundations: Penal Excess, Moderation, and Minimalism

This is a book about 'penal excess' – excessive use of the penal system. But what exactly does 'excess' mean? When will a particular practice become 'excessive'? We should discuss these conceptual issues at quite a basic level, and in particular, consider how excess relates to the concepts of *moderation* and *minimalism*, as a

[1] See, eg, Stanley Cohen, *Visions of Social Control: Crime, Punishment, and Classification* (1985, Polity Press); David Garland, *The Culture of Control: Crime and Social Order in Contemporary Society* (2001, Oxford University Press); Jonathan Simon, *Governing through Crime: How the War on Crime Transformed American Democracy and Created a Culture of Fear* (2007, Oxford University Press); Nicola Lacey, *The Prisoners' Dilemma: Political Economy and Punishment in Contemporary Democracies* (2008, Cambridge University Press); and Loïc Wacquant, *Punishing the Poor: The Neoliberal Government of Social Insecurity* (2009, Duke University Press).

starting point for a more situated analysis. Since an 'excess' is something more than necessary, 'penal excess' must mean *too much punishment*. It follows that any definition of penal excess must involve taking a stance on *how much punishment is enough*. We could speak about this at a micro-level: it is possible to conceive of a single individual receiving *too much punishment* relative to our purposes in punishing them.[2] However, we shall see that the problems criminologists identify in relation to what I am calling penal excess are more macro-level; that is, they concern *too much reliance on punishment* across society as a whole; that we turn to it too quickly and too often, and that this causes a range of problems for society. It should be clear that any conception about this 'too much' must be socio-politically situated, because it is closely linked to the specific goals of the penal system, and indeed those of the State more generally. But we can begin to map out its features by comparing it to its conceptual opposites – *moderation* and *minimalism*.

Although the concepts of (penal) moderation and minimalism are sometimes used interchangeably,[3] their meanings are qualitatively different. Minimalism is about doing *strictly no more than is necessary* – the bare minimum, and no more. Moderation, by contrast, involves steering a course between extremes – not too much, but also not too little.[4] Minimalism represents an *absolute* account of action, in other words, whereas moderation is *relative* to the extremes being avoided. Moderation is somewhere in 'the middle' between too little (a *deficiency*) and too much (an *excess*), relative to the possible actions that may be taken. Minimalism, by contrast, is relative to the principles that guide how we should act, *ab initio*.

In practice, this distinction may not be particularly substantial. For instance, suppose that we have two statements about criminal punishment, A and B. Statement A argues that *we should burn anyone who commits a criminal offence at the stake until dead*, and Statement B posits that *we should never punish anyone for criminal wrongs, under any circumstances*. We are unlikely to view a position that falls midway between A and B as 'moderate' because we bring our presuppositions and expectations to the table when deciding which political statements are thinkable. Our conception of what is 'moderate' is unlikely to fall exactly halfway within the range of all possible responses to a problem, because only some of those responses will be socio-politically and -culturally acceptable in the place and time we are making the relevant decision in. Our frame of reference will not be solely

[2] See, eg, Dirk van Zyl Smit and Andrew Ashworth, 'Disproportionate Sentences as Human Rights Violations' (2004) 67 *MLR* 541.

[3] See especially Jonathan Simon, 'Do These Prisons Make Me Look Fat? Moderating the US's Consumption of Punishment' (2010) 14 *Theoretical Criminology* 257; Sonja Snacken, 'Resisting Punitiveness in Europe?' (2010) 14 *Theoretical Criminology* 273; and Ian Loader, 'For Penal Moderation: Notes towards a Public Philosophy of Punishment' (2010) 14 *Theoretical Criminology* 349; compare Sonja Snacken, 'Punishment, Legitimate Policies and Values: Penal Moderation, Dignity, and Human Rights' (2015) 17 *Punishment & Society* 397.

[4] This conception of moderation is deeply ingrained in Western political philosophy: see generally Aristotle, *The Nicomachean Ethics* (2009, David Ross, trans, Lesley Brown, ed, Oxford University Press), II.6–II.9; Alisdair MacIntyre, *After Virtue: A Study in Moral Theory*, Third edn (2007, University of Notre Dame Press), pp 146–164.

contingent on the outermost extremes of the debate, but also on the particular prejudices, presuppositions, and foundational values we bring to the discussion, individually and as a polity. Moreover, it will rarely be possible to find a mathematically exact midpoint among all possible alternatives relative to one another, because social activity is determined by *qualitative* as well as *quantitative* differences that affect the nature of our actions. For example, is the moderate midpoint between Statements A and B above burning half of all criminals to death, burning all criminals halfway to death, or inflicting a punishment of half the severity of execution by burning? Assuming the latter, how do we even begin to identify such a punishment?

I make the distinction between moderation and minimalism because, at least in a penal sense, minimalism is more prescriptive than moderation: it is going *absolutely no further* than one has to, whereas moderation is the *avoidance of excess* (and deficiency). Both conceptions are necessarily conditioned by the penal theory that one is pursuing, to say nothing of one's wider political assumptions. Across penal theory (with the exception of the strongest penal abolitionists, for whom criminal punishment is always unjustified and unjustifiable),[5] moderation and minimalism offer more and less leeway, respectively, in the pursuit of constrained penal aims. By analogy, imagine the sentencing judge (and the wider architecture of the penal State that backs up their decision-making) as an archer aiming at a target. From the minimalist's perspective, there is an acceptable zone on and around the bullseye that will indicate 'success'; for the moderate, that zone is wider. An amateur archer might settle for just hitting the target at all, whereas for the most proficient professionals, only the bullseye will be a satisfying result. In criminal justice, we are unlikely to ever be able to be so accurate, because punishment is a social experience, marked by qualitative as well as quantitative differences. Any metric of penal 'success', whether in terms of proportionate punishment or effective interventions, will be reductive to the extent that it insists on mathematical precision, because there is no basis on which to say that a punishment is 'worth 42 penal units' – or for that matter, a crime is '42% serious'.[6] These judgements are neither natural nor inevitable, and cannot, for that reason, be specified in advance of a particular penal system or its wider political context.[7]

Indeed, these concepts can only carry us so far, and they still leave us a long way from a practical definition of penal excess. We need more detail about the range of alternatives that are possible, including the political, historical, economic, cultural, and social situation of the criminal justice system in question. What I have argued so far, however, is that moderation and minimalism *do* reflect subtly but significantly different approaches to the challenge of avoiding excess. If I am going to

[5] See generally Vincenzo Ruggiero, *Penal Abolitionism* (2010, Oxford University Press).

[6] Compare Duff's 'positive' and 'negative' proportionality: RA Duff, *Punishment, Communication, and Community* (2001, Oxford University Press), pp 137–139.

[7] See also Ted Honderich, *Punishment: The Supposed Justifications Revisited* (2006, Pluto Press), pp 35–41.

make out the claim that polities such as England and Wales ought to commit to penal minimalism as a public good, I must therefore explain why moderation is not enough in the context of the (Anglo-Welsh) penal State. To do this, we need to situate our concepts within the particular *political* context in which England and Wales, as a jurisdictional subset of the wider United Kingdom, operates.

II. Political Foundations: Penal Minimalism as a Public Good

By 'politics', I mean the broad set of processes and relationships by which we live together, in everything from small groups to the whole of humanity, on a global scale. Politics is therefore both a normative realm concerning what sort of society we *want* to live in, and what sort of principles we *ought to* live by in the abstract (so-called *political philosophy*); and on the other, a *pragmatic* realm concerned with how we bring those normative values into play in an imperfect and socioeconomically bounded world. This realm of the socioeconomically possible acts as a medium between abstract political philosophy (the realm of what we want to do) and particular *policies* (the policy arena being the realm of how the State actually arranges its institutions, systems, and agents, and for which purposes). By exploring these political contexts, we can ground the concept of penal excess in the specific challenges, values, and institutional frameworks of contemporary England and Wales. In particular, I argue that we ought to pursue penal minimalism, rather than mere moderation. This is because of the specific type of political model that prevails in England and Wales, and the wider United Kingdom: *liberal democracy*.

A. The UK as a Liberal Democracy

'Liberal democracy' is an unfashionable concept in contemporary criminology, for two reasons. Firstly, the concept is at least somewhat *ahistorical*, either because 'liberal democracies' have never really existed, or because they did exist but have since been undermined by a more authoritarian and/or anti-democratic direction in (Anglophone) politics. Certainly, the concept of 'liberal democracy' does not really appear in normative social, political or legal theory before the mid-twentieth century. 'Liberal democracy' was a way of describing 'the free world', defined less by what the polities it purported to describe had in common, than by the fact that the States in question were *not* fascist, and *not* communist.[8] Using this concept as if it were an accurate depiction of (say) post-Revolutionary France, the

[8] See generally Duncan Bell, 'What is Liberalism?' (2014) 42(6) *Political Theory* 682–715; Abbott Gleason, *Totalitarianism: The Inner History of the Cold War* (1995, Oxford University Press).

post-independence US, or indeed the post-1832 UK, is inaccurate. It applies a normative framework that the authors of those reformed and/or revolutionary societies were not pursuing, or at least, recasts it in terms of an ahistorical battle with very modern forms of State authoritarianism. Thus, calling a modern State a liberal democracy runs the risk of muddying its historical and modern origins (especially in a non-revolutionary liberal democracy like the UK, which emerged from and still inhabits the institutional, cultural and socio-political bones of its feudal and imperial past). Moreover, the label tells us something about what the State is not, but not a lot about what the State *is*.[9]

Secondly, speaking about 'liberal democracy' risks treating liberalism and democracy as essentially compatible goals, when they may well come into tension.[10] A liberal-democratic State may, without undermining its democratic credentials, pursue non-liberal ends. Indeed, at least some nineteenth-century liberals were very mistrustful of 'democracy', which was associated with radical threats to the existing socio-political order and the interests of its elite.[11] On the one hand, left-wing influences within liberal-democratic societies may pull the State towards a more interventionist, *social-democratic* State in which individual liberty is sacrificed to some extent to ensure collective security, equality, and social justice; and on the other, right-wing influences such as *neoliberalism* and *neo-conservatism* tend to pull the liberal-democratic State away from its fundamental commitment to meaningful equality and universal respect.[12] So claiming that a State is a 'liberal democracy' risks suggesting entirely too much settlement in terms of the shape, values, and practices guiding public institutions, public discourse, and indeed, public life.

I do not deny that these are compelling problems. But 'liberal democracy' is a well-recognised and widely-used concept, and its vagueness need not undermine our discussion of what the sort of society that England and Wales is a part of claims to be. So, we might as well use this language, bearing in mind its limitations as a precisely accurate descriptor of a class of historical or contemporary political orders, to describe a broad range of institutional and normative commitments. I do not mean to deny the possibility that there are gaps between what the State claims to pursue and what it actually does, but my starting point is that enough agents of the British State think of themselves as pursuing liberal-democratic agendas enough of the time, that we can meaningfully call it a 'liberal democracy', and hold it to account as such. This does not mean that the UK must (or could) fit a single platonic ideal of a perfectly liberal and perfectly democratic society.

[9] See Bell, ibid, arguing not that we should reject 'liberal democracy' so much as be very careful about how we use the concept and what it means.

[10] See generally Norberto Bobbio, *Liberalism and Democracy* (1990, Martin Ryle and Kate Soper (trans), Verso).

[11] Ibid, especially pp 45–49.

[12] See generally Nicola Lacey, 'Punishment, (Neo)Liberalism, and Social Democracy', in Jonathan Simon and Richard Sparks (eds), *The SAGE Handbook of Punishment and Society* (2013, SAGE); Anthony Giddens, *Beyond Left and Right: The Future of Radical Politics* (1994, Polity Press).

However, we can at least say something about the shared values such a society must hold: a commitment to liberty, to democracy, and to the pragmatic management of the State in the pursuit of those aims. To the extent that the UK government derives rhetorical force from its claim to be a 'liberal democracy', it can be held to account according to the fundamental values that that label implies. In particular, in the next two sections I argue that there are compelling reasons for both good-faith liberals and democrats to commit to a robust standard of penal minimalism.

B. Liberal Arguments for Penal Minimalism: Autonomy and Control

(i) Liberal Political Philosophy: An Overview

The first thing that a liberal democracy ought to be is *liberal.* I mean this in the theoretical sense – a commitment to pursuing individual liberty – rather than in the modern vernacular sense, in which 'liberal' means 'left-winger' (and 'conservative', 'right-winger'). The point is that the claim that a 'liberal' democracy is not one dominated by the political programme of its left-wing parties,[13] but rather, a society in which *the individual's freedom* is held to be a primary public good.

To be able to pursue freedom as a public good, we need to be able to say what freedom actually *is*, however. Liberal conceptions differ slightly from other freedom-loving political philosophies, and notably from *anarchist* approaches, in that they emphasise the importance of the political authority of the State in mediating between free individuals and ensuring maximum freedom for every individual across society. Hence Joseph Raz makes the revealing claim that, 'The doctrine of freedom is part of the doctrine of authority'.[14] This perspective is ultimately rooted in Hobbes's political theory of the citizen and the State. Hobbes famously posited that before the invention of States and other such hierarchical conglomerations that governed human activities, human beings lived in a 'state of nature' characterised by absolute freedom of action and by absolute insecurity. In the state of nature, ungoverned by law and beholden to the social and moral censure of no one, my freedom of action is limited only by the limitations of my body, my perception, and my lifespan. *However*, I am also vulnerable, because everybody else is equally free, and that includes the freedom to dominate, to pillage and plunder, and to exploit the hard work of others through manipulation and force of arms. Thus, in Hobbes's famous terms, the state of nature is 'a war of every man, against every man', in which life is invariably 'poor, solitary, nasty, brutish, and short.'[15]

[13] See generally Norberto Bobbio, *Left and Right: The Significance of a Political Distinction* (1996, Allan Cameron (trans), Polity Press).

[14] Joseph Raz, *The Morality of Freedom* (1984, Oxford University Press), p 23. Compare the famous anarchist *bon mot*: 'Liberty is the mother, and not the daughter of order'. See Stephen Marshall, *Demanding the Impossible: A History of Anarchism*, Third edn (2008, Harper Perennial), p 236.

[15] Thomas Hobbes, *Leviathan* (1996, JCA Gaskin (trans), Oxford University Press), XIII.8–XIII.9.

Thus, because of the inherent fallibility and selfishness of the human condition, Hobbes posits that a centralised State is necessary to secure meaningful freedom by creating conditions of relative peace and stability through a *social contract*. We all surrender a piece of our total freedom so that we are protected from the exercise of those same freedoms by others. This enables us to live our lives more fully, in pursuit of our autonomous desires.[16]

One does not need to accept Hobbes's radically pessimistic view of human nature in order to buy into a liberal social contract. John Locke, for instance, considered a social contract governed by a State hierarchy to be not so much a fundamental necessity for peaceful coexistence, so much as an *instrumentally* valuable way of achieving greater collective prosperity and security. Under the terms of a social contract, Locke argues that we are better equipped to *positively* rely upon each other's support, as well as being freer of the *negative* risk that Hobbes conceives of individuals as posing to one another.[17] Locke's position is not that individuals are *incapable* of selfishness and depravity, so much as that these tendencies are not *all* we are. However, particularly in criminal justice discussions, Locke's shadow tends to be remarkably shorter than Hobbes's, and his influence on the institutions, approaches, and operating logics of the penal State is much lower. The result is that liberal defences of the criminal justice system tend to start from a much stronger presumption of the necessity of State governance and social control against the errant desires of the citizen.[18]

Still, for both Hobbes and Locke, liberty is *ambiguous* rather than dangerous. Humans are free and equal by nature, and both accounts view that ability to decide one's future for oneself as an essential good.[19] This requires the State to be carefully controlled as a means of protecting individuals' *autonomy* from too much State control. The typical liberal justification for why this is necessary draws upon Immanuel Kant's conception of *human dignity*.[20] Kant's argument, in brief, is that all human beings possess an apparently unique capacity to make rational *moral choices*, to at least some degree and at least some of the time, by considering the likely consequences of their actions and then acting accordingly. As a

[16] Ibid. See also John Rawls, *A Theory of Justice*, Revised edn (1999, Oxford University Press); and Matt Matravers, 'Political Theory and the Criminal Law', in RA Duff and Stuart Green (eds), *Philosophical Foundations of Criminal Law* (2011, Oxford University Press).

[17] See John Locke, 'An Essay Concerning the True, Original, Extent, and End of Civil-Government'; in John Locke; Mark Goldie (ed), *Second Treatise of Government and A Letter Concerning Toleration* (2016, Oxford University Press), pp 4–10, 63–65; although see Henrique Carvalho, *The Preventive Turn in Criminal Law* (2017, Oxford University Press), pp 81–108, critiquing Locke's commitment to his own ideals.

[18] See Henrique Carvalho, 'Liberty and Insecurity in the Criminal Law: Lessons from Thomas Hobbes' (2017) 11 *Criminal Law and Philosophy* 249, especially pp 266–271; compare Simon Hallsworth and John Lea, 'Reconstructing Leviathan: Emerging Contours of the Security State' (2011) 15 *Theoretical Criminology* 141.

[19] Hobbes, above n 15, chs XIV–XV; Locke, above n 17, pp 63–81.

[20] See Immanuel Kant, *Groundwork on the Metaphysics of Morals*, revised translation (2012, Mary Gregor and Jens Timmerman (trans); Jens Timmerman (ed), Cambridge University Press), pp 45–48.

result, one person's autonomous moral decisions cannot be reasonably privileged over another's.[21] It follows that, if you think that your own desires are valuable, then *everybody's* wishes must also be equally valuable, and should therefore be respected. Moreover, that value cannot be quantified or compared (in Kant's language it has a 'dignity' rather than a 'value').[22] As a result, Kant famously argues that we must never treat individuals only as a means to an end. To do so would be to treat their moral autonomy as inherently less valuable than our own, and their human dignity as less worthy of respect.[23] In a liberal society, then, everyone must be free to exercise their moral autonomy *unless and until* their doing so would impinge upon the capacity of others to engage in the pursuit of their own autonomous wishes.[24] Thus, liberal political theory tends to conceive of an ideal society not so much as a utopia, a Good Society where everyone follows the same broad plan, as by an arena within which each citizen can freely pursue their own conception of the Good Life. To do this, each citizen needs to enjoy a *sphere of influence* in which they, and they alone, are capable of deciding how to act. The job of the State is twofold: firstly, through the ordering and stabilising of society, it should provide as much opportunity to exert one's autonomous desires as possible; but secondly, the State must police the borders of each person's autonomy 'bubble', ensuring that no-one is afforded greater respect for their autonomous desires than anyone else, and that no-one's liberty intrudes upon another's enjoyment of their own liberty illegitimately.

Different liberal theories place different levels of focus on these two roles of the State – the liberty-respecting State, from which we enjoy *negative liberty* and the autonomy-supporting State, which enhances our ability to pursue *positively* our autonomous wishes.[25] Thus, while the State is usually conceived of as a necessary evil, liberalism is capable of recognising its utility for enhancing the freedoms of the individual in certain circumstances. We see these tendencies in explicitly liberal theories of punishment: *liberal retributivism* focussing on small penal States and limited aims for the criminal justice system; and *liberal paternalist* strategies, typically employing some mix of deterrence and rehabilitation to simultaneously protect citizens *from* crime and enable criminals to engage with society in more productive and pro-social ways in future.[26] Criminal justice is typically conceived of as a means of preventing one citizen from intruding into the sphere of autonomy

[21] Ibid.

[22] Ibid, p 46.

[23] See also Dan Markel, 'Are Shaming Sanctions Beautifully Retributive? Retribution and the Implications for the Alternative Sanctions Debate' (2001) 54 *Vanderbilt Law Review* 2157, pp 2194–2198.

[24] See generally Kant, above n 20, pp 56–62; Raz, above n 14.

[25] See, eg, John Gray, 'On Negative and Positive Liberty', in John Gray (ed), *Liberalisms: Essays in Political Philosophy* (1989, Routledge). For a stridently 'negative' approach, see FA Hayek, *The Constitution of Liberty* (1960, Routledge). For a more 'positive' account, see LT Hobhouse, *Liberalism and Other Writings* (1994, James Meadowcroft (ed), Cambridge University Press).

[26] See generally Barbara Hudson, *Justice in the Risk Society: Challenging and Re-Affirming Justice in Late Modernity* (2003, SAGE), pp 3–39.

of another – if you will, using the illegitimate liberty they would enjoy in the state of nature to deprive another of the freedom and security to which they are entitled under the terms of the liberal social contract.[27] Under a liberal theory of criminal law, the most important justification for criminalisation is the *harm principle* – that your conduct causes a setback to their legitimate and autonomous interests of another individual.[28]

(ii) Liberalism, Penal Moderation, and Penal Minimalism

Criminal justice, then, can be conceived of as being both productive of liberty, rather than as (just) a challenge to liberty; it is like any other limb of the State and can be used to achieve a liberal State's social and political aims more generally.[29] From this, we might conclude that liberals are essentially agnostic as to whether we should pursue penal minimalism or the more flexible standard of penal moderation. After all, if criminal justice is one of the ways in which the State regulates each citizen's autonomy, then too little State intervention can be as bad as too much. Too little intervention can leave the individual vulnerable to the depredations of their fellow-citizens – a state of penal deficiency. But on the other hand, if the (penal) State polices autonomy decisions too heavily, then everyone's overall degree of freedom is reduced. A moderate liberal approach to penal control would therefore involve a balance between positive and negative State interventions, in which the *positive production of liberty* by the State (through social welfare and defence from external threats to security, for instance) and the *residual natural liberty* one would have been able to exercise in a hypothetical state of nature, absent any other forms of social control, outweighs both the State's and fellow-citizens' negative intrusions into our ability to act freely and autonomously. So, liberalism implies at the very least a concern with penal *moderation* – using the penal State to steer society between individual freedom and public protection.[30]

However, this account assumes that there is nothing different about penal State interventions that affect individual liberty, *relative to other forms of State intervention*. If we accept the liberal contention that the State can produce and restrict individual liberty simultaneously then the ideal liberal intervention is one in which the State produces as much 'artificial' liberty as possible whilst restraining 'natural' liberty as little as possible. From this perspective, criminal punishment is an inherently problematic institution, because of its high cost to individuals' freedoms. In particular, there are four key reasons for liberals to distrust criminal

[27] Compare Carvalho, 'Liberty and Insecurity in the Criminal Law', above n 18.

[28] See Joel Feinberg, *Harm to Others: The Moral Limits of the Criminal Law, Volume One* (1984, Oxford University Press), especially pp 31–64; JS Mill, 'On Liberty', in JS Mill, *On Liberty, Utilitarianism and Other Essays*, New Edition (2015, Mark Philp and Frederick Rosen (eds), Oxford University Press).

[29] See generally Barbara Hudson, *Penal Policy and Social Justice* (1993, Macmillan).

[30] Compare Loader, above n 3.

punishment compared to other State institutions for producing and maintaining social order.

Firstly, punishment involves the liberal State directly restraining its citizens' liberty, in stark contrast to its usual role. This is not to say that criminal punishment cannot be beneficial to individuals or to society as a whole, including the offender, or that there are no such liberty costs associated with other forms of State intervention. It is only to say that criminal justice interventions involve an inherent harm to liberty that does not exist with other forms of State intervention, and that at least sometimes, that cost may not be worth the benefit derived by the subject, their victim/s, and wider society.[31] Thus, liberals should be more sceptical about the use of criminal justice interventions, all else being equal, than less inherently coercive alternatives.[32]

Secondly, criminal punishment is *painful*, in addition to depriving liberty from citizens who break the law. That is, criminal punishment exposes the offender to a range of circumstances that are unpleasant, and which may cause the subject to experience physical pain, psychological suffering, and/or emotional trauma.[33] These features of criminal punishment are often deeply ingrained in penal processes, which have evolved out of systems designed for straightforward 'pain delivery'.[34] However, they may also be the result of responses to the penal subject's conviction or punishment by the wider community. Even in these cases, however, the State bears at least some responsibility for inflicting these pains – they are part and parcel of the punishment that is imposed, to the extent that they arise in *proximity* to State activities.[35] The pains of punishment may or may not be said to be *part* of the punishment in terms of attempts to measure severity (such as retributive proportionality),[36] but at the very least they are a sociological reality of the experience of punishment, and need to be recognised as attending punishment so that they can be confronted and minimised.[37] To the extent that we know that punishment involves the *intentional* infliction of pain, liberals ought to be

[31] See, eg, Edwin Schur, *Radical Non-Intervention: Rethinking the Delinquency Problem* (1973, Prentice Hall).

[32] Compare Feinberg, above n 28, pp 22–25.

[33] See, eg, GM Sykes, *The Society of Captives: A Study of a Maximum Security Prison* (1958, Princeton University Press), ch 4; David Hayes, 'Experiencing Penal Supervision: A Literature Review' (2019) *Probation Journal*, (2018) 65 *Probation Journal* 387.

[34] See generally Nils Christie, *Limits to Pain: The Role of Punishment in Penal Policy* (1982, Martin Robinson).

[35] See, eg, David Hayes, 'Proximity, Pain and State Punishment' (2018) 20 *Punishment & Society* 235.

[36] Jesper Ryberg, 'Punishment and the Measurement of Severity', in Jesper Ryberg and JA Corlett (eds), *Punishment and Ethics: New Perspectives* (2010, Palgrave Macmillan), pp 74–82; compare Esther van Ginneken and David Hayes, '"Just" Punishment? Offenders' Views on the Meaning and Severity of Punishment' (2017) 17 *Criminology and Criminal Justice* 62.

[37] See, eg, Ioan Durnescu, 'Pains of Probation: Effective Practice and Human Rights' (2011) 55 *International Journal of Offender Therapy and Comparative Criminology* 530; Lori Sexton, 'Penal Subjectivities: Developing a Theoretical Framework for Penal Consciousness' (2015) 17 *Punishment and Society* 114; compare Dan Markel and Chad Flanders, 'Bentham on Stilts: On the Bare Relevance of Subjectivity to Retributive Justice' (2010) 98 *California Law Review* 907.

reluctant to rely upon criminal punishment. One cannot show respect to someone's human dignity without also being humane,[38] and humanity must include an attempt to avoid the infliction of intentional pain if there is any alternative: 'Sorrow is inevitable, but not hell created by men'.[39]

Thirdly, criminal punishment inevitably exposes innocent individuals to hardship, in two senses. On the one hand, there are inherent deprivations associated with participation in the criminal process, which is intrusive and highly demanding in terms of the time and resources required to argue one's case from the first contact with police officers and prosecutors, through to the trial itself – pains that must be borne even by factually innocent defendants, who are found not guilty (or who experience miscarriages of justice).[40] On the other hand, punishment inevitably impacts upon third parties to the punishment, such as dependent family members and employers.[41] Punishment cannot only affect the individual being punished because it is a social process, and therefore causes ripple effects that pass throughout society. Again, this is not to say that third-party and procedural limitations to liberty are not associated with other forms of State intervention (consider, for instance, the awful knock-on effects that can be associated with taking a child into the care of the State for its parents and wider family), but only that these impacts are particularly prevalent given the inherent intrusiveness of the penal system.

Fourthly, criminal punishment is inevitably *reactive* to social harms, and therefore limited in terms of what it can achieve in terms of protecting and producing liberty.[42] The criminal justice system is set up to respond to criminality after it has already happened, and however much it may hope to target events in future, it is foundationally grounded in principles that target individuals' conduct, only when it has been labelled as transgressive in advance. Within the criminal justice system whose institutions have been bequeathed to us by history: we ought not to (intentionally) punish the innocent;[43] we should only punish individuals, rather than groups or communities;[44] and we should not punish retroactively what was not clearly expressed to be a criminal offence at the time the act was committed.[45]

[38] See generally Tony Ward, 'Dignity and Human Rights in Correctional Practice' (2009) 1 *European Journal of Probation* 110; Loader, above n 3; Snacken, 'Punishment, Legitimate Policies, and Values', above n 3.

[39] Christie, above n 34.

[40] See Marcus Feeley, *The Process is the Punishment: Handling Cases in a Lower Criminal Court* (1979, Russell Sage Foundation).

[41] See Nigel Walker, *Why Punish?* (1991, Oxford University Press), pp 106–110; Richard Lippke, 'Punishment Drift: The Spread of Penal Harm and What We Should Do About It' (2017) 11 *Criminal Law and Philosophy* 645.

[42] Compare Andreas von Hirsch, *Deserved Criminal Sentences* (2017, Hart), pp 122–125.

[43] Although see Duff, *Punishment, Communication and Community*, above n 6, pp xii–xiii.

[44] See, eg, Mark Drumbl, 'Collective Violence and Individual Punishment: The Criminality of Mass Atrocity' (2005) 99 *Northwestern University Law Review* 539.

[45] Enshrined in Art 7 of the European Convention on Human Rights; see also, eg, Jeremy Horder, *Ashworth's Principles of Criminal Law*, Eighth Edition (2016, Oxford University Press), pp 82–85; Tom Bingham, *The Rule of Law* (2010, Penguin), pp 73–74.

These are the key features of how the criminal justice system approaches those it exerts penal control over: as individuals, responsible for their conduct, and only for things that they already knew (or ought to have known) were wrong.[46] We might well change the penal institutions we have inherited, so that they are better suited to responding to wider social problems, and better equipped to be proactive. But if we changed the institutions of criminal justice away from the imposition of formal consequences in response to criminal acts by individuals, *it would no longer be the criminal justice system*. It would no longer be criminal punishment and would need to be justified in its own right, as a new creature, with new moral and political implications.[47]

If the liberal is committed to retaining the institutions of criminal justice that we have, then they must accept the limitations of that system. We can certainly intervene to attempt to reduce the likelihood of (criminal or non-criminal) social harms arising in future, but only in cases where someone has already committed a serious social wrong, been detected by the system's investigators, convicted, and singled out for stigmatisation and unpleasant treatment by the system (and society's response to that singling out). On the face of that, prevention seems better overall than cure. This is easier said than done, of course, and does not necessarily mean that we should not attempt to 'cure' deviant behaviour that does end up putting somebody under penal control. But at least in the abstract, if we can avoid waiting for harm to be done before responding to it in order to prevent further harm, we should do so. As a result, criminal justice ought to be seen as a much less effective tool than other instruments available to the State in ensuring maximum respect for every individual's human dignity, and should accordingly be used as little as possible.[48]

For these reasons, liberal States ought to be committed not just to *moderation* in the use of criminal justice interventions, but *minimalism*, too. The penal State carries a number of intrinsic harms that other aspects of State intervention, such as welfare provision and public education, do not, or at least do not have to the same extent. For these reasons, there should always be an expectation that criminal justice should be used as a last resort for resolving social problems.[49] This conclusion also provides a useful metaphor for measuring penal excess: the overall *size* of the penal State, in terms of how much it intrudes into the overall level of positive liberty enjoyed by society. A penal State that is minimalist in terms of size is therefore one that intrudes into each individual's autonomy *no more than is strictly necessary* to protect citizens from the setback to their liberty caused by criminal wrongdoing.

[46] Duff, *Punishment, Communication, and Community*, above n 6, pp 179–188; see also RA Duff, *Answering for Crime: Responsibility and Liability in the Criminal Law* (2007, Hart), pp 37–77.

[47] Compare Nicola Lacey and Hanna Pickard, 'To Blame or to Forgive? Reconciling Punishment and Forgiveness in Criminal Justice' (2015) 35 *OJLS* 665.

[48] See generally Andreas von Hirsch, *Deserved Criminal Sentences* (2017, Hart).

[49] Compare Feinberg, above n 28, pp 22–25; Horder, above n 45, pp 65–77.

C. Democratic Arguments for Penal Minimalism: Equality and Solidarity

However, we cannot quite conclude that liberal-democratic States must use criminal justice systems minimally, for two reasons. Firstly, liberal political theory does not properly explain why we turn to criminal justice systems at all, since criminal justice is also part of the architecture of illiberal States, and predates the emergence of liberalism as a political ideology.[50] Secondly, liberal-democratic societies are not *just* liberal, and do not *just* pursue liberal ends, because they conduct their business through *democratic* decision-making. As we have seen already, liberalism and democracy do not always pursue the same ends. After all, at its most basic, democracy means direct control by the people (the '*demos*'), and freedom must mean the freedom to make bad decisions, including decisions that make one less free.[51] So does democracy also support penal minimalism – or for that matter, penal moderation? To answer this question, we must firstly identify what we mean by 'democracy' more fully, and in particular, distinguish between 'formal' and 'substantive' conceptions of democracy. Whilst the former is essentially apathetic about penal excess, the latter does carry a series of particular commitments to penal minimalism. As a result, in a *liberal* democracy, penal minimalism must always be a significant feature of any penal-political philosophy.

'Democracy', like 'liberalism', has meant profoundly different things at different points in history. In classical (Western) history, 'democracy' was associated with Hellenic city-states, and notably with Athens, in which citizens (that is, men over the age of majority who were not slaves or foreign-born) could contribute directly to public discourse and policy-making.[52] What we would now call *representative democracy* – the election of representatives to engage in public decision-making on our behalf – was defined by Enlightenment theorists not as democracy but as *elective aristocracy* – the periodic election of a temporary ruling class.[53] After the Enlightenment (and the French and American revolutions), however, 'aristocracy' became a dirty word, and 'democracy' came to be conceived of as something that could be done at arm's length, through intermediaries.[54] Especially with the rise of authoritarian opponents of democracy in the form of fascism and communism, rule by the people, in which everyone had some say in the running of the State, became valued as a good in its own right in Western societies.[55]

[50] Paul Roberts, 'Criminal Law Theory and the Limits of Liberalism', in AP Simester, Antje du Bois-Pedain, and Ulfrid Neumann (eds), *Liberal Criminal Theory: Essays for Andreas von Hirsch* (2014, Hart).

[51] Recall generally Bobbio, *Liberalism and Democracy*, above n 10.

[52] See Aristotle, *Politics* (1995, Ernest Baker (trans), RF Stalley (ed), Oxford University Press), III.9–13.

[53] Jean-Jacques Rousseau, *The Social Contract* (1994, Christopher Betts (trans), Oxford University Press), pp 102–104.

[54] Bobbio, *Liberalism and Democracy*, above n 10, pp 25–29.

[55] Recall Bell, above n 8.

This 'democracy' – performed by representatives and therefore through institutions, processes, and practices *designed* to represent – is the one that has taken root in the liberal-democratic tradition.

'Democracy' is best understood as a mode of delivery rather than a commitment to any particular ideal – which is why the early liberal theorists did not consider it necessary to pursue individual freedom through a system in which everyone had an individual voice. Moreover, its definition of 'everyone' is fluid – the process towards universal suffrage (which usually is not universal, because it excludes people below a certain age) has been a distinct feature of twentieth-century politics. It is a way of doing politics in which power is invested in the people making up the polity – the citizens who have to live together – rather than in any specified subset of that populace.[56] But beyond this, there are two major approaches to democracy that we need to be aware of: *formal* and *substantive* democracy. Let us consider each conception, and consider how concerned they are with penal minimalism, moderation, and excess.

(i) Formal Democracy and Penal Minimalism

Formal democracy, in brief, consists of ensuring the constitutional arrangement of the State such that there is a minimum level of democratic oversight of the institutions of government: in the UK, the lower House of Parliament is periodically elected, and the party (or coalition) with a majority (or in rare cases, as at the time of writing, the largest minority) of seats forms the government, and is therefore indirectly democratically accountable. The government exercises control over the judiciary, appoints new peers to the House of Lords, and is otherwise answerable to Parliament, which enjoys so-called 'Parliamentary Sovereignty' over both the executive and the judiciary in the event of a conflict between them.[57] Likewise, in local government, directly elected representatives are periodically appointed and generally command unelected officers. One central function of juries and lay magistrates is to act as a democratic stay on the powers of unelected judges, given the severe consequences of a criminal conviction,[58] and increasingly, new positions such as the Police and Crime Commissioner are being created to provide a more direct level of democratic control (however tokenistic) over historically unelected public services, such as the police.[59] Importantly, not every government institution needs to be democratically elected in order for the system to be 'democratic', so long as the people have overall control over the State's activities

[56] See generally Jorge Nef and Bernd Reiter, *The Democratic Challenge: Rethinking Democracy and Democratization* (2009, Palgrave Macmillan), ch 1.

[57] For an accessible oversight of Parliamentary Sovereignty, see Bingham, above n 45, pp 160–170.

[58] See generally Albert Dzur, *Punishment, Participatory Democracy, and Juries* (2012, Oxford University Press).

[59] See, eg, Stuart Lister and Michael Rowe, 'Electing Police and Crime Commissioners for England and Wales: Prospecting for the Democratisation of Policing' (2015) 25 *Policing and Society* 358.

(through formal expressions of the *vox populi* such as elections and referendums). Every so often, the people speak, and the State derives political legitimacy from their having spoken, until either a formal period of time has elapsed, or a political crisis fatally undermines that legitimacy.

In a purely formal democracy, criminal punishment does not meaningfully bear upon the question of whether or not a State is democratic. The reliance of a State upon criminal punishment as a means of keeping society in check is generally independent of *how* (and *for whom*) public institutions are run. Since a purely formal democracy contains no commitments to any values that might urge restraint in penal activities, a formal democrat seems to be – at best – indifferent about the reliance of democratic States upon criminal punishment. If that is the case, then in a *liberal* democracy, strong liberal concerns about securing penal minimalism ought to trump the lack of interest in penal minimalism on the part of democrats, and so our commitment to a minimal penal State should not waver. However, in practice, formal democracy is vulnerable to illiberal shifts in policy and public discourse. It cannot resist changes in the political climate that undermine liberal principles, because it lacks inherent commitment to any principles upon which 'healthy' democracy depends. Liberal paternalist criminologists, in particular, have argued that a campaign of *penal populism* (or 'populist punitiveness') has been driven by shifts in public discourse that have tended to actually militate against penal minimalism *and* moderation, and in favour of penal excess.[60] Whilst this complaint is probably overblown, both in the sense that there is little evidence of a unidirectional shift in public attitudes towards a rabid punitiveness,[61] it illustrates how formal democracy's principled apathy can be overcome by short-term policy imperatives.[62]

(ii) Substantive Democracy and Penal Minimalism

Substantive democracy – sometimes also called 'democracy as a way of life' – is less embodied in institutions, and more about the *flavour* of democratic processes.[63] In a substantively democratic society, the institutions by which the people exert

[60] See generally Julian Roberts et al, *Penal Populism and Public Opinion: Lessons from Five Countries* (2003, Oxford University Press); Nicola Lacey, *The Prisoners' Dilemma*, above n 1, especially ch 4; Anthony Bottoms, 'The Philosophy and Politics of Punishment and Sentencing', in: Chris Clarkson and Rod Morgan (eds), *The Politics of Sentencing* (1995, Clarendon Press).

[61] See, eg, Shadd Maruna and Anna King, 'Public Opinion and Community Penalties', in Anthony Bottoms, Sue Rex, and Gwen Robinson (eds), *Alternatives to Prison: Options for an Insecure Society* (2004, Willan); Roger Matthews, 'The Myth of Punitiveness' (2005) 9 *Theoretical Criminology* 175. Compare Will Jennings, Stephen Farrall, Emily Gray, and Colin Hay, 'Penal Populism and the Public Thermostat: Crime, Public Punitiveness, and Public Policy' (2017) 30 *Governance* 463.

[62] See, eg, Ian Loader and Richard Sparks, *Public Criminology?* (2011, Routledge), chs 3–5; Lisa Miller, *The Myth of Mob Rule: Violent Crime and Democratic Politics* (2016, Oxford University Press).

[63] See, eg, Elizabeth Anderson, 'Democracy: Instrumental vs. Non-Instrumental Value', in Thomas Christiano and John Christman (eds), *Contemporary Debates in Political Philosophy* (2009, Wiley-Blackwell), especially pp 214–222.

control over the various levels of government must not only exist, *but must actually be used effectively.* After all, the democratic ideal – rule by the people – is easy to express and normatively attractive, but it is difficult to achieve in practice. Indeed, there are various nightmare scenarios in political theory, in which democracy falls apart through misuse, abuse, or neglect. Some are as old as the resurgence of democracy within the political lexicon, such as the 'tyranny of the majority', in which minority interests are suppressed and marginalised by a large but not total majority, to the extent that genuine rule by all is supplanted by a new *de facto* elite.[64] Others are new, such to the supposed threat that right-wing populism poses to European (and wider Western) democracy, or the problem of 'failed democracy,' in which the formal institutions of democracy are dominated by authoritarian forces that use corruption, coercion, fraud, violence, propaganda, and censorship to retain control.[65] While 'failed' democracies are usually subverted from the top down, it is also possible for *political apathy* to cause failures in the democratic process – if one can vote, but nobody does, then in what sense do 'the people' rule? To be sure, apathy, like ignorance, can be produced[66] – but for the substantive democrat there is also the problem of investing voters in genuine deliberation to begin with, which becomes increasingly difficult where political problems are discussed in technical language, involve opaque institutions, and deal with ever-more complex issues.[67] Under such circumstances, democracy is simply *exhausting*, and it can be very tempting to give up the responsibility of freedom – to go with the flow, and trust the know-betters to get it right.[68] But a healthy, meaningful democracy requires active discourse and widespread participation in deliberation if it is to endure.[69]

In short, the only way for substantive democrats to be satisfied that democracy is meaningfully at work is to ensure the presence of *democratic values* in the actions of electors and of government. Two key commitments in particular compel the substantive democrat to pursue penal minimalism: to *socio-political equality*; and to *communal solidarity*.

[64] See generally Alexis de Tocqueville, *Democracy in America, Volume One*, Third American edn (1889, Henry Reeve (trans), John Spencer (ed), George Adlard), ch 15; Mill, above n 28; Bobbio, *Liberalism and Democracy*, above n 10, pp 51–61.

[65] See, eg, MS Fish, *Democracy Derailed in Russia: The Failure of Open Politics* (2012, Cambridge University Press), pp 30–81; Nic Cheeseman, *Democracy in Africa: Successes, Failures and the Struggle for Political Reform* (2015, Cambridge University Press), pp 143–170; compare Nef and Reiter, above n 56, pp 149–165.

[66] See generally Robert Proctor and Londa Schiebinger (eds), *Agnotology: The Making and Unmaking of Ignorance* (2008, Stanford University Press).

[67] See generally Peter Berger and Thomas Luckmann, *The Social Construction of Reality: A Treatise in the Sociology of Knowledge* (1966, Penguin).

[68] See Erich Fromm, *The Fear of Freedom* (1942, Routledge and Kegan Paul), ch 7.

[69] See Amartya Sen, *Development as Freedom* (1999, Oxford University Press), pp 146–159; Amartya Sen, *The Idea of Justice* (2009, Penguin), pp 321–354. For the concept of 'deliberative democracy', see also Jürgen Habermas, *Moral Consciousness and Communicative Action* (1990, Christian Lenhardt and Shierry Nicholson (trans), Polity Press).

The democrat's belief in *equality* is more immediate and substantive than the liberal commitment to a *fair* and equitable distribution of abstract political rights to exercise autonomous choices. Indeed, for the democrat, there is a strong *socio-economic* dimension to equality in terms of *equality of opportunity* to pursue different agendas, and to enjoy scarce *resources*.[70] This fuller equality is important to substantive democracy because it ensures fuller equality of *voice* in public discourse. If one group is very rich, then they are able to monopolise media channels and drive discourses to serve their vested interests whether lobbying, media consolidation, and campaign funding (to say nothing of outright bribery and corruption) become open to the landed few.[71] Information cannot freely flow, and the interests of less well-off groups may well be marginalised and obscured in favour of elite vested interests – especially in the context of identifying particular problems as the object of criminal law.[72] The greater the level of socio-economic and – political inequality in practice, therefore, the lower the prospects for genuine equality of voice in public deliberations, and the lesser the chances of meaningful contribution of everyone to public decision-making. For this reason, the democratic tradition has proven decidedly ambivalent about free-market *capitalism* as a mode of political economy, with its focus on individual property ownership and unconstrained exchanges in market conditions. To be sure, liberalism, democracy and capitalism can coexist, but democracy is just as welcoming of the socialist tradition as the capitalist one.[73]

However, this is by no means a zero-sum game. Even in extremely unequal societies it is possible for the better- and worse-off to feel part of the same project, and to at least feel as though they are travelling in the right direction. A healthy democracy is one in which all the members of an electorate feel attachment to one another, such that they are willing to peacefully coexist with one another. This is particularly important in a democracy, where people can be deeply and intractably divided over the best course of action to pursue, but must continue to live together once a decision has been taken. In other words, in a healthy democracy there must be *room to disagree, without that disagreement being a barrier to interaction*. This sense of belonging to the same in-group, even when we disagree vehemently with one another, is called *solidarity*, a concept popularised by the work of Émile Durkheim.[74] Solidarity can arise *mechanically*, from a common purpose between members of a society, or *organically*, as a result of interactions

[70] See Bobbio, *Liberalism and Democracy*, above n 10, pp 31–35.

[71] Recall nn 65–69; compare Joseph Stiglitz, *The Price of Inequality* (2012, Penguin), pp 148–182.

[72] See, eg, Steven Box, *Power, Crime, and Mystification* (1983, Routledge); compare Douglas Hay, 'Property, Authority and the Criminal Law', in Douglas Hay, Peter Linebaugh, John Rule, EP Thompson, and Cal Winslow (eds), *Albion's Fatal Tree: Crime and Society in Eighteenth-Century England*, Revised edn (2011, Verso); EP Thompson, *Whigs and Hunters: The Origins of the Black Act* (1976, Penguin).

[73] See, eg, Bobbio, *Liberalism and Democracy*, above n 10, pp 73–78.

[74] See, eg, Émile Durkheim, *The Division of Labor within Society* (1984, WD Halls (trans), Macmillan), pp 31–87.

arising out of different purposes and approaches. But both forms serve the purpose of creating an internal sense of commitment to other members of the society – that we are 'all in it together' and therefore deserve the respect, support, and care of our neighbours.[75] Social institutions serve to protect solidarity, whether by reinforcing the community's interior ties ('I am like my neighbour') or by demonstrating the 'otherness' of the outsider ('I am unlike strangers').[76] On this account, criminal punishment in particular is less an attempt to control crime, and more an attempt to express messages to society at large that shore up social solidarity, by reaffirming moral norms and by stigmatising those who have broken them, either temporarily or permanently, as outcasts from the group.[77] By simultaneously castigating the wrongdoer *as such* and restating the values of the group, punishment serves powerful and important expressive roles that serve the political purpose of holding society together in the face of the challenge posed by the crime.[78] Solidarity helps to smooth over socio-economic, -cultural, and -political tensions and enable citizens to walk a mile in each other's shoes. It gives them a reason to care about each other's problems, and therefore be committed to democratic deliberation, even when their own interests are not directly affected by an issue. Solidarity, then, is crucial to the ongoing viability of the polity; it gives citizens a reason to care about one another, and therefore, to care about how we live with one another.

The substantive democrat's normative commitments to *solidarity* and *equality* create strong incentives to reject penal excess and embrace robust standards of penal minimalism. Simply put, if a society wishes to remain cohesive *as* a substantive democracy in the long-term, it must use the extremely stigmatising and fragmentary sledgehammer of criminal justice to deal with as few social problems as possible. Criminal justice is, after all, a very intrusive and disruptive process – which is at least partly why its interventions are so often so painful and so harmful to both formally guilty offenders, who may or may not 'deserve to suffer', and formally innocent third parties.[79] It is also a deeply stigmatising and othering process. By definition, a breach of the criminal law is a *public wrong* – not just a private wrong against the individual victims (assuming that there are any), but a breach of the fundamental tenets upon which the polity itself is based.[80] As such,

[75] Ibid.

[76] Compare Lacey, *The Prisoners' Dilemma*, above n 1, ch 3; Jock Young, *The Exclusive Society: Social Exclusion, Crime and Difference in Late Modernity* (1999, SAGE).

[77] See Jock Young, *The Vertigo of Late Modernity* (2007, SAGE); David Garland, 'Punishment and Social Solidarity', in Jonathan Simon and Richard Sparks (eds), *The SAGE Handbook of Punishment and Society* (2013, SAGE). See also Émile Durkheim; TA Jones and Andrew Scull (trans), 'Two Laws of Penal Evolution' (1973) 2 *Economy and Society* 285.

[78] Recall Markel, above n 23; compare Joel Feinberg, 'The Expressive Function of Punishment' (1965) 49 *The Monist* 397; Joshua Glasgow, 'The Expressivist Theory of Punishment Defended' (2015) 34 *Law and Philosophy* 601.

[79] Recall n 41 and accompanying text.

[80] See, eg, Richard Dagger, Republicanism and the Foundations of Criminal Law', in RA Duff and Stuart Green (eds), *Theoretical Foundations of Criminal Law* (2011, Oxford University Press); Ambrose Lee, 'Public Wrongs and the Criminal Law' (2015) 9 *Criminal Law and Philosophy* 155.

to break the criminal law is to become an 'other' – to hold oneself apart from and above the standards of everyone else. It is very tempting to conceive of criminal offenders – however unintentionally or unconsciously – as enemies of the people, to be rejected forever.[81]

Now, we might say that some people have done such heinous wrongs that they *deserve* exclusion – if only temporarily.[82] Or we might say that, however much exclusion of certain persons harms the solidarity between those persons and the community, the benefits of that exclusion outweigh the harms. Or that that exclusion can be reframed to be less exclusive and in fact heal the rupture in social solidarity that the crime should be properly understood as in the first place. These are, essentially, the claims of retributivist, consequentialist, and restorative justifications of punishment, respectively. To say that punishment is in *tension* with the norms of egalitarian solidarity in a substantive democracy – that it requires justification – is not to say that such a justification is impossible.[83] But anything that does create tension with those values ought to be undertaken only when absolutely necessary – only as a bare minimum. It follows that in a genuinely, substantively democratic society, the rule of the people (as a whole) ought not to be interfered with. In particular, concern with protecting social groups and individuals from marginalisation within decision-making processes should imply a particular concern with the *shape* of the penal population – that is, the footprint of the penal State's control on different sections of society, and how its control overlaps and intersects with already-marginalised sections of society. Unless there is a good reason for crime to be more associated with one community than another, in an egalitarian (and solidarian) society, one would expect the Rule of (Criminal) Law to apply equally across society. A system that perpetuates or exacerbates existing forms of social marginalisation must necessarily therefore be excessive, from a democratic perspective.

III. Conclusion: Two Spatial Metaphors for Penal Excess

Both liberals and democrats, in other words, have compelling reason to commit to penal minimalism as an important part of their theory of the State, as it relates to the criminal justice institutions and processes undertaken by that State. These are not the only reasons to be committed to penal minimalism, of course, because not everyone is straightforwardly a liberal or a democrat.[84] Rather the point is that,

[81] See Young, *The Exclusive Society*, above n 76; and Young, *The Vertigo of Late Modernity*, above n 12.
[82] Compare Duff, *Punishment, Communication, and Community*, above n 6 at pp 148–155.
[83] Ibid, pp xii–xv.
[84] Ibid, pp 127–130.

if the UK (and therefore, England and Wales) is a 'liberal democracy', and we aim to take the philosophical commitments of liberal democracy seriously, then the State *ought* to be committed to penal minimalism. By ignoring the principles of 'liberal democracy' as a sphere of debate, critical criminology has tended to cede an important evaluative (and rhetorical) battleground in penal policy debates, which a focus on liberal democracy allows us to contest. The normative claim to be a liberal democracy matters, even if it is disingenuous or even illusory; to borrow one of Kurt Vonnegut's witticisms: 'We are what we pretend to be, so we must be very careful what we pretend to be'.[85] So long as we use the label of liberal democracy to identify particular States, that leaves those States and their citizens open to the charge of being *bad faith* liberal-democrats, who ought to change direction. For this reason, we ought not to ignore those foundational principles, however abstract and distant from practice they seem.

Moreover, the picture of penal minimalism that emerges from this analysis of liberal and democratic values tells us something about the particular contours of penal minimalism, and give us some means for more meaningfully mapping out what 'excessive' over-reliance on the penal State actually looks like: excessive overall *size*, and disproportionately uneven *shape*. By *size*, I mean the overall interference with liberty and autonomy across each member of the polity; and by *shape*, I mean the extent to which different sections of society are subjected to the penal State's coercive control. In the next chapter, we can put this framework to use, drawing together several themes of academic scholarship on recent Anglo-Welsh criminal justice in terms of the liberal-democratic conception of penal excess.

[85] Kurt Vonnegut, Jr, *Mother Night: A Novel* (1961, Random House), p v.

2

Penal Excess in England and Wales

For all my attempts to flesh out the concept in the last chapter, 'penal excess' is not a term of art in the academic literature so much as an umbrella term for a number of related observations across the social sciences. This chapter gives an overview of the most significant forms of what I am calling penal excess identified in contemporary England and Wales. Following on from the last chapter, it groups these around two overlapping but distinct indicators of excess: the excessive growth in the *size* of the penal State, as reflected in debates around 'mass punishment', 'over-criminalisation', and 'the dispersal of discipline'; and developments that have rendered the *shape* of the penal State's footprint excessively uneven in terms of its impact on society, centred around a more nebulous discourse of 'punishing the poor'. This overview will enable us to focus in on precisely what retributive penal theory is allegedly complicit in bringing about since the decline of the rehabilitative ideal – a charge we discuss in the next chapter from the Criminal Justice Act 1991 onwards. For this reason, the present overview focuses on changes in the three decades from 1989 to 2018, covering the time immediately before, during, and after the time when retributive theory was most influential on penal policy.

I. Mass Punishment: Excesses of Size

The first feature of penal excess in a liberal democracy is excessive *size*. In the last chapter, I identified size in terms of (predominantly) liberal concerns with *socio-political* incursion into the individual citizen's freedoms. In this sense, the penal State's size can increase in terms of the *number* of people subject to its control and the *extent* to which that control intrudes upon their lives. This section therefore considers the charge that England and Wales has become excessively large, relative to the time before the decline of the rehabilitative ideal, in the context of three key literatures: 'mass punishment', or increase in the *number* of people subjected to penal control; 'over-criminalisation' of human conduct through the *law*; and the 'dispersal of discipline', by which criminal justice *permeates* more intrusively into wider social life. In each case, we must consider not only whether the penal State has grown, but also whether or not that growth is *excessive* – that is, whether or not increases in size can be excused by any penal policy aim. For instance, if crime rates rise, that would be at least a prima facie reason to expand the penal population, too. We will discuss possible excuses for a larger penal State as they arise.

A. Mass Imprisonment and Mass Supervision

The first way we might measure the penal State's size is simply to look at the raw number of people subject to its control – and especially, the number of subjects of imprisonment and of probation supervision (which may include those serving non-custodial sentences, released early from prison, or subject to pre-trial oversight).[1] We could draw this net still wider: to those subject to fines, discharges, and other non-custodial sentences; to those subject to police detention, stop-and-search, or investigation. But probation and prison populations provide a useful shorthand for the most direct and intrusive interventions of the Anglo-Welsh penal State into its subjects' lives, and at least advances on the generally prison-focussed literature that has been carried on up to this point – albeit mostly in the US.[2] For this reason, much of this literature is not just concerned with the growth of imprisonment as such, but also with racial and class-based disproportionalities in penal populations, which we will encounter more fully when we discuss the penal State's shape, below.[3] It has also tended to ignore the comparable expansion of supervision, and indeed, the phenomenon of 'mass punishment' more generally.[4] For now, however, let us consider the situation in England and Wales, and focus purely on the size dimension.

If the penal system *has* expanded over the period since the rise of retributive penal policies in England and Wales in the early 1990s, then that produces a substantial challenge to the claim that retributive proportionality can constrain penal States in practice. So, we need to be able to answer two key questions: firstly, have rates of punishment risen; and secondly, is this rise in the use of punishment excused by other factors, such as a rise in crime? Figure One and Table One below

[1] See, eg, Fergus McNeill and Kristel Beyens, 'Introduction: Studying Mass Supervision', in Fergus McNeill and Kristel Beyens (eds), *Offender Supervision in Europe* (2013, Palgrave Macmillan), pp 1–6.

[2] See, eg, David Garland, 'Introduction: The Meaning of Mass Imprisonment' (2001) 3 *Punishment and Society* 4; Mona Lynch, 'Mass Incarceration, Legal Change, and Locale: Understanding and Remediating American Penal Overindulgence' (2011) 10 *Criminology & Public Policy* 673; Marc Mauer, 'Addressing the Political Environment Affecting Mass Imprisonment' (2011) 10 *Criminology & Public Policy* 699; Michelle Phelps, 'The Paradox of Probation: Community Supervision in an Age of Mass Incarceration' (2013) 35 *Law & Policy* 51.

[3] See, eg, Michael Tonry, *Malign Neglect: Race, Crime, and Punishment in America* (1995, Oxford University Press); Bruce Western, *Punishment and Inequality in America* (2006, Russell Sage Foundation); Michelle Alexander, *The New Jim Crow: Mass Imprisonment in an Age of Colorblindness* (2010, The New Press); Loïc Wacquant, *Punishing the Poor: The Neoliberal Government of Social Insecurity* (2010, Duke University Press); Judah Schept, *Progressive Punishment: Job Loss, Jail Growth, and the Neoliberal Logic of Carceral Expansion* (2015, New York University Press); Elizabeth Brown and Amy Smith, 'Challenging Mass Incarceration in the City of Care: Punishment, Community, and Residential Placement' (2018) 22 *Theoretical Criminology* 4. Compare Loïc Wacquant, 'Class, Race, and Hyperincarceration in Revanchist America' (2010) 139 *Daedelus* 74.

[4] See particularly Phelps, *The Paradox of Probation*, above n 2; Marcelo Aebi, Natalia Delgrande, and Yann Magruet, 'Have Community Sanctions and Measures Widened the Net of the European Criminal Justice Systems?' (2015) 17 *Punishment & Society* 575; Fergus McNeill, 'Mass Supervision, Misrecognition, and the "Malopticon"' (2018) *Punishment and Society*, forthcoming; Fergus McNeill, *Pervasive Punishment: Making Sense of 'Mass Supervision'* (2018, Emerald Publishing), pp 16–18.

map the development of trends in four metrics over the last 30 years: the *recorded crime rate* (that is, the number of crimes officially noted by the police); the *recorded homicide rate* (as a way of measuring change in the most *serious* crime over the same period);[5] the *mean prison population* over a 12-month period; and the *total probation population*, that is, every unique person subject to probation supervision either as part of a non-custodial sentence or before or after release from imprisonment.

Table One Crime and Punishment in Numbers over Time, 1989–2018[6]

Year	Recorded Crime Rate (Homicide)	Prison Pop'n.	Probation Pop'n.	Year	Recorded Crime Rate (Homicide)	Prison Pop'n.	Probation Pop'n.
1989	3,870,748 (641)	48,600	130,420	2004	6,013,759 (904)	74,657	177,387
1990	4,543,611 (669)	45,600	131,157	2005	5,637,511 (868)	75,979	181,211
1991	5,267,173 (725)	45,900	132,754	2006	5,555,172 (764)	78,127	192,583
1992	5,591,717 (687)	45,800	132,662	2007	5,427,558 (758)	80,126	242,722
1993	5,526,255 (670)	44,552	141,284	2008	4,952,277 (775)	82,572	243,434
1994	5,252,980 (726)	48,800	151,926	2009	4,702,697 (664)	83,559	241,504
1995	5,100,241 (745)	51,000	153,645	2010	4,338,295 (620)	84,725	238,973

(Continued)

[5] On the use of homicide as a proxy for serious crime, see Lisa Miller, *The Myth of Mob Rule: Violent Crime and Democratic Politics* (2016, Oxford University Press), ch 2.

[6] Data on crime rates are drawn from three sources: Home Office, *A Summary of Recorded Crime Data from 1898 to 2001/02*, published 19 July 2012; Home Office, *A Summary of Recorded Crime Data from Year Ending Mar 2003 to Year Ending Mar 2015*; and Office for National Statistics, *Crime Data in England and Wales: Quarterly Data Tables*, online at: www.ons.gov.uk/peoplepopulationandcommunity/crimeandjustice/datasets/crimeinenglandandwalesquarterlydatatables. Both Home Office sources are available for download at: www.gov.uk/government/statistics/historical-crime-data. NB: data after 1998 is recorded from March of the previous year to March of the current year. From 2015, to maintain comparability I have used the figures excluding fraud offences. Prisons and probation population information dating back to 2012 are available from: Ministry of Justice, 'Quarterly Offender Management Statistics', online at: Ministry of Justice, *Statistics at MOJ*, online at: www.gov.uk/government/organisations/ministry-of-justice/about/statistics#topics. Older data were drawn from annual *Probation Statistics* documents and the *Home Office Statistics Bulletin*. It would be tedious to note every discrete document, which can be found by reviewing the National Archives, *UK Government Web Archive*, at: webarchive.nationalarchives.gov.uk/. NB: for 1989–1997, prison population data were rounded to three significant figures. The more accurate data for 1993 and 1998–2012 are taken from Michael Cavadino, James Dignan, and George Mair, *The Penal System: An Introduction*, Fifth edn (2013, SAGE), p 13.

Table One ***(Continued)***

Year	Recorded Crime Rate (Homicide)	Prison Pop'n.	Probation Pop'n.	Year	Recorded Crime Rate (Homicide)	Prison Pop'n.	Probation Pop'n.
1996	5,036,552 (679)	55,300	158,169	2011	4,150,916 (639)	88,179	234,528
1997	4,598,327 (739)	61,100	164,365	2012	4,023,007 (553)	86,634	224,823
1998	4,545,337 (748)	65,298	173,467	2013	3,733,059 (558)	84,249	219,588
1999	5,109,089 (750)	64,771	173,644	2014	3,717,768 (533)	85,291	217,359
2000	5,301,187 (766)	64,602	168,529	2015	3,811,268 (534)	85,678	241,144
2001	5,170,843 (850)	66,301	165,491	2016	3,949,500 (689)	85,130	267,146
2002	5,525,024 (891)	70,778	173,701	2017	4,503,500 (685)	83,263	264,649
2003	5,974,960 (1,047)	73,038	175,266	2018	4,978,455 (719)	82,773	262,758

Measuring either the rate of crime or of punishment is harder than one might think. Crime data are notoriously difficult to get at, given that not every crime will be reported, investigated, or recorded in official statistics.[7] Punishment data is easier to verify, but note that prison and probation populations are calculated differently and so are not directly comparable, especially since these data include some overlap if persons both in prison and on probation at some point during the same 12-month period. Moreover, the probationary population has been particularly subject to change as new forms of probation-based penalties (such as unpaid work) have emerged, and have been used very differently over this period. This accounts, in particular, for the jump in the probation population after 2005, when the entire prison population became part of the probation caseload under what was then the National Offender Management Service (NOMS), and after 2015, when the Offender Rehabilitation Act 2014 imposed further mandatory periods of probation supervision on offenders serving short sentences.[8] Finally, we should

[7] See generally Mike Maguire and Susan McVie, 'Crime Data and Crime Statistics: A Critical Reflection', in Alison Liebling, Shadd Maruna, and Lesley McAra (eds), *The Oxford Handbook of Criminology*, Sixth edn (2017, Oxford University Press).

[8] See, eg, Lol Burke and Steve Collett, '*Transforming Rehabilitation*: Organisational Bifurcation and the End of Probation as We Knew It?' (2016) 63 *Probation Journal* 120; Matthew Cracknall, 'Post-Release Reform to Short Prison Sentences: Re-Legitimising and Widening the Net of Punishment' (2018) 65 *Probation Journal* 302.

also note that these crime and punishment statistics bear only a limited relationship to one another. The recorded crime rate consists of the crimes reported to the police that are considered worth investigating. Of these, only some investigations will result in a prosecution. Of those cases that do progress to trial, not every defendant will be convicted, and not every offender will be sentenced to prison or to probation supervision. As a result of this rate of attrition, it is not necessarily surprising that the recorded crime rate is many orders of magnitude above the combined penal population for prisons and probation.[9]

Figure One Graph of Crime Rate and Probation/Prison Population, 1989–2018

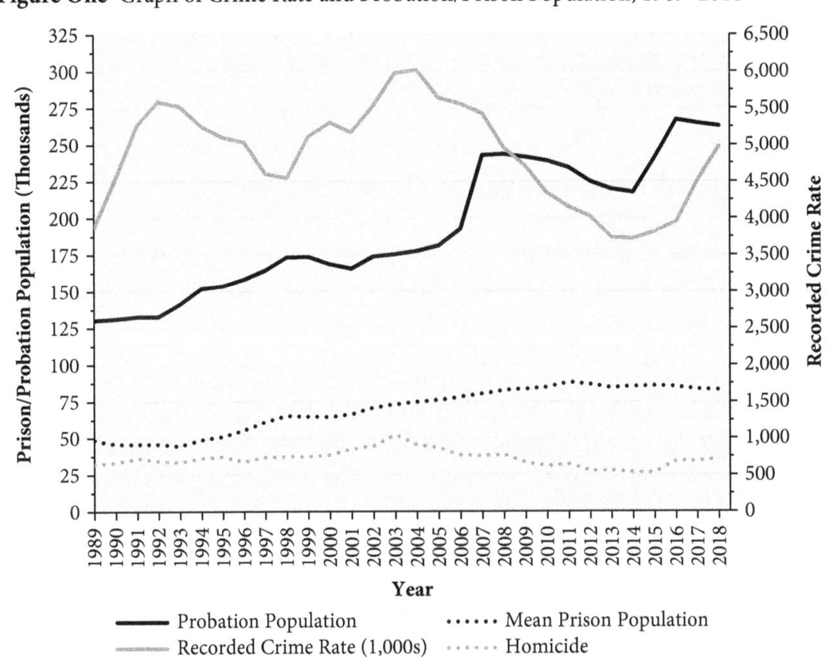

For this reason, the sheer inequality of scales between the crime rates and punishment rates do not indicate that any increase is necessarily a good thing – even though the punishment of the factually guilty is one of the key rationales of criminal justice in a liberal-democratic polity.[10] We should not assume, in other words, that penal excess is not a possible explanation of the growth in prison and probation populations over this period. Indeed, what these data do tell us is that both prison and probation populations have expanded substantially over the

[9] See generally Andrew Sanders and Richard Young, 'From Suspect to Trial', in Mike Maguire, Rod Morgan and Robert Reiner (eds), *The Oxford Handbook of Criminology*, Fifth edn (2012, Oxford University Press).

[10] See generally Herbert Packer, 'Two Models of the Criminal Process' (1964) 113 *University of Pennsylvania Law Review* 1.

last 30 years. The prison population has nearly doubled between 1989 and 2018 (and has doubled earlier prison populations in the 1970s),[11] and the probation-supervised population has more-or-less doubled since 1989. Although probation population has been relatively stable since 2016, and prison population since its peak in 2011, neither is there any sign of a sustained cycling back down to the values of earlier decades. Meanwhile, the recorded crime rate rose throughout the 1990s (despite a dip in 1997–1998), but has more or less remained constant in a cycle between three and five million recorded offences. Looking at homicide rate does not suggest a spike in violent crime, either. Something else must be driving penal expansion, and it does not seem to respond in any meaningful way to the crime rate – as a last-resort penal system should within a liberal democracy. In other words, therefore, this expansion of raw penal population provides evidence of worsening penal excess over the last 30 years.

B. Over-Criminalisation and 'The Preventive Turn'

The raw number of people subject to direct penal control is only one aspect of potential penal excess in a liberal polity. After all, criminal law has a generally proscriptive effect upon human behaviour, because the threat of punishment tends to discourage at least some people from acting as they otherwise might, at least some of the time.[12] Even if the penal State does not exert direct control over free citizens, however, its size can also indirectly restrict their autonomous decision-making. For this reason, criminal law theorists have written extensively about the *principled* limits of criminal law – the normative principles governing how far the criminal law *should* reach, according to the polity's purported values.[13] Whatever the precise principles that should limit the criminalisation of previously non-criminal conduct, these theories tend to call for minimal reliance upon the criminal law, especially when alternative systems of legal regulation and social control are available.[14] These authors also indicate a growing phenomenon of *over-criminalisation*, where more conduct than is strictly

[11] See Cavadino, Dignan, and Mair, above n 6, p 13.

[12] See, eg, Andrew von Hirsch, *Deserved Criminal Sentences* (2017, Hart), pp 9–10.

[13] See, eg, John Stuart Mill, 'On Liberty', in John Stuart Mill, *On Liberty, Utilitarianism, and Other Essays* (2015, Mark Philp and Frederick Rosen (eds), Oxford University Press); Joel Feinberg, *The Moral Limits of the Criminal Law*, Four Volumes (1984–1988, Oxford University Press); and AP Simester and Andreas von Hirsch, *Crimes, Harms and Wrongs: On the Principles of Criminalisation* (2014, Hart). Compare Nicola Lacey and Lucia Zedner, 'Criminalization: Historical, Legal, and Criminological Perspectives', in Alison Liebling, Shadd Maruna, and Lesley McAra (eds), *The Oxford Handbook of Criminology*, Sixth edn (2017, Oxford University Press).

[14] See, eg, Joel Feinberg, *Harm to Others: The Moral Limits of the Criminal Law*, Volume One (1984, Oxford University Press), 22–25; Simester and von Hirsch, above n 13, pp 189–232. Compare Edwin Schur, *Radical Non-Intervention: Rethinking the Delinquency Problem* (1973, Prentice Hall); and Nils Christie, *A Suitable Amount of Crime* (2004, Routledge).

necessary for the legitimate aims of a liberal-democratic State becomes subject to criminal law.[15]

With that said, quantifying 'how much' criminal law there is in a given polity is surprisingly hard. We cannot simply count the number of crimes, because some offences may overlap, while others may be antiquated and no longer in de facto use by the penal system.[16] Moreover, fewer offences may be able to cover the same amount of human conduct. For instance, English law has three offences dealing with non-consensual sexual penetrations, whereas substantively the same conduct is covered by one offence under the regime of the International Criminal Court.[17] Likewise, it would be a mistake to quantify criminal law purely in terms of the *volume* of the law – in terms of the number of pages, sections, or words of text in binding legal sources. After all, a four-word statute: "Thou shalt not kill" may criminalise more conduct than a wordier framing of the prohibition on murder that allows more nuance in attributing liability.[18] Finally, measuring the 'amount' of law and its overall intrusiveness into private life requires an engagement with the practical procedural impact of the diversity, complexity, and opacity of the law to lay (and even expert) practitioners, and the impact of discretion on the effect the criminal law actually has in regulating social conduct. Our attention cannot be confined purely to legal doctrine.[19] In sum, a qualitative study of the spread of criminal law is prohibitively hard to do in any meaningful way.

More significant (and rather easier to explore) are the *qualitative* changes expressed through recent over-criminalisation – that is, the different spheres of life that criminalisation is seeping into.[20] These changes are particularly implicated in the recent so-called 'preventive turn' in English criminal law:[21] a general shift in the focus of criminalisation away from responding to harm, and towards a

[15] See generally Douglas Husak, *Overcriminalization: The Limits of the Criminal Law* (2008, Oxford University Press).

[16] See, eg, ibid, pp 8–13; James Chalmers and Fiona Leverick, 'Tracking the Creation of Criminal Offences' [2013] *Crim LR* 543; James Chalmers, '"Frenzied Law-Making": Overcriminalisation by Numbers' (2014) 67 *Current Legal Problems* 483; James Chalmers, Fiona Leverick, and Alasdair Shaw, 'Is Formal Criminalisation Really on the Rise? Evidence from the 1950s' [2015] *Crim LR* 177.

[17] Sexual Offences Act 2003, ss 1–2 and 4(4); International Criminal Court, *Elements of Crimes* (2011, ICC): Arts 7(1)(g)-1 and 8(2)(b)(xxii)-1.

[18] Husak, above n 15, pp 9–11. Compare the fictitious legal issue in Lon Fuller, 'The Case of the Speluncean Explorers' (1949) 62 *Harvard Law Review* 616.

[19] Husak, above n 15, pp 17–20. Compare Nicola Lacey, 'Historicising Criminalisation: Conceptual and Empirical Issues' (2009) 72 *Modern Law Review* 936.

[20] See, eg, James Chalmers and Fiona Leverick, 'Criminal Law in the Shadows: Creating Offences in Delegated Legislation' (2018) 38 *Legal Studies* 221; Peter Cartwright, 'Crime, Punishment, and Consumer Protection' (2007) 30 *Journal of Consumer Policy* 1.

[21] See especially Peter Ramsay, *The Insecurity State: Vulnerable Autonomy and the Right to Security in Criminal Law* (2012, Oxford University Press); Andrew Ashworth, Lucia Zedner, and Patrick Tomlin (eds), *Prevention and the Limits of the Criminal Law* (2013, Oxford University Press); Andrew Ashworth and Lucia Zedner, *Preventive Justice* (2014, Oxford University Press); Henrique Carvalho, *The Preventive Turn in Criminal Law* (2017, Oxford University Press).

preoccupation with avoiding the mere risk of harm.[22] Prevention itself is far from a new concept in criminalisation theory; indeed, the most foundational liberal accounts justify criminalisation as a way of *preventing* future harm to others.[23] Moreover, risk is hardly a new preoccupation of the criminal law. Indeed, one of the essential requirements of a criminal justice system that respects us as rights-bearing citizens is that we are protected from crimes.[24] However, recent reforms have brought more and more remote forms of risk under criminal law's control, with the result that criminal justice has leaked into more aspects of everyday life.[25]

The construction of newer offences extends the traditional ambit of criminal law in three crucial respects. Firstly, the last three decades have seen a prominent shift towards strict liability offences, which require no substantive standard of mens rea, including for offences which can be punished by imprisonment, and therefore place no requirement on the prosecutor to prove any particular mental wrongdoing on the part of the defendant.[26] Secondly, a range of newer offences, especially those concerned with preventing terrorist attacks, are 'pre-inchoate' – going further back even than the already-nebulous class of 'incomplete' offences such as attempts, to address conduct that *only might* eventually become dangerous.[27] Thirdly, and partly as an extension to the 'pre-inchoate' offences, the law has also seen an expansion of *status offences*, such as those based purely on possession (eg of firearms or knives), or of membership of prohibited organisations. Together, these new classes of offences provide a pretext for wider preventative interventions by increasingly empowered police forces.[28] The upshot is that previously anodyne realms of public life, albeit ones that could materialise into a future harm, are now the subject of criminal control. This is a general increase in the reach of the criminal justice State into everyday life, in the service of protecting the public from severe threats. Moreover, in order to preserve the general public from its

[22] See, eg, Andrew Ashworth and Lucia Zedner, 'Defending the Criminal Law: Reflections on the Changing Character of Crime, Procedure, and Sanctions' (2008) 2 *Criminal Law and Philosophy* 21.

[23] See Feinberg, *Harm to Others*, above n 14, pp 10–13, 26. Compare Frederick Schauer, 'The Ubiquity of Prevention', in Ashworth, Zedner, and Tomlin (eds), *Prevention and the Limits of Criminal Law*, above n 21.

[24] See, eg, Ashworth and Zedner, *Preventive Justice*, above n 21, pp 10–13; Françoise Tulkens, 'The Paradoxical Relationship between Criminal Law and Human Rights' (2011) 9 *Journal of International Criminal Justice* 577.

[25] Ibid; compare Peter Ramsay, 'Overcriminalization as Vulnerable Citizenship' (2010) 13 *New Criminal Law Review* 262; Ana Aliverti, *Crimes of Mobility: Criminal Law and the Regulation of Mobility* (2013, Routledge); Lucia Zedner, 'Terrorizing Criminal Law' (2014) 8 *Criminal Law and Philosophy* 99; Mary Bosworth and Sarah Turnbull, 'Immigration, Detention, and the Expansion of Penal Power in the United Kingdom', in Keramet Reiter and Alexa Koenig (eds), *Extreme Punishment: Comparative Studies in Detention, Incarceration, and Solitary Confinement* (2015, Palgrave Macmillan).

[26] Ashworth and Zedner, 'Defending the Criminal Law', above n 22, pp 31–33.

[27] Peter Ramsay, 'Democratic Limits to Preventive Criminal Law', in: Andrew Ashworth, Lucia Zedner, and Patrick Tolmin (eds), *Prevention and the Limits of the Criminal Law* (2013, Oxford University Press), p 215 and fn 4. See more generally, Ashworth and Zedner, *Preventive Justice*, above n 21, pp 96–102.

[28] Ashworth and Zedner, *Preventive Justice*, above n 21, pp 51–73, 99–100. See generally Kent Roach, *The 9/11 Effect: Comparative Counter-Terrorism* (2011, Cambridge University Press), pp 238–308.

worst excesses, much of this extension is governed only by police and prosecutorial discretions, which raise potential concerns about bias and corruption (which we will discuss again when it comes to the shape of penal excess, below).[29]

Not all of these extensions are necessarily evidence of over-criminalisation – indeed, some of the most innovative and broad offences (such as fraud and offences of failure to prevent corporate bribery and tax evasion)[30] are designed to target white-collar and corporate crime, areas that have been historically *under*-criminalised.[31] However, they do suggest a leakage of the criminal law into new areas, and a new level of omnipresence of law in people's lives, ostensibly in response to changing threats requiring new legal solutions in the name of public protection. But then, protecting the public *is* a major justifying aim of liberal criminal justice, and so the liberal criminal theorists have struggled to produce clear guidelines as to how much prevention is "too much" in order to challenge this qualitative over-criminalisation. The sorts of factors that are typically mentioned – threats to autonomy, to public safety, to security, prosperity, and the core values of liberal democracy – are just the sort of aims that underpin all criminal law.[32] Of course this does not mean *all* prevention is justified under a liberal approach: we might accept some new offences but not others, or express a cautious willingness to allow some (but not all) preventive criminal law on principled grounds.[33] But where those lines are to be drawn is an open question, and orthodox liberal criminal theory has tended to be relaxed, in principle, about most types of preventive criminal offences.

This seems like a problem – the preventive turn intuitively *feels* like a sign of penal excess, but we cannot say *how* excessive, because I have defined the size of the penal State in predominantly (post-Hobbesian) liberal terms. This orthodox liberal perspective defines freedom in a fundamentally ambiguous manner, as something to at once prize and protect, but also fear and control. This conception makes it difficult to make clear distinctions between when freedom should be protected, and when constrained, and therefore to resist excesses arising in the name of public protection.[34] While we could resolve this issue by reconfiguring liberal conceptions of Statehood to better reflect the balance between 'freedom to' and 'freedom from',[35] that would entail a lengthy period of introspection

[29] See generally Husak, above n 15, pp 25–30.

[30] See, respectively the Fraud Act 2006, ss 1–4; the Bribery Act 2010, ss 7–9; and the Criminal Finances Act 2017, ss 44–50.

[31] See generally Michael Levi and Nicholas Lord, 'White-Collar and Corporate Crime', in Alison Liebling, Shadd Maruna, and Lesley McAra (eds), *The Oxford Handbook of Criminology*, Sixth edn (2017, Oxford University Press); Steven Box, *Power, Crime and Mystification* (1983, Routledge), ch 2.

[32] Ramsay, 'Democratic Limits', above n 27; Tulkens, above n 24; Henrique Carvalho, 'Liberty and Insecurity in the Criminal Law: Lessons from Thomas Hobbes' (2017) 11 *Criminal Law and Philosophy* 249.

[33] This is broadly the position taken by Ashworth and Zedner: above n 21, pp 104–116, 250–267.

[34] See generally Ramsay, 'Democratic Limits', above n 27, pp 219–223; Carvalho, 'Liberty and Insecurity in the Criminal Law', above n 32.

[35] As Carvalho, ibid, suggests.

preventing any immediate confrontation with contemporary penal excess, and a loss of the rhetorical force derived from orthodox liberalism's commitment to penal minimalism. Fortunately, Ramsay offers a means of avoiding this, by arguing against preventive criminal law based on *democratic* objections to the penal excess.[36] In particular, Ramsay concludes that the preventive turn represents a challenge to the democratic citizen's right to *self-determination* – that is, to exercise free control over oneself as part of the patchwork of 'collective self-government' that makes up rule by the people.[37] While liberalism is willing to surrender positive liberty if it secures an overall greater degree of freedom from the threat posed by others, the right to self-determination requires:[38]

> that the substantive law not be used as a means to subvert the institutions of formal trust among citizens which is a necessary condition of the executive being held to account for its accusations against citizens. It requires the state's normal surveillance powers be limited to identifying *dangerous acts* rather than dangerous actors (emphasis added).

Whilst orthodox liberals can accept a reining-in of that right to a private life, at least to some extent, so long as it does not endanger the citizen's overall personal *autonomy*, substantive democrats cannot, because it undermines the fundamental basis of a genuinely democratic society. Ramsay therefore provides us with a persuasive basis on which to argue, from a liberal-democratic criminal law theorist's perspective, that the 'preventive turn' in English criminal law is a form of penal excess, because the criminal justice State oversteps its bounds to protect from harm at an unacceptable cost to democratic self-determination.

C. The Dispersal of Discipline: Blurring the Boundaries of the Penal State

Since the late 1970s, criminologists have mapped a *dispersal of discipline*, in which the penal State does not so much grow larger as much as it *penetrates* the daily lives of its citizens to a greater extent.[39] These discussions specifically relied upon Foucault's account of the emergence of the modern penal State in general, and of the industrialised prison in particular. During this process, the aim of the penal system ceased to be the spectacular bodily torture of those who challenged the monarch's power, and became instead about *disciplining* the mind of the errant citizen who could not satisfy an increasingly industrialised society's needs for

[36] Ramsay, 'Democratic Limits', above n 26.
[37] Ibid, p 230.
[38] Ibid, p 232.
[39] See especially Stanley Cohen, 'The Punitive City: Notes on the Dispersal of Social Control' (1979) 3 *Contemporary Crises* 339; Thomas Mathiesen, 'The Future of Control Systems – The Case of Norway' (1980) 8 *International Journal of the Sociology of Law* 149; Stanley Cohen, *Visions of Social Control: Crime, Punishment and Classification* (1985, Polity Press).

politically passive and untroublesome labour.[40] Part of this process involved the concentration of penal power away from public displays of cruelty and into a private correctional spaces: 'complete and austere institutions' cut off from the external society as much as possible.[41] However, Foucault also imagined a generalisation of the sort of discipline most obvious in non-penal institutions like schools, barracks, workhouses, factories, and prisons, across entire cities, and indeed, beyond them.[42] In the 1980s, Foucault's sociological inheritors began to explore ways in which discipline had extended out of the custodial centre and merged into external social life. While we have covered some of the phenomena they identified in our discussion of mass punishment and over-criminalisation, above, they also pointed to a *blurring* of penal institutions, processes, and actions with the non-penal spheres of citizens' everyday lives.[43] In particular, Stanley Cohen highlighted the growing trend towards community penalties as evidence of a dispersal of discipline: probation supervision was being co-opted into a means of supervision, intrusive rehabilitative control, and eventually, punishment, which took place alongside the individual's day-to-day life. Moreover, other forms of community penalty, such as unpaid work, represented a direct movement of previous custodial concepts (such as the penitential value of unpaid work) into the community.[44] However, the dispersal of discipline also occurs in terms of the blurring of crime prevention technologies with daily life, and of public and private spheres more generally – the replacement of imprisonment with curfews enforced by electronic monitoring, but also the replacement of monitoring of specific suspects with the mass surveillance of crowds (and of online metadata).[45]

A dispersal of discipline *into* society does not necessarily amount to an (excessive) increase in the overall size or intrusiveness of the State. What would need to be shown is a general increase in the *reach* of the penal State – over people and into their lives. Indeed, the move towards community corrections has been driven at least in part by attempts to replace disruptive, coercive and expensive custodial punishment with 'alternatives to imprisonment' in the community.[46] In practice, however, community sanctions have widened the net of carceral control, in two

[40] Michel Foucault, *Discipline and Punish: The Birth of the Prison* (1977, Alan Sheridan (trans), Penguin).

[41] Ibid, p 231; compare the 'total institution': Erving Goffman, *Asylums: Essays on the Social Situation of Mental Patients and Other Inmates* (1961, Anchor Books), p 11.

[42] Ibid, pp 195–228; Cohen, *Visions of Social Control*, above n 39, pp 208–210.

[43] Cohen, 'The Punitive City', above n 39, pp 346–347.

[44] Ibid, pp 347–357.

[45] See, eg, Benjamin Goold, Ian Loader, and Angélica Thumala, 'The Banality of Security: The Curious Case of Surveillance Cameras' (2013) 53 *British Journal of Criminology* 977; Mike Nellis, 'Understanding the Electronic Monitoring of Offenders in Europe: Expansion, Regulation and Prospects' (2014) 62 *Crime, Law and Social Change* 489; Cohen, 'The Punitive City', above n 39, pp 353–356; Mathiesen, above n 39; Richard Fox, 'Someone to Watch Over Us: Back to the Panopticon?' (2001) 1 *Criminology and Criminal Justice* 251. See also the Investigatory Powers Act 2016.

[46] See, eg, Dirk van Zyl Smit, *Handbook of Basic Principles and Promising Practices on Alternatives to Imprisonment* (2007, UN Office on Drugs and Crime), pp 25–45; Helen Mills, *Community Sentences: A Solution to Penal Excess?* (Centre for Crime and Justice Studies, July 2011); Ioan Durnescu, 'Pains of

key respects. Firstly, community orders and suspended sentence orders (especially since the latter have become able to incorporate the same 'requirements' as the former) have tended to act more as alternatives to one another, and to other non-custodial sentences such as fines, than they have tended to reduce reliance on imprisonment.[47] Secondly, community penalties have faced a need to 'toughen up' from either a punitive or a public-protection perspective. This has, in part, driven the increasing imposition of imprisonment being against those who breach their orders.[48] But whatever the upshot, we are seeing a general increase of the size of the penal State, despite (if not because of) attempts to provide non-custodial alternatives to imprisonment. The dispersal of criminal-justice discipline into wider public (and private life) has also been driven by three major trends in criminal law and procedure: the increased use of fast-tracked *'fixed penalty notices'*, colloquially known as 'on-the-spot fines'; the emergence of 'hybrid' *quasi-criminal orders*, most infamously the Anti-Social Behaviour Order (ASBO); and the emergence of new patterns of formal and informal post-conviction *civil disqualification*.

Fixed penalty notices are hardly new, having been used for decades in road traffic and parking offences,[49] and being part of a legacy of less formalised police intervention to ensure social order dating back to at least the fourteenth century.[50] However, in 2001 a new 'Penalty Notice for Disorder' (PND) enabled the use of 'on-the-spot fines' to deal with those involved in low-level public nuisances, such as public drunkenness, harassing or alarming individuals, or wasting police time.[51] As their colloquial name suggests, they involve a police officer imposing a binding order to pay a fixed sum of money (either £50 or £80), without trial or conviction (although the fined subject has a right to contest the order at court). This fine will not appear on the individual's criminal record, although it does remain in the police's own records and can inform subsequent policing decisions regarding the subject. Most of the offences covered by PNDs have maximum sentences well in excess of the fixed penalties imposed. Indeed, PNDs were intended to help to speedily punish lower-level offending with less intrusive and invasive penalties, and thereby reduce penal excess overall.[52]

Probation: Effective Practice and Human Rights' (2011) 55 *International Journal of Offender Therapy and Comparative Criminology* 530; Helene De Vos and Elli Gilbert, 'Freedom, So Close But Yet So Far: The Impact of the Ongoing Confrontation with Freedom on the Perceived Severity of Punishment' (2017) 9 *European Journal of Probation* 132; McNeill, 'Mass Supervision, Misrecognition, and the "Malopticon', above n 4.

[47] See also Aebi et al, above n 4; Gwen Robinson, 'Three Narratives and a Funeral: Community Punishment in England and Wales', in Gwen Robinson and Fergus McNeill (eds), *Community Punishment: European Perspectives* (2016, Routledge), pp 41–44. Compare Nicola Padfield, 'Time To Bury the Custody "Threshold"?' [2011] *Crim LR* 593.

[48] See generally Gwen Robinson and Pamela Ugwudike, 'Investing in "Toughness": Probation, Enforcement, and Legitimacy' (2012) 51 *The Howard Journal of Criminal Justice* 300.

[49] Ashworth and Zedner, 'Defending the Criminal Law', above n 22, pp 26–27.

[50] See *R v Howell* [1982] QB 416, at 427f. Compare the power of magistrates to 'bind over' individuals without conviction to 'keep the peace', under s 115 of the Magistrates Courts Act 1980.

[51] Criminal Justice and Police Act 2001, s 1; see also ss 2–5.

[52] Ashworth and Zedner, 'Defending the Criminal Law', above n 22, p 27.

'Hybrid' or 'quasi-criminal' orders, by contrast, blurred the boundaries of criminal and civil law by enabling civil orders to be imposed that had potential penal consequences should they be breached. ASBOs, for instance, could be imposed against those whose (of itself usually non-criminal) behaviour was problematised by neighbours and community members (such as rough sleeping, begging, public drunkenness, and noise violations), but which was not of itself criminal. However, breach of the order by repeating the 'anti-social' activity was a criminal offence, punishable by up to five years' imprisonment.[53] Both PNDs and hybrid orders could be considered a mild form of *diversion*, allowing low-level offending (and problematic behaviour that could potentially degenerate *into* criminality in future, if unchallenged) to be dealt with at a relatively minor level and with minimal long-term repercussions for the wrongdoer.

However, in practice, both innovations tended to widen the net by pulling more people into the criminal justice system's ambit.[54] PNDs in particular were overwhelming used against those who would normally have received formal cautions or warnings, rather than those facing the more serious consequences of full-blown prosecution.[55] As a result, minor offences that might previously have been ignored fell into the formal system, in effect increasing rather than decreasing the number of people being punished. Moreover, the truncation of policing and prosecutorial decisions about whether to investigate and prosecute a crime involved in these measures raises troubling implications for a potential suspect or defendant protesting their innocence. In the case of PNDs, the prosecutorial discretion that prevents cases against the public interest, or those without sufficient evidence to back them up, is replaced with a presumed punishment that can only be challenged if the subject of the PND is willing to invest time and resources into seeking a trial, and is prepared to risk the (usually much more costly) consequences conviction in court would bring.[56] In the case of ASBOs and other hybrid orders, the procedural safeguards of a criminal trial are partially avoided by moving the initial imposition of the order into the civil courts, where fewer fair-trial protections exist.[57] Whilst the offence of breach of an ASBO would have to be pursued as a criminal offence, under the more rigorous safeguards of criminal procedure, the upshot is that the order not to commit more anti-social behaviour – which the ordinary

[53] Crime and Disorder Act 1998, s 1.

[54] See Andrew Ashworth, 'Is the Criminal Law a Lost Cause?' (2000) 116 *LQR* 225.

[55] Rebecca Roberts and Richard Garside, 'Punishment before Justice? Understanding Penalty Notices for Disorder' (Crime and Society Foundation Briefing #1, March 2005), especially pp 5–6; Elizabeth Burney, *Making People Behave: Anti-Social Behaviour, Politics and Policy* (2005, Willan), pp 40–41.

[56] Compare Ashworth and Zedner, 'Defending the Criminal Law', above n 22, pp 27–28. See also, more generally, Rod Morgan, 'Austerity, Subsidiarity and Parsimony: Offending Behaviour and Criminalisation', in Arianna Silvestri (ed), *Lessons for the Coalition: An End of Term Report on New Labour and Criminal Justice* (Centre for Crime and Justice Studies, January 2011).

[57] See, eg, Andrew Ashworth, 'Social Control and "Anti-Social Behaviour": The Subversion of Human Rights?' (2004) 120 *LQR* 263; Simon Hoffman and Stuart McDonald, 'Should ASBOs Be Civilised?' [2010] *Crim LR* 457, p 460.

citizen is not under – is imposed through a procedural sleight-of-hand that erodes the protection of the citizen from the improper infliction of State punishment.[58] As a result, both impositions have tended to expand penal populations rather than reduce them, and therefore, have tended to (unjustifiably) increase the overall size of the penal State. Although ASBOs in particular were functionally abolished and replaced by the 2010–2015 Coalition government,[59] they were not reversed entirely, and retain an enclave of criminal-style social control within the civil law – an expansion of the penal State, embedded in wider State processes, and entrenched within a separate framework that criminal justice policy will find difficult to influence in future.[60]

Our third category of quasi-criminal order, *civil disqualifications*, consists of limitations imposed after criminal conviction, which restrict the offender's capacity to engage in particular activities thereafter, temporarily or permanently. Formal post-conviction restrictions (such as bans on holding political office or possessing a driver's licence)[61] are old and ingrained features of criminal justice.[62] However, the period since the 1980s has seen a considerable expansion of civil society's informal *collusion* in effectively disqualifying offenders from economic participation in some or all lines of work, due to the imposition of a public, highly stigmatising, and long-lasting *criminal record*.[63] Criminal records have existed for at least the last three centuries due to concerns about the risk posed by preventable reoffending,[64] but since 1980 the law has changed to make it far easier for prospective employers to find out information about previous convictions, in response to several high-profile examples of violence and sexual predation, typically against young children. The result has been an explosion of the number of criminal record checks being made against prospective employees, with over three million checks made in the 2007 calendar year.[65] At the same time, it is becoming harder in

[58] Ashworth and Zedner, 'Defending the Criminal Law', above n 22, pp 29–31; see also Peter Ramsay, 'Substantially Uncivilised ASBOs' [2010] *Crim LR* 761; Andrew Ashworth and Lucia Zedner, 'Preventive Orders: A Problem of Undercriminalization?' in: RA Duff, Lindsay Farmer, SE Marshall, Massimo Renzo, and Victor Tadros (eds), *The Boundaries of the Criminal Law* (2014, Oxford University Press), especially pp 80–85.

[59] See generally the Anti-Social Behaviour, Crime and Policing Act 2014, ss 1–33.

[60] See generally Hoffman and McDonald, above n 57; Ramsay, 'Substantially Uncivilised ASBOs', above n 58, and Simon Hoffman and Stuart McDonald, 'Substantively Uncivilised ASBOs: A Response' [2010] *Crim LR* 764.

[61] See generally Andrew von Hirsch and Martin Wasik, 'Civil Disqualifications Attending Conviction: A Suggested Conceptual Framework' (1997) 56 *CLJ* 599.

[62] See ibid, pp 601–604 for a brief discussion of examples in English law.

[63] See Terry Thomas and Bill Hebenton, 'Dilemmas and Consequences of Prior Criminal Record: A Criminological Perspective from England and Wales' (2013) 26 *Criminal Justice Studies* 228.

[64] See generally Nageen Mustafa, Paul Kingston, and Derek Beeston, 'An Exploration of the Historical Background of Criminal Record Checking in the United Kingdom: From the Eighteenth to the Twenty-First Century' (2013) 19 *European Journal on Criminal Policy and Research* 15.

[65] Chris Baldwin, 'The Vetting Epidemic in England and Wales' (2017) 81 *Journal of Criminal Law* 478.

practice to remove (or 'spend') convictions from one's criminal record.[66] This then makes it easier for prospective employers to – implicitly or explicitly, lawfully or unlawfully – discriminate against those with criminal records, even if their previous offending has nothing to do with the employment they are seeking.[67] This broad concern for public protection has produced a wide-ranging legal right to know about one's prospective employees' criminal pasts. By all means in at least some circumstances, this practice is defensible, especially where the employment in question involves access to positions of power or trust, or responsibility for vulnerable people.[68] But that is precisely what the law did before the passage of the Police Act 1997, which established a *general* right of access to criminal records checks (albeit with differentiated levels of access to information, depending upon context). The extension of a general right to access to previous information is therefore out of step with minimalistic intervention in the name of public protection. Simply put, we did not have to go this far to protect specific communities of vulnerable people from harm.

The modern law on criminal records checks is also remarkable in its dispersal of discipline *out of the hands of the State* entirely – the imposition of negative consequences with the tacit knowledge of the State to allow exceptions to its claimed monopoly on the right to punish offenders. To an extent, this is inevitable, and part of the challenge of trying to measure the severity of punishment, especially in the community. But as with the partitioning off of previously criminal powers into the civil legal system in the Coalition's ASBO reforms, this increasing of public access, potentially in perpetuity, is necessarily difficult to control. Each prospective employer will judge every type of criminal conviction in different ways, and even if the overall effect on job-hunting by convicted offenders is negative, some individuals will not be materially affected. There is a loss of consistency and certainty, substantially undermining Rule of Law values.[69]

Indeed, when punishment ceased to take place only within complete and austere institutions (to the extent that any prison has ever been entirely cut off from the world), the claim of liberal punishment to monopolise legitimate punishment became fatally compromised. Liberal criminal theory claims that one is subjected to criminal punishment so that you can 'pay your debt to society' – the punishment is a form of 'answering' for the crime that enables you to return to society as a full and equal citizen in good standing with the community at large.[70] But if the offender never leaves society then they cannot *return*, and particularly as

[66] See Nicky Padfield, 'Judicial Rehabilitation? The View from England' (2011) 3 *European Journal of Probation* 36.

[67] Ibid.

[68] See, eg, Thomas and Hebenton, above n 63, pp 230–234; von Hirsch and Wasik, above n 61, pp 606–611.

[69] See, eg, Nigel Walker, *Why Punish?* (1991, Oxford University Press), pp 108–110.

[70] See, eg, Barry Vaughan, 'Punishment and Conditional Citizenship' (2000) 2 *Punishment & Society* 23, pp 24–32; Antje du Bois-Pedain, 'Punishment as an Inclusionary Practice: Sentencing in a Liberal

the public and private penal domains blur, it becomes ever harder to tell who has answered for their crimes, who is doing so, and who has not.[71] The basis for trust between mutually respectful citizens breaks down, undermined by the very penal processes designed to defend it. And all the while, the penal State grows, without any underpinning justification in liberal or democratic political theory.

II. Punishing the Poor: Excesses of Shape

In sum there is strong evidence of excessive growth in the size of the penal State in England and Wales over the last four decades. But what about the *size* dimension of penal excess? Here, as well, there is a rich literature on the maladaptation of the penal State since the 1970s, particularly in terms of the disproportionate inclusion of marginalised groups within the penal system (usually the prison, given the historical, and to some extent ongoing, side-lining of non-custodial sentences in academic circles)[72] relative to the white, mentally healthy, affluent, and powerful. The over-representation of socially side-lined communities within the penal system is certainly nothing new, given that elite interests have always been able to control the definition of crimes, and to influence the shape of penal institutions.[73] However, what has generally changed in the last 30 years is the scale with which social control has shifted away from more proactive and supportive mechanisms for maintaining social control (such as physical or mental healthcare, education, and social welfare) and towards the more reactive, coercive, and stigmatising penal system.[74] The result is that social control systems aimed at ameliorating social marginalisation and empowering the dispossessed (at least in theory) are replaced with an additional level of social exclusion.

The conventional explanation for this is a movement from one form of social control into another, driven either by shifts in the social structure caused by movements towards *late modernity* in (Anglophone) Western culture, and/or by *neoliberal* political economy.[75] Although these explanations differ in terms of the root causes of this transfer, the symptoms are broadly the same: a favouring of the free market over State intervention in the economy from the 1970s and 1980s onwards leads to a shrinking welfare State (as a result of lower taxation, and a

Constitutional State', in Antje du Bois-Pedain, Magnus Ulväng, and Petter Asp (eds), *Criminal Law and the Authority of the State* (2017, Hart).

[71] Compare Cohen, 'The Punitive City', above n 43, pp 344–346, 356–357.

[72] See Gwen Robinson, 'The Cinderella Complex: Punishment, Society, and Community Sanctions' (2016) 18 *Punishment & Society* 95.

[73] Recall ch 1, n 114, for examples on this point.

[74] See generally David Garland, *The Culture of Control: Crime and Social Order in Contemporary Society* (2001, Oxford University Press), pp 89–102; Wacquant, *Punishing the Poor*, above n 3, especially pp 41–109.

[75] See, eg, Garland, ibid; Wacquant, ibid. See also Jock Young, *The Exclusive Society: Social Exclusion, Crime and Difference in Late Modernity* (1999, SAGE), for an account mixing both explanations.

favouring of privatisation of areas of State control), leading to an imbalance in the 'penal-welfare complex'.[76] Since the welfare State no longer provides (or at least, claims to provide) a system of joined-up care with the penal system, and since the absence of welfare support removes a key means of previous arrangements for social control, penal rationales had to shift. Punishment could no longer be a means of rehabilitating social misfits, because the wider welfare State apparatus no longer existed to the same extent to back it up. The result is a political-economic collapse into an overly simplistic rugged individualism, a return of personal moral responsibility to the social policy equation in all spheres of traditional governmental responsibility, including criminal punishment.[77]

This shift towards greater recognition of the individual has, it should be noted, had some positive effects, especially for historically (and presently) marginalised identity groups. Individualism is, after all, part of the same current that brought us emancipatory movements such as feminism, critical race theory, race-related civil rights movements, queer theory, and the LGBTQ+ movement, which we should not simply throw away to return to some rose-tinted vision of the past.[78] So there is nothing wrong with holding people individually responsible for their successes, or for their moral wrongdoing – necessarily. Rather, the issue is that a strategy of *total* personal responsibility neglects any and all roles for structural and systemic causes of crime. The wider social and other contexts of crime and criminal justice are flattened down to individual faults – in popular discourse, the criminal becomes a feckless, selfish monster to be feared, ostracised, and punished; and in expert discourse, macro-social causes of crime become individualised criminogenic risk factors. As a result, high crime rates become an assumed fact of life, something that cannot ever be eradicated, because some people (that is, usually, a criminal underclass) are just going to commit crime.[79] Meanwhile, historical forms of pre-emptive social control such as education, physical and mental healthcare, State welfare, and informal community control, are crumbling, and we might at least expect to see the loss of these proactive, less stigmatising and intrusive safety nets giving way to a concomitant increase in the criminal justice system's inclusion of marginalised groups as a result.[80]

However, in practice there are a number of reasons why this relationship is more complex. Firstly, just because one is marginalised does not mean that one will offend and/or be punished for offending. Secondly, not every form of marginalisation tracks with over-inclusion in the criminal justice system. To the extent

[76] See generally David Garland, *Punishment and Welfare: A History of Penal Strategies* (1985, Ashgate).

[77] See Garland, *The Culture of Control*, above n 74, pp 180–182.

[78] See Young, above n 75, pp 190–199.

[79] Garland, *The Culture of Control*, above n 74, pp 175–182. See also George Mair (ed), *What Matters in Probation* (2004, Willan).

[80] See, eg, Garland, *The Culture of Control*, above n 74, pp 124–127; Wacquant, *Punishing the Poor*, above n 3, especially chs 2–3. Compare Barbara Hudson, *Justice through Punishment: A Critique of the 'Justice' Model of Corrections* (1987, Macmillan), especially pp 113–114, 125–129, and 162–170.

that we remain a *patriarchal* society, for instance, it is noteworthy that women account for only 5 per cent of the 2016/17 prison population, and 15 per cent of the probationer population, despite accounting for 51 per cent of the general population at the 2011 census.[81] Theoretical positions differ as to why this might be the case, but at least for the sorts of offences that tend to be punished by imprisonment or community penalties, criminality may simply be a set of cultural behaviours that are associated with masculine gender norms.[82] Thus, we should remember that we are considering collective trends at a society-wide level, over long periods of time. Discriminatory patterns of social exclusion may well emerge that have nothing to do with conscious choices or *explicitly* discriminatory practices.

This is not to deny the role of discrimination, however. In terms of ethnicity, for instance, persons from a Black, Asian, or other Minority Ethnic (BAME) background made up 12.5 per cent of the general population at the 2011 census, and yet they represented a combined total of 26 per cent of the prison population in 2017, and 18 per cent of probationers subject to community or suspended sentence orders. This over-representation is evident at every level of the criminal justice system: BAME suspects are more likely to be stopped and searched, arrested, prosecuted, convicted, and denied bail. Moreover, BAME offenders are more likely to be sentenced to imprisonment, and generally receive longer prison sentences.[83] These statistics form part of a long history of *institutional racism* that has long haunted British policing, long before the term was popularised by the Macpherson inquiry into the failed investigation of the racially-motivated killing of Stephen Lawrence in 1993.[84] At least part of the problem is that policing, prosecutions, conviction and sentencing involve the exercise of discretion, which is vulnerable to *implicit bias* – unconsciously prejudiced ways of thinking to which we are all vulnerable, intentionally or not, either as a result of ingrained racism in modern society or as an ingrained cultural hangover of our more explicitly racist past (or both).[85] This tendency may or may not be unintentional, but the upshot

[81] See Ministry of Justice, *National Offender Management Service Annual Offender Equalities Report, 2016/17* (Ministry of Justice, 30 November 2017), p 5; Office for National Statistics, *Statistical Bulletin: 2011 Census: Population Estimates for the United Kingdom, March 2011* (Office for National Statistics, 17 December 2012).

[82] See Ann Oakley, 'Crime, Justice and "The Man Question"', in Stephen Farrall, Barry Goldson, Ian Loader, and Anita Dockley (eds), *Justice and Penal Reform: Re-Shaping the Penal Landscape* (2016, Routledge).

[83] See generally Ministry of Justice, above n 81; Ministry of Justice, *Statistics on Race and the Criminal Justice System 2016* (Ministry of Justice, 30 November 2017).

[84] See William Macpherson, Tom Cook, John Sentamu, and Richard Stone, *The Stephen Lawrence Inquiry*, Cm 4262, 24 February 1999; Janet Foster, Tim Newburn and Anna Souhami, *Assessing the Impact of the Stephen Lawrence Enquiry*, Home Office Research Study 294 (Home Office, October 2005); compare Coretta Phillips and Ben Bowling, 'Ethnicities, Racism, Crime, and Criminal Justice', in: Alison Liebling, Shadd Maruna, and Lesley McAra (eds), *The Oxford Handbook of Criminology*, Sixth edn (2016, Oxford University Press).

[85] See, eg, Katheryn Russell-Brown, 'Making Implicit Bias Explicit: Black Men and the Police', in: Angela Davis (ed), *Policing the Black Man: Arrest, Prosecution, and Imprisonment* (2017, Pantheon Books).

is an over-representation for reasons that have nothing to do with the relative rate of offending.[86]

A third, and final, issue affecting the relationship between social marginalisation and criminality is that both of those concepts are inter-related and socio-politically, -economically, and -culturally contingent. We have encountered one problem that this causes already, on a few occasions: crime tends to be defined by the already-powerful, and therefore tends to problematise the wrongful behaviours of the less-well-off over those of the wealthy.[87] Although we are beginning to see greater proscription of traditionally middle-class (or 'white collar') crime by the criminal law, even if only in the 'law on the books', criminalisation has historically focussed upon lower-class offending and preserving the wider interests of the higher socio-economic orders, and overturning that bias without radical legal and institutional overhaul will take some time. So the very definition of crime (as a social problem and as a legal designation for particular courses of conduct) is likely to skew the definition of criminality in ways that affect the already-marginalised, but which have nothing to do with whether or not one is more likely to commit a particular offence *because* of that marginalisation. In other words, if criminal justice is really (at least in part) about 'punishing the poor',[88] then this is more about the way the 'crime' itself is defined (and enforced) than about any characteristics of 'the poor' as a socioeconomic group. Indeed, it is difficult to measure the effects of (socioeconomic) class upon offending, if only because 'class' is not covered by the Equalities Act 2010, and therefore is not a required subject for Ministry of Justice statistics on penal populations.[89] Three studies over the last quarter-century suggest that symptoms (or causes) of poverty, such as unemployment, reliance upon welfare benefits, a history of social care and/or domestic abuse, truancy, expulsion from school, or a general lack of education, are far more prevalent in offender populations than in the general public, but since 2012 there has been no new data for England and Wales (and most of what does exist is focussed solely on prisoners).[90] In other words, there is still evidence, albeit weak

[86] See, eg, Luc Faucher, 'Revisionism and Moral Responsibility for Implicit Attitudes', in: Michael Brownstein and Jennifer Saul (eds), *Implicit Bias and Philosophy, Volume Two: Moral Responsibility, Structural Injustice, and Ethics* (2016, Oxford University Press); Clare Sharp and Tracey Budd, *Minority Ethnic Groups and Crime: Findings from the Offending, Crime and Justice Survey*, Second edn, Online Report 33/05 (2005, Home Office), pp 7–12.

[87] Recall Box, above n 31; Douglas Hay, 'Property, Authority and the Criminal Law', in: Douglas Hay, Peter Linebaugh, John Rule, EP Thompson, and Cal Winslow (eds), *Albion's Fatal Tree: Crime and Society in Eighteenth Century England* (1975, Pantheon Books).

[88] See, eg, Wacquant, above n 3; Barbara Hudson, 'Punishing the Poor: A Critique of the Dominance of Legal Reasoning in Penal Policy and Practice', in RA Duff, Sandra Marshall, Rebecca Emerson-Dobash, and Russell Dobash (eds), *Penal Theory and Practice: Tradition and Innovation in Criminal Justice* (1994, Manchester University Press). Compare Jeffery Reiman and Paul Leighton, *The Rich Get Richer and the Poor Get Prison*, Eleventh edn (2017, Routledge).

[89] See Ministry of Justice, *NOMS Annual Offender Equalities Report, 2016/17*, above n 81, pp 3–4.

[90] See generally Dee Cook, *Poverty, Crime and Punishment* (1997, Child Poverty Action Group); Social Exclusion Unit, *Reducing Reoffending by Ex-Prisoners* (2002, Social Exclusion Unit); and Prison

evidence, of the over-inclusion of socio-economically marginalised classes within the penal State's control.[91]

Individuals with mental health treatment needs are also substantially over-represented within the criminal justice system. Generally, mental health issues are relatively common in general society, with about one in four people in the UK facing some such issue over the course of their lifetime.[92] Even so, the rate amongst penal subjects is significantly higher. Two reports, in 2002 and 1998 (respectively), have suggested that as many as 70 per cent or 90 per cent of offenders suffer from five categories of mental disorders (neurotic disorder, psychotic disorder, personality disorder, drug addiction, and hazardous drinking).[93] Comparable data for other penal populations do not exist, but one would expect similar statistics.[94] Notably, self-inflicted deaths in prison and on probation occur at remarkably similar rates.[95] While not all such deaths are suicides, and not all suicides are necessarily evidence of mental illness, the similar rates provide at least some evidence of an equivalent crisis of over-representation in community-based penal populations to that inside prisons. Indeed, diagnosed and undiagnosed mental health disorders are over-represented at every stage of criminal proceedings, especially those where criminal behaviour has been at least partly driven by the disorder (such as cravings in drug or alcohol dependency, for example).[96]

Altogether, then, there is evidence of ongoing inequality in the distribution of the penal State's social footprint. However, this is part of longer-term and more widespread social problems than those that have specifically emerged over the last 30 years. Rather, these trends reflect longer-standing issues of race, class, and the definition of crime; of the interaction between social justice and criminal justice. That we have not resolved these disproportionalities is evidence of penal excess, to be sure, but it is not a form of penal excess that has been *exacerbated*

Reform Trust, *Bromley Briefings Prison Factfile: Autumn 2018* (2018, Prison Reform Trust), p 20, comparing data collected on prisoners between 2010 and 2012 with general population data from between 2012 and 2013.

[91] See also Cavadino et al, above n 5, pp 283–287; Robert Reiner, 'Political Economy, Crime, and Criminal Justice', in Alison Liebling, Shadd Maruna, and Lesley McAra (eds), *The Oxford Handbook of Criminology*, Sixth edn (2017, Oxford University Press), pp 123–125. Compare McNeill, *Pervasive Punishment*, above n 4, pp 50–62, providing more recent and similar data from Scotland.

[92] See JUSTICE, *Mental Health and Fair Trial* (2017, JUSTICE), pp 10–11.

[93] See, respectively, Social Exclusion Unit, above n 90; Nicola Singleton et al, *Psychiatric Morbidity among Prisoners in England and Wales* (1998, Office for National Statistics).

[94] Compare, eg, Colin Roberts, Barbara Hudson, and Rachel Cullen, *The Supervision of Mentally Disordered Offenders: The Work of Probation Officers and their Relationship with Psychiatrists in England and Wales* (1995) 5 *Criminal Behaviour and Mental Health* 75; Charlie Brooker, 'Healthcare and Probation: The Impact of Government Reforms' (2015) 62 *Probation Journal* 268, pp 271–272.

[95] See generally Ministry of Justice, *Safety in Custody Statistics, England and Wales: Deaths in Prison Custody to September 2018, Assaults and Self-Harm to June 2018* (Ministry of Justice, 25 October 2018); Ministry of Justice, *Deaths of Offenders in the Community, England and Wales, 2017/18* (Ministry of Justice, 25 October 2018); Jake Phillips, Loraine Gelsthorpe, and Nicola Padfield, 'Non-Custodial Deaths: Missing, Ignored, or Unimportant?' (2017) *Criminology and Criminal Justice*, forthcoming.

[96] See generally Jill Peay, *Mental Health and Crime* (2010, Routledge); compare JUSTICE, above n 92.

by the last three decades. That ethnic minorities, men, the impoverished, and the mentally ill are over-represented in the criminal justice system relative to the general population reflects long-standing tensions and problems in the ways we define and respond to crime, rather than a problem peculiar to recent times.[97] That is not an excuse for the ongoing penal excess – but it does suggest that the rise of retributive sentencing in the 1990s is not a relevant factor in that excess, in this context.

With this said, however, a lack of meaningful improvement is problematic in itself. We know from the 'mass punishment' literature that penal expansion has occurred over the last 30 years. But if over-representation has remained the same, then that means that: (a) the increasing size of the penal State has not corrected its disproportionate footprint on society; and (b) there is a larger overall community of marginalised groups within the penal system overall (which is only to say that one quarter of 1,000 is a bigger number than one quarter of 500). So it is worth going one step further here. Let us take the BAME population as an indicative example, on whose penal populations we have reliable data going back to 2003/04, due to a legal requirement that the government publish annual statistics on race and ethnicity in the criminal justice system.[98] Table Two gives an overview of these data, charting the combined percentage of persons from a BAME background (in the data sets referred to, this meant: 'mixed race'; 'Asian', 'Black', and 'Other Non-White') in the general population as against their representation in the prison population and in the probationer population. Note, as ever, that there are some changes from report to report in terms of how data are gathered and presented, which limits the comparability of these data.[99] What is interesting about these data is their relative stability, both in percentage and bare number terms. What this tells us is that there *was* a relative reduction in the proportion of BAME prisoners over this time period (up 3.3 per cent), since the estimated proportion of BAME persons in the general population generally rises slightly more quickly (up 3.8 per cent). However, there is a proportionate increase of 9.2 per cent in the probation population over the same period that the overall probation population on court orders fell 2.68 per cent.[100] In other words, overall, fewer offenders from ethnic minority

[97] Compare Nicola Lacey, *In Search of Criminal Responsibility: Ideas, Interests, and Institutions* (2016, Oxford University Press).

[98] Criminal Justice Act 1991, s 95. Earlier years are not included because of a historical failure of probation administrators to compile sufficient data on their subjects' ethnicity.

[99] General population data in the sources listed below seem to have been taken either from the last census or from projections based on that census, without any explanation. Data are available for June 2006 but they are exactly the same as the figures for 2006/07. Probation population could not be located in the National Archives for 2010/11 or 2011/12. In 2005/06, 2006/07, and 2016/17, prisoner and probationer population data appear to have been rounded to the nearest 1%.

[100] See Ministry of Justice, *Offender Management Statistics Quarterly: October to December 2017 and Annual 2017* (Ministry of Justice, 26 April 2018), p 10; and National Offender Management Service, *Probation Statistics: Quarterly Brief: October to December 2004, England and Wales* (Home Office, nd, archived 4 December 2007), p 2. NB: These figures are lower than in Table One because they exclude those offenders supervised during, or after imprisonment.

backgrounds are being sent to prison compared to 2004, but more are being placed under penal control overall. These data only provide a rough snapshot, but they tell us that overall, racial over-representation within the penal system is getting worse, in spite of attempts to combat explicit and institutional racism in criminal justice. This is (weak) evidence of a more uneven footprint of penal State intervention across society – of penal excess.

Table Two Changes in Ethnic Minority Representation in Criminal Justice, 2003–2017[101]

Year	BAME (%) General Pop'n.	BAME (%) Prison Pop'n.	BAME (%) Probation Orders	Year	BAME (%) General Pop'n.	BAME (%) Prison Pop'n.	BAME (%) Probation Orders
2003/04	8.7	22.7	8.8	2010/11	11.0	26.2	---
2004/05	8.7	19.8	13.0	2011/12	11.0	26.2	---
2005/06	8.7	26.0	14.0	2012/13	12.9	25.3	14.9
2006/07	8.7	26.0	14.0	2013/14	12.4	25.9	15.7
2007/08	8.8	26.9	14.6	2014/15	12.4	25.7	15.8
2008/09	10.6	26.7	14.6	2015/16	12.5	25.8	16.1
2009/10	11.3	25.7	15.0	2016/17	12.5	26.0	18.0

III. Conclusion: The Age of Excess

On the whole, then, the English penal State is growing bigger and intruding further into its citizens' lives, and is at least replicating historical unevenness in which parts of society it impacts upon. Both in terms of size and shape, therefore, the penal State has become more excessive over the last three decades. But what caused this worsening excessiveness, and to what extent do these causes indicate a *failure* of the retributivist claims that a robust commitment to proportionate sentencing can constrain the penal State? I turn to these questions in the next chapter.

[101] These data were collated from: Ministry of Justice, *National Offender Management Service Annual Offender Management Statistics* 2008/09-2016/17; Ministry of Justice, *Statistics on Race and Criminal Justice*, 2006/07-2007/08; and Home Office, *Statistics of Race and Criminal Justice*, 2003/04-2005/06. The same online repositories described in the note to Table One, above, were used to gather recent and more historical data.

3

Penal Excess as the Failure of Retribution

Retributivists argue that punishment is only capable of being morally justified where it is *deserved*. A key aspect of this principle is that the punishment must fit the crime – the principle of *proportionality*. Although this principle operates at the level of individual sentencing decisions in particular cases, its proponents have argued that proportionality provides a limiting principle for constraining the penal State – that is, retributive sentencing ought to provide a brake against penal excess. This claim, made against the backdrop of declining faith in rehabilitation and the subsequent politicisation of criminal justice led to a far more conscious embracing, however temporarily, of retributive principles in the Anglo-Welsh criminal justice system. But given the evidence of growing penal excess over the last three decades in England and Wales, it seems hard to deny the charge that retributive penal policies have failed to avoid penal excess in practice. This chapter examines the evidence for and against that claim.

We should begin this discussion with a brief overview of the *history* in which penal excess increased. This will establish the role that retributivism has played in recent penal policy, setting the scene for the role that it *could* have played in preventing the penal excess we discussed in the Chapter 2. Having done so, I lay out the retributivist claim to be able to constrain the penal State in more detail. I then consider three separate critiques of that claim, together with the often insufficient counterarguments that retributivism's luminaries have subjected them to. I conclude that retributivism *has* played a role in facilitating the excessive penal State, but as a result of political rather than inherently theoretical failures. This, however, is still a problem: if retributivism *could not* resist the political rise of penal excess in the 1990s, 2000s, and 2010s, that at least raises the spectre that it *never could*. A penal theory that is only workable in a clockwork utopia is useful to no-one. This conclusion, in turn, opens up a question for the next two chapters to answer – to what extent should we give retributivism another chance to constrain the penal State?

I. The Historical Context of Retributivism and the Rise of Penal Excess

Increasing conditions of penal excess over the last three decades can be explained in part by changes in patterns of crime, and especially the high-profile and frightening threat of terrorism. However, they also need to be understood against the backdrop of specific policy changes, which were at least in part attempts to impose particular penal theories on contemporary penal practice in England and Wales. This history of policy change is well-rehearsed in the criminological literature, and runs as follows:

Up to the mid-1970s, criminal justice was a relatively settled political question in the English-speaking Western world, and rarely a topic of heated exchanges between competing political parties. Punishment was generally governed by a liberal-paternalist *treatment model* that saw criminality as broadly analogous to a disease, to be treated through predominantly custodial correctional interventions. However, in the 1970s, this approach came under attack on two fronts in Anglo-American policy discourse: on an ethical level, for its willingness to support very long and disproportionate sentences;[1] and on an empirical level, when meta-analytical data about existing rehabilitative interventions appeared to show that 'Nothing Works' in terms of reducing reoffending rates.[2] Since treatment-model rehabilitation was a consequentialist justification of punishment, the suggestion that it was not achieving its ends was fatal to its political legitimacy, and left it vulnerable to the broader ethical challenge. State attitudes towards rehabilitation accordingly hardened, and more restrained alternative justifications were sought.

The solution came, in the US, in the form of the 'Justice Model' – central to which was the 'just deserts' theory of retributivism, advanced primarily by Andreas von Hirsch.[3] On this account, criminal justice could be defended as a terrain for expressing censure and reinforcing social norms in the aftermath of crimes. Retributive punishment was a way of showing that the offender had received their 'just deserts', and would be self-restraining because of the central role played by *proportionality* in sentencing.[4] The Justice Model represented a relative pessimism about the utility of the criminal justice system as a response to social problems,

[1] See American Friends Service Committee, *Struggle for Justice* (1971, Hill & Wang).

[2] On the historical provenance of this phrase, see George Mair, 'The Origins of What Works in England and Wales: A House Build on Sand?', in: George Mair (ed), *What Matters in Probation* (2004, Willan), pp 14–15.

[3] See Andrew von Hirsch, *Doing Justice: The Choice of Punishments* (1976, Hill & Wang). Throughout this book, I use whichever variant (the German "Andreas" or Anglicised "Andrew") von Hirsch himself used in that source.

[4] Ibid; see also Andrew von Hirsch, *Past or Future Crimes: Deservedness and Dangerousness in the Sentencing of Criminals* (1986, Manchester University Press); Andrew von Hirsch, *Censure and Sanctions* (1993, Clarendon Press); and Andreas von Hirsch, *Deserved Criminal Sentences: An Overview* (2017, Hart).

and recommended winnowing down the principal focus of criminal justice to punishing wrongdoing, rather than trying to 'fix' the actor or their wider social circumstances. Punishment lost its benevolent sheen and became more explicitly concerned with the moral condemnation of criminal harms.[5]

Anglo-Welsh criminal justice responded relatively slowly to the Justice Model, compared to the US. However, in the Criminal Justice Act 1991, the Conservative government subscribed to a remarkably pure 'just deserts' model.[6] The 1991 Act created a stripped-down sentencing regime in which community sanctions were reconceived as an intermediary punishment between imprisonment (for the worst crimes) and fines, discharges, and other non-supervisory, non-custodial orders (for the least serious crimes). Judges were severely curtailed from taking any factors other than the current offence into account – particularly previous convictions. However this – together with the adoption of 'day fines' imposing a proportionate loss of income based on daily income, rather than a flat sum – proved politically unpopular, and the purity of English sentencing law's retributivism was swiftly diluted by a succession of legislative compromises in 1993, 1994, 1997, and finally, the Criminal Justice Act 2003.[7] Retributivists criticised the 2003 Act in particular as creating a confusing 'smorgasbord' of penal aims, none of which was ranked more highly than the other.[8] However, it at least reserved the structuring of prisons, community penalties, and other non-custodial sanctions from the 1991 Act, such that no higher-severity sentence was to be imposed unless the lower class of penalties was insufficient to satisfy it – preserving a basic degree of proportionality at the heart of the system.[9] This has recently been further entrenched by the work of the Sentencing Council, which issues guidelines for sentencing decision-making. These guidelines are framed first and foremost in the context of harm and culpability, the retributive building blocks of offence seriousness used in 'just deserts' proportionality-based sentencing.[10] By all means, non-retributive questions can be brought in at a later stage, particularly when considering aggravating and mitigating factors, but by that point the rough outline of a sentence has typically begun to form, guided along retributive lines.[11]

[5] See generally Barbara Hudson, *Justice through Punishment: A Critique of the 'Justice' Model of Corrections* (1987, Macmillan).

[6] See, eg, Austin Lovegrove, 'Sanctions and Severity: To the Demise of Von Hirsch and Wasik's Sanction Hierarchy' (2001) 40 *The Howard Journal of Criminal Justice* 126.

[7] See Andrew Ashworth, 'Prisons, Proportionality, and Recent Penal History' (2017) 80 *Modern Law Review* 473, especially pp 475–480.

[8] See ss 142–142A of the Criminal Justice Act 2003; Andrew von Hirsch and Julian Roberts, 'Legislating Sentencing Principles: The Provisions of the Criminal Justice Act 2003 Relating to Sentencing Purposes and the Role of Previous Convictions' [2004] *Crim LR* 639.

[9] See the Criminal Justice Act 2003, ss 148(1) and 152(2); Gavin Dingwall, 'Deserting Desert? Locating the Present Role of Retributivism in the Role of Sentencing Adult Offenders' (2008) 47 *The Howard Journal of Criminal Justice* 400.

[10] See Andrew von Hirsch and Nils Jareborg, 'Gauging Criminal Harm: A Living Standard Analysis' (1991) 11 *OJLS* 1.

[11] See, eg, Julian Roberts (ed), *Mitigation and Aggravation at Sentencing* (2011, Cambridge University Press); Nicola Padfield, 'Time to Bury the Custody "Threshold"?' [2011] *Crim LR* 593.

Policy change has also occurred more generally, beyond formal legislation. Two tendencies in particular have been associated with penal excess: on the one hand, the much-discussed *punitive turn* in the rhetoric and practice of punishment; and on the other, a shift towards *penal managerialism*. The concept of a 'punitive turn', or 'new punitiveness' became a popular explanation in criminological scholarship for the expanding size of the penal State in the 1990s and 2000s, and a number of the specific policy changes that drove it, such as: increasing sentence length; preference of short prison sentences over long community orders; more frequent use of imprisonment to punish breaches of non-custodial sanctions' requirements; and mandatory minimum sentencing regimes (such as 'Three Strikes' laws).[12] These policies responded to a (perceived) hardening of public attitudes towards offenders – as existential risks to security and as violators of an increasingly venerated social contract. Punishment, after all, is emotionally satisfying – on a very basic level we like to see people get some sort of comeuppance when they have done wrong.[13] Growing social insecurity and the decline of traditional forms of communal cohesion (along with the withering of the welfare State) could well have encouraged greater punitiveness and insistence on 'law and order' as a means of reinforcing perceived social security.[14] With punishment increasingly a matter of political debate, and increasingly a feature of mass-mediated public discourse, a 'punitive turn' helps to explain some manifestations of penal excess – particularly the emergence of 'mass punishment'.

The risk agenda has also contributed to the emergence of *penal managerialism* – an approach to criminal justice that takes an explicitly *actuarial* and *palliative* approach to the threat of crime. In other words, managerialism rejects the claim that it is possible to live in a world without crime, and therefore seeks to reduce (or avoid) the risks of crime occurring instead of attempting more profound social change. It is therefore less optimistic than treatment-era rehabilitation, but more so than classical incapacitation.[15] The reconceptualising of crime as a routine risk of life in a complex society has, in particular, encouraged the dispersal of discipline

[12] See generally John Pratt, David Brown, Mark Brown, and Simon Hallsworth (eds), *The New Punitiveness: Trends, Theories, Perspectives* (2005, Willan); Tim Newburn, '"Tough on Crime": Penal Policy in England and Wales' (2007) 36 *Crime and Justice* 425; and compare Ian Loader, 'The Fall of the "Platonic Guardians": Liberalism, Criminology and Political Responses to Crime in England and Wales' (2006) 46 *British Journal of Criminology* 561.

[13] Rob Canton, 'Crime, Punishment and the Moral Emotions: Righteous Minds and their Attitudes towards Punishment' (2015) 17 *Punishment & Society* 54. See also Henrique Carvalho and Anastasia Chamberlen, 'Why Punishment Pleases: Punitive Feelings in a World of Hostile Solidarity' (2018) 20(2) *Punishment & Society* 217–234.

[14] See, eg, Peter Ramsay, *The Insecurity State: Vulnerable Autonomy and the Right to Security in the Criminal Law* (2012, Oxford University Press).

[15] See, eg, Malcolm Feeley and Jonathan Simon, 'The New Penology: Notes on the Emerging Strategy of Corrections and its Implications' (1992) 30 *Criminology* 449; Barbara Hudson, *Justice in the Risk Society: Challenging and Re-Affirming Justice in Late Modernity* (2003, SAGE), especially ch 2; Paula Maurutto and Kelly Hannah-Moffatt, 'Assembling Risk and the Restructuring of Penal Control' (2006) 46 *British Journal of Criminology* 438; and Kelly Hannah-Moffatt, 'Punishment and Risk', in Jonathan Simon and Richard Sparks (eds), *The SAGE Handbook of Punishment and Society* (2013, SAGE). Compare Pat O'Malley, *Risk, Uncertainty, Government* (2004, Glasshouse Press).

into our everyday lives to protect us from the risk of victimisation. Given the tendency of crime to be associated with socioeconomic marginalisation, it can also be linked to the developments around the malformation of the shape of the penal State. Most significantly in penal practice, however, penal managerialism is visible in the resurrection of rehabilitation as a penal rationale in England and Wales, under the auspices of the 'What Works' movement.

As the name suggests, 'What Works' emerged as a conscious riposte to the 'Nothing Works' fatalism of the 1970s and 1980s, challenging the meta-analyses that had purported to show the failure of rehabilitative interventions to reducing rates of reoffending. In fact, the authors of the first 'What Works' papers argued, a significant effect on reoffending rates *could* be found for tailored, individualised responses to the particular causes of crimes in particular cases. A pragmatic and pluralistic approach to rehabilitation, insisting on no one system of treatment or one pathway to corrections, stood a chance of making a real dent in the crime rate.[16] Their approach was conditioned by psychology, and particularly, by the 'Risk-Needs-Responsivity' (RNR) model of crime prevention, discussed in more detail in Chapter 4.[17] Over time, however, the 'What Works' movement morphed away from having policies that responded to evidence that they were failing, and towards spinning the evidence to suggest that policy was succeeding. This was partly in response to the propaganda needs of the day,[18] but was also a consequence of the scale of penal intervention at the time – one of the perils of doing punishment on a 'mass' scale is that it is very time- and resource-intensive to individualise every intervention. Particularly as a result of the need for prisoners on indefinite sentences of Imprisonment for Public Protection (IPP) to prove that they were no longer 'dangerous', the demand for rehabilitative interventions quickly outstripped supply, requiring a paring-back of the ambitious individualisation of the original interventions.[19] As a result, 'What Worked' became increasingly predetermined: group-based rehabilitative programmes that applied a largely 'one-size fits all' approach to solving criminogenic needs. A new 'National *Offender Management* Service' incorporated the Probation and Prison Services, giving voice to the position that offenders were now to be viewed less as liberal rights-bearing subjects and more as bundles of risks to be managed down, and returned to their communities not so much 'fixed' as citizens, as much as being made into less of a nuisance to the law-abiding majority.[20]

[16] See Mair, 'The Origins of What Works in England and Wales', above n 2, pp 15–20.

[17] See generally Rob Canton and Jane Dominey, *Probation: Working with Offenders*, Second edn (2018, Routledge), pp 114–132.

[18] George Mair, 'Research on Community Penalties', in: Roy King and Emma Wincup (eds), *Doing Research on Crime and Justice*, Second edn (2007, Oxford University Press).

[19] See, eg, Jessica Jacobson and Mike Hough, *Unjust Deserts: Imprisonment for Public Protection* (2010, Prison Reform Trust), pp 35–43.

[20] See, eg, Gwen Robinson, 'Late-Modern Rehabilitation: The Evolution of a Penal Strategy' (2008) 10 *Punishment & Society* 429; Mona Lynch, 'Waste Managers? The New Penology, Crime Fighting, and Parole Agent Identity' (1998) 32 *Law & Society Review* 839.

Not all rehabilitation workers, policy-makers, or theorists bought into the 'What Works' movement, and the extent to which probation practice changed on the ground is debateable.[21] But the 'What Works' approach, and the policies it gave rhetorical weight to, are indicative of the trends in penal managerialism, in which the traditional liberal-democratic conception of the citizen controlling the State becomes a strategy of *governance* of risky materials. If punitiveness is the excessive double of the restrained penal system pursued by retributivists in England and Wales, managerialism has been the same to rehabilitation. It emerged out of (and achieved greater political and academic credibility through) earnest attempts to make rehabilitation more effective, humane, and moderate in practice.[22]

The lesson here is that specific penal policies promote or resist penal excess, in ways not entirely reducible to broad trends in penal philosophy or economy. Penal theories have a normative force, at the policy level and in the academic discussions that surround it and provide grist for the politician's mill. But just as not every advocate of rehabilitation, in theory or practice, is a treatment-model authoritarian or a 'What Works' managerialist,[23] then by analogy, retribution needs to be interpreted in a certain way and put into a certain form of practice in order to support increasingly excessive penal conditions. In other words, policy-level decisions about the pursuit of retributive proportionality *could potentially* have made a difference, and it follows that retributive policies *might potentially* have failed to constrain the penal State. To consider whether they *did*, in fact, fail, however, we need to look more closely at the retributivist claim that proportionality does serve as a limit on penal excess.

II. Retributive Proportionality and the Limited Penal State

Retributivism, like any penal theory, is a broad church accommodating many different variant theories. However, they are united by some form of commitment to *proportionality* – the principle that the punishment should 'fit' the crime. This commitment is central to both the retributivists' claim to have an ethical justification for (problematic) punishment, *and* its claim to be able to constrain the size and shape of the penal State. Thus, proportionality has received much

[21] See, eg, Raynor, above n 18; Fergus McNeill, 'A Desistance Paradigm for Offender Management' (2006) 6 *Criminology & Criminal Justice* 39; Fergus McNeill, 'Four Forms of "Offender" Rehabilitation: Towards an Interdisciplinary Perspective' (2012) 17 *Legal and Criminological Psychology* 18.

[22] Compare Stanley Cohen, *Visions of Social Control: Crime, Punishment and Classification* (1985, Polity).

[23] Compare Rob Canton, 'Probation and the Philosophy of Punishment' (2018) 65 *Probation Journal* 252.

attention from both retribution's champions and its critics.[24] The idea of punishment 'fitting' a crime requires an understanding of how serious crimes are, relative to each other and to other crimes of the same type, and an analogous understanding of punishment. It therefore requires a *metric* – some measurable feature of punishment that can be compared consistently between cases.[25] In orthodox retributive theory, the seriousness of an offence is understood as a factor of the *harm* it causes and the *culpability* of the offender for that harm. Punishment is, in theory, always imposed intentionally,[26] so the only question is how much harm it does. In both cases, harm is constructed objectively: as a setback to the interests of the party involved; as a deprivation of liberty; or as a diminution of one's socio-economic standard of living.[27] This metric may be used to set hard limits on precisely how many 'units' of punishment can be imposed ('positive' proportionality), or more flexible boundaries that determine when a punishment is *not disproportionate* ('negative' proportionality).[28]

These ingredients produce a *penal tariff*, which allows us to rank each family of offences against all other offences (so-called *ordinal* proportionality). Individual offences can then be compared against the range of appropriate punishments that are maximally and minimally 'fitting' for that class of wrong, to be deployed according to the relative severity of the offence, and any other aggravating and mitigating factors in play. This is *cardinal proportionality* – the measurement of the severity of the sentence against the seriousness of the offence.[29] Different retributive theories take distinct approaches to defining a metric, and to setting ordinal and cardinal proportionality. However, on their account, it is this determination of 'fittingness' of the punishment for the crime that ensures restraint in the use of punishment.

[24] See, eg, Andrew von Hirsch and Andrew Ashworth, *Proportionate Sentencing: Exploring the Principles* (2005, Oxford University Press); Jesper Ryberg, 'Punishment and the Measurement of Severity', in Jesper Ryberg and Angelo Corlett (eds), *Punishment and Ethics: New Perspectives* (2010, Routledge); John Kleinig, 'What Does Wrongdoing Deserve?', in Michael Tonry (ed), *Retributivism Has a Past: Has It a Future?* (2011, Oxford University Press); Michael Tonry, 'Can Deserts Be Just in an Unjust World?', in AP Simester, Antje du Bois-Pedain, and Ulfrid Neumann (eds), *Liberal Criminal Theory: Essays for Andreas von Hirsch* (2014, Hart).

[25] See, eg, Mara Schiff, 'Gauging the Intensity of Criminal Sanctions: Developing the Criminal Punishment Severity Scale (CPSS)' (1997) 22 *Criminal Justice Review* 175; von Hirsch and Jareborg, above n 10; David Hayes, 'Penal Impact: Towards a More Intersubjective Measurement of Penal Severity' (2016) 36 *OLJS* 724.

[26] But compare David Hayes, 'Proximity, Pain and State Punishment' (2018) 20 *Punishment & Society* 235.

[27] See, eg, Schiff, above n 25; von Hirsch and Jareborg, above n 10; and compare Hayes, 'Penal Impact', above n 25. On harm as a setback to one's liberal interests, see Joel Feinberg, *Harm to Others: The Moral Limits of the Criminal Law, Volume One* (1984, Oxford University Press), pp 31–64.

[28] See generally RA Duff, *Punishment, Communication, and Community* (2001, Oxford University Press), pp 132–143.

[29] See generally von Hirsch, *Censure and Sanctions*, above n 4, chs 4–5; von Hirsch and Ashworth, above n 24; Julian Roberts, 'Punishing, More or Less: Exploring Aggravation and Mitigation at Sentencing', in Julian Roberts (ed), *Mitigation and Aggravation at Sentencing* (2011, Cambridge University Press).

This might seem like an over-reaching claim. After all, proportionality judgements are made according to limits that are external to the penal tariff itself. A sentencing scheme in which the range of penalties goes from 1–21 years' imprisonment is, in theory, just as proportionate as one that goes from 31–51 years' imprisonment.[30] In sociological terms, proportionality is wholly concerned with relating the *macro* level of the overall size and shape of the penal system to the micro level of an individual sentence's 'fit' in relation to a particular crime. The principle seems to contain no inherent principle about how to relate the micro back to the macro level.[31] It is at this point where the retributivist's claim to meaningfully limit the penal State divides into two separate strands: the essential, or *theoretical*; and the pragmatic, or *political*. Briefly, the first asserts that there *are*, in fact, meaningful limits built into a system of proportionality that encourage penal minimalism in practice; while the second argues that specific retributive programmes were constructed in ways that would enable proportionality to maintain pre-existing limits on penal excess created by forces outside of sentencing by encouraging interests within the penal system that create political pressure *against* increasing penal excess. We should explore these two arguments in some depth, since different critiques of retributivism's claim to encourage penal minimalism focus to a greater or lesser extent on both levels.

A. Theoretical Arguments for Retributive Penal Minimalism

The idea that micro-level proportionality imposes a theoretical limit on macro-level penal excess predates the Justice Model – for instance, it appears in the 'side-constrained' punishment model proposed by HLA Hart, and in Norval Morris's 'limiting retributivism'.[32] Both accounts are *hybrid models* that attempt to set the relationship between different penal theories in a way that enables policy to enjoy the best of both – imposing *theoretical constraint* on the potential excesses of consequentialist penal theories through retributive proportionality. After all, none of the traditional consequentialist justifications of criminal punishment contain intrinsic systems of self-restraint: deterrence maximises the

[30] See, eg, von Hirsch, *Censure and Sanctions*, above n 4, pp 36–38; Ted Honderich, *Punishment: The Supposed Justifications, Revisited* (2006, Pluto Press), pp 193–194; and See Nicola Lacey and Hanna Pickard, 'The Chimera of Proportionality: Institutionalising Limits on Punishment in Contemporary Social and Political Systems' (2015) 78 *MLR* 216.

[31] See Vincent Chiao, 'Mass Incarceration and the Theory of Punishment' (2017) 11 *Criminal Law and Philosophy* 431.

[32] See, respectively: HLA Hart, 'Prolegomenon to the Principles of Punishment', in HLA Hart (ed), *Punishment and Responsibility: Essays in the Philosophy of Punishment*, Second edn (2007, Oxford University Press), pp 8–13; and Norval Morris, *The Future of Imprisonment* (1974, University of Chicago Press).

discouragement of crime by maximising the threat that punishment represents (as in the semi-mythical Athenian Code of Drakon, where virtually every crime was punishable by death);[33] incapacitation and rehabilitation both prescribe long (potentially indeterminate) and intrusive sentences until the offender is either no longer a threat, or has had their criminogenic tendencies in some sense resolved.

To be sure, those theories have generally embraced various external limiting principles (notably parsimony, the principle of minimum *necessary* intervention). But proportionality attracted Hart and Morris because it was a neat, *intrinsic* commitment to self-restraint on the part of the penal State, to go no further than was deserved by the individual, for the specific offence. Moreover, as a limiting principle it emphasised the *distribution* of punishment, not its *content*: a sentence could satisfy the retributive metric in the amount of punishment imposed, while still pursuing rehabilitative or other consequentialist ends in the enforcement. For penal hybridists, proportionality therefore offered a way of justifying *some* preventive or rehabilitative intervention, subject to hard limits that were entirely determined by the offence in question.[34] This focus on offence rather than offender – a retrospective focus on the gravity of the wrong done as the basis for the intervention, rather than the 'good' that might be obtained prospectively – helped to make proportionality seem attractive as a side-constraint on consequentialist ambitions from bubbling over into authoritarian penal excess.[35]

Pure retributive accounts have also argued that proportionality protects penal minimalism. von Hirsch himself responds to the challenge of 'anchoring' the penal scale with an argument based on *comparative harshness*. Recall the hypothetical situation illustrated above, where two penal systems offer ranges of sentences amounting to 20 years' imprisonment (1–21 and 31–51 years, respectively), but differ on the upper and lower ends of those ranges. It is impossible to say which of the two better 'fits' the crime – but von Hirsch alleges that nevertheless, a comparison between the two systems would lead to a preference for the less intrusive one, because the latter is less punitive towards less 'reprehensible' offences and would therefore seem like an intuitively better fit in practice.[36] This is because harsher punishment interferes unduly with central elements of decent standards of living in a liberal democracy, whilst communicating relatively little censure when applied to less reprehensible crimes.[37] As a result, the disproportionate sentencing system will be compared with other regimes that apply the same principles and will be found unduly demanding, and therefore less likely to

[33] See Aristotle (attrib.), *The Athenian Constitution* (1984, PJ Rhodes (trans), Penguin), chs IV–VI; Plutarch; Philip Stadter (ed), *Greek Lives: A Selection of Nine Greek Lives* (1998, Robin Waterfield (trans), Oxford University Press), p 61.

[34] See, eg, Hart, above n 32, pp 11–13.

[35] See, eg, Morris, above n 32, pp 73–76.

[36] von Hirsch, *Censure and Sanctions*, above n 4, p 37.

[37] Ibid; and recall von Hirsch and Jareborg, above n 10. Compare Joel Feinberg, 'The Expressive Function of Punishment' (1965) 49 *The Monist* 397.

be politically popular within a liberal-democratic polity. Moreover, there was no corresponding lower limit – punishment could feasibly become merely a series of 'token impositions' and it would still communicate the necessary censure, even for the most heinous of crimes, so long as the system as a whole still cohered to proportionate limits.[38]

For von Hirsch, this provided an admittedly weak guarantee of penal restraint, but a meaningful one.[39] Moreover, it was supported by key principles of liberal State governance that militate for minimal restriction of liberty, and maximum avoidance of the intentional infliction of suffering upon subjects of coercive State force. At first blush, this might seem like a cop-out – proportionality has to rely upon socio-political and -cultural restraining values that are not automatically associated with the pursuit of proportionate punishment in order to really achieve any meaningful restriction.[40] But remember that von Hirsch's proposed 'justice model' of criminal justice was not *just* a sentencing schematic, even if that is where it was most successfully adopted in the English-speaking world. Rather it attempted to justify the criminal justice system as a whole in liberal polities, and therefore assumed the wider institutional, procedural, and political context of a liberal democracy.[41] In other words, von Hirsch's account argues more that proportionality is *less excessive* than its consequentialist rivals (and certainly in comparison to the treatment-based rehabilitation that it generally responded to), than that proportionality *ensures* some objective level of restraint.

This linking of penal theory to wider political philosophy is a still more significant characteristic of RA Duff's increasingly influential 'communicative model' of retributive justice. Although Duff embraces rehabilitation and reparation as important values alongside retribution, he is still a retributivist, first and foremost. Indeed, his recognition of the desirability of rehabilitation and reparation are corollaries of his view of the role of proportionality within a liberal community.[42] To Duff, mere expression of censure is one-sided and of limited use, offering a poor alternative to two-way *communication* between the offender and the punishing community (represented by State institutions).[43] Thus, rehabilitation and reparation are *desired* outcomes of genuine communication: hopefully, the offender sees that they have done wrong, takes steps to change their ways in future because of that recognition, and tries to make amends for that wrong. But the State cannot force the offender to undertake the 'moral rehabilitation'[44]

[38] von Hirsch, *Censure and Sanctions*, above n 4, p 38.

[39] Ibid, p 37. Compare Dirk van Zyl Smit and Andrew Ashworth, 'Disproportionate Sentences as Human Rights Violations' (2004) 67 *MLR* 541.

[40] Compare Lacey and Pickard, above n 30.

[41] See generally Hudson, *Justice as Punishment*, above n 5, ch 2.

[42] See, eg, RA Duff, 'In Defence of One Kind of Retributivism: A Reply to Bagaric and Amarasekara' (2000) 24 *Melbourne University Law Review* 411; Duff, *Punishment, Communication, and Community*, above n 28, pp 35–73.

[43] Ibid, pp 79–82.

[44] Recall McNeill, 'Four Forms of "Offender" Rehabilitation', above n 21.

needed for either task – it can only impose a proportionate sentence that hopes to start a dialogue through the punishment imposed.[45] This conception of punishment presents offenders as (recalcitrant) citizens who have violated widely shared values, rather than wicked outsiders incapable of changing their ways.[46]

For this reason, Duff does not place a substantial focus on proportionality as an *inherent* safeguard against penal excess. Rather, he argues that the setting of modest aims for the criminal justice and penal systems focussed on communication and persuasion, rather than coerced rehabilitation or risk avoidance, will ensure a modest penal State.[47] They owe duties to their fellow-citizens – and criminal trial and punishment is a way of calling on them to answer for breaches of those duties.[48] Indeed, Duff's model of criminal justice is expansive, arguing that any theory of punishment must also engage with criminalisation, criminal trials, and the framework of the substantive criminal law. By consistently focussing on the values of a liberal community throughout the criminal process, Duff argues, penal restraint will follow naturally.[49]

Again, it is the liberal principles underpinning proportionality that seem to be doing most of the work of resisting penal excess on Duff's account, and not proportionality as such. With that said, Duff's conception emphasises a link between proportionality, citizenship, and *solidarity*. We only adopt the relatively modest and open-textured aims of the communicative model because we view the offender as 'one of us'. Moreover, and importantly, on Duff's account the *metric* of proportionality is radically different to von Hirsch's perspective, in that not all modes of punishment are created equal. Rather than attempting to rationalise all punishments down to a single criterion, Duff treats the *mode* of punishment imposed as an important part of the message to be communicated. Prison, for example, is a period of 'temporary exile', while probation represents (as the name etymologically implies) a 'time of proving' in which the offender's full rights of citizenship needs to be justified by a period of commitment to (mandatory) pro-social behaviours in the community.[50] This places normative pressure on the State to minimise the use of imprisonment to a bare minimum. After all, exile, however temporary, is a major, disruptive, and socially damaging act with profound consequences for the exiled party and those around them, and should therefore only be used for truly awful breaches of the community's criminal code.[51] Indeed, longer prison sentences necessarily undercut the message that the offender is

[45] See Duff, *Punishment, Communication, and Community*, above n 28, pp 107–125; see also RA Duff, 'Probation, Punishment and Restorative Justice: Should Al Truism Be Engaged in Punishment?' (2003) 42 *The Howard Journal of Criminal Justice* 181.

[46] Duff, *Punishment, Communication, and Community*, above n 28, pp 51–52; 86–87.

[47] Ibid; compare RA Duff, 'A Criminal Law for Citizens' (2010) 14 *Theoretical Criminology* 293.

[48] See RA Duff, *Answering for Crime: Responsibility and Liability in the Criminal Law* (2009, Hart).

[49] Ibid; see also RA Duff, *Punishment, Communication, and Community*, above n 28, pp 66–68; Duff, 'A Criminal Law for Citizens', above n 47.

[50] RA Duff, *Punishment, Communication, and Community*, above n 28, pp 99–106, 143–155.

[51] Ibid, pp 148–152.

awaiting their return to a fully integrated citizenship.[52] Thus, Duff's claim to have a theoretical argument for penal minimalism is still dependent upon wider liberal values, but the construction of the metric from citizenship-based concepts makes his account stronger than von Hirsch's.

B. Political Arguments for Retributive Penal Minimalism

The retributivists who influenced the Criminal Justice Act 1991 as a response to the decline of the rehabilitative ideal also offered a range of purely political arguments about how retributive proportionality commitments would ensure penal restraint. In particular, we should focus on three situated political benefits that would tend to reduce penal excess, despite being ancillary to the aims of the 'just deserts' model of retributive punishment. These are: firstly, the *downplaying of actor-based aggravating factors* in the wider Justice Model; secondly, a *radical rejection of the problem-solving capacities of the penal State*; and thirdly, a relative rejection of *euphemism*, at least compared to other penal policy approaches.

One feature of the decline of the rehabilitative ideal was a rejection of paternalistic (and downright authoritarian) focuses in sentencing, particularly the 'treatment' of offenders and the pursuit of incapacitating and preventative interventions with, at best, rather murky evidential foundations.[53] These lengthy, costly, and freedom-restricting interventions focussed on the offender's characteristics: the treatment model calls for incarceration until one's offending behaviour has been 'fixed', and preventive detention takes the more pessimistic approach of simply locking offenders up to physically prevent reoffending. To be sure, the Justice Model allowed some role for consequentialist aims, but it was firm in its primary focus on wrongful *acts* rather than problematic *actors*.[54] In England and Wales, the Criminal Justice Act 1991 adopted this approach for the most part, although it took a more preventative line with respect to serious violent and sexual offences (even above the fact that these are generally very serious crimes in their own right).[55]

Importantly, the role of previous convictions was cast as a *progressive loss of mitigation*, rather than a perpetually aggravating factor. In other words, the maximum sentence was determined by offence seriousness, and after this determination had been made, the amount of mitigation should be higher for those

[52] Marguerite Schinkel, 'Punishment as Moral Communication: The Experience of Long-Term Prisoners' (2014) 16 *Punishment and Society* 578; compare von Hirsch and Ashworth, above n 24, p 77.

[53] See, eg, American Friends Service Committee, above n 1, pp 67–99.

[54] See generally von Hirsch, *Doing Justice*, above n 3, pp 124–131.

[55] Home Office, *Crime, Justice and Protecting the Public: The Government's Proposals for Legislation* (1990, The Stationery Office, Cm 965), [2.19]; s 2(2) of the Criminal Justice Act 1991.

with fewer previous convictions than those with a longer criminal history.[56] Conversely, mitigating factors were embraced in the statutory regime, providing for a hard border at the top of the penal tariff, but more discretion at the bottom to reduce overall severity.[57] Actor-relevant criteria were to be reinterpreted as only relevant in stepping back from the proportionate sentence, not over-stepping it. The only aggravating criteria built into the 1991 Act were for violent and sexual offenders who pose a serious risk of further harm – a class of *actors*, but one delineated (however broadly) by a class of acts.[58]

As noted above, these changes to make the sentencing process almost exclusively acts-focussed were almost immediately reversed in the face of negative public (and judicial) reaction.[59] But the claim was that a desert model would redefine the contours of a judicial decision from the old law, under which sentences could be extended (potentially indefinitely) to respond to repeat offenders' failure to desist after their last punishment.[60] By refocussing judges' (and the wider public's) imagination of what constituted an 'appropriate' sentence on a response to the specific acts and omissions that led to conviction, the aim was to deny salience to a range of aggravating factors, at least in terms of their ability to influence the sentence beyond an act-proportionate level. In the context of England and Wales in the early 1990s, this was a political argument for comparative penal restraint – and one that proportionality was directly intended to advance.

This increasing focus on acts rather than actors was part of the wider normative reasoning of the Justice Model, which posits that *criminal justice is a poor mechanism for solving social problems*. On this account, the cosy alliance of the 'penal-welfare complex'[61] is ineffective and deeply problematic, and its downfall actively desirable, because the consequences of criminal punishment are much worse than other forms of State control, and incapable of properly addressing the (structural) root causes of (individual) criminal offending. By forcing social justice concerns out of the criminal justice system, von Hirsch sought to compel liberal democracies to deal with the persistent inequalities and social-structural problems that led to crime being disproportionately defined, policed and prosecuted to suit vested social interests, and to engage with more effective and respectful systems of social control.[62] By washing its hands, the criminal justice system could

[56] Ibid, [2.18]; see also Andrew von Hirsch, 'Proportionality and the Progressive Loss of Mitigation: Some Further Reflections', in Julian Roberts and Andrew von Hirsch, *Previous Convictions at Sentencing: Theoretical and Applied Perspectives* (2010, Hart); s 29(1) of the Criminal Justice Act 1991.

[57] See s 28(1) of the Criminal Justice Act 1991.

[58] See generally s 2(2) of the Criminal Justice Act 1991.

[59] See, eg, George Mair, 'Community Penalties in England and Wales' (1998) 10 *Federal Sentencing Reporter* 263, p 264 for a compact summary. Recall also von Hirsch and Ashworth, above n 24, pp 79–80.

[60] On which, see, eg, Youngjae Lee, 'Repeat Offenders and the Question of Desert', in Julian Roberts and Andrew von Hirsch, *Previous Convictions at Sentencing: Theoretical and Applied Perspective* (2010, Hart).

[61] Recall David Garland, *Punishment and Welfare: A History of Penal Strategies* (1985, Ashgate).

[62] See von Hirsch, *Censure and Sanctions*, above n 4, pp 97–99.

force those concerned about the impact of social injustice on punishment to look to the root causes, while still recognising criminal wrongdoing as wrongful.[63] By arguing for a modest set of criminal justice objectives, in other words, von Hirsch argued that proportionate focus on offence seriousness would prevent the penal State from becoming a mere sponge to mop up those spilled out of the social welfare bucket. Given the differing harms and costs of the penal and welfare States, the Justice Model prefers to force States to adopt ambitious programmes of proactive solidarity-building, rather than relying on the purely reactive criminal justice system. Better to stop people being brought into a harmful, painful, and costly system in the first place than to try to ensure they do not come back once they are there![64]

In this regard, von Hirsch takes a very German approach to the conception of the liberal State. In German constitutional law, the State must preserve not only the (negative) liberties of the citizen from the State by respecting their rights and upholding the Rule of Law (the so-called *Rechtsstaat* – literally, the 'rights-State' or 'legal State'). It must also ensure a minimum level of personal empowerment to positively *pursue* one's autonomous wishes in a world of scarce economic resources and social capital (the *Sozialstaat* – literally, 'social State').[65] It is natural, from such a perspective, to identify a robust welfare State as a means of covering for the social justice blindness taken on by the criminal justice system. Indeed, von Hirsch has frequently observed (against the charge that just deserts ignore structural inequalities) that Sweden and Finland – two other liberal States with strong welfare safety-nets – have adopted relatively pure versions of 'just deserts' proportionality in sentencing, and have relatively constrained penal systems overall.[66]

The desert model is also notable for its comparative rejection of *euphemism*, relative to the previous treatment-oriented regime. Cohen strongly rejected the euphemistic 'Controltalk' associated with the treatment model and other penal strategies (including the Justice Model) prevalent at the time. Influenced by Nils Christie's rejection of 'the shield of words' as a way of quieting moral concerns about the problem of punishment,[67] Cohen argued that 'progressive crime control ideology has developed a special vocabulary to soften or disguise the essential (and defining) feature of punishment systems – the planned infliction of pain'.[68]

[63] Ibid, pp 97–98. Compare von Hirsch, *Deserved Criminal Sentences*, above n 4, pp 122–125.

[64] Cohen, above n 22, p 236, after Charles Wright Mills.

[65] See, eg, Dirk van Zyl Smit, 'Prison Law', in Markus Dubber and Tatjana Hörnle (eds), *The Oxford Handbook of Criminal Law* (2014, Oxford University Press), p 998.

[66] See von Hirsch, *Censure and Sanctions*, above n 4, p 98; von Hirsch and Ashworth, above n 24, p 78; and von Hirsch, *Deserved Criminal Sentences*, above n 4, pp 4–7, 115–118. See also Ashworth, 'Prisons, Proportionality, and Recent Penal History', above n 7, pp 480–485. However, compare Nicola Lacey, *The Prisoners' Dilemma: Political Economy and Punishment in Contemporary Democracies* (2008, Cambridge University Press), pp 144–169.

[67] Nils Christie, *Limits to Pain: The Role of Punishment in Penal Policy* (1982, Martin Robertson), pp 13–19.

[68] Cohen, above n 22, p 276.

By focussing attention on the punishment and not on what we mean to achieve thereby, the rhetorical focus shifts. It takes one at least closer to what Christie called an 'absolute' theory of punishment:[69]

> You punish because you punish, just as you are sad because you are sad. An absolute theory of punishment is completely out of fashion among modern penal thinkers. It gives no reason, shows no utility. I like the theory because of that. If there were no purpose behind the pain, it would be more of a clear moral matter. The parties would have to think again about whether pain was right. *Not whether it was necessary, but right*. The chances are great that the more they thought, the less they would find it right. Reflection would exile anger (emphasis added).

Importantly, the purpose of punishment under the desert model is *not* 'absolute' in Christie's sense: it is not to inflict pain, as in the Biblical *lex talionis*.[70] Rather, painful hard treatment is only a means of *expressing* the amount of censure necessary to recognise the gravity of the offender's wrong.[71] So retributivism as it is expressed in its modern form is not an absolute theory in Christie's sense, because it sees pain only as a necessary means of delivering *censure*.[72]

With that being said, however, a purely retributive model at least takes us closer to a focus on the painfulness of the punishment. The negative consequences for the subject are not swept aside to the same extent as in the consequentialist weighing up of the net benefit to society. The suffering that normally accompanies the punishment is the vocabulary and grammar of moral condemnation, and therefore, while necessary, it is necessary in a more intrinsic way than in penal rehabilitation, where care, support, and 'treatment' could, in theory, be imposed without imposing the substantial negative consequences of criminal punishment at all. By focusing attention on what the wrongful act deserves, a retributive sentencing regime made it easier to conduct a political discussion of punishment in absolute terms, by focussing public attention on responses to wrongdoing before an amorphous concept of social improvement. Almost certainly this was unintentional: notably, the 1990 Home Office White Paper bends over backwards to clarify that crime prevention and public protection were still features of governmental policy.[73] But by moving the debate towards what wrongdoers deserve, the Criminal Justice Act 1991 provided more room to discuss whether

[69] Christie, above n 67, pp 100–101.

[70] See, eg, von Hirsch and Ashworth, above n 24, p 81.

[71] See, eg, von Hirsch, *Censure and Sanctions*, above n 4, pp 6–19; and compare Duff, *Punishment, Communication, and Community*, above n 28, pp 88–99; Dan Markel and Chad Flanders, 'Bentham on Stilts: The Bare Relevance of Subjectivity to Retributive Justice' (2010) 98 *California Law Review* 907, pp 929–941, 945–947; Joshua Glasgow, 'The Expressivist Theory of Punishment Defended' (2015) 34 *Law and Philosophy* 601; and Matt Matravers, 'Punishment, Suffering and Justice' in: Stephen Farrall et al (eds), *Justice and Penal Reform: Re-Shaping the Penal Landscape* (2016, Routledge).

[72] See, eg, RA Duff, 'Punishment, Communication and Community', in: Matt Matravers (ed), *Punishment and Political Theory* (1998, Hart), p 50; Kleinig, above n 24.

[73] See, eg, Home Office, above n 55, [1.6]–[1.9].

punishment was a necessary consequence of criminal wrongdoing at all,[74] shifting the rhetorical terrain of penal policy-making such that penal minimalism was easier to bring onto the agenda.

III. Critiques of Retributive Penal Minimalism

What emerges from these defences of retributive proportionality is a belief that a genuine commitment to (just-deserts) proportionality would impose inherent constraints on the growth and malformation of the penal State, and provide political reasons to reject penal policies likely to result in penal excess. In Chapter 2, however, we saw an overall increase in penal excess in terms of both size and shape over the period between 1989 and 2018. To what extent does the correlation of the rise of Justice Model retribution and increases in penal excess indicate a *causal* relationship between them? Three distinct arguments that allege a failure to prevent penal excess on the part of retributivism deserve particular attention: firstly, the 'desert-severity' hypothesis, alleging that retributivism provides succour for punitive penal politics; secondly, the inability of desert to take account of social injustices – the challenge of 'just deserts in an unjust world'; and thirdly, the argument that *proportionality is a 'chimera'* – a vacuous concept with no internal basis for forcing State restraint. von Hirsch and Ashworth have responded to (and rejected) each allegation, and we will consider their ripostes alongside the broader critiques. I will discuss their responses to each of the three critiques, and consider the extent to which each argument reveals either a *theoretical* or a *political* failure on retributivism's ability to resist penal excess.

A. The 'Desert-Severity' Hypothesis: Desert, Blame, and Punitiveness

The first charge against retributivism is that it has a tendency, with all its talk of wrongdoing, blameworthiness, and morally deserved hardship, to give credence to 'mere' punitiveness – that is, to the idea that punishment is always good, regardless of proportionality or offence-seriousness. Certainly there are conceptual linkages between retribution, which rests upon the intuitive appeal of seeing people 'get what is coming to them', and punitiveness, which speaks to our desire to enact revenge upon wrongdoers.[75] Indeed, retributive justice has always been justified as a response to the threat of 'rough justice' by private vigilantes – an

[74] Compare Kleinig, above n 24.

[75] See generally Michael Moore, *Placing Blame: A General Theory of Criminal Law* (1997, Oxford University Press), especially chs 3–4; Canton, above n 13.

explicit concern of the drafters of the Criminal Justice Act 1991,[76] but also more foundationally in English criminal law, which emerged out of the replacement of a system of (pagan) clan-based blood-feuds with the centralised legal system of a (Christian) monarch in early medieval England.[77] Retributive criminal justice is therefore foundationally linked to retaliation. The aim is that, by imposing hardships dispassionately, the State avoids cycles of internecine violence that are socio-economically and -politically destabilising. Private desires for vengeance are channelled into a more 'civilised' form, and thus, the desire for revenge is sated without overstepping its bounds.[78]

The specific assertion that (desert-based) retributivism *leads to* and *rhetorically reinforces* mere punitiveness does not follow from the mere presence of conceptual overlap between the two approaches. Despite this, the claim has been made with considerable vehemence, in a number of different contexts, since the success of the Justice Model. For Cullen and Gilbert, retribution's foundational concern with offenders' moral guilt and blameworthiness inevitably ceded ground to the conservative law-and-order lobby active in 1980s American politics, while a (treatment-based) rehabilitative approach was more resistant in that it placed care and respect for the offender at the centre of its vision.[79] Braithwaite and Pettit echo this sentiment, claiming that retributivism provides normative aid and succour to those who wish to 'play to the sense of the normality of the majority' and 'tyrannize the minority'.[80] Most recently, Lacey has expressed a 'foundational conviction' in a conference presentation that:[81]

> [T]he tendency of our public debate on penal policy to focus on the question of calibrating the punitiveness of penal measures adequately to reflect society's censure of wrongdoing has had some really bad effects in terms of narrowing the way in which we think about criminal justice, and in some ways has had the effect of rather distancing the idea of justice.

Garland alleges, more charitably, that desert was effectively in the wrong place at the wrong time: it encouraged penal excess only because it spoke of blame

[76] Home Office, above n 55, [2.4].

[77] See generally Marc Bloch, *Feudal Society, Volume 2: Social Classes and Political Organisation* (1964, Routledge), pp 408–437; Peter Wormald, *The Making of English Law: King Alfred to the Twelfth Century, volume 1: Legislation and its Limits* (1999, Blackwell), pp 39–40, 311–312.

[78] See, eg, John Gardner, 'Crime: In Proportion and in Perspective', in: Andrew Ashworth and Martin Wasik (eds), *Fundamentals of Sentencing Theory: Essays in Honour of Andrew von Hirsch* (1998, The Clarendon Press); David Garland, *Punishment and Modern Society: A Study in Social Theory* (1990, Clarendon Press), ch 10.

[79] See generally Francis Cullen and Karen Gilbert, *Re-Affirming Rehabilitation*, Second edn (2013, Anderson Publishing), ch 5 (originally published in 1982). Compare Cohen, above n 22, pp 246–248, summarising and critiquing their position.

[80] John Braithwaite and Phillip Pettit, *Not Just Deserts: A Republican Theory of Justice* (1990, Oxford University Press), pp 15–16.

[81] Nicola Lacey, 'Rethinking Justice: Penal Policy Beyond Punishment', *What is Justice?*, 1–2 October 2013. An audio recording of this paper is available at: https://howardleague.org/what-is-justice-conference-podcasts/ (accessed 8 August 2018). The quoted text is from 03:38–04:15.

and wrongdoing *at the time* when social and cultural stability were weakening, and concern with the interests of victims, under conditions of 'late modernity' (a period in which socioeconomic globalisation and cultural individualisation create considerable increases in (perceived) social, political, and existential insecurity).[82] In another time and another place, Garland suggests, proportionality could have worked as a limiting factor – it is just that, in the UK and US of the 1980s and 1990s, it did not. So Garland's claim is that retributivism failed, but only on a *political* level – not in the *theoretical* terms that Cullen and Gilbert, Braithwaite and Pettit, and Lacey allege.

The theoretical version of the claim is stronger: that the very narrowing of the focus of criminal justice towards the act and away from the actor had negative as well as liberty-positive effects. Although the paternalistic impulses of the treatment and prevention strategies of the 1970s were removed from sentencing authorities' formal ambit, this also removed the *benevolence* that rehabilitation in particular had inserted into the system. Whilst treatment's humanity may well have been a veneer for paternalistic and authoritarian control in practice, that veneer was at least rhetorically significant in reminding policy-makers, sentencing authorities, and public commentators that crimes were the result of systemic problems as well as individual responsibility, and that the State owes certain minimum duties of care towards (and basic respect for the humanity of) those who had thumbed their nose at its moral codes. This silenced valuable support for penal minimalism on the traditionally liberal-paternalist left at the same time as redefining the grammar and vocabulary of penal policy debate to terms amenable to traditionally punitive conservative concerns with moral responsibility and preserving 'law and order'. The classically liberal retributivists – sitting in between the further-left liberal-paternalists and further-right punitive 'law and order' crowd – had unintentionally stacked the deck in favour of penal excess, as an inherent consequence of their use of desert as their model's limiting factor.

Ashworth and von Hirsch have both emphatically rejected this hypothesis.[83] They rely on comparative evidence that, in countries such as Sweden and Finland, where desert principles have been highly influential, penal excess has generally been lower overall than in the UK and US. This suggests that there is no *inherent* connection between the adoption of a criminal justice system focussed on proportionate punishment of offences and the overuse of the penal State.[84] Turning to England and Wales, they observe that the Criminal Justice Act 1991 was almost immediately undercut – first by interpreting court judges, and then by subsequent Acts of Parliament. At the same time, penal politics were shifted by high-profile

[82] See David Garland, *The Culture of Control: Crime and Social Order in Contemporary Societies* (2001, Oxford University Press), p 9.

[83] See von Hirsch, *Censure and Sanctions*, above n 4, pp 91–94; von Hirsch and Ashworth, above n 24, ch 6; von Hirsch, *Deserved Criminal Sentences*, above n 4, pp 115–121; Ashworth, 'Prisons, Proportionality, and Recent Penal History', above n 7, pp 486–488.

[84] See, eg, von Hirsch and Ashworth, above n 24, pp 77–78.

events such as the killing of James Bulger, 9/11, and 7/7 in the direction of a more punitive and managerial penal policy, in ways that had nothing to do with the terrain left by the vocabulary of desert. Likewise, post-1997 penal excess was driven by explicitly managerial interventions, such as imprisonment for public protection, mandatory minimum sentences and 'three strikes' laws, which had little or no rhetorical basis in the desert of the offenders, and so could hardly be blamed on retributivist theories.[85]

What should we make of these competing claims? Certainly, von Hirsch and Ashworth offer strong reasons to reject any inherent causal connection between desert-based retributivism on the one hand, and punitive increases in severity on the other. In particular, it is worth drawing out a distinction that neither these scholars, nor their critics, make particularly clearly the difference between the role of *punitiveness* in driving up penal excess, and that of *penal managerialism*. The two are related, undoubtedly, but as I have laid them out above, these two expansionist tendencies in recent penal policy are worlds apart. The desert/severity hypothesis argues that *punitiveness* is supported by the desert model's focus on calibrating painful hard treatment to express a certain amount of censure, because it opens up the emotional floodgates to a focus on the offender as a moral enemy of the State and of civil society more generally. But that is not an explanation of the parallel success of penal managerialism over the same period – an approach to reducing reoffending and protecting the public that is about as emotionally-driven as a commercial audit, even if it responds to the fear of crime. Given the success of managerialism cannot easily be linked to the language of desert, the claim of a theoretical failure of desert is overblown, and neglects the role of other penal theories – particularly 'What Works' era rehabilitation – in doing the same.

However, by the same token it is unfair to say that desert had *nothing* to do with increases in penal excess over the past 30 years. In focussing purely on prisons as the site of penal severity, von Hirsch and Ashworth ignore the massive expansion of the probationer population since the 1990s. This is significant because, in the 1991 Act, community penalties were recognised as alternative punishments to imprisonment for offences of intermediate seriousness. The problem was that this reconceptualisation created normative pressure to 'toughen up' community penalties, and demonstrate their punitive potential.[86] Part of the problem here was the choice of liberty deprivation as the *metric* for proportionality in the 1991 Act regime. The deprivation of liberty (that is, of freedom of movement and of

[85] See, eg, ibid, pp 79–80; Ashworth, 'Prisons, Proportionality, and Recent Penal History', above n 7, pp 474–479.

[86] See, eg, Mair, 'Community Penalties in England and Wales', above n 59, p 263; Gwen Robinson, 'Three Narratives and a Funeral: Community Punishment in England and Wales', in Gwen Robinson and Fergus McNeill (eds), *Community Punishment: European Perspectives* (2016, Routledge), pp 36–39. Compare Michael Tonry and Mona Lynch, 'Intermediate Sanctions' (1996) 20 *Crime and Justice* 99, for equivalent US developments at the time.

choice regarding one's actions) is actually a relatively minor part of the 'pains of probation',[87] but is inherent to the very nature of imprisoning someone (although different prison regimes can certainly limit the degree of intrusiveness into liberty involved). As a result, community penalties inevitably seemed like pale alternatives to imprisonment in the retributive hierarchy.[88] At least part of the policy reasons underpinning the 'toughening up' of probation-based penalties in the 1990s had to do with concerns around the regularity of breaches of those orders[89] – a concern at least as managerial as punitive. However, it was legitimised and underwritten by the wider transformation of community sanctions into *community penalties* that were appropriate punishments for offences of intermediate severity.

Conversely, excessive use of non-custodial sentences has not *solely* been driven by the need to speak in the language of desert. Probationary penalties have no more been free from the effects of preventive and managerial interventions than imprisonment in this regard. Indeed, Robinson notes that the 'punishment in the community' rhetoric only really began to take off from 1994 – by which time a robust, monistic commitment to desert had already begun to crumble in Anglo-Welsh penal policy.[90] The point is not that desert is the only or even the primary driver of penal expansion – it is just that the protestations that it has had *nothing* to do with enabling punitiveness (and managerialism) ring hollow in this instance. Ultimately, this weakness is not a theoretical failure of proportionality – we might just have well have kept the relatively 'soft' community penalties of the pre-1991 Act period, and lowered prison sentences to ensure overall ordinal and cardinal proportionality.[91] But we *did* not, because it was ultimately easier to anchor the scale to intrusive but popular imprisonment rather than relatively less intrusive probation. The effect was punitive overall (it increased the total intrusiveness of the sentencing tariff), and it was undertaken in the name of securing effective proportionality in practice. So it is not fair to say that proportionality *never* gives any ground to the pursuit of ever-greater severity.

Moreover, Ashworth's and von Hirsch's defences both utterly concede the *political* failure version of the desert/severity hypothesis. Their argument is that retributivism (especially in England and Wales) was swiftly abandoned and replaced by a confused, 'law and order' jumble – and that *this* was what drove up the level of excess in the penal system:[92]

> In assessing the link between sentencing rationale and penal severity, a certain realism is needed. A sentencing theory cannot, Canute-like, stop the waters from rising.

[87] See, eg, Ioan Durnescu, 'Pains of Probation: Effective Practice and Human Rights' (2011) 55 *International Journal of Offender Therapy and Comparative Criminology* 530; David Hayes, 'The Impact of Supervision on the Pains of Community Penalties in England and Wales: An Exploratory Study' (2015) 7 *European Journal of Probation* 82.

[88] See also Hayes, 'Penal Impact', above n 25.

[89] See, eg, Home Office, *Crime, Justice and Protecting the Public*, above n 55, [4.18], [4.21].

[90] Robinson, 'Three Narratives and a Funeral', above n 86, p 39.

[91] Recall nn 36–38 and accompanying text above, for discussion of 'anchoring' the penalty scale.

[92] von Hirsch, *Censure and Sanctions*, above n 4, pp 93–94.

> Where the law-and-order pressures in a particular jurisdiction are sufficiently strong, punishments will increase, and no penal theory can prevent that. [...]All a penal theory can do is offer reasons for limiting penalty increases.

For an audience concerned with whether desert is a coherent and ethically justifiable theory, this is an entirely consistent and reasonable position. But penal minimalism is *not* a justification of punishment, so much as it is a theory of how we should *respond* to the use of the penal system in a particular sort of polity. It offers an argument that too much punishment is bad, but not a reason to impose criminal punishment in the first place. The result is that, while von Hirsch and Ashworth can quite happily chalk the failure of desert to persuade policy-makers and voters to continue to support minimalism *and still remain committed retributivists*. However, anyone who specifically endorsed desert as a way of resisting penal excess in response to the decline of the rehabilitative ideal must be disappointed, and ask whether it is worth granting retributivism another chance. There is no reason to think that the political tide will not turn again. von Hirsch may be happy to simply try again – but someone primarily committed to penal minimalism is unlikely to be satisfied with that political option. Indeed, it may be an admission that proportionality cannot ever really succeed in restraining the penal State, except temporarily and more by political luck than by skill.

B. 'Just Deserts in an Unjust World': Blind Proportionality and Social Injustice

In Chapter 2 we saw that the criminal justice system over-represents subjects from a range of already-marginalised social groups, in ways that do not seem to have anything to do with the characteristics of those groups or their propensity towards criminality. This propensity of the penal system to replicate and exacerbate social inequality is at the heart of the 'just deserts in an unjust world' critique, which was named (and recognised) by von Hirsch himself, but which is particularly embodied in British criminology by the work of Barbara Hudson.[93]

Hudson's version of the 'unjust world' critique is based, foundationally, upon a rejection of 'legal reasoning' as the sole or primary basis of penal decision-making. Her concern is that proportionality limits our attention to factors that are relevant to the question of legal guilt (around how much blame is deserved for one's actions, omissions, and mental state), to the exclusion of important *social factors* that ought to have some influence on how we respond to criminal justice.[94]

[93] In the US, see Michael Tonry, *Malign Neglect: Race, Crime, and Punishment in America* (1995, Oxford University Press), pp 149–160; Tonry, 'Can Deserts Be Just in an Unjust World?', above n 24.

[94] See especially Hudson, *Justice through Punishment*, above n 5; Barbara Hudson, *Penal Policy and Social Justice* (1993, Macmillan); Barbara Hudson, 'Beyond Proportionate Punishment: Difficult Cases and the 1991 Criminal Justice Act' (1995) 22 *Crime, Law & Social Change* 59; Barbara Hudson, 'Punishing the Poor: Dilemmas of Justice and Difference', in William Heffernan and John Kleinig (eds),

The result is that criminal justice constructs the offender as a bundle of abstract rights, as a perfectly rational actor, and solely as an individual, rather than as an embodied and socio-economically, -politically and -culturally situated human animal. The resultant blindness to the social problems that at least play *some* role in causing at least *some* crimes undermines the ability of the desert model to claim any sort of moral high ground, in the context of any liberal-democratic polity with a genuine commitment to meaningful social equality.[95] For Hudson, in other words, it is not an advantage that retributive punishment separates acts from actors – because you *cannot* separate the act from the actor, or the actor from their social context.[96]

Moreover, the separation of social justice concerns from criminal sentencing creates the risk that social injustices are simply acquiesced to, rather than being forced into the wider State's concern. It is all very well to say that one thinks social justice should be a matter of social welfare and other, looser forms of social control. But if one does not match word to deed, the statement that "This is better dealt with elsewhere" all too readily becomes a dismissal: "This isn't part of our concern, and so we don't have to worry about it".[97] Making such a claim effectively prevents the theorist from dealing with systemic problems around the way that the criminal justice system has been defined (in the interests, overwhelmingly, of social elites),[98] and in doing so, bakes those problems into the system. More prosaically, it ties the hands of the criminal justice system to do things to address the social factors that have caused the offender to end up under penal social control in the first place. Hudson's critique ultimately comes down to a question of political strategy among different subspecies of liberal penal policy-making. Both she and von Hirsch conceive of the 'unjust world' problem as concerning the relationship between criminal justice and wider social justice. They are opposed not because they disagree about the problem, but because they offer contrasting *solutions* to that problem. Whereas von Hirsch takes the view that welfare is better served by non-penal institutions with fewer and less severe negative consequences, for Hudson criminal justice ought to be viewed as just another tool in the social policy toolbox.[99] At this level, then, the argument is really about a failure to follow through on the desert model's insistence on a robust social welfare State, as much as about a theoretical defect.

A penal minimalist is liable to side more with von Hirsch than with Hudson in this dispute. At her most proactively rehabilitation-oriented, Hudson downplays the serious negative consequences of the penal State's control, whilst, at her more

From Social Justice to Criminal Justice: Poverty and the Administration of Criminal Law (2000, Oxford University Press); Hudson, *Justice in the Risk Society*, above n 15.

[95] See, eg, Hudson, *Justice through Punishment*, above n 5, p 169

[96] See, eg, Hudson, *Penal Policy and Social Justice*, above n 94, chs 2–3.

[97] See Hudson, *Justice through Punishment*, above n 5, pp 162–163.

[98] See Hudson, 'Punishing the Poor', above n 94, pp 201–210.

[99] See generally Hudson, *Penal Policy and Social Justice*, above n 94.

nuanced, she is willing to accept that desert ought to impose at least some hard limits, albeit further reinforced by the limiting effects of the parsimony principle.[100] But the penal minimalist's objection is that there *is* something problematic about using criminal justice as a source of social control. The problem of punishment is not the same as the problem of social welfare, and it is generally more problematic for the liberal-democratic State. So Hudson's critique is more of the Justice Model's focus on criminal punishment rather than the causes (and definition) of crime. It does not result in a robust theoretical rejection of proportionality as such – but it warns that a meaningfully minimalist model using proportionality must provide an answer to the question of what it will do about the social justice concerns that it is exorcising from criminal justice. Penal minimalism, in other words, cannot be installed and then permanently guaranteed only through a proportionate system of punishment – routine maintenance work is required both inside and out of penal policy.

There is one aspect of Hudson's critique, however, which reaches into at least some retributive theories: the hardening of their hearts towards the (collateral) consequences of criminal punishment. In discussing the social context and consequences of punishment, von Hirsch displays a telling lack of sympathy:[101]

> It is unquestionably true that the stigma of a criminal record narrows [a convicted] person's opportunities. But such disabilities are the consequences of the person's *own* actions in having violated the law.

Given the sort of social-contract approach typical amongst liberal accounts, it *is* fair to say on the basis of von Hirsch's conception of the (penal) State that we as citizens can be taken to know the consequences of breaking the law.[102] However, this claim reduces the infliction of collateral harms to something that is *solely* the offender's fault. Compare a later adoption of this position by Dan Markel and Chad Flanders, which takes this observation to its logical extreme:[103]

> The contingent harms third parties may experience as a result of offender's actions culminating in state punishment – sometimes called spillover effects on the offender's family or loved ones – are in our view *morally attributable to the offender* as reasonably foreseeable consequences arising from the offender's conduct (emphasis added).

Again, if offenders are responsible for their actions, even in part, then they are responsible for the consequences of their actions. Moreover, in a State governed by the rule of law, to the extent that laws are transparent and accessible to the lay public,[104] it is right that we treat offenders as knowing that if they commit

[100] Hudson, 'Beyond Proportionate Punishment', above n 94, pp 60, 72–75.

[101] von Hirsch, *Doing Justice*, above n 3, p 148. Compare, however, p 149.

[102] See generally Matt Matravers, 'Political Theory and the Criminal Law', in RA Duff and Stuart Green, *Philosophical Foundations of Criminal Law* (2011, Oxford University Press).

[103] Markel and Flanders, above n 71, p 971.

[104] Recall Kim Stevenson and Candida Harris, 'Breaking the Thrall of Ambiguity: Simplification (of the Criminal Law) as an Emerging Human Rights Imperative' (2010) 74 *Journal of Criminal Law* 516.

a crime, they are running a risk of punishment, and that that punishment may affect not only their life, but also the lives of those around them. Where this argument becomes morally indefensible is the implication (by Markel and Flanders but not, in context, by von Hirsch) that because the offender could see it coming, that absolves the State of *any* responsibility for the imposition of the well-documented and reliably observable collateral consequences of punishment.[105] This reasoning takes us uncomfortably close to the language of a domestic abuser: *Look what you made me do*! It effectively pretends that the collateral consequences of punishment, for offenders and for formally innocent third parties, do not exist, or at least that the State is not responsible for addressing or ameliorating them. But that claim seriously undermines the liberal ideology underpinning the Justice Model, in its claim to respect citizens equally and to treat them first and foremost as ends in themselves.[106] That we do so is a result of the narrowing of focus of what matters when we fix the sentence only to the acts of the offender, treating their wider context as though it does not matter.

Notice, however, that nothing in this is an inevitable result of adopting proportionality as a limiting principle upon punishment. Indeed, in the Criminal Justice Act 1991 there was room for 'personal mitigation' for circumstances affecting the hardship imposed by punishment arising from the penal subject's social situation.[107] It is more a question of *how* proportionality is pursued than something inherent in proportionality that encourages blindness to the potential collateral consequences of punishment. The solution is not to amend the theory of proportionality, necessarily, but to ask its proponents to take seriously their claim to think of criminal justice as a limited system capable of achieving only modest ends, and to speak to what goes on outside of that system. If one wants a robust *Sozialstaat*, one had best actually argue for it, in other words! This is the crux of Barbara Hudson's point, which is inherently minimalistic: that we should always punish in bad conscience.[108] But it only alleges a political failing on the part of the desert model.

C. The Conceptual Emptiness of Proportionality

The final (and most direct) critique of proportionality's role in limiting the size of penal States, is Nicola Lacey's and Hanna Pickard's claim that proportionality

[105] See, eg, Christopher Bennett, 'Invisible Punishment is Wrong – But Why? The Normative Basis of Criticism of Collateral Consequences of Criminal Conviction' (2017) 56 *The Howard Journal of Crime and Justice* 480.

[106] Compare Hudson, *Justice through Punishment*, above n 5, pp 166–167.

[107] Recall s 28(1) of the Criminal Justice Act 1991; and see generally Roberts (ed), above n 11.

[108] See, eg, Hudson, *Justice in the Risk Society*, above n 94, p 35; Willem de Haan, 'Abolition and the Politics of "Bad Conscience"' (1987) 26 *The Howard Journal of Crime and Justice* 15; Thomas Mathiesen, *The Politics of Abolition Revisited* (2015, Routledge), pp 227–230.

is a *chimera* – that is, a nebulous and uncertain concept lacking in meaningful content.[109] Lacey and Pickard present two arguments in support of their assertion that proportionality is a mere chimera. Their argument is historical and comparative, as well as normative. They note that different penal systems throughout history have demonstrated a commitment to some degree of proportionality in their sentencing systems, but with vastly different outcomes in terms of the size, shape, and intrusiveness of their penal systems. While a consensus *does* emerge across space and over time for the ordinal ranking of offences (murder and rape are typically seen as more serious than shop theft, for example), no such pattern emerged for the cardinal 'fitting' of punishments to crimes.[110] This is, of course, consistent with what von Hirsch and Ashworth have already said in the context of the desert/severity hypothesis – a hypothesis that Lacey and Pickard substantially reproduce in the final part of this argument.[111] But their argument is also broader and more conceptual in nature.

Whereas von Hirsch and Ashworth are willing to take the differentiated penal climates between different penal regimes as a vindication of the desert model under conditions of more effective social welfare provision, for Lacey and Pickard this is to treat the symptom as the cause. They argue that retributive proportionality is only successful in the right institutional context – that is, in a set of criminal justice institutions amenable to self-restraint, against a wider social background of welfare and other institutions that support that – because the successes of proportionality are actually *the successes of those institutional arrangements*. Proportionality has no independent effect in terms of reducing or restraining penal excess, and is wholly reliant upon underlying conventions, social structures, institutions, and value systems.[112] Lacey and Pickard point to a range of early-modern and contemporary examples, noting the importance of strong socio-cultural ties of association, and to the historical importance of the quasi-sacred nature of punishment and State authority in historically devout Christian nations.[113] The problem, as they see it, is that proportionality used to rely upon these shared values about social hierarchy, religious morality, and shared political symbolism. However, those shared precepts have decayed, and as a result proportionality serves as a code for an underlying set of socio-cultural values and expectations about the institutions of government (including those of criminal justice) that no longer exist.[114] We have tended the branches of penal restraint while letting the roots wither.

[109] See Lacey and Pickard, 'The Chimera of Proportionality', above n 30; Nicola Lacey, 'The Metaphor of Proportionality' (2016) 43 *Journal of Law and Society* 27.

[110] Lacey, 'The Metaphor of Proportionality', above n 109, pp 39–41.

[111] See, eg, Lacey and Pickard, 'The Chimera of Proportionality' above n 30, pp 220–221, 226–228. See also Nicola Lacey and Hanna Pickard, 'To Blame or To Forgive? Reconciling Punishment and Forgiveness in Criminal Justice' (2015) 35 *OLJS* 665.

[112] Lacey, 'The Metaphor of Proportionality', above n 109, pp 40–41.

[113] See Lacey and Pickard, 'The Chimera of Proportionality', above n 30, pp 221–232.

[114] Ibid, pp 232–237.

The response to Lacey and Pickard's argument by the desert model's champions has been, to put it lightly, insufficient. Ashworth offers the benefit of a full retort in a paper developed solely for that purpose,[115] but his response is framed solely in terms of the Lacey-Pickard critique's repetition of the desert/severity hypothesis, and does not specifically address the 'chimerical' aspect of the allegations against proportionality. By contrast, von Hirsch does address that aspect of the critique, but out of hand, in a total of three paragraphs.[116] To strip the desert model of its liberal underpinnings, and so to focus on just proportionality, is in his view reductive and disingenuous. It does not represent the whole of the desert model, but only part of it, taken out of context. But von Hirsch misses an important element of the Lacey-Pickard critique: that the desert model as a whole presumes liberal underpinnings *but does nothing to preserve them*. Indeed, by focussing so heavily on retrospective sentencing judgments, the desert model largely ignores the wider institutional architecture in which sentencing operates, preventing wider critique of the role of the sentencing authority within the social, political, and cultural institutions that surround the (penal) State. Indeed, we saw that von Hirsch himself notes above that desert's systems are not proof against wider political shifts, in and of themselves, in response to the desert-severity critique, above.[117] The point is not that the desert model *can never emerge* in a way that promotes proportionate sentencing, but that its systems for self-maintenance and propagation lie wholly outside the penal system upon which it focuses virtually all of its rhetorical attention. It is therefore extremely vulnerable to wider-scale policy shifts.[118]

Again, this is not so much a critique of retributivism as a penal theory – Lacey and Pickard concede that other penal theories are just as vulnerable to wider institutional changes.[119] Their critique, however, is of the wider use of proportionality *as a limiting principle in its own right*, both within and beyond the criminal justice context.[120] But whatever its target, von Hirsch has missed the point in his too-brief dismissal of the Lacey-Pickard argument, and has engaged in an important conceptual slip in doing so. The positioning of the Justice Model has always had a substantial focus on 'realism' and the modern world. von Hirsch and his contemporaries were grappling with the challenges of what to do in *these* (Western) penal systems at *this* moment (after the decline of the rehabilitative ideal). However, in defending desert from the Lacey-Pickard critique, he resorts to a retreat into the normative realm, arguing that desert-based proportionality *can* have and *has had* an impact but only where the wider institutional architecture is capable of maintaining the wider liberal ideals it needs, and that desert *should* be based upon certain limited, substantive bases. But that is to concede the point

[115] See Ashworth, 'Prisons, Proportionality, and Recent Penal History', above n 7.
[116] von Hirsch, *Deserved Criminal Sentences*, above n 4, pp 125–126.
[117] Recall n 92 and accompanying text.
[118] Lacey and Pickard, 'The Chimera of Proportionality' above n 30, pp 238–239.
[119] Ibid, pp 239–240.
[120] See generally Lacey, above n 109.

that proportionality, *in and of itself*, has no power to limit the State, and is reliant on broader institutional superstructure to do the heavy lifting in resisting penal excess – which is precisely what Lacey and Pickard claim! This certainly suggests a political failure on the part of proportionate sentencing regimes in England and Wales to constrain the impulse towards penal excess after the Criminal Justice Act 1991.

However, Lacey and Pickard's critique is also a substantial *theoretical* critique of the value of proportionality as a penal constraint, because their argument suggests that proportionality *can never substantially* constrain the penal State. Instead of quibbling with penal theory, penal minimalists should focus on building consensus for changes to the underlying normative and institutional structures.[121] However, Lacey and Pickard do not really make out the claim that proportionality can *never* have a substantive effect. To do so would require a larger historical and comparative analysis of levels of penal excess within different legal codes with different levels of commitment to proportionality than they provide. That would, in fairness, be a herculean task – not least because 'penal excess' would mean different things at different times historically, and would be anachronistic in illiberal non-democracies in the liberal-democratic terms I have defined it here. One would also struggle to construct a sample of comparable States or legal codes. Comparing criminal justice systems is a challenging endeavour, even at the best of times,[122] but across vast geographic and cultural differences, and over great periods of time, it is harder. Is it fair, for instance, to compare Hammurabi's Babylon with Drakon's Athens, or Manu's India, or Tang China? These are questions that could potentially be answered, but only with great difficulty. The problem is that, while Lacey and Pickard draw upon a considerable range of historical and current States that *do* commit to proportionality, and argue that they show a wide disparity in terms of levels of excess. However, they do not point to a control group of historical and/or contemporary penal systems that make *no such rhetorical commitment* to proportionality. What we would need to see to say, definitively, that proportionality has no independent effect, would be that there is just as much variation between non-proportionate and proportionate States. If proportionate States tend on average to be more restrained than non-proportionate ones, notwithstanding variations between those two groups, then that is a sign that proportionality is doing *something*, no matter in how limited and attenuated a manner. In the absence of that kind of robust historical comparative data, however, we must be circumspect about claiming that proportionality *can never work*. Indeed, Lacey appears to accept this in her restatement of the Lacey-Pickard critique, because she assumes that under certain institutional

[121] Lacey, 'The Metaphor of Proportionality' above n 109, p 41.

[122] See generally David Nelken, *Comparative Criminal Justice: Making Sense of Difference* (2010, SAGE).

circumstances, proportionality can be a valid metaphor, if only because a broken clock is at least right twice a day.[123] Her overall point is that we should not *rely* on proportionality to consistently defend penal moderation (or minimalism), not that it never does or never could. So, the Lacey-Pickard critique does not provide evidence of total theoretical weakness on reliance on proportionality. It does raise important questions, however, about the conceptual coherence of proportionality and its relationship to restraint in the exercise of penal State coercion.

D. Normative Retributive Theory and the Failures of Desert

These critiques suggest a failure of retributivism, as expressed in the Justice Model – albeit a partial and mostly political one. I have focussed on critiques of the just deserts model, partly because von Hirsch and Ashworth have been so active in challenging each of these critiques, but mainly because the 'just deserts' model has been the most influential theory of retribution at the level of penal policy throughout the English-speaking world (and the wider Global West). It is therefore the best theory to use to distinguish and separately consider the charges of *political* and *theoretical* failure – since we actually have a historical record of its operation. Given, however, that the three critiques outlined above have indicated some theoretical limitations in retributive solutions to penal excess, it is worth asking whether these critiques are restricted to the desert model, or can apply more generally to other retributive theories.

At least in the case of Duff's communicative approach, the answer is, 'probably not,' because of that account's *normative abstraction*. Duff's model is vulnerable to the same failures as von Hirsch's in the short term, on a *pragmatic* level. This problem is well-known, to the extent that Duff himself admits it. Duff starts from an idealised view of what life in a liberal community *should* look like – the relationship between 'I' and 'We', and the institutions that reinforce them.[124] Only then can he turn to questions of criminal punishment and its justification. So Duff only attempts to justify a model of punishment insofar as it coheres with a pre-defined and delimited 'rational reconstruction' of what society and the people within it look like and how they relate to one another. As a result, he makes no claims about existing real-world practices, going so far as to observe that it would be a 'callously bad joke' to use his communicative model to justify existing penal systems.[125] But in effect, this means that Duff's solution is to define away problems arising from the messy practical context at a preliminary stage.

[123] Lacey, 'The Metaphor of Proportionality', above n 109.

[124] See generally Duff, *Punishment, Communication, and Community*, above n 28, pp 35–73; Duff, *Answering for Crime*, above n 48, pp 37–56; Duff, 'A Criminal Law for Citizens', above n 47.

[125] RA Duff, 'Penance, Punishment, and the Limits of Community' (2003) 5 *Punishment & Society* 295, p 304.

If society is messier and more complicated than he conceives of it as being, then his theory is limited to the extent that no such tidy society actually exists, and probably it never will. Duff's community is a place that can never be anyone's home – and certainly cannot be for anyone actually alive at present. There is, certainly, value in exploring ideal types, even when they are simplified, because they tell us important things about what it would mean to live up to the ideals that we so flippantly express. Rational reconstruction at a purely normative level can therefore tell us as much about the shortcomings of our normative ideals as of our actual practices.[126] But if the question is about how to achieve a more minimal penal State in the short term, a purely ideal-type vision of penal systems in some sort of perfect liberal community will not suffice. At best it will be vulnerable to the same political challenges, limitations and failures that have dogged the desert model; and at worst it will be still more vulnerable, because Duff's theory does not emerge from responses to problems (and so has not weathered the challenges of specific policy drives towards penal excess) in existing penal systems in the way that von Hirsch's has.

Nevertheless, might we, as penal minimalists, take his account as something to aspire to? I am sceptical, but to explain why, I must explain more about the scope of the problem facing retributivism, and wider penal theory, and the sort of approach needed to break us out of the quagmire of worsening penal excess that contemporary England and Wales finds itself in. I therefore forestall further discussion of that point until Chapter 6. For now, suffice it to say that Duff's account, in relying to such an extent upon a presupposed series of extra-penal institutions of liberal community, bakes a series of wider biases and perspectives into his model. His is no utopian vision of a better system, so much as a set of gears that assumes an *a priori*, more-or-less-perfect set of wider socio-political clockwork for them to mesh into. Duff ultimately asks a profoundly *static* question about criminal justice: 'In the sort of society that we claim to be in countries like England and Wales, Scotland, and the USA, what would it mean to genuinely take seriously our claimed commitments to liberty and community? How would that influence our commitments to criminal law, trial, and punishment?' Rather than attempting to press an ambitious vision of socio-penal reform, his enduring interest is in taking seriously the (criminal justice) values that we claim to live by today. But for all the value of that task, it will not and cannot show the way to a better criminal justice *from where we are now*, because it assumes that the problems with existing criminal justice are generally localised and isolated in particular institutions and processes. I am not, therefore, convinced that we should trust Duff's model to resist the challenges to penal minimalism that, we have seen, triumphed politically over the desert model.

[126] See generally RA Duff and Stuart Green, 'Introduction: Searching for Foundations', in: RA Duff and Stuart Green (eds), *Philosophical Foundations of Criminal Law* (2011, Oxford University Press), pp 6–10.

IV. Conclusion: Catching Chimera by the Tail

Overall, we have seen that retributivism *did* fail to prevent the emergence and worsening of penal excess in England and Wales over the last three decades. However, these failures were generally political, rather than theoretical – retributive proportionality could not resist the rising tides of punitiveness and penal managerialism that gripped England and Wales in the 2000s and 2010s. This political failure has been partially caused and partially exacerbated by the crumbling and fracturing of wider socio-political and -cultural institutions and processes tending to support liberal values, and by their appropriation by more authoritarian, punitive or managerial influences. In this, the retributivist's tight focus upon act-proportionality and the rigid insistence that social justice concerns are best dealt with outside the penal State have tended to distract retributivist theorists from bigger-picture problems, and hobble their capacity to speak meaningfully to the wider conditions necessary to justify (minimal) punishment. Most worryingly, the Lacey-Pickard critique alleges that proportionality is a 'chimera' in that it never has any independent effect on penal decision-making in a way that will tend to reduce overall conditions of penal excess. Although we have dismissed the Lacey-Pickard critique's theoretical dimensions, we have only been able to do so on a rather tenuous basis, and so much doubt remains. To extend Lacey and Pickard's metaphor (perhaps beyond its proper limits), and to mangle an aphorism regarding tigers, if proportionality is a chimera then we have *caught that chimera by the tail*. On the one hand, we have put ourselves in danger by latching onto proportionality as a means of doing something it might be incapable of. However, one the other it will also be dangerous to let go and face the angry three-headed monster, because abandoning proportionality if it *does* serve the interests of penal restraint, however weakly, would be to give up an important, if not necessarily principal, means of confronting penal excess.[127]

That it is dangerous to let go of proportionality's tail, of course, does not mean that we should not. If we can find one or more alternative principles that will be better suited (theoretically and politically) to ameliorating penal excess, then it is better for minimalists to commit to those approaches, rather than to indulge in the cognitive, normative, and political work of retooling proportionality to better confront penal excess. In Part II, I therefore commit to thinking carefully about the value and limitations of retributivism against its alternatives in existing penal theory, both orthodox and radical, in the pursuit of penal minimalism.

[127] On the chimera as myth and as metaphor, see Jorge Borges and Margarita Guerrero, *The Book of Imaginary Beings* (1974, Jorge Borges and Norman di Giovanni (trans), Vintage), pp 41–42.

PART II

Pursuing Penal Minimalism

4

Other Routes to Penal Minimalism

Even if retributive proportionality held the seed of restraining the penal State, in practice it was incapable of defending its underlying rationales against the twin interventionist tides of punitiveness and penal managerialism. At least some penal minimalists may have remained retributivists in spite of this failure, but what about those who did not? What are the prospects for the pursuit of penal minimalism elsewhere in penal theory? This chapter considers three non-retributive strategies for promoting penal minimalism, which ought to at least be attractive to a hypothetical penal minimalist, disenchanted with retributivism. These are, in turn: *rehabilitation*, particularly in its more agency-focussed forms; secondly, *restorative justice*; and finally, *penal abolitionism*. Although we should not treat these three as the only possible alternatives to retributivism, they have been influential in penal theory and policy over the last 30 years, and so are the most deserving of attention for the purposes of this enquiry. As in the Chapter 3, we will focus our attention on the extent to which these three theories provide *an effective means of constraining the penal State*, rather than on whether these theories are *internally consistent or persuasive justifications of coercive State punishment*, in and of themselves.

I. Rehabilitation and Penal Minimalism

The rehabilitative ideal famously 'declined' in the 1970s, due to empirical scepticism about its effectiveness at reducing reoffending, and complaints about the illiberal tendencies of the Treatment Model (especially in the US).[1] Rather than fading away, however, rehabilitation underwent a series of 'paradigm shifts' as traditionally rehabilitative interventions (notably including probation supervision) were retrofitted into changing expectations about the aims and functions of the penal system.[2] These developments are critical for understanding rehabilitation

[1] See generally AE Bottoms, 'An Introduction to "The Coming Crisis"', in: AE Bottoms and RH Preston (eds), *The Coming Penal Crisis: A Criminological and Theological Exploration* (1980, Scottish Academic Press).

[2] See generally Anthony Bottoms and William McWilliams, 'A Non-Treatment Paradigm for Probation Practice' (1979) 9 *British Journal of Social Work* 160; Fergus McNeill, 'A Desistance Paradigm for Offender Management' (2006) 6 *Criminology & Criminal Justice* 39; Gwen Robinson, 'Late-Modern Rehabilitation: The Evolution of a Penal Strategy' (2008) 10 *Punishment & Society* 429.

as a contemporary movement – not just because its critics tend to ignore these changes in favour of a crude stereotype of the treatment-based authoritarianism,[3] but also because these resurgent forms of rehabilitation are at least somewhat opposed to penal excess, and particularly, to the endemic *punitiveness* of criminal justice policy. These newer rehabilitative approaches have at least some capacity to encourage minimalism (directly or indirectly) through an insistence on *humaneness* and *respect for penal subjects' agency* within the system.[4] To explore these arguments in more detail, we should separate out the various strands of rehabilitative theory in play in modern academic and policy circles. Firstly, however, I must explain why I focus *only* on rehabilitation, and not also on its usual theoretical bedfellows, *deterrence* and *incapacitation*.

A. An Aside about Deterrence and Incapacitation

As we discussed in the introduction to this book, rehabilitation is typically taken together with deterrence and incapacitation: three 'reductivist' theories linked by a *consequentialist* commitment to reducing reoffending. I separate out rehabilitation in this enquiry for three reasons. Firstly, rehabilitative theory is not *necessarily* reductivist. Not every theory of rehabilitation begins and ends with the aim of reducing reoffending. Secondly, rehabilitation's strategies *for* reducing reoffending differ from those of incapacitation (containment until offenders are no longer considered dangerous) or deterrence (threatening the offender and/or public into compliance). While different theories of rehabilitation have different methods and criteria for success in terms of what 'works' at reducing reoffending,[5] they generally take a more positive approach, in terms of adding something to the offender and their social context, rather than on coercing or constraining their behaviour. Thirdly, and most significantly, good-faith penal minimalists (especially those motivated by the liberal-democratic values in Chapter 1) simply *ought not to* endorse either deterrence or incapacitation as overarching penal strategies. In Georg Hegel's famous terms, deterrence is particularly incompatible with the purposes of a liberty-respecting State:[6]

> To justify punishment in this way is like raising one's stick to a dog; it means treating a human being like a dog instead of respecting his honour and freedom. But a threat,

[3] See Fergus McNeill, 'Four Forms of "Offender" Rehabilitation: Towards an Interdisciplinary Perspective' (2012) 17 *Legal and Criminological Psychology* 18; Rob Canton, 'Probation and the Philosophy of Punishment' (2018) 65 *Probation Journal* 252.

[4] See, eg, Francis Cullen and Karen Gilbert, *Re-Affirming Rehabilitation*, Second edn (2013, Anderson Publishing); but recall Nils Christie, *Limits to Pain: The Role of Punishment in Penal Policy* (1982, Martin Robinson), pp 11–19.

[5] See, eg, Chris Trotter, 'Reducing Recidivism through Probation Supervision: What We Know and Don't Know from Four Decades of Research' (2013) 77 *Federal Probation* 43.

[6] Georg Hegel, *Elements of the Philosophy of Right* (1991, HB Nisbet (trans), Allen Wood (ed), Cambridge University Press), §99, p 125.

> which may ultimately provoke someone into demonstrating his freedom in defiance of it, sets justice aside completely.

In this general attitude Hegel expresses fundamentally liberal attitudes to the relationship between individual citizen and State, and democratic ideals of solidarity and respect. If one can only speak to criminal offenders as though they are dogs, then they are not citizens in any meaningful sense, as much as they are victims of a protection racket. To be comfortable with even a minimal penal system that does these things is inconsistent with the expansive, freedom- and solidarity-based aims of liberal democratic societies.[7] The same applies to incapacitation, *mutatis mutandis* – rather than raising a stick to a dog, incapacitation resorts to the muzzle.

It would be over-simplistic and ahistorical to claim that deterrence and incapacitation can never form any part of valid liberal-democratic criminal justice policy. However, I do not see how a penal minimalist can pursue either theory *as a primary means* of pursuing penal minimalism, because of this tendency to reduce offenders to risks to be managed. Both have historically tended to justify lengthy and otherwise severe interventions. Moreover, their essentially actuarial conception of the offender is too vulnerable to the twin tides of punitiveness and (especially) penal managerialism that have encouraged Anglo-Welsh penal excess. But ultimately, even if deterrence and incapacitation *could* provide a means of achieving penal minimalism, such a route would be inappropriate from the start, because it would place a fundamentally illiberal and anti-democratic conception of the State at the centre of penal governance. By contrast, rehabilitation is at least rhetorically about responding to the offender as a wrongdoing fellow-citizen in need of support, as someone to be improved. Although in practice different theories tend to be much less straightforwardly benevolent, this at least raises the possibility that, after punishment, the individual will be better-equipped to pursue their own social, political, economic, and personal aims – not just as a law-abiding *ex-offender* but as a more truly self-determining *citizen*. To the extent that rehabilitation *can* produce benefits that outweigh the costs of criminal punishment in terms of one's autonomy and self-determination, there is at least a closer proximity between liberal-democratic values and the practice of a rehabilitative penal State. However, the mere existence of this possibility does not mean that *every* rehabilitative theory will always tend to serve liberal-democratic values, or that *any* rehabilitative theory can or will necessarily achieve penal minimalism in practice. We must therefore consider the full range of contemporary rehabilitative theory in more detail, to see how each fares as a means of confronting penal excess.

[7] Compare RA Duff, *Punishment, Communication and Community* (2001, Oxford University Press), p 85; see also JR Edwards and AP Simester, 'Prevention with a Moral Voice', in AP Simester, Antje du Bois-Pedain, and Ulfrid Neumann (eds), *Liberal Criminal Theory: Essays for Andreas von Hirsch* (2013, Hart).

B. Species of Rehabilitation: From Treatment to the 'Desistance Paradigm'

Modern rehabilitative theories are diverse, and vary wildly in their presuppositions, aims, and methods of changing the offender. They also vary in terms of how they construct the process of rehabilitation, and from whose perspective: that of the authority imposing a specific sentence, the penal policy-maker reviewing the system as a whole, or the rehabilitation worker working with particular penal subjects. Indeed, the survival of rehabilitation as a penal strategy after the rejection of the treatment model in the 1970s was partly due to the robust commitment of probation officers to entrenched occupational 'probation values' emphasising benevolence and humanity, which have tended to resist and conflict with more managerial developments in rehabilitative penal policy and strategy.[8] In short, we must be careful to distinguish between rehabilitation *as an intended outcome* in individual cases, and rehabilitation *as a principle of distribution* of punishment. Any account of rehabilitation focussing on penal minimalism must focus on the latter, recognising the former only indirectly. Moreover, we can accept rehabilitation as an aim at one level without necessarily embracing it at the other. They are separate concerns.[9]

At the level of determining the *distribution* of punishment, and therefore the macro-level ability of the penal State to commit to the constraint of penal excess, rehabilitative theory is currently dominated by the orthodox Risk-Needs-Responsivity ('RNR') model, which influenced the 'What Works' movement discussed in the Chapter 3. However, this orthodoxy is increasingly challenged by a newer, more nebulous *'Good Lives'* or *'agentic'* approach to rehabilitation, associated with but distinct from the wider criminological literature on *'desistance'* from crime. This development, in turn, is related to but distinct from Edgardo Rotman's conception of *deontological rehabilitation* – as something to which offenders might have a right.

The historical interplay between different rehabilitative theoretical traditions in the last half-century of Anglo-Welsh penal policy has been driven by shifts in the theoretical backdrop against which rehabilitative work and policy has formed.[10] The old Treatment Model itself succeeded a *penitentiary* conception of rehabilitation as saving immortal souls by encouraging moral reflection and repentance

[8] See, eg, McNeill, 'A Desistance Paradigm', above n 2; John Deering, 'Attitudes and Beliefs of Trainee Probation Officers: A "New Breed"?' (2010) 57 *Probation Journal* 9; Fergus McNeill, *Pervasive Punishment: Making Sense of 'Mass Supervision'* (2018, Emerald Publishing), especially chs 2 and 4.

[9] See, eg, Canton, 'Probation and the Philosophy of Punishment', above n 3.

[10] See generally Michael Ignatieff, *A Just Measure of Pain: The Penitentiary in the Industrial Revolution, 1750–1850* (1978, Peregrine); Philip Goodman, Joshua Page, and Michelle Phelps, *Breaking the Pendulum: The Long Struggle over Criminal Justice* (2017, Oxford University Press), chs 2–4; Michel Foucault, *Discipline and Punish: The Birth of the Prison* (1977, Alan Sheridan-Smtih (trans), Penguin); but compare Michael Ignatieff, 'State, Civil Society, and Total Institutions: A Critique of Recent Social Histories of Punishment' (1981) 3 *Crime & Justice* 153.

from sin. It replaced this ideology with a focus on *correcting* defective characteristics of the offender, their thinking, and their broader life through psycho-medical interventions aimed at identifying and palliating (or altogether removing) the causes of offending behaviour. However, increasingly, this *correctional* focus on attitudes and values became absorbed into a more *managerial* approach, driven by a concern with effectively preventing criminal behaviour rather than necessarily changing minds. This process was marked by radical optimism, and by pluralism: the emphasis was on flexible, dynamic interventions that focussed rehabilitative resources where they could do the most good (generally in terms of best reducing the rate of reoffending).[11] This pragmatism was driven by the rise to dominance of the RNR model of rehabilitation, which viewed offenders' risk of reoffending as being dynamically related to *criminogenic needs* – factors in the offender's life, behaviour, and attitudes that encourage criminality.[12] The model also aims to be *responsive* in that the offender's characteristics rendered them more or less amenable to certain approaches, such that rehabilitation ought to be tailored towards the most effective solution for driving down risk. Managerialism, in this sense, was less about managing risk as such, so much as *offender management* aimed at producing effective, more-or-less bespoke solutions to the unique rehabilitative needs and receptivity to interventions of individual subjects.[13]

In practice, however, this managerialism proved remarkably susceptible to a *late-modern* focus on insecurity, condemnation, and oversight.[14] Pragmatic individualisation proved to be extremely difficult, and failed to produce politically useful results for a government that had placed electoral capital on being able to show it had an 'evidence base' for its policies. As a result, the emphasis of penal policy shifted from *doing* what worked to *showing* that what was done was working, by spinning official data and adopting an increasingly dogmatic approach to defining effectiveness in practice, with the result that responsivity became increasingly neglected in comparison to 'risk' and 'need'.[15] At the same time, the focus on risk became increasingly all-encompassing, to the extent that RNR was being operationalised (at the level of distributing punishment, at least) in a way that shifted the focus from managing the offender so as to allocate scarce rehabilitative resources in the most effective way, towards treating the offender as a cluster of risk factors to be managed. Increasingly, wider social factors contributing to

[11] See, eg, DA Andrews, James Bonta, and JS Wormith, 'The Risk-Need-Responsivity (RNR) Model: Does Adding the Good Lives Model Contribute to Effective Crime Prevention?' (2011) 38 *Criminal Justice and Behavior* 735.

[12] See, eg, Gwen Robinson, 'Power, Knowledge, and "What Works" in Probation' (2001) 40 *The Howard Journal of Crime and Justice* 235, pp 236–240.

[13] See generally Tony Grapes, 'Offender Management', in: Rob Canton and David Hancock (eds), *Dictionary of Probation and Offender Management* (2007, Willan).

[14] Recall Robinson, n 2.

[15] See generally George Mair, 'Research on Community Penalties', in: Rod King and Anna Wincup (eds), *Doing Research on Crime and Justice*, Second edn (2008, Oxford University Press); Kathleen Kendall, 'Dangerous Thinking: A Critical History of Correctional Behaviourism', in: George Mair (ed), *What Matters in Probation* (2004, Willan).

individuals' criminality were not being challenged in their own right, so much as they were conceived as problematic extensions of the penal subject themselves, limiting the ability of the penal State to respond effectively to their needs, and tending to encourage a dehumanising account of offenders as mere clusters of risk.[16]

This is, to be fair, a *policy imperative* driven by the scarcity of rehabilitative resources (especially after the 2008 Great Recession), and not an inherent theoretical failing of RNR.[17] Nevertheless, the tendency of practical applications of RNR to be compatible with increasingly dehumanising, atomising, and actuarial approach has trigged a substantial *humanitarian* backlash, at least at the level of penal theory. Importantly, there has been much recent emphasis engaging with the elements of a 'good' life in terms of personal capacities for self-empowerment and -improvement, and not just in terms of risk-avoiding skills, attitudes, and behaviours. The Good Lives Model ('GLM') in particular focuses on providing the offender with the agency to determine the wider purpose of their own rehabilitation, at least to some extent. The GLM amends traditional RNR approaches comparatively modestly, focussing on the management of risk but filtered through a humanitarian lens of reflecting and respecting the ex-offender as a person in their own right.[18]

The GLM approach is part of a general turn within rehabilitation theory and practice towards concern with the wider phenomenon of *desistance* – that is, the way in which offenders actually stop offending. Desistance is wider than rehabilitation, especially at the level of determining the overall distribution of punishment – it is best thought of as the goal at which the rehabilitative intervention is aiming, and can sometimes occur without any State intervention at all. But an increasing desistance focus in rehabilitative theory marks a shift towards a greater focus on individualisation and agency, which sees the offender less as a lump of clay to be shaped into a more desirable shape, and more as an essential *partner* – someone who cannot be forced to change without their collaboration.[19]

A final noteworthy trend in rehabilitative theory, less influential on policy but with a related focus on humanity and individual agency is Edgardo Rotman's rights-based argument for rehabilitation as something that the offender *deserves*, rather than as something whose legitimacy depends upon empirically demonstrable

[16] See generally Tony Ward, Joseph Melser, and Pamela Yates, 'Reconstructing the Risk-Need-Responsivity Model: A Theoretical Elaboration and Evaluation' (2007) 12 *Aggression and Violent Behavior* 208.

[17] See, eg, Tony Ward, Pamela Yates, and Gwenda Willis, 'The Good Lives Model and the Risk Needs Responsivity Model: A Response to Andrews, Bonta and Wormith (2011)' (2012) 39 *Criminal Justice and Behavior* 94.

[18] Ward, Yates, and Willis, ibid; see also Tony Ward and Clare-Ann Fortune, 'The Good Lives Model: Aligning Risk Reduction with Promoting Offenders' Personal Goals' (2013) 5 *European Journal of Probation* 29.

[19] See McNeill, 'A Desistance Paradigm', above n 2.

effectiveness.[20] Rotman offers three defences of this account. Firstly, he notes, punishment can (and routinely does) cause significant harm (and pain) to its subjects. These negative outcomes can damage the offender's prospects upon release, which can encourage the offender to remain in a criminal lifestyle during and after their punishment. Given that a liberal State ought not to do unnecessary harm to its citizens, the argument runs, by the end of the sentence there should be both 'negative' (ie "making things no worse") and 'positive' rehabilitation (ie "making things better").[21]

Secondly, and relatedly, a right to rehabilitation arises out of any explanation of crime as being at least partly rooted in social context, upbringing, and personal characteristics of the offender. The offender's autonomous choice in committing crimes is generally conceived of as being, at the very least, heavily influenced by their wider social, economic, and cultural context on the retributive schema. That, after all, is why one rehabilitates – there is a cause of the offending behaviour, and we can do something about that cause (whatever causes and solutions one's particular theory might recognise).[22] If so, then it follows that any crime represents a failure of the State and/or wider society *as well as* by the offender.[23] This does not necessarily affect the offender's responsibility for the wrongdoing involved in their crime.[24] However, it can influence our perspective on how to treat them *during* their punishment, with a view to restoring them to a community where they have freedom, capacity, and desire to desist from crime, from which the State has at least played a part, through inaction, in excluding them.[25]

A third, less essential basis for a right to rehabilitation is drawn from the liberal commitment to human *dignity*, and the specific rights that have emerged in international human rights law to defend it. Thus, on this account, the absence of opportunities for meaningful rehabilitation may breach fundamental human rights norms such as prohibitions on cruel and unusual, or inhuman or degrading punishments.[26] States therefore have minimum legal responsibilities to make criminal punishment benefit penal subjects, especially where (as with imprisonment) the costs of time away from one's home and family include economic

[20] See generally Edgardo Rotman, 'Do Criminal Offenders Have a Constitutional Right to Rehabilitation?' (1987) 77 *Journal of Criminal Law and Criminology* 1023; Edgardo Rotman, *Beyond Punishment: A New View of the Rehabilitation of Criminal Offenders* (1990, Greenwood Press).

[21] See Rotman, *Beyond Punishment*, ibid, pp 69–70. See also Barbara Hudson, *Penal Policy and Social Justice* (1993, Macmillan), pp 160–169.

[22] See, eg, Rotman, ibid, pp 1–9.

[23] Compare Ilsa Koch, 'Moving Beyond Punitivism: Punishment, State Failure, and Democracy at the Margins' (2017) 19 *Punishment & Society* 203.

[24] See Christopher Bennett, 'Punishment and Rehabilitation', in Jesper Ryberg and JA Corlett (eds), *Punishment and Ethics: New Perspectives* (2010, Palgrave Macmillan).

[25] See Rotman, *Beyond Punishment*, above n 20, pp 76–78; compare Pat Carlen, 'Crime, Inequality, and Sentencing', in Pat Carlen and Dee Cook (eds), *Paying for Crime* (1989, Open University Press).

[26] See Rotman, 'Do Criminal Offenders Have a Constitutional Right to Rehabilitation?', above n 20, pp 1039–1059; Dirk van Zyl Smit and Sonja Snacken, *Principles of European Prison Law and Policy: Penology and Human Rights* (2009, Oxford University Press), chs 2 and 4–6. Compare Dirk van Zyl Smit, 'Outlawing Irreducible Life Sentences: Europe on the Brink?' (2010) 23 *Federal Sentencing Reporter* 39.

deskilling and the destruction of key relationships that may enable offenders to avoid future offending.[27]

Overall, this brief overview suggests that rehabilitation has adopted a variety of approaches to 'improving the offender' over the last four decades, seesawing back and forth between more humanistic and more paternalistic policy imperatives over the last 40 years.[28] Each approach is characterised by a range of assumptions, methods, and objectives that, from a policy perspective, imply different conclusions for the overall size and shape of the penal State. Having complicated the question, we can now examine the prospects for rehabilitative penal minimalism, in terms of actually existing rehabilitative theory. Can rehabilitation – and especially more agentic and individualistic approaches – pay dividends for the penal minimalist cause?

C. Rehabilitation and Penal Minimalism: Effectiveness, Benevolence, and Managerialism

There are essentially two arguments for rehabilitation as a route to penal minimalism. The first is the claim that *effectiveness is itself a route to penal restraint*; and the latter is a claim, associated with the 'new rehabilitation' movement of the 1980s and 1990s,[29] that the *humanistic* nature of rehabilitation is rhetorically forceful in encouraging restraint through 'civilised' benevolence.

The first claim is that effective rehabilitation would, in and of itself, produce a more restrained criminal justice system. 'Effectiveness' is the key metric of a consequentialist theory's success – but what it is 'effective' at is a subject for some dispute.[30] Most commonly in policy discussions, and in the Treatment, RNR and 'Good Lives' models outlined above, the question of effectiveness is judged in terms of *reducing reoffending* – in other words, an effective sentence is one which plays some role in causing the offender to become an ex-offender – and as a *non*-offender going forward.[31] There is a simple logic in the claim that if we make all repeat offenders unlikely to reoffend through rehabilitation (or other penal aims) then the penal system will necessarily be small. If the body politic is imagined as a literal body, and criminal justice is (part of) its immune response, then a strong immune response will keep the body healthy. Infections and other maladies can be dealt with as they arise, but importantly, they are prevented from spreading,

[27] Compare van Zyl Smit and Snacken, ibid, chs 5–6.

[28] See Rotman, *Beyond Punishment*, above n 20, pp 8–9.

[29] See, eg, Cullen and Gilbert, above n 4; Hudson, *Penal Policy and Social Justice*, above n 21.

[30] See, eg, Lesley Frazer et al, 'Rehabilitation: What Does "Good" Look Like Anyway?' (2014) 6 *European Journal of Probation* 92.

[31] Compare Keith Soothill and Brian Francis, 'When Do Ex-Offenders Become Like Non-Offenders?' (2009) 48 *The Howard Journal of Crime and Justice* 373.

and thereby, the overall need for penal interventions is kept low.[32] By contrast, under a purely retributive strategy, in which no attempt is made to solve the social problems that crime represents, serial criminals face no State-imposed incentive to desist from crime, making it less likely that they will, and increasing the risk that they will continue to harm other liberal citizens.

To take away the metaphor: does effectively reducing reoffending (through rehabilitative interventions, or more generally) create a long-term pressure towards penal minimalism? It is difficult to say. We know, for instance, that the Treatment and 'What Works' Models have been associated with penal strategies that have increased overall penal severity. However, just because the Treatment Model occurred alongside a drive towards lengthy and intrusive prison sentences does not mean that those were an *inherent* feature of the Treatment Model, instead of a policy choice that merely accompanied it. After all, in England and Wales, the Treatment Model did not encourage the indeterminate sentences that characterised equivalent US policy.[33] So we cannot simply assume that historical correlation implies causation – just as we could not in the case of the desert/severity hypothesis.[34] However, we can address the capacity of the penal system's rehabilitation of convicted offenders to reduce crime rates – and the underlying assumptions that this makes about who commits crime and why.

The Treatment Model was predicated on this sort of faith in the ability of the penal system to change the world. The Justice Model claimed that, in trying to do so much, the criminal justice system was overreaching its capacity to effect longer-term social change, and as a result, tended towards over-punishment rather than minimalism.[35] A treatment-oriented system assumed that more-or-less the same kinds of people committed crimes, and that at least some crimes were likely to be committed by repeat offenders. But this ignores the empirical facts that, on the one hand, different types of crime are typically committed by different social groups,[36] and on the other, that repeat offenders tend to desist over time independently of State intervention.[37] To the extent that it made these errors, the Treatment Model simply put too much stock in rehabilitation. After all, only a small minority of all

[32] Compare Peter Kropotkin, 'Prisons and their Moral Influence on Prisoners', in: Peter Kropotkin; Roger Baldwin (ed), *Anarchism: A Collection of Revolutionary Writings*, Second Edition (2002, Dover Press), pp 228–235.

[33] See, eg, Rotman, *Beyond Punishment*, above n 20, pp 102–109; Francis Allen, *The Decline of the Rehabilitative Ideal: Penal Policy and Social Purpose* (1981, Yale University Press), p 60.

[34] Recall Andrew Ashworth, 'Prisons, Proportionality, and Recent Penal History' (2017) 80 *MLR* 473.

[35] See, eg, Andrew von Hirsch, *Doing Justice: The Choice of Punishments* (1976, Hill & Wang), pp 11–18, 124–131.

[36] See generally Pat Carlen, 'Against Rehabilitation; For Reparative Justice', in Kerry Carrington, Matthew Ball, Erin O'Brien, and Juan Tauri (eds), *Crime, Justice and Social Democracy: International Perspectives* (2013, Palgrave Macmillan). Compare Rotman, *Beyond Rehabilitation*, above n 20, pp 113–120.

[37] See, eg, David Farrington, 'Age and Crime' (1986) 7 *Crime and Justice* 189; Richard Tremblay and Daniel Nagin, 'The Developmental Origins of Aggression in Humans', in: Richard Tremblay, Willard Hartup, and John Archer (eds), *Developmental Origins of Aggression* (2005, The Guildford Press).

crimes believed to occur ever result in conviction, and so offender rehabilitation can only deal with the tip of the iceberg of the 'true' criminal population.[38]

For this reason, and because of the negative associations that the Treatment Model came to occupy in penal policy discourse, contemporary supporters of rehabilitation tend not to argue that effectiveness is itself a route to minimalism. This is especially true of more humanitarian, agency-focussed, and rights-respecting forms of rehabilitation that ought to be attractive to the frustrated penal minimalist. Rather, they argue for minimalism because, by committing to rehabilitation, the State is forced into a role that is at least partly *benevolent*, and focussed on improving the offender's situation.[39] Although rehabilitation is usually constructed primarily in terms of overall social benefit, this impetus can encourage the State to maintain 'at least the pretense' of benevolence towards the offender, enhancing the rhetorical argument for humanity and minimalism.[40] Further, the focus of rehabilitation on the contextual causes of criminality force sentencing authorities and policy-makers into a confrontation with the inequalities that the penal system tends to overlook, in terms of the definition of crimes, the selection and exercise of criminal justice discretions, and the over-representation of socially marginalised communities within the system.[41] In the process, rehabilitation focuses sentencing attention onto those systemic inequalities, either directly or indirectly, and so creates tensions in the political and social legitimacy of the system, encouraging direct engagement with social context (for instance, as mitigating factors) during sentencing, and driving penal and wider social reform.

Both of these defences of rehabilitation's capacity to constrain the penal State were largely developed in the period before the emergence of 'late-modern' rehabilitation – its reformulation along punitive and managerial grounds to speak to a more vengeful and risk-averse policy environment.[42] As such, neither really takes into account the way that rehabilitation's meanings have shifted since the 1990s, and the way that its rhetoric has played into the hands of the *managerial* agenda in penal policy. In particular, there has been a rhetorical shift from a supportive model of rehabilitation, enabling the contrite offender to change their ways for the 'better' (from a social but also potentially individual perspective), to a narrative about the management and expulsion of risk factors, and indeed to a straightforwardly Foucauldian, disciplinary construction that sees offenders

[38] See generally Andrew Sanders and Richard Young, 'From Suspect to Trial', in Mike Maguire, Rod Morgan, and Robert Reiner (eds), *The Oxford Handbook of Criminology*, Fifth edn (2012, Oxford University Press).

[39] Cullen and Gilbert, above n 4, p 149.

[40] Ibid, pp 149–150.

[41] Recall Hudson, *Justice through Punishment: A Critique of the 'Justice' Model of Corrections* (1987, Macmillan Education), pp 93–129; Hudson, *Penal Policy and Social Justice*, n 21, generally; Barbara Hudson, 'Punishing the Poor: Dilemmas of Justice and Difference', in William Heffernan and John Kleinig (eds), *From Social Justice to Criminal Justice: Poverty and the Administration of Criminal Law* (2000, Oxford University Press).

[42] See generally Robinson, above n 2.

'[not simply as] liabilities to be managed, but as *assets to be harnessed*' (emphasis added).[43] In the main, rehabilitation's response to its period in the policy wilderness was pragmatic: it repackaged itself for an increasingly hostile and demanding policy audience, or else it went underground and focussed on the level of rehabilitation workers' practice rather than the level of distribution.[44] In doing so, rehabilitative discourse was co-opted by the forces of managerialism, and its rhetoric used to serve a broader agenda of actuarial, paternalist, or even outright authoritarian social control.[45] So at the very least, in cannot be the case that rehabilitation *always* forces the State to think benevolently about the offender as a human being. Risk management has done away with that rhetoric, at least to some extent.

Indeed, this is just as true, of the humanising rhetoric of more agency-focussed theories of rehabilitation. An extreme example of this can be found in Judah Schept's ethnography of a new Indianan 'justice campus'. Punishment was 'progressive' in Schept's study, in that it continued to expand, both geographically and in terms of population, but also in that it was justified by the humanitarian and benevolent rhetoric of left-wing US politics.[46] The logic – deployed because of the strong Democratic voting patterns of the local population – was that the comprehensive suite of non-custodial options could form a seamless bridge between the penal and welfare States, and their positioning within the shadow of the custodial facility would enable that benevolent concern with welfare to bleed into the prison estate, too. In practice, however, this provided an excuse to substantially develop the reach of the penal State into the lives of (especially) the poor, unemployed, and culturally marginalised – ie, expanding both the size and shape of the penal State. For Schept, this showed the impossibility of meaningful reform without radical change: whichever penal policy one votes for, the general tendency remains towards penal expansion.[47]

Although limited to a single case study in a single moment, Schept's study provides two reasons to be sceptical about the capacity of humanistic rehabilitation, *in and of itself*, as a means of constraining penal excess: the *quietist* effect of its euphemistic language; and secondly, the *nostalgia* that tinges at least some of its thinking. Both upshots have had the effect of disguising penal expansion beneath benevolent care.

Euphemism is a major feature of the appeal of rehabilitative interventions. The claim that rehabilitative interventions are justified because they achieve a benevolent social good (for the subject or for wider society) can lead to the use

[43] David Cameron, 'Prison Reform: Prime Minister's Speech', Policy Exchange, London, 8 February 2016. Available at: www.gov.uk/government/speeches/prison-reform-prime-ministers-speech.

[44] Recall Bottoms and McWilliams, n 2; McNeill, 'A Desistance Paradigm', n 2.

[45] See, eg, Barbara Hudson, *Justice in the Risk Society: Challenging and Re-Affirming Justice in Late Modernity* (2003, SAGE), p 66; recall Robinson, n 2.

[46] See generally Judah Schept, *Progressive Punishment: Job Loss, Jail Growth, and the Neoliberal Logic of Carceral Expansion* (2015, New York University Press), especially chs 1–4.

[47] Ibid, chs 7–8.

of rehabilitative language to make punishment seem straightforwardly positive. Indeed, the 'Treatment Model', in its very name, exposed this tendency, by making criminal justice just another wing of the palliative functions of the medical State.[48] But in doing so, we reify punitive interventions as an unproblematic part of the core functions of the State, in the same way that any humane modern Western State provides medical healthcare to its citizens. The possibility that we could solve the social problems that rehabilitation fixes *outside* the penal system is therefore never raised, and neither are rehabilitation's underlying assumptions about the pre-crime position of the offender within their community.[49] Any moral concerns about penal intervention are *quieted* by rehabilitation's rhetoric. The problem of punishment is sidestepped, rather than confronted.

This danger is equally present in more agentic theories of rehabilitation, such as the Good Lives Model. We should not assume that the GLM will automatically fall foul of the euphemistic harshness of the Treatment Model, or the dogmatic essentialism that RNR has defaulted to in practice. In order to achieve a distributive model of the GLM, we would be forced to ask in each offender's case: how much punishment will enable the offender to adopt a pro-social life? What sorts of interventions will encourage them to desist from crime? What will the State need to do to address the risk factors in the offender's life, and the offender's needs in terms of learning to address and overcome them? Despite the focus on individual offender agency and collaboration in one's own rehabilitation,[50] the GLM's central metaphor of the 'good' life ultimately assumes that the penal subject must compromise with the status quo, and therefore offers limited room to critique systemic inequalities and problems in the institutional and communal arrangements outside that subject's control. More pragmatically, I see no reason why the GLM will not repeat the RNR model's failure to make the penal State responsive to individuals' dynamic needs. Mass rehabilitation has so far tended to make individualisation fiscally impractical, and the GLM does not challenge the institutional backdrop that enables penal populations to reach such high levels. In the face of this, which intervention encourage the 'Good Life' is liable to either be very economically limited, or else dogmatically determined by the centre. The former outcome would undercut GLM's capacity to meaningfully overcome the failures of RNR-based initiatives. The latter would substantially replicate the reasons why they failed. For this reason, I am pessimistic about the capacity of the GLM – and other agency-focussed rehabilitation regimes – to succeed without fairly radical institutional changes in the way that punishment is funded, its modes (given that agentic rehabilitation is a lot easier in the community rather than outside of it, in a total institution), and the quality of its sentencing decisions. By itself,

[48] See also Stanley Cohen, *Visions of Social Control: Crime, Punishment and Classification* (1985, Polity), pp 273–281; Nils Christie, *Limits to Pain*, above n 4, pp 13–19.
[49] See Carlen, 'Against Rehabilitation', above n 36.
[50] Recall nn 17–19 and accompanying text.

as a principle of distribution, I have no faith that it would do any better than its forerunners at constraining penal excess.

Although Rotman's approach is far less vulnerable to euphemistic masking of penal excess, because of its fundamental rejection of consequentialist concerns with 'effectiveness', it is for similar reasons unlikely to promote penal minimalism in the distribution of punishment. The question of quantum ("How much punishment?") can be answered to an extent, because at a bare minimum every offender should receive enough 'negative' rehabilitation to minimise the longer-term harms that their punishment subjects them to. Indeed, Rotman especially uses this point to defend a campaign of vastly reducing the number of offenders sent to prison, due to its especially deleterious effects on offenders' social capital and personal wellbeing.[51] If you are doing less harm to an offender's ability to live peacefully alongside their neighbours once the punishment is over, then less 'negative rehabilitation' is needed to ameliorate that harm. However, things get more difficult for the sentencing authority when considering how much punishment will make the offender *better off* (rather than just *no worse off*). If that is a matter of right, then the offender must enforce that right against the State, and then *choose* to engage with it when delivered. But it is not clear to what extent that can be factored into a sentencing hearing. Even though offenders can and should speak in their own sentencing hearings, they cannot always accurately predict how they will engage with their own rehabilitation in future. Nor should they tie their hands in that way – that would be to surrender their rights on the basis of a prior decision.[52] For this reason, the rights-based account of rehabilitation is poor at setting principled limits on the distribution of punishment, and must rely upon external limiting factors. Notably in this respect, Rotman himself argues for the Norval Morris's hybrid approach, involving proportionality and parsimony.[53]

A second problem with rehabilitative rhetoric is its particular *nostalgia* with respect to non-custodial sentences. This tendency (which, it should be said, is increasingly isolated and critically re-examined)[54] views the transition of probationary supervision into the penal regime as an 'alternative punishment to imprisonment' as an error that has completely undermined the traditional role of probation officers as advisors, assistants, and friends to their clients.[55] This has resulted in a tendency to insist upon the benevolent and productive capacities of probation

[51] Rotman, *Beyond Punishment*, above n 20, pp 143–182.

[52] Ibid, pp 76–78.

[53] Ibid, pp 105–109; Norval Morris, *The Future of Imprisonment* (1974, University of Chicago Press).

[54] See, eg, Rob Canton, 'Probation and the Tragedy of Punishment' (2007) 46 *The Howard Journal of Crime and Justice* 236; Peter Raynor, 'Is Probation Still Possible?' (2012) 41 *The Howard Journal of Crime and Justice* 173; and Steve Collett, 'Riots, Revolution and Rehabilitation: The Future of Probation' (2013) 52 *The Howard Journal of Crime and Justice* 163.

[55] See, eg, Finola Farrant, 'Knowledge Production and the Punishment Ethic: The Demise of the Probation Service' (2006) 53 *Probation Journal* 317; Greg Mantle, 'Counterblast: Probation: Dead, Dying or Poorly?' (2006) 45 *The Howard Journal of Crime and Justice* 321; Judy McKnight, 'Standing Up for Probation' (2009) 48 *The Howard Journal of Crime and Justice* 327.

supervision, whilst either downplaying its punitive features, or isolating them to an 'enforcement role' that the offender management approach has forced onto a group of historically benevolent social-work oriented practitioners.[56] This nostalgia is at least partly an accurate reflection of the profound historical changes in the nature and function of probation practice, and particularly the reconceptualisation of the probation officer from a critical friend and social worker, into a managerial overseer of punishment. However, even if probation was historically an alternative to punishment, rather than an alternative punishment, the insistence that probation is not punishment *because* it is rehabilitation: (a) waves away the pains (and harms) of probation as more-or-less inevitable features to be minimised but largely ignored in the justification of imposing community-based interventions;[57] (b) gives succour to punitive rhetoric that insists that probation is 'not really punishment' and therefore needs 'toughening up';[58] and (c) simultaneously supports the managerial rhetoric that views the imposition of additional probation supervision as a non-punitive add-on that does not affect the proportionality of custodial sentences.[59] In other words, the insistence that the probation-as-punishment genie should be put back in the bottle enables policy-makers to simultaneously treat supervision as a possible (but insufficient) site of punishment, and a lossless extension of the rehabilitative capacity of short prison sentences.

None of this is inevitable, and a more consistent defence of agency-focussed, 'humane' rehabilitation should be part of the fightback against penal excess. But by itself, it has failed to resist the forces of punitiveness and penal managerialism, because its rhetoric has tended to play into their broader policy agendas in ways that are superficially opposed to one another, but which in combination have tended to legitimate and excuse worsening penal excess. This is exactly the same brand of political failure we charged the desert model with in Chapter 3: it folded in the face of punitiveness and managerialism, and rehabilitative rhetoric and policy has proven no stronger. That political failure is just as damning here as it was there. For the penal minimalist, then, a focus on rehabilitation is no guarantee of benevolence, let alone of restraint.[60]

[56] See, eg, Marilyn Gregory, 'Practical Wisdom and the Ethic of Care in Probation Practice' (2011) 3 *European Journal of Probation* 60; David Hayes, 'The Impact of Supervision on the Pains of Community Penalties in England and Wales: An Exploratory Study' (2015) 7 *European Journal of Probation* 85, p 93.

[57] Ioan Durnescu, 'Pains of Probation: Effective Practice and Human Rights' (2011) 55 *International Journal of Offender Therapy and Comparative Criminology* 530, pp 539–543. Compare Louise Brangan, 'Civilizing Imprisonment: The Limits of Scottish Penal Exceptionalism' (2019) *British Journal of Criminology*, forthcoming.

[58] See, eg, Gwen Robinson, 'Three Narratives and a Funeral: Community Punishment in England and Wales', in Gwen Robinson and Fergus McNeill (eds), *Community Punishment: European Perspectives* (2016, Routledge), pp 36–39.

[59] See, eg, Matthew Cracknall, 'Post-Release Reform to Short Prison Sentences: Re-Legitimising and Widening the Net of Punishment' (2018) 65 *Probation Journal* 302–315.

[60] Compare Nicola Lacey and Hanna Pickard, 'The Chimera of Proportionality: Institutionalising Limits on Punishment in Contemporary Social and Political Systems' (2015) 78 *MLR* 216, pp 239–240.

II. Restorative Justice and Penal Minimalism

If penal minimalists have no basis to choose between the four traditional penal theories, what are the prospects of more radical approaches? We might, first, be tempted to adopt a more-or-less radical reformation of penal practices around a *restorative* paradigm. 'Restorative' justice, as the name suggests, is aimed at addressing the damage caused by the crime – or on some accounts, at addressing the wider harms that have contributed to the crime coming about in the particular context of the community or communities in question.[61] The restorative church is very broad, ranging from rather modest changes to the sorts of punishments imposed at trial, to radical reappraisals of existing trial proceedings, to the abandonment of criminal justice altogether. However, these approaches emphasise moving away from the traditional paradigm of 'retributive' criminal justice – which means not (necessarily) a penal system governed by retributive penal theory, but also any non-retributive criminal justice system focussed on disadvantaging the offender, rather than healing the rift caused (and/or represented) by the crime.[62] To avoid confusion, and for present purposes only, I will describe this conception of punishment as a disadvantageous response to an individual's wrongdoing as 'orthodox' criminal justice.

The key features of any restorative justice intervention are: a concern with the involvement and empowerment of victims within criminal justice decision-making;[63] a bottom-up value-system with little or no State involvement in the determination of key features of the offender's responsibility; a focus on community rather than State as the locus of any reference to shared aims, values, and goals; and an emphasis on criminal justice as a means of seeking proactive solutions to social problems, rather than delivering pain in the hope that two wrongs will make a right.[64] In theory, this suggests a preference for informal interactions between the offenders, victims, and wider communities (potentially but not necessarily mediated by State agents), rather than an orthodox State-versus-citizen approach dominated by monistic conceptions of wrongdoing and due process. In practice, however, restorative justice has proven quite capable of operating within the orthodox criminal justice system, and a spectrum of possible levels of restorative engagement has emerged. For present purposes, let us distinguish: 'weak'

[61] See generally Gerry Johnstone and Daniel van Ness, 'The Meaning of Restorative Justice', in: Gerry Johnstone and Daniel van Ness (eds), *Handbook of Restorative Justice* (2007, Willan).

[62] See especially Howard Zehr, *Changing Lenses: A New Focus for Crime and Justice* (1990, Herald Press); see also Declan Roche, 'Retribution and Restorative Justice', in: Gerry Johnstone and Daniel van Ness (eds), *Handbook of Restorative Justice* (2007, Willan).

[63] On the relationship (and only partial overlap) between restorative justice and the victims' justice movement, see generally Inge Vanfraechem, Daniela Bolívar, and Ivo Aertsen (eds), *Victims and Restorative Justice* (2015, Routledge); compare Simon Green, 'The Victims' Movement and Restorative Justice', in: Gerry Johnstone and Daniel van Ness (eds), *Handbook of Restorative Justice* (2007, Willan).

[64] See Lode Walgrave, 'Integrating Criminal Justice and Restorative Justice', in: Gerry Johnstone and Daniel van Ness (eds), *Handbook of Restorative Justice* (2007, Willan), p 559.

or *in-system* restorative justice, where restorative interactions take place either during the sentencing hearing, or as part of the punishment;[65] from 'strong' or *extra-systemic* interventions that divert suspects or defendants from the orthodox criminal justice system prior to sentence, into either parallel systems or less formalised, case-by-case arrangements. The strongest theories of restorative justice phase into penal abolitionism, in that they advocate substantial and/or total abolition of orthodox criminal justice, in favour of ad hoc restorative alternatives.[66]

Restorative scholarship, however 'weak' or 'strong', is concerned more with prescribing *processes* than *outcomes*.[67] Although restorative justice encourages individualised procedures suited to specific cases, interventions often use similar methods, including: *mediation*, where stakeholders are led in a semi-structured discussion about the causes and impacts of the crime, and what ought to be done about it; or *conferencing*, in which numerous stakeholders (including the victims and offenders) are gathered together in wider discussion.[68] Three key principles are essential in all restorative processes: firstly, that all stakeholders (including the potentially traumatised victim and the offender) must participate *consensually*;[69] secondly, that the offender must recognise and not contest their own guilt (although they may offer mitigating factors or explanations for their behaviour, without the threat of this being used against them in any future criminal trial);[70] and finally, that outcomes should pursue some sort of positive resolution in the future, rather than focussing solely on the attribution of retrospective blame.[71] As a result, restorative processes tend to accentuate relationships, human foibles, and social detail, over the formal abstractions involved in orthodox legal proceedings.[72] If the needs

[65] See, eg, RA Duff, 'Probation, Punishment, and Restorative Justice: Should Al Truism Be Engaged in Punishment?' (2003) 42 *The Howard Journal of Crime and Justice* 181, pp 183–189; s 201(2) of the Criminal Justice Act 2003.

[66] See generally Vincenzo Ruggiero, 'An Abolitionist View of Restorative Justice' (2011) 39 *International Journal of Law, Crime and Justice* 100.

[67] See, eg, Jim Dignan, 'Restorative Justice: Towards a Systemic Model of Restorative Justice: Reflections on the Concept, its Context, and the Need for Clear Constraints', in: Andrew von Hirsch et al (eds), *Restorative Justice or Criminal Justice: Competing or Reconcilable Programmes?* (2003, Hart), pp 136–138.

[68] See, eg, Inge Vanfraechem and Daniela Bolívar, 'Restorative Justice and Victims of Crime', in: Inge Vanfraechem, Daniela Bolívar, and Ivo Aertsen (eds), *Victims and Restorative Justice* (2015, Routledge); Joanna Shapland et al, 'Situating Restorative Justice within Criminal Justice' (2006) 10 *Theoretical Criminology* 505, pp 506–507.

[69] See, eg, United Nations, *Basic Principles for the Use of Restorative Justice Programmes in Criminal Matters*, UN Doc E/2000/INF/2/Add.2 at 35 (2000), §§7 and 12(c). Compare Andrew Ashworth, 'Responsibilities, Rights, and Restorative Justice' (2002) 42(3) *British Journal of Criminology* 578; with Martine Herzog-Evans, 'Consent and Probation: An Analogy with Contract Law' (2015) 7 *European Journal of Probation* 143.

[70] UN *Basic Principles*, above n 69, §8. See also Kay Pranis, 'Restorative Values', in: Gerry Johnstone and Daniel van Ness (eds), *Handbook of Restorative Justice* (2007, Willan).

[71] See, eg, Shapland et al, above n 68, pp 512–519.

[72] See, eg, Pranis, above n 70, especially pp 61–66; Barbara Hudson, 'Victims and Offenders', in: Andrew von Hirsch et al (eds), *Restorative Justice or Criminal Justice: Competing or Reconcilable Programmes?* (2003, Hart).

of the community and the wider context of the harm are foregrounded during the 'trial' phase of restorative interventions, then this must have some impact on the 'punishment' phase, because different values, facts, and expectations will be emphasised when the stakeholders consider how to restore the parties to their pre-crime position (or indeed, to a better overall distribution of social capital and responsibilities).

In particular, the increasing focus over the course of restorative processes on finding viable solutions for the future means that outcomes will generally be discussed purely in terms of what is *to be done* to make things right, rather than focussing entirely on the past. This implies certain assumptions about the *modes* of punishment – capital and corporal punishment are inherently unable to restore the pre-crime position of the community, and imprisonment is highly unlikely to do so. To be sure, one can impose restorative interventions in prisons,[73] but the burden must lie on the State to show why restorative aims cannot be achieved by a non-custodial intervention that situates the offender within the very community with which they are being restored. In other words, there a different range of preconditions exist about what makes for 'good' or effective punishment, based on the needs, values, and expectations of the offenders, victims, and communities involved, rather than those of society and the State.[74]

At the level of penal objectives, this shift towards a prospective focus inevitably entails the rejection of retributivism, given its wholly retrospective outlook. However, the focus on fixing social problems involving a wide range of stakeholders also dismisses incapacitation and deterrence, which ignore the offender's interests and longer-term personal growth as a community member.[75] Restorative justice is therefore likely to favour rehabilitative outcomes (particularly more agentic, desistance-focussed versions),[76] while also favouring *reparative* interventions. We should consider the latter's approach to penal distribution more fully.

Reparative justice assumes the rationale that punishment should be used, as the name suggests, to *repair the harm done* by the crime.[77] The use of penal interventions to repair harms is associated with the restorative justice movement, but can also be an aim in itself, and has been adopted as a core aim of contemporary English sentencing law.[78] 'Repair' can be interpreted narrowly – I steal two £5 notes from your wallet, and I must repay you £10 – but is usually drawn wider, to encompass more nebulous losses such as psychiatric damage, deprivation of perceived personal security, or the loss of sentimental value. These less tangible

[73] See, eg, Mandeep Dhami, Greg Mantle, and Darrell Fox, 'Restorative Justice in Prisons' (2009) 12 *Contemporary Justice Review* 433; compare Ottmar Hagemann, 'Restorative Justice in Prison?' in: Lode Walgrave (ed), *Repositioning Restorative Justice* (2003, Willan).

[74] Compare Nils Christie, *A Suitable Amount of Crime* (2004, Routledge), pp 1–31.

[75] Recall Shapland et al, n 68, pp 512–519.

[76] See Gwen Robinson and Joanna Shapland, 'Reducing Recidivism: A Task for Restorative Justice?' (2008) 48 *British Journal of Criminology* 337.

[77] See generally Carlen, 'Against Rehabilitation', n 36.

[78] Criminal Justice Act 2003, s 142(1)(e).

harms can still be compensated. Firstly, I might make reparations through direct financial *compensation*, as above (by calculating an extra amount of compensation for the additional physical, psychiatric, and emotional harms I have caused). Any such compensation is likely to be arbitrary, but it can be standardised in ways that at least make that arbitrariness more consistent across different cases, and therefore fairer in practice. Secondly, I might 'pay back' in other ways: by doing work to your benefit. Reparative labour can develop ties between offender, victim, and community,[79] but in any event can be added into our schema of relative compensatory values: x hours of unpaid work for the victimised individual or community might be equivalent to £y of direct compensation. Again, we could vary this on a case-by-case basis, thinking about the appropriateness of work versus compensation for particular offences.

Thirdly, an apology might form part of the reparative mix. Apologies are not always the best form of compensation, but may well help to ease some of the pains of victimisation, particularly those involved in the insecurity and trauma attending upon being the target of crime.[80] The penal State might even *order* an apology – and while we might be tempted to reject this as unlikely to be perceived as sincere, there is empirical evidence that victims (and indeed, offenders and other stakeholders) can find the process useful in recovering from the crime.[81] Neither does an apology have to lead to forgiveness in order to be useful to one or both parties: it might only act as a first step towards forgiveness, or as a sign of remorse and putative change for the better.[82]

This last point raises a wider question for reparative approaches, about *who* is being repaired, as against *what*. Financial compensation and other forms of 'paying back' imply a pseudo-tortious relationship between an individual offender and an individual victim. However, the victim in this relationship need not be an individual, but rather a community or a particular group affected by the crime and the response to it.[83] More radically, the offender themselves may be included amongst those to be repaired – in terms of the harms that their own offending (and their communities' responses to it) may do to them, or in terms of their wider ability to function in society, as an effective, empowered and critical citizen. In other words, the 'habilitation' of the offender as someone who is *both* a useful and productive member of their communities, *and* a genuinely autonomous

[79] See, eg, Gill McIvor, 'Paying Back: 30 Years of Unpaid Work by Offenders in Scotland' (2010) 2 *European Journal of Probation* 41.

[80] See generally Christopher Bennett, *The Apology Ritual: A Philosophical Theory of Punishment* (2008, Cambridge University Press); Peter Chau, 'Bennett's Expressive Justification of Punishment' (2017) 11 *Criminal Law and Philosophy* 661.

[81] See, eg, Gijs van Dijk, 'The Ordered Apology' (2017) 37 *Oxford Journal of Legal Studies* 562; but compare Christopher Bennett, 'Taking the Sincerity Out of Saying Sorry' (2006) 23 *Journal of Applied Philosophy* 127.

[82] See, eg, Joanna Shapland, 'Forgiveness and Restorative Justice: Is it Necessary? Is it Helpful?' (2016) 5 *Oxford Journal of Law & Religion* 94.

[83] See, eg, Loraine Gelsthorpe and Sue Rex, 'Community Service as Reparation: Exploring the Potential', in: George Mair (ed), *What Matters in Probation* (2004, Willan).

individual capable of pursuing their desires within their social setting, can become part of the reparative agenda, and not just the rehabilitative one.[84] These differences ultimately come down to questions of the *metric* – how we measure reparation, and which harms (inflicted upon whom) we take into account when we do so.

You have probably spotted my broader point: the logic of a reparative approach reinvents a principle of proportionality, with a range of sentencing options that one must organise into some sort of tariff if one is to apply them fairly, and a metric for measuring the extent of reparation. However, importantly, reparative justice does not merely recreate *retributive* proportionality. After all, reparative proportionality does not communicate censure, it compensates harms. As a result, forms of punishment that have historical or present value as retributive expressions of censure – notably imprisonment, but also capital and corporal punishment – will not necessarily have any reparative content. I might conceivably make some amends to you from within prison, but it is unlikely to be the act of confining me in a prison that *causes* that reparation, and it is highly likely that in most cases I could have made that reparation in a non-custodial setting instead. So reparative proportionality is not just old retributive wine in new bottles – it applies the proportionality principle in a different way, and with vastly different ramifications for the shape, structure, and institutional backdrop to the criminal justice system.

However, reparation is still reliant on an essentially proportionality-based approach to distributing punishment, and is therefore vulnerable to those critiques of proportionality that have been made in the retributive context. There is certainly an argument, at the theoretical level, that a proportionality model built around repairing harms rather than inflicting them would have a stronger internal basis for resisting both the punitive and the managerial imperatives towards penal excess, especially if our approach to proportionality uses a metric that takes some account of harms to the offender as part of what is to be repaired. But that is dependent upon wider public acceptance of the legitimacy of that metric, and therefore, of that system. The underlying social processes, principles, and values again seem to be doing the heavy lifting in driving proportionate limits on punishment. Moreover, the language of reparation is liable, as with rehabilitation, to abuse and conceptual slippage. After all, 'payback' has rhetorical value to both a reparative and a punitive agenda: in the latter case, inflicting suffering upon the offender in proportion (or out of it) to the victim's own suffering as simple revenge ('It's payback time!').[85] So while adopting a reparative approach can enable us to

[84] See generally Carlen, 'Against Rehabilitation', above n 36; compare Alessandro de Giorgi, *Rethinking the Political Economy of Punishment: Perspectives on Post-Fordism and Penal Politics* (2006, Ashgate).

[85] See, eg, Gelsthorpe and Rex, above n 85; Nicholas Pamment and Tom Ellis, 'A Retrograde Step: The Potential Impact of High Visibility Uniforms within Youth Justice Reparation' (2010) 49 *The Howard Journal of Crime and Justice* 18.

avoid some of the euphemistic presumptions that have bedevilled rehabilitation there is no guarantee that its language could automatically avoid being co-opted for perverse effects by political agendas encouraging penal excess.[86]

General theories of restorative justice do not (necessarily) adopt a reparative logic, and offer three other strategies of limiting the penal State: firstly, by specifically embracing a proportionality limit on the harms to be restored;[87] secondly, by including external limiting factors, most commonly the *parsimony* principle;[88] and thirdly, by treating certain minimal socio-political conditions of fairness, justice, and equality as necessary preconditions for restorative justice, with the result that restorative justice would not be possible *unless* it took place under conditions where minimalism would naturally occur.[89] The first approach is subject to the same general critique that we have just discussed in the context of reparative metrics and tariffs, applied *mutatis mutandis* to the remit of that particular restorative model. The second will stand and fall on the ability of those other external limiting principles to resist penal excess in practice – a question I forestall until Chapter 5, which discusses parsimony in detail. The third approach, however, only seems amenable to stronger restorative accounts, where there are relatively revolutionary changes in the social and political institutions underpinning criminal justice. These changes would encourage fellow-citizens to impose limits on punishment naturally, as a result of the mutual respect and recognition inherent in the fabric of the new social order. To the extent that is the case, however, it is not clear how to restrain the penal State while those social-structural shifts are taking place, and therefore how to restrain penal excess in the meantime in a way that does not simply resort to pre-existing limiting principles.[90] Either we should prioritise wider-ranging socio-political change (in which case, once again, it is the socio-political institutions *behind* criminal justice that really cause penal restraint), or we are reliant upon external limiting factors – potentially including proportionality. So either restorative justice provides a long-term goal offering little prospect of short- or medium-term restraint, or it is reliant on similar limiting factors, and no better an antidote to penal excess than retributivism or rehabilitation.

[86] See, eg, Lucia Zedner, 'Reparation and Retribution: Are They Reconcilable?' (1994) 57 *MLR* 228; compare Giuseppe Maglione, 'The Political Rationality of Restorative Justice' (2018), *Theoretical Criminology*, forthcoming.

[87] Recall Walgrave, n 64; Dignan, n 67.

[88] See, eg, John Braithwaite and Philip Pettit, *Not Just Deserts: A Republican Theory of Criminal Justice* (1990, Clarendon Press), pp 78–80; Lode Walgrave, 'Imposing Restoration Instead of Inflicting Pain', in: Andrew von Hirsch et al (eds), *Restorative Justice or Criminal Justice: Competing or Reconcilable Programmes?* (2003, Hart).

[89] See Philip Pettit and John Braithwaite, 'Not Just Deserts, Not Even in Sentencing' (1993) 4 *Current Issues in Criminal Justice* 222.

[90] Recall Braithwaite and Pettit, n 88, pp 78–80.

III. Penal Abolitionism and (Post-)Penal Minimalism

Let us therefore turn our attention to the other major radical response in penal theory: *penal abolitionism*. This term covers a series of more or less radical rejections of the justifiability of punishment, challenging either: certain *modes* of punishment (notably the death penalty and, more recently, imprisonment);[91] certain *subjects* of punishment (notably young or female offenders);[92] or indeed, the entire edifice of criminal justice.[93] As a result, abolitionist stances are fundamentally concerned with limits on the distribution of penal interventions in society, and so provide an obvious (if crude) means of pursuing penal minimalism.[94] But would doing so overcome the problems we have described as penal excess? To answer this question we must take account of the full range of abolitionist thought, which, in line with the previous section, I reduce into *weaker* (ie partial abolition) and *stronger* positions (ie total abolition). In the case of weaker abolitionism, we must ask whether their proposed amendments to the modes and subjects of criminal justice would be enough to prevent penal excess. In the case of strong abolitionism, we should ask what, if anything, would replace criminal justice, what that would entail, and how desirable that would be from the perspective of (liberal-democratic) penal minimalist values.

A. Weaker Abolitionism: Root and Branch Minimalism

Weaker abolitionist positions effectively place limits on the forms of punishment that can be imposed in particular cases. Rather than claiming that a particular form of punishment (say) is *disproportionate*, abolitionists of these sorts will claim that it is outright *inappropriate*, on either instrumental or intrinsic-value grounds. Intrinsic-value arguments claim that there is something inherently indefensible about the use of certain forms of punishment, such as corporal or capital punishment, on the basis of contemporary socio- political norms.[95] But the abolitionist argument can also be made instrumentally. For instance, Edwin Schur argues that

[91] See, eg, Joe Sim, *Prisons and Punishment: Power and the Carceral State* (2009, SAGE); Mick Ryan and Tony Ward, 'Prison Abolitionism in the UK: They Dare Not Speak its Name?' (2015) 41 *Social Justice* 107; compare David Garland, *Peculiar Institution: America's Death Penalty in an Age of Abolition* (2010, The Belknap Press).

[92] See, eg, Edwin Schur, *Radical Non-Intervention: Rethinking the Delinquency Problem* (1973, Prentice Hall); Pat Carlen, *Alternatives to Women's Imprisonment* (1990, Open University Press); David Frank, 'Abandoned: Abolishing Female Imprisonment to Prevent Sexual Abuse and Herald an End to Incarceration' (2014) 29 *Berkeley Journal of Gender, Law and Justice* 1.

[93] See generally Vincenzo Ruggiero, *Penal Abolitionism* (2010, Oxford University Press).

[94] Indeed, many prominent abolitionist scholars have tended to adopt penal minimalist stances in the short- or long-term. See Johannes Feest, 'Abolitionism: Some Answers to Frequently Answered Questions' (2015) 7 *Sortuz: Oñati Journal of Emergent Socio-Legal Studies* 141, p 144.

[95] See, eg, John Pratt, 'Punishment and "The Civilizing Process"', in: Jonathan Simon and Richard Sparks (eds), *The SAGE Handbook of Punishment and Society* (2013, SAGE).

criminal justice ought not to be applied against deviant children because, paradoxically, the use of the youth criminal justice system can actually lead to an increased likelihood of reoffending compared to not intervening at all.[96] Likewise, if a penal system uses the death penalty for deterrent purposes (say), and it can be shown that executions do not actually discourage the sorts of crimes against which they are applied, then there is no justification for that imposition of capital punishment.[97] From this perspective, particular punishments should be abandoned not because they are inappropriate, but merely because they are counterproductive according to the aims of the system.

The reasons for which weaker strands of abolitionism propose to end certain forms of punishment for certain people imply important consequences about the distribution of those punishments that remain. For instance, stances rejecting certain forms of punishment typically target interventions towards the top of retributive sentencing tariffs. If sentences at the top of the sentencing tariff are abolished, then to maintain parity in the expression of censure, a proportionality advocate would be obliged to generally reduce the rest of the tariff, encouraging overall movement towards a more minimal penal system.[98] The same can be said of other penal rationales and limiting principles other than retributive proportionality. For instance, imagine a system predicated on deterrence and incapacitation that uses the death penalty as the most serious means of dissuading (or removing) offenders from society. A successful abolitionist policy predicated on the belief that capital punishment is inappropriate in that society would compel the State to adopt different sorts of punishments to try to achieve its deterrent and preventative ends, *even if execution would otherwise have achieved those ends*. So in both examples, principled abolition of particular modes of punishments encourages a substantial reduction of the size of the penal State, in terms of its overall interference with autonomy if not necessarily in a straightforwardly beneficial way in every case.[99] The exclusion of marginalised groups from the penal State's ambit can play a similar role in confronting problems with the shape of the penal State, therefore encouraging penal minimalism in practice.

However, none of this is guaranteed. There are any number of reasons why a removal of options at the top of the range of available sentences would not lead to a general reduction in penal severity. For example, concerns other than proportionality, such as for public protection, may resist the general downward shift of punishment; or a tendency of experienced judges to import the previous system's

[96] Schur, above n 92.

[97] See, eg, John Donohue and Justin Wolfers, 'The Uses and Abuses of Empirical Evidence in the Death Penalty Debate' (2006) 58 *Stanford Law Review* 791; Daniel Nagin and John Peppers (eds), *Deterrence and the Death Penalty* (2012, National Academies Press).

[98] Recall Andrew von Hirsch, *Past or Future Crimes: Deservedness and Dangerousness in the Sentencing of Criminals* (1985, Manchester University Press), pp 92–101; Andrew von Hirsch, *Censure and Sanctions* (1993, Clarendon Press), pp 36–46, on 'anchoring' the penalty scale.

[99] See, eg, Dirk van Zyl Smit and Catherine Appleton, *Life Imprisonment: A Global Rights Analysis* (2019, Harvard University Press).

basic notions of 'trustworthy', 'effective', and/or 'fair' sentences may encourage the continuing use of relatively harsh penalties.[100] Moreover, abolitionist policies are likely to face considerable political resistance, given the endemic reliance of States on criminal justice in existing institutional orders, and the emotive, symbolic, and political significance of punishing criminal wrongdoing in particular ways.[101] The success of the abolitionist urge is dependent upon socio-political institutions' support, in other words – and we are back to the Lacey-Pickard critique about where the heavy lifting is really taking place. To be fair, moderate abolitionist accounts are typically more explicit about the political nature of the struggle to constrain the penal State.[102] But we are left with the charge that, again, the criminal justice system cannot contain itself, and cannot really contribute much internally to the wider institutional systems of control that underpin it.

B. Strong Abolitionism: Penal Minimalism After Punishment?

In a sense, the strongest abolitionists, who would do away with all criminal punishment, could solve penal excess at a stroke, because there would no longer be a penal system to be excessive! However, the claim that we could simply do away with criminal justice without any implications for other systems of social control would be over-simplistic to the point of parody. Legitimate or not, criminal justice *does* play a role in maintaining social order in contemporary societies, and so any system that seeks to abolish criminal justice altogether must explain what other institutions would replace it as a means of ensuring the minimum necessary level of peace and stability to enable individual and social flourishing. Like any broad movement, strong abolitionism offers a diverse range of answers to these questions, short of a mere return to a violent, Hobbesian state of nature. It is also instructive to look to the wider tradition of *anarchist* political theory, since the anarchist rejection of the State necessarily implies strong penal abolitionism.[103] In particular, these sources suggest: *radical decriminalisation*; *mental health alternatives*; and *exile*.

A programme of *radical decriminalisation* would abolish most (if not all) crimes as such, replacing them with either: claims in civil law;[104] ad hoc arrangements

[100] Compare Nicola Padfield, 'Time to Bury the Custody "Threshold"?' [2011] *Crim LR* 593.

[101] See, eg, Garland, *Peculiar Institution*, above n 91, pp 248–255, on US death penalty retention.

[102] See, eg, Thomas Mathiesen (ed), *The Politics of Abolition Revisited* (2015, Routledge); Sim, above n 91, chs 7–8.

[103] On the (partial) overlap between penal abolitionism and anarchism, see, eg, Ruggiero, above n 93, especially ch 8; and compare Larry Tifft and Dennis Sullivan, *The Struggle to Be Human: Crime, Criminology, and Anarchism* (1980, Cienfuegos Press), especially ch 2.

[104] See Gary Chartier, *Anarchy and Legal Order: Law and Politics for a Stateless Society* (2013, Cambridge University Press), chs 4–5; Nils Christie, 'Conflicts as Property' (1977) 17 *British Journal of Criminology* 1.

similar to restorative justice proceedings;[105] strong community-based moral censure;[106] or, indeed, with nothing. Indeed, given the modern tendency towards over-criminalisation, on the one hand, and the emphasis that strong abolitionism gives to wider-scale socio-political changes alongside the abandonment of criminal justice, on the other, we could potentially do away with a good deal of criminality overnight. For instance, if we live in a society without a concept of individual property, there can be no property crime.[107] Since strong abolitionism is typically associated with a radical reconstitution of the status quo, their approach to crime can lead to a substantial reduction, in real terms, of both the size and shape of the post-revolutionary equivalent of the penal State.[108] However, this effect is dependent upon, and really a corollary of, that wider radical social change.

A second alternative is to use radical *mental health alternatives*. In an analogy advanced by the anarcho-communist Peter Kropotkin, for instance, crime is a sort of 'social disease' caused by the breakdown of good interpersonal relationships.[109] Kropotkin assumes that crimes occur for several reasons, each of which is really a failing of the aggregate social 'organism' rather than of any one individual alone. After all, society forms the environmental backdrop against which 'human nature' forms: if every socio-cultural cue throughout your life is telling you to amass wealth, to compete, to prefer your needs over those of your fellows, then that will encourage tendencies towards (potentially criminal) rapacity, greed, and selfishness instead of those towards mutual aid and solidarity.[110] But Kropotkin also points to characteristics that modern terminology would describe as the offender's mental health: their capacity to live amongst the neighbours they happen to cohabit with may be limited as a result of that community's inability to support their needs and wishes. For Kropotkin, the solutions are humane interaction with a genuine effort towards understanding, and in the last resort, the creation of specific, voluntary communities of non-coercive care and support where those incapable of living according to 'conventional' standards can find other, more personally rewarding, ways of being.[111]

[105] See, eg, Ruggiero, 'An Abolitionist View of Restorative Justice', above n 80. See also Chris Cunneen, 'Reviving Restorative Justice Traditions', in: Gerry Johnstone and Daniel van Ness (eds), *Handbook of Restorative Justice* (2007, Willan); Wade Mansell, *A Critical Introduction to Law*, Fourth edn (2015, Routledge), pp 26–69.

[106] See, eg, Christie, *A Suitable Amount of Crime*, above n 74, ch 1; Ruggiero, *Penal Abolitionism*, above n 93, ch 2.

[107] See, eg, Peter Kropotkin, 'Law and Authority', in: Peter Kropotkin; Roger Baldwin (ed), *Anarchism: A Collection of Revolutionary Writings* (2002, Dover), pp 210–212. Compare Vincenzo Ruggiero, 'Crime and Punishment in Classical and Libertarian Utopias' (2013) 52 *The Howard Journal of Crime and Justice* 414.

[108] On the value of this kind of utopian project, see, eg, Ruggiero, ibid; Simon Critchley, *The Faith of the Faithless: Experiments in Political Theology* (2012, Verso); Ruth Levitas, *Utopia as Method: The Imaginary Reconstitution of Society* (2013, Palgrave Macmillan).

[109] Kropotkin, 'Prisons', above n 32, p 228.

[110] Ibid, pp 228–235. See also Murray Bookchin, *The Ecology of Freedom: The Emergence and Dissolution of Social Hierarchy*, Third edn (2005, AK Press), pp 20–21.

[111] Kropotkin, 'Prisons', above 32, pp 233–235. Compare (the not explicitly anarchist) David Scott, *Against Imprisonment: An Anthology of Abolitionist Essays* (2018, Waterside Press), p 227.

Kropotkin foresaw, however, the danger in this line of thinking: a straightforward trans-incarceration of 'the criminally insane' into the mental healthcare system could only amount to making prisons of mental hospitals, which would prove just as deleterious to the pursuit of individual liberty.[112] Regardless of what we think about Kropotkin's *fin de siècle* anarcho-communism, or his understanding of the causes of crime (before or after the Revolution), he raises an important point for all (strong) abolitionists – that the new institutions may turn out to be just as bad as the old. Mental healthcare, too, is a field enfolded with power relationships and hierarchies that, in its current form, also imposes substantial implications for the liberty and democratic citizenship of its inmates.[113] The use of secure mental healthcare facilities, analogous to prisons, is in and of itself deeply controversial, and its use as an alternative to penal State coercion is not a straightforward 'win' for the penal minimalist concerned with securing maximum personal autonomy more generally.[114] Penal minimalists (especially of the type I have described) ought to oppose *medical* as well as penal excess, in other words. Thus, for the strong abolitionist to consistently rely on mental healthcare and other forms of social control in a way that satisfies penal minimalist concerns, they must commit to building non-coercive (and *less coercive*) institutions in those areas, too. An only partial revolution, in other words, is no revolution at all.[115]

The final, and potentially most worrying alternative to criminal justice offered by strong abolitionism is *exile*, where the offender is removed from a community altogether.[116] For the typical liberal criminal theorist, exile is a relic of a barbaric pre-history of blood-feuds and Bloody Codes that civilised society has outgrown. A banished individual is effectively made stateless, which can have dreadful consequences for the protection of their (human) rights at a national or international level, and makes it practically impossible (without at supportive third State) for them to pursue their autonomous desires. This perspective is somewhat overblown, however. In the first instance, England and Wales continues to effectively

[112] Kropotkin, 'Prisons', above 32, p 233.

[113] See generally Michel Foucault, *Discipline and Punish*, above n 10; see also Michel Foucault, *Abnormal: Lectures at the* Collège de France, *1974–1975* (2003, Graham Burchell (trans), Valerio Marchetti and Antonella Salomoni (eds), Verso); Nicola Lacey, *In Search of Criminal Responsibility: Ideas, Interests, and Institutions* (2016, Oxford University Press), especially pp 64–78.

[114] See, eg, Jill Peay, *Mental Health and Crime* (2011, Routledge), chs 9–11; Andrew Ashworth and Lucia Zedner, *Preventive Justice* (2014, Oxford University Press), ch 9; Jill Peay, 'Mental Health, Mental Disabilities, and Crime', in: Alison Liebling, Shadd Maruna, and Lesley McAra (eds), *The Oxford Handbook of Criminology*, Sixth edn (2017, Oxford University Press). Compare Eoin O'Sullivan and Ian O'Donnell, 'Introduction: Setting the Scene', in: Eoin O'Sullivan and Ian O'Donnell (eds), *Coercive Confinement in Ireland: Patients, Prisoners and Penitents* (2012, Manchester University Press).

[115] See, eg, Laurence Davis, 'The Dynamic and Revolutionary Utopia of Ursula K Le Guin', and Chris Ferns, 'Future Conditional or Future Perfect? *The Dispossessed* and Permanent Revolution', both in: Laurence Davis and Peter Stillman (eds), *The New Utopian Politics of Ursula K Le Guin's* The Dispossessed (2005, Lexington Books). Compare Christie, *Limits to Pain*, above n 4.

[116] See, eg, Matthew Wilson, *Rules without Rulers: The Possibilities and Limits of Anarchism* (2014, Zero Books), pp 60–70; Delfina Vannucci and Richard Singer, *Come Hell or High Water: A Handbook on Collective Process Gone Awry* (2010, AK Press), pp 57–62.

exile foreign nationals who break (criminal and immigration) law through post-conviction deportation.[117] Secondly, temporary exile – whether in the historical form of transportation to penal labour colonies, or in the more ongoing figurative banishment involved in imprisonment[118] – has remained a much more recent feature of English criminal justice. Moreover, thirdly, exile has not necessarily always meant what the increasing-civilisation hypothesis implies – in late antiquity, for instance, 'clerical exile' was a way of gaining Church sanctuary by being removed to a distant part of the Empire, to proselytise for the church, in lieu of formal punishment for one's crime. Exiles could potentially be escorted by friends and loved ones, and because of the unifying influence of the Church in their new diocese, were able to form strong and effective social bonds in their new environment.[119]

None of this makes exile unproblematic, or necessarily compatible with penal-minimalist values. Even in an anarchist setting, banishment can be harmful, painful, and coercive.[120] However, it is naïve to dismiss all exile as inherently *more* coercive than the penal status quo out of hand, especially in the context of radically different social orders that tend to underpin strong abolitionist accounts. In particular, anarchist abolitionists defend the potential practice of exile on the basis of their wider pursuit of a society founded on the principles of *mutual aid* and *solidarity*, which would dissuade communities from the othering of criminal wrongdoers, and enable them to find support elsewhere. An anarchist society on the level of the modern UK (or even contemporary England) would really be made up of small, nested, and only loosely interconnected communities, each connected more by common values and loose trade networks than by an imposed, external set of rules.[121] Unlike in a liberal society – where the social contract means that no one person needs to really get along with any other, so long as they respect the 'terms' of the social contract – an anarchist society depends upon mutual respect arising out of shared moral and social values. However, moral censure would tend to be localised and parochial, with differences in the particular expectations and interests of each community. It would be quite possible, therefore, for someone who simply cannot fit in to one community to fit in to others. Those socio-political and -cultural conditions of radical solidarity would

[117] See, eg, Jordanna Bailkin, 'Leaving Home: The Politics of Deportation in Postwar Britain' (2008) 47 *Journal of British Studies* 852; Mary Bosworth and Sarah Turnbull, 'Immigration, Detention, and the Expansion of Penal Power in the United Kingdom', in: Keramet Reiter and Alexa Koenig (eds), *Extreme Punishment: Comparative Studies in Detention, Incarceration, and Solitary Confinement* (2015, Palgrave Macmillan). Compare Beth Caldwell, 'Banished for Life: Deportation of Juvenile Offenders as Cruel and Unusual Punishment' (2013) 34 *Cardozo Law Review* 2261.

[118] See Duff, *Punishment, Communication, and Community*, above n 7, pp 148–152.

[119] See generally Julia Hillner, Jörg Ulrich, and Jakob Engberg (eds), *Clerical Exile in Late Antiquity* (2016, Peter Lang).

[120] See Vannucci and Singer, above n 116, pp 59–62; Wilson, above n 116, pp 66–68.

[121] Examples abound in anarchist and libertarian utopias: see generally Ursula K Le Guin, *The Dispossessed: An Ambiguous Utopia* (1976, Gollancz); Ursula K Le Guin, *Always Coming Home* (1985, Gollancz); and Ruggiero, 'Crime and Punishment in Classical and Libertarian Utopias', above n 93.

make exile a very different institution than our current, historically informed (and partly stereotyped) conception of it. We must consider the most extreme abolitionist alternatives in the context of the similarly extreme social changes that would accompany them.

Three lessons arise from this overview of strong abolitionist alternatives to State punishment. Firstly, none of these approaches is a 'magic bullet' that unambiguously resolve the challenges posed by the problem of punishment. Each brings its own limitations, tensions with penal-minimalist values, and opportunities for new excesses. However, secondly, a real-terms reduction of coercive excess is at least possible under a radical abolitionist programme, in which formal punishment is supplanted by more organic, community- and solidarity-based approaches to resolving the disputes underlying criminal wrongdoing. With that said, thirdly, each system of dispute resolution relies, to a greater or lesser extent, upon profound, radical, and perhaps even revolutionary changes to social, cultural and political-economic institutions and concepts throughout society. Such change does not happen overnight, even when the Revolution is achieved through the violent overthrow of the old order. Strong abolitionists must therefore work out what to do in the meantime, to maximise the chances of bringing about the conditions of change. Fundamentally, abolitionists must engage with their goals as part of what Thomas Mathiesen calls 'The Unfinished' – as an incomplete sketch of a system to be filled in progressively as one comes closer to making it a reality:[122]

> A change through which we leave one order in favour of another *which is waiting*, is no abolishment. It is only a substitution, which certainly may involve differences in detail, and 'improvements' in detail, but which does not involve a change in structure. Structurally, a finalized fully formed new order perpetuates old solutions; our relationship to what is waiting is structurally like our relationship to the old order.

Key to this understanding is that reform is not enough – if we leave the institutions of criminal justice to reform themselves, history teaches us that the only solution will be more of the same.[123] If we have come to the point where the penal minimalist can only accept strong penal abolitionism, then the penal system is inherently unjust, inadequate, and broken. Moreover, attempts at reforming its brokenness can actually undermine the argument for reform – by making it seem that the indefensible is actually getting better, that our punishments are becoming more 'civilised'.[124] Reform ultimately has a *quietist* effect – it makes it seem less troubling that we engage in the deprivation of liberty and the infliction of pain upon criminal wrongdoers, because the pain is softened, and transmuted into less ugly and obviously unpleasant forms.[125] A penal minimalist might well be tempted

[122] Thomas Mathiesen, 'The Politics of Abolition', in: Thomas Mathiesen (ed), *The Politics of Abolition Revisited* (2015, Routledge), p 58.
[123] Cohen, *Visions of Social Control*, above n 48.
[124] Mathiesen, 'The Politics of Abolition', above n 122, pp 47–61. Compare Schept, above n 46.
[125] Compare McNeill, *Pervasive Punishment*, above n 8.

to radically reject the existing status quo, and in so doing commit to an entirely different vision of a future world. But to get there would take substantial recalibration and restructuring at the level of the very ideas and institutions that formulate our current social order, rather than focussing on the penal system on its own. While all this was going on, penal excess would only continue.

IV. Conclusion: Is Penal Minimalism Possible?

This chapter has offered a targeted overview of retributive theory's main competitors in terms of their prospects for confronting, resisting, and reversing penal excess. It suggests that these theories offer at best poor prospects of (short- to medium-term) restraint. Rehabilitation's quietist effects, and vulnerability to penal managerial agendas, suggest that it has a limited capacity, at the level of the *distribution* of criminal punishment, to fight the progressive expansion of the penal system. Altogether, less radical alternatives (including 'weaker' abolitionism and restorative justice) tend to rely upon external limiting factors to constrain penal excess, and therefore offer nothing in and of themselves, whilst more radical alternatives offer promising long-term trends but little in the meantime, absent radical (and perhaps revolutionary) social change. So, even if we agree that those long-term social changes are desirable, where does this leave the penal minimalist seeking a reduction of penal excess today?

We might be tempted to return to retributivism at this point, and see what can be done to increase its resilience to the sort of political failures that dogged the desert model over the last three decades. However, before we do so there is one more possibility to consider, which Chapter 5 takes up. Both retributivism and its alternatives rely upon different sets of *limiting principles*, such as proportionality and parsimony. We should consider these in their own right, to see if there is any rational basis for minimalists to prefer one over the other, and therefore to choose between the particular penal theories that they support.

5

Proportionality and its Alternatives

The conclusion of Chapter 4 is fairly depressing: on the face of it, none of retributivism's existing rivals in penal theory offer any more hope than of it restricting penal excess. On the one hand, they may rely on external limiting principles that have nothing in particular to do with those theories, and therefore give the minimalist no inherent reason to adopt their theory over any other. On the other, those theories that *do* appear to offer the prospect of a genuine confrontation with penal excess either demand long-term revolutionary changes in the political and cultural framework of our society, or else are reliant upon the support of the socio-political institutions that do the lion's share of keeping the size and shape of the penal State under control. In the first case this means that penal minimalism can only be a distant aim in the context of contemporary penal-political conditions, and in the second it means that the confrontation of penal excess is outside of penal theorists' direct control to at least some extent. To an extent, penal theorists simply have to accept these possibilities. Penal policy relies upon the wider political processes and non-penal institutions that surround it, simply because punishment is an inherently political process, determined by political decisions about what counts as crime and how it is permissible to respond to it. Against such a backdrop, penal theory can only contribute partly to criminal justice reform, and therefore, to penal minimalism.

However, this is not to say that penal theories cannot say *anything* about the (political) quest for penal minimalism. In Part III, I develop a theory of criminal punishment that takes the pursuit of penal minimalism seriously, on the basis of retributive proportionality. To do so, however, I must first resolve a question I left open in Chapter 4 – can any external limiting factors do a better job of controlling penal excess than proportionality has? Specifically, this chapter engages with five principles aimed at limiting the scope and reach of the penal State, which have emerged from the criminal justice literature. It starts with a brief recap of *proportionality* and then considers: *parsimony*; *respect for human dignity*; the related concepts of *clemency* and *forgiveness*; and *solidarity*. I examine each of these principles against some of the challenges that limiting factors face in contemporary criminal justice contexts. We will see that no one principle can overcome all of these challenges, but that each adds something to the pursuit of penal minimalism. With that said, I argue that proportionality plays a particularly important role in this process, though not a determinative one. Rather than seeing proportionality as a superior, standalone principle, it is better to think of it as merely a first amongst equals.

This conclusion informs, and leads into, the model of proportionality-based sentencing and policy-making proposed over the next two chapters.

I. Five Limiting Factors

Our discussion in Chapter 4 identified some guiding principles that offer alternative means of imposing limits on the use of penal institutions to proportionality: *parsimony*; *respect for human dignity*; *forgiveness;* and (particularly in the light of our discussion of radical restorative justice and penal abolitionism) *solidarity*. In this section, I discuss these four concepts in outline, exploring their key characteristics and internal concepts *as they relate to limiting the use of criminal punishment*. However, for clarity, and to allow better comparisons to be drawn across the rest of this chapter, I begin with a brief overview of these aspects in the context of proportionality, drawing on the fuller discussion in Chapter 3.

A. Proportionality, *Redux*: Cognitive and Institutional Restraints

The central claim of proportionality-based sentencing is that the punishment should 'fit' the crime. That 'fitness' is defined nebulously but in terms of a metaphor of balancing, depending upon the particular penal theory in question: under retributivism, for instance, proportionality requires that *the severity of the penal intervention should be in proportion to the seriousness of the offence*. For reparative proportionality, there is a similar equation between the ability of the punishment to heal the level of harm caused and/or represented by the crime. Establishing this proportion requires a means of effectively comparing the severity of punishments against all other punishments, another for comparing the seriousness of offences, and a means of identifying what level of seriousness on the one scale matches which degree of severity on the other.

Part of the appeal of proportionality as a limiting principle is that it is *relatively* unambitious compared to theories justifying punishment in terms of doing some prospective good. Although it may allow for the pursuit of rehabilitative or other aims, the overriding concern is that the sentence fits the seriousness of the offence, which imposes a hard limit on the potential aims (and therefore, on the overall size) of the penal State.[1] But proportionality's main draw is that its limitation of judicial reasoning in individual cases is *inherent* to the wider penal theory, in such a way as to prevent excessive punishments of individuals.[2] To get what you

[1] See, eg, Andrew von Hirsch, *Doing Justice: The Choice of Punishments* (1976, Hill & Wang), pp 124–131; Andreas von Hirsch, *Deserved Criminal Sentences* (2017, Hart), pp 111–115.

[2] See, eg, Alice Ristroph, 'Proportionality as a Principle of Limited Government' (2005) 55 *Duke Law Journal* 263. Compare RA Duff, 'A Criminal Law for Citizens' (2010) 14 *Theoretical Criminology* 293.

deserve, we need to be able to say how much you deserve, and on what basis. To understand how I can repair the harm I have done, we must be able to say how bad that harm is. This means that the limiting effect of balancing the punishment against the crime cannot be undone without undoing the very basis of the wider penal theory, the justification for why we punish at all.[3] This is not so much a claim about proportionality *in and of itself*, so much as certain (retributive/reparative) justifications that are inherently proportionate. If proportionality is simply grafted onto an otherwise non-proportionate 'general justifying aim', then it will be just as extrinsic as any other limiting factor.[4]

The trouble with limiting factors that are external to the penal rationales they limit is that they face a *cognitive* hurdle, by virtue of their very externality to the limited theory's logic. If a sentencing authority thinks, 'I must keep the public safe', then they may well bow to principles that impose limits on the sentence, regardless of the impact on public safety. But it may also be tempting to go beyond that – to be literally better safe than sorry! The constraint is an artifice, an interference with the punishment's wider theoretical justification of 'doing some good'.[5] That does not mean that an extrinsic limiting factor can be safely ignored – only that, because it is going against the internal calculation imposed by the penal intervention's goal, it is a barrier to what one is really trying to do, and not a core part of the solution one seeks.[6] It is therefore much easier to find justifications for working one's way around an external limiting principle in hard cases, because of the artificiality of the limit from the internal perspective of the task being limited.

The major issue with using proportionality as a *limiting* principle in punishment is that there is no guarantee that proportionality will be the only issue at play in judicial reasoning, and that proportionality may be ineffective at responding to other issues on the judge's mind. For instance, a judge may find it easier to aggravate a community sentence into a custodial one than to mitigate a prison term into a non-custodial one, because of lingering doubts about the punitive credentials of 'alternative punishments', or because of insufficient guidance about how many months of imprisonment is commensurate to how many months of community penalties.[7] Moreover, since the focus is solely on individual cases, the overall size

[3] See, eg, Joel Feinberg, 'The Expressive Function of Punishment' (1965) 49 *The Monist* 397; Joshua Glasgow, 'The Expressivist Theory of Punishment Defended' (2015) 34 *Law and Philosophy* 601; Lode Walgrave, 'Integrating Criminal Justice and Restorative Justice', in Gerry Johnstone and Daniel van Ness (eds), *Handbook of Restorative Justice* (2007, Willan).

[4] See, eg, HLA Hart, 'Prolegomenon to the Principles of Punishment', in: HLA Hart (ed), *Punishment and Responsibility: Essays in the Philosophy of Punishment*, Second edn (2007, Oxford University Press), pp 8–13.

[5] See generally Stanley Cohen, *Visions of Social Control* (1985, Polity Press), pp 245–254.

[6] Compare Sara Cate and Daniel HoSang, '"The Better Way to Fight Crime": Why Fiscal Arguments Do Not Constrain the Carceral State' (2018) 22 *Theoretical Criminology* 169.

[7] See Nicola Padfield, 'Time to Bury the Custody "Threshold"?' [2011] *Crim LR* 593. On the problem of commensurability, see: Dan Kahan, 'Punishment Incommensurability' (1998) 1 *Buffalo Criminal Law Review* 691; Peter Wood and Harold Grasmick, 'Toward the Development of Punishment Equivalencies: Male and Female Inmates Rate the Severity of Alternative Sanctions Compared to Prison' (1999) 16 *Justice Quarterly* 19; Jesper Ryberg, 'Punishment and the Measurement of

of the penal State can be increased if more formally guilty persons are criminalised, detected, investigated and prosecuted, or if fewer formally guilty persons are diverted or decriminalised, than was previously the case.[8] The problem is that, while the metaphor of fittingness itself makes some intuitive sense, the concept of how penal severity should be measured has been paid insufficient attention in the theoretical literature,[9] while the determinants of both the rankings of crime seriousness and of punishment severity are essentially *politically* determined, and not set at the point of the theory.[10] The problem is that seen objectively from outside the system, and in comparison with other penal systems, proportionality can fail to provide strong arguments against cruel punishments, or certainly punishments that go beyond those of other penal systems in similar societies.

Consider the satirical example provided by Franz Kafka's 'Harrow': a punishment machine that inscribes the wrongdoing of any person directly onto their body – inevitably causing death in the process. In the warped mind of the former colonial governor who developed the Harrow, and of the loyal officer who deploys it, the Harrow visits perfectly proportionate punishment, inflicting upon its subjects an agony that transforms into a purported religious ecstasy.[11] Another challenging thought experiment is Adam Kolber's 'truncation',[12] where one is made to stand against a wall while a blade passes at a fixed height along it. A short offender would be (physically) unaffected, one of middling height would receive 'a rather imprecise haircut',[13] and a taller one would be decapitated. While these examples are purposefully fanciful, and out of keeping with contemporary moral conceptions of acceptable punishment, they reveal tensions in terms of how we measure the degree of punishment imposed, and what makes it count as proportionate.

If we take Kafka's Harrow at face value, then we must recognise that it pursues some sort of proportionality. The result is always the same – death – but the meaning communicated, both in the claimed subjective rapture of the victim, and in the objective inscription of the wrong onto the wrongdoer's body, there is a differentiation of the message conveyed. In other words, the metric of proportionality under Kafka's Harrow is the *meaning expressed* by the punishment. This is not necessarily as fanciful as it might first seem. Different manners of execution can have different

Severity', in: Jesper Ryberg and JA Corlett (eds), *Punishment and Ethics: New Perspectives* (2010, Palgrave Macmillan); and David Hayes, 'Penal Impact: Towards a More Intersubjective Measurement of Penal Severity' (2015) 36 *OLJS* 724.

[8] See, eg, Vincent Chiao, 'Mass Incarceration and the Theory of Punishment' (2017) 11 *Criminal Law and Philosophy* 431; and compare Doug Husak, *Overcriminalization* (2007, Oxford University Press); Nicola Lacey, 'Historicising Criminalisation: Conceptual and Empirical Issues' (2009) 72 *MLR* 936.

[9] A claim I make more fully in Hayes, 'Penal Impact', above n 7.

[10] See Ted Honderich, *Punishment: The Supposed Justifications Revisited* (2006, Pluto Press), pp 35–41. Recall Andrew von Hirsch, *Censure and Sanctions* (1993, Clarendon Press), ch 5.

[11] Franz Kafka, 'In the Penal Colony', in: Franz Kafka; Joyce Crick (ed, trans), The Metamorphosis *and Other Stories* (2009, Oxford University Press).

[12] Adam Kolber, 'The Subjective Experience of Punishment' (2009) 109 *Columbia Law Review* 182, pp 188–189.

[13] Ibid, p 188.

cultural messages, despite leading to the same objective result: at the Nuremberg and Tokyo International Military Tribunals, for instance, there was some debate as to whether convicted war criminals should be executed by 'honourable' military firing squad rather than the more humiliating method of hanging, reserved as it was for 'common' criminals in contemporary German and Japanese penal law.[14] Likewise, in medieval codes, the power of the monarch could be expressed by punishing particularly audacious crimes with extremely gory and spectacular modes of execution.[15] The Harrow's calculus is similar to expressive theories of retributivism, in that pain is only a means of effectively communicating penal censure. It is just that (proportionate) censure is expressed not through the *mode* of punishment and its *duration*, as in most modern accounts, but the *manner* of that mode's execution.[16] Kafka's example illuminates the historical, cultural, and socio-political underpinnings of the claim that punishment needs to hurt, and in certain ways, to effectively communicate the extent of the polity's disapproval.[17] If it is shockingly inhumane and grotesque, *it is nonetheless proportionate.*

Likewise, the ridiculous claim in Kolber's example, that all 'truncated' offenders have undergone the same punishment, is meant as a critique of the *duration fetish* in US (and wider Western) sentencing practice. Kolber rejects the assumption that punitive value only attaches to the length of sentences to imprisonment (under the same prison regime), arguing that it obscures differences in the experience of punishment that affect its overall severity *as* a punishment.[18] Again, proportionality is maintained, but only at an objective and rather artificial level, with the effect that only injustice is achieved in practice. In both hypotheticals, some sort of proportionality is pursued. The concept is plastic enough to cover seemingly barbaric and *outre* examples – and it is not clear *why* a certain metric is or is not ridiculous, without reference to the wider cultural, political, and philosophical norms against the backdrop of which proportionality is invoked.[19]

In sum, (criminal) proportionality calculates a sentence in terms of the extent to which it counterbalances a justifying need, such as the existence of a harm one ought to repair, or a blameworthy wrong that one deserves censure for. This balancing guides the sentencing authority implicitly and intrinsically, but blinds

[14] See, eg, Michael Bazyler, 'The Role of the Soviet Union in the International Military Tribunal at Nuremberg', in: Herbert Reginbogin, Christoph Safferling, and Walter Hippel (eds) *The Nuremberg Trials: International Criminal Law Since 1945: 60th Anniversary International Conference* (2006, KG Saur), p 45 at fn 5 and accompanying text; and Richard Minear, *Victor's Justice: Tokyo War Crimes Trial* (1971, Princeton University Press), p 91 at fn 44 and accompanying text.

[15] See Michel Foucault, *Discipline and Punish: The Birth of the Prison* (1977, Alan Sheridan (trans), Penguin).

[16] See, eg, Glasgow, above n 3.

[17] Compare Matt Matravers, 'Punishment, Suffering and Justice', in: Stephen Farrall et al (eds), *Justice and Penal Reform: Re-Shaping the Penal Landscape* (2016, Routledge).

[18] See generally Kolber, above n 12; Ian O'Donnell, *Prisoners, Solitude, and Time* (2014, Oxford University Press). See also Hayes, 'Penal Impact', above n 7; David Hayes, 'Pain, Proximity, and State Punishment' (2017) 20 *Punishment & Society* 235.

[19] Recall Nicola Lacey and Hanna Pickard, 'The Chimera of Proportionality: Institutionalising Limits on Punishment in Contemporary Social and Political Systems' (2015) 78 *MLR* 216.

us to wider issues beyond sentencing in individual cases, without worrying overmuch about the wider attitudes, institutional shape, and socio-political terrain of acceptable modes of punishment that define a particular penal system.

B. Parsimony: Minimising Harm

Like proportionality, the principle of parsimony is straightforward in the abstract, but difficult to pin down. This 'utilitarian and humanitarian' principle[20] demands that *the penal State should make the least harmful intervention necessary to achieve its aims*.[21] It is a way of achieving the required (usually consequentialist) good by the least intrusive, restrictive, painful, or otherwise harmful means necessary. Parsimony enables one to focus on achieving some prospective benefit from penal interventions, while also enabling us to recognise the costs of punishment, and to operationalise the normative claim that it should only be used as a last resort.[22]

However, it also provides a useful subsidiary principle in tandem with some proportionality-based accounts, where the range of potential sentences is identified negatively, rather than insisting on some mathematical equivalence.[23] Such a principle of proportionality might tell us that a proportionate sentence falls within a range of (say), nine to twelve months' supervision, with parsimony then telling us where, within that range, the subsidiary aims of the sentence (perhaps, the rehabilitation of the offender, or their making of effective reparation) should fall. Perhaps we decide that the offender needs at least ten months to achieve these secondary aims: then the proper sentence is ten months. But if they would need 15 months to achieve the secondary aims, then the proportionality limit would kick in, constraining the sentence to 12 months, regardless of parsimony's recommendation. By having the two principles operate together, one achieves a system whereby one is bound *either* by proportionality *or* by parsimony, whichever produces the lesser sentence.[24] It is also a particularly useful guide for sentencing authorities when choosing *between* different modes of punishment, for instance, where the sentence might be imprisonment or a community penalty.[25]

[20] Norval Morris, *The Future of Imprisonment* (1974, University of Chicago Press), p 61.

[21] See ibid, pp 59–62; Richard Frase, 'Limiting Retributivism', in: Michael Tonry (ed), *The Future of Imprisonment* (2004, Oxford University Press); Richard Frase, *Just Sentencing: Principles and Procedures for a Workable System* (2013, Oxford University Press), pp 31–32.

[22] Compare Jeremy Bentham, 'An Introduction to the Principles and Morals of Legislation', in: Michael Tonry (ed), *Why Punish? How Much? A Reader on Punishment* (2011, Oxford University Press), ch 13.

[23] See, eg, Richard Lippke, 'Retributive Parsimony' (2009) 15 *Res Publica* 377.

[24] See, eg, Richard Lippke, 'Parsimony and the Sentencing of Multiple Offenders', in: Jesper Ryberg, Julian Roberts, and Jan de Keijser (eds), *Sentencing Multiple Crimes* (2017, Oxford University Press).

[25] See Michael Tonry, 'Proportionality, Parsimony, and Interchangeability of Punishments', in: Anthony Duff et al (eds), *Penal Theory and Practice: Tradition and Innovation in Criminal Justice* (1994, Manchester University Press).

One advantage that parsimony has over proportionality is that it can speak to the overall size and shape of the penal State as well as to the treatment of individual penal subjects. Indeed, the pursuit of penal minimalism is, at least to some extent, an expression of the desire for a parsimonious penal State, in which the use of criminal justice to pursue social stability and social order is kept to the lowest necessary level.[26] It makes no sense to talk of the penal State as a whole in terms of proportionality, since proportionality is a question of individual liability. However, particularly regarding the instrumental aims of criminal justice as an institution of social control, it *does* make sense to speak of a parsimonious penal State, which does the least necessary to keep the peace, communicate public values, and prevent future crime.

Nonetheless, parsimony faces a range of definitional challenges, similar to those facing proportionality. Simply put, what is the 'least necessary' intervention? Who decides how much punishment is enough to achieve one's ends? On what basis? On the one hand, this determination is rather more difficult for the sentencing judge than proportionality, which is retrospective in its focus on the criminal act. What is 'needed', however, is necessarily a predictive question depending heavily upon the individual context of the case, which makes it hard to specify clear limits in advance. On the other hand, however, this case-specificity produces *sources* that can tell us what is needed to achieve our ends – such as pre-sentence reports, which provide a key source of contextual information for sentencing decision-making in contemporary England and Wales.[27]

The *epistemic* objection ("How can we know?") is rather different from, and easier to solve than the underlying *ontological* ("What is there to know?") question. The latter depends highly upon the theory underpinning the intervention. Take (general) deterrence. We know what an excessively deterrent criminal justice system would look like: we have the example of the Code of Drakon, who prescribed the death penalty for virtually every crime. Assuming that this is the *most* intrusive punishment and that it has even some potential deterrent value,[28] what is the *least*? To know that would require empirical data of how crime rates interact with different forms of punishment and different lengths of sentence – and given that every penal system is situated in its own specific contexts, it is hard to draw clear direct conclusions from historical and comparative examples.[29] This makes

[26] See Mary Bosworth, 'Introduction: Reinventing Penal Parsimony' (2010) 14 *Theoretical Criminology* 251; Ian Loader, 'For Penal Moderation: Notes towards a Philosophy of Punishment' (2010) 14 *Theoretical Criminology* 349.

[27] See Mike Nash, 'Probation, PSRs and Public Protection: Has a "Critical Point" Been Reached?' (2011) 11 *Criminology & Criminal Justice* 471; Gwen Robinson, 'Stand Down and Deliver: Pre-Sentence Reports, Quality and the New Culture of Speed' (2017) 64 *Probation Journal* 337.

[28] See generally Anthony Bottoms and Andrew von Hirsch, 'The Crime-Preventive Impact of Penal Sanctions', in Peter Cane and Herbert Kritzer (eds), *The Oxford Handbook of Empirical Legal Research* (2010, Oxford University Press).

[29] Ibid; compare David Nelken, *Comparative Criminal Justice: Making Sense of Difference* (2010, SAGE).

it extremely hard to predict how long and of what form of sentence is needed to deter, meaning that either the parsimonious constraint must be interpreted harshly, defeating the pursuit of more effective deterrence in the longer-term by discouraging experimentation, or loosely, undermining the ability of parsimony to achieve minimalism through that very vagueness.

Indeed, in a purely consequentialist system, parsimony is really just a restatement of the fact that the aims of the criminal justice system justify the means (in other words that one's rationale *is* consequentialist): the best returns on the least investment, or the most gains for the fewest pains.[30] In other words, it is not really a limiting factor at all, except insofar as it redirects attention from maximising benefits to minimising the costs of sentence. I am not convinced that this is wholly meaningless, at the level of sentencing – accentuating the negatives over the positives may well encourage sentencing authorities to be more sceptical in the pursuit of prospective penal ends. For instance, it might help to mitigate the phenomenon highlighted above, in which judges are more willing to aggravate a non-custodial sentence into a sentence of imprisonment than they are to mitigate a custodial sentence into the community.[31] However, absent strong additional limiting factors, parsimony faces difficulties in making its voice heard.

Moreover, parsimony can struggle with problems of comparative fairness and equality.[32] Suppose that you and I both commit a serious offence – say, an assault occasioning actual bodily harm under section 47 of the Offences against the Person Act 1861. The maximum penalty on statute is five years' imprisonment. Now, suppose the judge is minded to take into account each of our capacities to be rehabilitated. You, the judge considers, have reasonably good prospects for responding to rehabilitation, while, I am much more unlikely to avoid reoffending as a result of penal interventions available to the sentencing authority. Under that statutory maximum, your parsimonious sentence is likely to be lower, and perhaps significantly lower, than mine, despite the fact that our crimes are relatively similar in nature. To the extent that this results in our unequal treatment of similar conduct, that looks fundamentally unjust.[33]

Frase (summarising Morris's rejoinders to von Hirsch and inferring some of his own)[34] identifies two problems with this critique, to which I add a third. Firstly, the claim that equality is the *only* or the *primary* concern of punishment is contested, and relies substantially upon accepting von Hirsch's own conception of punishment as a censure-attributing process focussing only on the

[30] See, eg, Andrew von Hirsch, 'Equality, "Anisonomy", and Justice: A Review of *Madness and the Criminal Law*' (1984) 82 *Michigan Law Review* 1093, pp 1105–1107.

[31] Compare Padfield, n 7 (although she analyses a system governed by proportionality, not parsimony).

[32] von Hirsch, 'Equality, "Anisonomy", and Justice', above n 30, pp 1106–1107.

[33] Ibid, pp 1102–1104; see also von Hirsch, *Censure and Sanctions*, above n 10, pp 55–56. Compare William Lucy, *Law's Judgement* (2017, Hart), chs 3 and 5.

[34] Richard Frase, 'Sentencing Principles in Theory and Practice' (1997) 22 *Crime & Justice* 363, pp 382–388.

criminal act.[35] Secondly, in Morris's example, parsimony operates *within* proportionality-based limits, and so his conception is not of a purely consequentialist approach, as we have explored it here. Although Morris and von Hirsch differ on how robust Morris's conception of proportionality is,[36] this means that there is at least some room for treating offenders 'mostly alike' within the limits of (positive) proportionality, without surrendering the ability to engage with particular cases' unique circumstances within that range. This raises a third question: what does it mean to treat offenders equally? The stance taken by von Hirsch is very duration- and modes-focussed, and so takes a strongly *objectivist* approach to the measurement of punishment.[37] However, it is not at all clear that this is the only or best means of securing equality in sentencing in practice. If we recognise the impact of *subjective* characteristics of sentences as part of what makes punishment severe, then we create an opportunity to take different circumstances into account when deciding what makes like cases alike.[38] Once again, the choice of metric is important, and must be calibrated carefully with our wider penal rationale and aims. It follows that the measurement of 'equal treatment' is profoundly reliant upon how the penal State defines 'equality'. Parsimony, in alerting us to harms, is predisposed towards at least some engagement with subjectivity as a feature of measuring penal severity, and this subjectivity can enable us to rethink the fundamentals of what makes two cases 'alike' in the first place.

In short, parsimony is intuitively appealing but lacks essential features of other limiting factors when deployed alone, and suffers from much of the rhetorical contingency and fuzziness around the edges that proportionality can fall into.

C. Clemency and Forgiveness: The Quality of Mercy

The concepts of mercy, clemency, and forgiveness are closely interrelated in terms of the values they uphold and their essential outlook on the nature of (penal) politics. However, insofar as they tend to limit penal severity, we ought to recognise their differences, which have considerable practical impact. Let us specifically discuss: the ancient role of *executive clemency* as a specific mechanism for showing mercy by mediating judicial harshness; the more structured role of *mercy* as a basis for mitigation during sentencing; and Lacey and Pickard's more recent attempt to radically recalibrate the notion of criminal justice around *forgiveness*.

The age-old prerogative of clemency entitles the executive to amend the sentences imposed upon offenders by the judiciary in the name of basic humanity, on the (usually extreme) facts of individual cases that legal rules are ill-equipped to

[35] Ibid, pp 384–386; Norval Morris and Michael Tonry, *Between Prison and Probation: Intermediate Punishments in a Rational Sentencing System* (1990, Oxford University Press), pp 168–173.

[36] See generally Frase, above n 34, p 383–385.

[37] See also Esther van Ginneken and David Hayes, '"Just" Punishment? Offenders' Views on the Definition and Severity of Punishment' (2017) 17 *Criminology & Criminal Justice* 62, pp 63–65.

[38] Ibid; see also Hayes, 'Proximity, Pain and State Punishment', above n 18.

engage with.[39] Clemency is an important means, firstly, of mediating the harshness of the law where judicial discretion is limited. Probably the most famous example of this form of clemency is the English case of Dudley and Stephens, in which two shipwrecked sailors killed and ate a cabin boy in order to survive, and whose mandatory death sentences were commuted to short prison terms in recognition of their exceptional circumstances.[40] Secondly, executive clemency can be used to reflect changes in the conditions of punishment, for instance where a prisoner becomes terminally ill and seeks early release on compassionate grounds. Just such an invocation of executive clemency motivated the Scottish Government's release (and extradition back to Libya) of Abdelbaset al-Megrahi, the Lockerbie bomber, after his diagnosis with terminal cancer. The then-Minister of Justice, Kenny MacAskill, provided a robust (if rhetorical) defence of clemency, even for mass murderers:[41]

> Mr Al Megrahi did not show his victims any comfort or compassion. […] But that alone is not a reason for us to deny compassion to him and his family in his dying days. Our justice system demands that judgment be imposed but that compassion should be available. Our beliefs dictate that justice be served, but mercy be shown. Compassion and mercy are about upholding the beliefs we seek to live by, remaining true to our values as a people.

If criminal justice is about saying that we, as a polity, are *better* than criminal wrongdoing (although not necessarily that we are morally superior to criminal wrongdo*ers*) then we must put our money where our mouth is, in other words. We must stand by the principles and values of a liberal democracy, which include minimum compassion for and recognition of other citizens (which, in this case, includes al-Megrahi as a non-citizen subject of Scottish power). To stand by these principles demands rigorous adherence by the State (or polity) to its own values, and systemic channels for doing so. Executive clemency fills this role in cases where there is an extraordinary change in circumstances, since criminal law lacks 'the quality of mercy' that equity brings to the private law.[42]

The limitations of executive clemency as a vehicle for penal restraint stem from its discretionary character. It falls outside the formal criminal justice system, and is dependent upon the support of a politician whose ministerial position is ultimately subject to public attitudes. It is not to be trusted robustly as a means of securing penal minimalism, because it can therefore only support penal minimalism if the public are in favour of a small and fairly distributed penal State to begin

[39] See generally Andrew Novak, *Comparative Executive Clemency: The Constitutional Pardon Power and the Prerogative of Mercy in Global Perspective* (2016, Routledge).

[40] *R v Dudley and Stephens* (1884) 14 QBD 273; see generally AWB Simpson, *Cannibalism and the Common Law* (1984, University of Chicago Press).

[41] Kenny MacAskill, *Decisions on the Applications for Prisoner Transfer and Compassionate Release in Relation to Abdelbaset Ali Mohamed Al-Megrahi*, Website of the Scottish Government, 20 August, 2009. Available online at: www.gov.scot/News/Speeches/Speeches/Safer-and-stronger/lockerbiedecision.

[42] See Stephen Cohen, '"The Quality of Mercy": Law, Equity, and Ideology in *The Merchant of Venice*' (1994) 27 *Mosaic* 35.

with. As a result, even at the best of times executive clemency has tended to have relatively little effect on the size and shape of the penal system overall.

More substantial and consistent is the role of *mercy* in the mitigation of sentences by judges. Mercy can play an important role in the 'personal mitigation' of sentences, that is, the reduction of the sentence given on account of the personal characteristics of the penal subject rather than the nature of the offence. For instance, an offender whose offence is close to the custody threshold, and who is therefore only just deserving of a prison sentence, may be given a non-custodial sentence because of a bereavement, or an emerging health problem, or some other grounds for staying the usual operation of justice.[43] The exact range of factors that can mitigate a sentence are up for debate: we might include the remorse of the offender, for instance, particularly when backed up with attempts at reparation or other acts of (secular) penance.[44] We might also take account of some of the collateral consequences of punishment, such as the loss of one's job, one's home, one's friends, or one's family – as well as the indirect effects on those other groups more generally.[45] Finally, we might consider some of the criminogenic causes of crime as potential grounds for mitigation, such as intoxication or poverty.[46] However, each of these possibilities is contentious, and open to debate. The English sentencing guidelines system take a particularly narrow approach in this sense, since they distance the question of aggravation and (personal) mitigation from the proportionality equation: the judge must first identify the harm and culpability caused by the offence and *only then*, once the upper and lower limits of the sentencing range have already been set, can questions of personal mitigation be considered.[47]

In all of these examples, mercy has been used to dull the edge of a (predominantly) retributive system. As a result, its role is necessarily small, bounded, and more or less exceptional. However much it is provided for in sentencing procedures, not every offender is going to raise factors that encourage mercy, and to the extent that they do, the ability of the sentencing authority to be lenient is bounded by the requirements of the proportionality principle. Mercy is also compatible with parsimony – indeed, Morris describes that principle as humanitarian as well as utilitarian because it creates room for mercy as well as culpability judgments to

[43] See generally Jessica Jacobson and Mike Hough, 'Personal Mitigation: An Empirical Analysis in England and Wales', in: Julian Roberts (ed), *Mitigation and Aggravation at Sentencing* (2011, Cambridge University Press).

[44] See generally Hannah Maslen, *Remorse, Penal Theory and Sentencing* (2015, Hart); compare Doug Husak, '"Already Punished Enough"' (1990) 18 *Philosophical Topics* 79.

[45] Recall Richard Lippke, 'Punishment Drift: The Spread of Penal Harm and What We Should Do About It' (2017) 11 *Criminal Law and Philosophy* 645.

[46] See respectively Nicola Padfield, 'Intoxication as a Sentencing Factor: Mitigation or Aggravation?', in: Julian Roberts (ed), *Mitigation and Aggravation at Sentencing* (2011, Cambridge University Press); William Heffernan and John Kleinig (eds), *From Social Justice to Criminal Justice: Poverty and the Administration of Criminal Law* (2000, Oxford University Press).

[47] See generally Andrew Ashworth and Julian Roberts (eds), *Sentencing Guidelines: Exploring the English Model* (2013, Oxford University Press).

be made.[48] However, the ability of mercy to mitigate a parsimonious sentence is inevitably limited by the utilitarian component: it is the least necessary intervention *to achieve the overall aims of sentencing*, and so mercy is always competing with the need to achieve the goods one is trying to achieve. On its own, mercy is simply the recognition of a basis to hold back from what is deserved (or needed), and for that reason must always be an external limit on punishment.[49] If mercy is all we have to argue for penal minimalism, then it will either only affect some cases (possibly only a minority of cases) in which we have *reason* to be merciful; or it is an argument against punishment as a whole. If mercy were the only factor in play, we would never punish at all: it is hard to think of harm (and pain) infliction as a way of being merciful.[50] For that reason, as a limit on punishment, the quality of mercy is always ephemeral. It must face the challenges of externality discussed above, and is unlikely to have a sustained limiting effect at the aggregate level on its own.

This is exactly how Lacey and Pickard's reconstitution of punishment around *forgiveness* differs from mercy in mitigation. Their argument is that criminal justice, by its very structuration around liability and punishment, encourages us to blame but stifles our equally inherent capacity to forgive criminal wrongdoing at the State level. Blaming is a useful psychological response to wrongdoing as it helps castigate and ultimately remove group members whose presence endangers the group's survival. However, forgiveness is an equally (or perhaps even more) important response, because without it, blame would lead to atomisation and the failure of the group as a cohesive unit. Blame is condemnatory, retrospective, and reinforces social values, whereas forgiveness can encourage the wrongdoer to make reparation, while also abandoning negative emotions and recriminations that might have a long-term disruptive effect on group stability. The privileging of blaming over forgiveness within contemporary criminal justice systems is therefore problematic, because it creates a disintegrative and unduly stigmatising system of pain imposed for its own sake.[51]

We should not, therefore, make forgiveness dependent on prior punishment (as in Duff's secular penance model), but 'punish *with* forgiveness – [foreswearing] vengeance and affective blame *in* punishment, not just afterwards'.[52] Lacey and Pickard offer two justifications for this conclusion. Firstly they argue that morally *blaming* someone is distinct from *holding them formally responsible*. This should not be a troubling proposition. In private law, I can be responsible for causing a loss to the claimant, even if I am not morally blameworthy for *causing* that loss. I might have morally discharged my duties but still nevertheless bear *legal* liability.

[48] Norval Morris, *Madness and the Criminal Law* (1982, University of Chicago Press). See also Frase, 'Sentencing Principles', above n 34, pp 373–375, 380, 383–384.

[49] Maslen, above n 44, pp 120–123; Nicola Lacey and Hanna Pickard, 'To Blame or to Forgive? Reconciling Punishment and Forgiveness in Criminal Justice' (2015) 35 *OJLS* 665, pp 673–675.

[50] Morris, *Madness and the Criminal Law*, above n 48, p 180.

[51] See Lacey and Pickard, 'To Blame or to Forgive?' above n 49, pp 672–684.

[52] Ibid, p 678.

From here, secondly, Lacey and Pickard adopt a conception of responsibility used in the context of misbehaviour in clinical psychiatric settings. Blaming may be unnecessary or even impossible in this context: because of the mental capacity of group members, for example. It can also frustrate efforts towards therapeutic change, by encouraging the blamed patient to become resentful, or by stigmatising the blamed patient from other patients' and the therapist's perspective. Against this backdrop, and given the need to prevent misconduct from derailing group therapy, responsibility is conceived of as a capacity to change one's behaviour, and an accountability for it, without any associated moral demand that one should be thought less of if one fails to do so. In short, responsibility is a cognitive capacity, and blame is only one moral response to that capacity.[53]

Although there is much to commend Lacey and Pickard's distinction between moral blame and legal responsibility, I am deeply uncomfortable with their conclusions. Some of my problems arise from the paternalistic analogy of prisoners with clinical patients, in a way that downplays penal subjects' autonomy and reifies the distorted shape of the penal system as an inevitable feature of criminal justice. Lacey and Pickard assume that the over-representation of mental health difficulties and other forms of social marginalisation amongst the penal population is inevitable, ignoring other offenders from privileged backgrounds, such as tax evaders and white-collar fraudsters.[54] But more importantly, and substantially, I am concerned with the limits of their imagination. What Lacey and Pickard derive from this radical re-imagination of the *basis* of punishment is plainly little different from the modes and institutions of the status quo. They propose to re-evaluate punishment as the imposition of 'consequences – no doubt typically negative but occasionally not, so long as they are serious and appropriate to the crime and the context',[55] instead of hard treatment or retaliatory costs. Careful readers of previous chapters will have foreseen my disquiet about the euphemism involved in this recasting of hard treatment as 'consequences'. This change in rhetoric downplays and fundamentally quiets concerns about the pains and harms of punishment in favour of their reparative and reformative consequences, just as the treatment model and more managerial conceptions of rehabilitation have. In this sense their account is a straightforward example of Cohen's 'controltalk' – a means of avoiding rather than confronting the problem of punishment, by pretending that the institutions of rehabilitation and reparation they like in the current penal system (including processes taking place in prisons) can be repurposed with fairly minor changes: the only solution, when the system fails, is more of the same.[56] On one reading,

[53] Ibid, pp 670–672. See generally Nicola Lacey and Hanna Pickard, 'From the Consulting Room to the Court Room? Taking the Clinical Model of Responsibility without Blame into the Legal Realm' (2013) 33 *OJLS* 1.

[54] Recall Barbara Hudson, *Penal Policy and Social Justice* (1993, Macmillan); Barbara Hudson, *Justice through Punishment: A Critique of the 'Justice' Model of Corrections* (1987, Macmillan Education), pp 162–170.

[55] Lacey and Pickard, 'To Blame or to Forgive?', above n 49, p 669.

[56] Cohen, above n 5, pp 273–281.

their account is little more than an attempt to provide new normative support for the treatment model; on a more charitable viewing, it is a rather weak version of restorative justice through the criminal justice system that suffers the pitfalls of weak restorative justice, discussed in Chapter 4. Indeed, it is not clear to me why, given their rejection of the blaming penal State, they do not engage with the (strong) restorative justice movement as a way of trying to change the institutional and normative structure of criminal justice in favour of a human confrontation of the stakeholders with one another and the rupture caused by the offence. That would seem to be a better means of achieving their wider goals, although it would be subject to the limitations of a strong restorative account discussed above.

Moreover, Lacey and Pickard's account runs afoul of more conceptual issues about the role of the State in expressing forgiveness, as opposed to blame. Just because both blame and forgiveness are essential human responses to serious norm violations, it does not follow that the artificial gestalt that we call the State is best placed to offer normatively satisfying versions of both. I am not at all sure that the State *can* forgive a wrongdoer in the same way that they can express blame towards them on their citizens' behalf. Importantly, Lacey and Pickard accept that the State's forgiveness cannot and should not replace (or force) the victim's forgiveness of the wrongdoer,[57] but they do not go quite far enough. On the orthodox, blame-based account, a crime is a *public* wrong – not just the concern of the victim, but of society as a whole. The State steps in to punish that wrong, according to this approach, to ensure that the individual is held responsible, to ensure that justice is done.[58] In practice, however, criminal punishment also played an important role in the historical replacement of private revenge with centralised State justice. By making the crime into an offence against the medieval 'King's Peace', the nascent English State not only claimed a great deal of political power from the regional level, but also sought to supplant disruptive traditions of private revenge and vendetta.[59] So while we can attach a certain normative value to the State's vicarious blaming of the subject (for breaches of a democratic social contract, rather than a monarchical King's Peace), there is also a political purpose at play: to avoid the costly bloodshed and unfairness of vigilantism and vendetta. In Lacey and Pickard's terms, the State is blaming, but in blaming seeks to attach fewer negative consequences *to* that blame than private revenge would, in order to defuse and disarm the private desire for revenge.[60] Victims and private citizens may not feel that *enough* blame has been attached in individual cases, but in most cases they accept that *enough* justice has been done to mollify their desire for revenge.

[57] Lacey and Pickard, 'To Blame or to Forgive?' above n 49, p 677, fn 38.

[58] See, eg, Ambrose Lee, 'Public Wrongs and the Criminal Law' (2015) 9 *Criminal Law and Philosophy* 155.

[59] See generally Marc Bloch, *Feudal Society, vol. 2: Social Classes and Political Organisation* (1964, Routledge), pp. 408–437; compare Home Office, *Crime, Justice and Protecting the Public: The Government's Proposals for Legislation* (1990, The Stationery Office, Cm 965), [2.4].

[60] See also John Hostettler, *A History of Criminal Justice in England and Wales* (2009, Waterside Press), pp 13–17.

But it makes no sense to say of me (as a victim or a third party) that I accept the partial forgiveness offered by the State as enough to satisfy my own urge to forgive. The State may call someone to moral account on my behalf but it does not (as Lacey and Pickard accept) forgive on my account. Moreover, the State itself cannot actually forgive – it is an aggregate institution and has no inherent emotional reaction of its own.[61] So what is it doing, besides trying to express forgiveness as a rationale that the public *should* embrace? The State has no good reason to act as an intermediary for forgiveness in the same way that it currently monopolises blame. It can certainly facilitate *opportunities* to forgive, but it is not clear that existing criminal justice institutions are a good way to do this. Restorative processes, again, offer a better mode for pursuing forgiveness rationales in punishment, by bringing the victim, offender, and community into direct contact, without such intrusive State mediation. In so doing, they offer a framework for (actual or potential) forgiveness[62] and reintegration, which avoids the historical authoritarianism and abstraction of the contemporary criminal justice system. However, as we discussed in Chapter 4, this is not an effective short-term means of limiting penal excess.

To sum up, forgiveness, like mercy and clemency, offers strong humanitarian support for mitigating penal harshness, and there must be some room for it in the system. But it is better conceived of as mercy in individual cases than as a raison d'être for the apportionment of punishment. Accordingly, it cannot have much of an independent effect, although it can add additional rationales for at least penal moderation in particular cases – so long as the sentencing authority is already predisposed to recognise the subject as *deserving* of mercy. This is a comparatively small effect on penal severity, in the aggregate, but within existing criminal justice institutions there is not much room for much more. That said, in more radical, long-term alterations of the penal landscape, we might find better ways of institutionalising forgiveness as a State (or post-State) institutional rationale – as a reason for avoiding pain infliction altogether, or as a justification for causing less pain overall.[63]

D. Human Dignity: Hard Lines and Blurred Boundaries

Human dignity is an entrenched value of liberal political philosophy, post-Kant.[64] Respecting the inherent capacity of the individual for moral autonomy is also more practically important in national and international legal regimes, however, following the advent of *international human rights law*, which (typically) relies

[61] Lacey and Pickard, 'To Blame or to Forgive?' above n 49, pp 683–684.
[62] See Joanna Shapland, 'Forgiveness and Restorative Justice: Is It Necessary? Is It Helpful?' (2016) 5 *Oxford Journal of Law and Religion* 94.
[63] See Nils Christie, *Limits to Pain: The Role of Punishment in Penal Policy* (1982, Martin Robinson), p 11.
[64] Recall Immanuel Kant, *Groundwork for the Metaphysics of Morals*, Revised edn (2012, Mary Gregor and Jens Timmerman (trans); Jens Timmerman (ed), Cambridge University Press), pp 45–48.

upon the defence of respect for human dignity as a core ideological tenet.[65] So, whether for principled or practical reasons, English criminal justice must confront the conception of human beings as innately *dignified*: that there is something intrinsically valuable about human beings that grants them the right to freedom and self-determination, up to the point where the exercise of those freedoms intrude on the ability of others to exercise their own.[66] We ought, therefore, never to do anything that fails to respect an individual's capacity for self-determination, autonomous moral decision-making, and personal growth (what is sometimes called 'human flourishing' or the 'pursuit of happiness').[67] In practice, respect for human dignity has a range of moral and legal implications, embodied in individual fundamental rights that may have an impact upon the operation of the criminal justice system. Specific examples include the right to life, to freedom from torture and slavery, to a fair trial, to non-retroactive criminal liability, and to the judicial determination and oversight of any deprivation of liberty.[68]

The general impact of the human rights agenda on criminal punishment has been threefold.[69] Firstly, human rights regimes have identified *modes* of punishment so offensive to human dignity that they ought never to be used by rights-respecting States. Examples in modern penal discourse include the (ongoing) international campaign to abolish capital punishment,[70] and the more successful prohibitions (at least, in the global West) on corporal punishment,[71] and on removing citizenship where it would leave the punished offender stateless.[72] In this context, human dignity has also been invoked in its own right as a reason to abhor certain modes of punishment – certainly on the part of pre-human rights era advocates of prison reform.[73]

[65] See generally Jürgen Habermas, 'The Concept of Human Dignity and the Realistic Utopia of Human Rights' (2010) 41 *Metaphilosophy* 464; AWB Simpson, *Human Rights and the End of Empire: Britain and the Genesis of the European Convention* (2001, Oxford University Press).

[66] Kant, above n 64, pp 56–62.

[67] On the former, see, eg, Richard Arneson, 'Human Flourishing Versus Desire Satisfaction' (1999) 16 *Social Policy and Philosophy* 113. On the latter, see, eg, Patrick Charles, 'Restoring "Life, Liberty, and the Pursuit of Happiness" in Our Constitutional Jurisprudence: An Exercise in Legal History' (2011) 20 *William and Mary Bill of Rights Journal* 457, especially pp 470–477.

[68] See, eg, respectively: Arts 2, 3–4, 6, 7, and 5(4) of the European Convention on Human Rights 1950.

[69] See generally Dirk van Zyl Smit, 'Punishment and Human Rights', in: Jonathan Simon and Richard Sparks (eds), *The SAGE Handbook of Punishment and Society* (2013, SAGE).

[70] Ibid, pp 398–402; see also William Schabas, *The Abolition of the Death Penalty in International Law*, Third edn (2002, Cambridge University Press), ch 7. On the difficult and attenuated role of human dignity in the abortive moratorium on capital punishment in the US, see generally David Garland, *Peculiar Institution: America's Death Penalty in an Age of Abolition* (2010, The Belknap Press), especially ch 8.

[71] See, eg, Application No 5856/72 *Tyrer v United Kingdom* (1978) 2 EHRR 1, 25 April 1978.

[72] See generally Shai Lavi, 'Revocation of Citizenship as Punishment: On the Modern Duties of Citizens and their Criminal Breach' (2011) 61 *University of Toronto Law Review* 783; Michelle Foster and Hélène Lambert, 'Statelessness as a Human Rights Issue: A Concept Whose Time Has Come' (2016) 28 *International Journal of Refugee Law* 564; compare Sandra Mantu, '"Terrorist" Citizens and the Human Right to Nationality' (2018) 26 *Journal of Contemporary European Studies* 28.

[73] See generally Michael Ignatieff, 'State, Civil Society, and Total Institutions: A Critique of Recent Social Histories of Punishment' (1981) 3 *Crime & Justice* 153. See also: John Howard, *The State of the*

Secondly, human rights have encouraged reductions in penal severity by specifying limits on *how* punishment can be imposed. Principal amongst these are procedural requirements about the *legality* and *non-retroactivity* of crimes and mechanisms for their punishment, and their overall *proportionality* as responses to a legitimate aim (to use the language of European human rights law).[74] However, human rights law also has something to say about the proper limits of *criminalisation* – although its impact here is mixed. On the one hand, human rights law acts as a 'shield' against undue interventions into one's private sphere by defending key opportunities to act in certain ways from absolute prohibitions.[75] The concept of human dignity also provides an argument for rationalising and simplifying the law, reducing the number of different offences available, and expressing the language of the law more straightforwardly, to enable lay readers to better understand (and so act upon) the legal limits placed around their free behaviour.[76] On the other, however, human rights law also requires the creation of protective criminal laws, to discharge States' positive duties to protect their subjects' human rights.[77] Human rights law must inevitably balance multiple rights-holders' interests, including the interests of actual or potential victims of crime – and so human dignity is not straightforwardly a decriminalising influence.[78] From the perspective of *over*-criminalisation, however, its rhetorical force is more towards the limited penal State rather than the excessive one, if only because it tends to mirror the broader liberal pursuit of penal minimalism. It follows that a robust commitment to respect for human dignity would tend to resist over-criminalisation, as well as supporting the sort of due process requirements that would lead to unfair, illegitimate, and excessive punishment more generally.

Thirdly, human rights law sets limits on the *nature* of those modes of punishment that remain permissible in principle.[79] In quantitative terms, human rights norms provide a strong argument against extremely long sentences. This can lead

Prisons in England and Wales: With Preliminary Observations and an Account of Some Foreign Prisons, Second edn (1784, Cambridge University Press); Charles Dickens, *American Notes for General Circulation, Volume One* (1842, Cambridge University Press), pp 231–268; Charles Dickens, 'Mr Charles Dickens and the Execution of the Mannings,' *The Times*, 13 November 1849. Collected in: Georgina Hogarth and Mamie Dickens (eds), *Letters of Charles Dickens, Book II: 1843–1857* (1893, Cambridge University Press).

[74] van Zyl Smit, above n 69, pp 403–406.

[75] See Françoise Tulkens, 'The Paradoxical Relationship between Criminal Law and Human Rights' (2011) 9 *Journal of International Criminal Justice* 577, pp 579–582; Miriam Gur-Ayre, 'Human Dignity of "Offenders": A Limitation on Substantive Criminal Law' (2012) 6 *Criminal Law and Philosophy* 187. Compare Andrew Ashworth, 'A Decade of Human Rights in Criminal Justice' [2014] *Crim LR* 325.

[76] See Kim Stevenson and Candida Harris, 'Breaking the Thrall of Ambiguity: Simplification (Of the Criminal Law) as an Emerging Human Rights Imperative' (2010) 74 *Journal of Criminal Law* 516.

[77] See Tulkens, above n 75, pp 582–587; Tatjana Hörnle, 'Criminalizing Behaviour to Protect Human Dignity' (2012) 6 *Criminal Law and Philosophy* 307; John Kleinig, 'Paternalism and Human Dignity' (2017) 11 *Criminal Law and Philosophy* 19.

[78] See, eg, Andrew Ashworth and Mike Redmayne, *The Criminal Process*, Fourth edn (2010, Oxford University Press), ch 2; Andrew Sanders, Richard Young, and Mary Burton, *Criminal Justice*, Fourth edn (2010, Oxford University Press), ch 1.

[79] See van Zyl Smit, above n 69, pp 406–411.

to the effective abolition of certain punishments, such as life imprisonment (with or without parole), which seems to be a possible direction for future European human rights jurisprudence.[80] However, human dignity also provides an independent argument against *grossly* disproportionate sentences in its own right, since these sentences treat their subjects wholly as ends of penal objectives, without respecting their autonomy by focussing on the character of their actions.[81] In both cases, sentences of undue *duration* can have an unacceptable impact upon the dignity of the offender, and ought to be avoided. Moreover, human rights norms impose qualitative limits on the nature of modes of punishment in practice. In prison, this includes the *regime* to which one is subjected, including the architecture, hygiene, and provision of good food and clothing, access to work (and rehabilitation), contact with the outside world to maintain family and friendship relationships, and fair treatment by prison officers (including during disciplinary proceedings).[82] Equivalent provisions for minimum rules in non-custodial penalties also create minimum expectations about fairness, transparency, and the intrusiveness of orders taking place beyond prison walls.[83] These rules aim to ensure a basic level of decency in punishment against the inherently coercive nature of the penal State.

In each of these cases, human dignity provides a purely macro-level account that prohibits certain forms of punishment in certain contexts, and that requires certain legal impositions *on* judicial sentencing, rather than providing any detailed guidance on the sentencing of individual cases. Human rights and human dignity offer powerful rhetorical and ideological incentives for democratic institutions to resist the 'tyranny of the majority', where it might encourage penal excess in the overall institutional structuring of the penal system,[84] but they also offer political reasons for potentially sceptical individuals to accept the importance of respecting the human dignity of (even very serious) offenders, too.[85] Human dignity, after all, is not a zero-sum game, even in the aftermath of a crime that displays contempt for the victim's dignity. Certainly two individuals' human rights *can* be in conflict,[86]

[80] See ibid, pp 402–403; Dirk van Zyl Smit and Catherine Appleton (eds), *Life Imprisonment and Human Rights* (2016, Hart); Dirk van Zyl Smit and Catherine Appleton, *Life Imprisonment: A Global Human Rights Analysis* (2019, Harvard University Press).

[81] See Dirk van Zyl Smit and Andrew Ashworth, 'Disproportionate Sentences as Human Rights Violations' (2004) 67 *MLR* 541.

[82] See generally Dirk van Zyl Smit and Sonja Snacken, *Principles of European Prison Law and Policy: Penology and Human Rights* (2009, Oxford University Press).

[83] See, eg, Recommendation CM/Rec(2017) 3 of the Council of Ministers *on the European Rules on Community Sanctions and Measures*, 23 March 2017; and the United Nations *Standard Minimum Rules for Non-Custodial Measures ('The Tokyo Rules')*, adopted by UN General Assembly Resolution 45/110, 14 December 1990.

[84] Sonja Snacken, 'Resisting Punitiveness in Europe?' (2010) 14 *Theoretical Criminology* 273; Sonja Snacken, 'Punishment, Legitimacy, and the Role of the State: Reimagining More Moderate Penal Policies', in: Stephen Farrall et al (eds), *Justice and Penal Reform: Re-Inventing the Penal Landscape* (2016, Routledge).

[85] See Sonja Snacken, 'Punishment, Legitimate Policies and Values: Penal Moderation, Dignity and Human Rights' (2015) 17 *Punishment & Society* 397.

[86] See especially App No 6538/74 *Sunday Times v UK* (1979) 2 EHRR 245, 26 April 1979.

but there is no intrinsic reason that they inevitably should be. In particular, although an offender's crime has violated some interest (and potentially, one or more of the human rights) of the victim/s, that does not automatically mean that each of the victim's rights are *in conflict* with each of the offender's. Why should the demeaning of the victim be affected in any way by the degradation of the offender? Reasons can be found, but the argument for a minimum standard of decency in criminal justice is made strongly, and the burden of proof shifted to those who wish to remove or deny rights.[87]

However, it is harder to pin down the role of human dignity in limiting severity *in individual cases*. There will always be hard cases demanding guidance at the level of individual cases, and overall the concept of human dignity tends to be too imprecise to specify that a sentence of mode x and duration of n days is acceptable, but that $n + 1$ days of x would not be. To do this, it must rely upon other limiting factors. Where it has set standards for dealing with individual cases above, notice that it tends to fall back on *proportionality* judgements. Indeed, human dignity frequently only provides a protection against *grossly* disproportionate sentences – a weaker standard than the proportionality principle itself demands.[88] Moreover, the declaration that a mode of punishment is not, of itself, incompatible with respecting human dignity, tends to reinforce the moral credentials of that punishment in practice. This is exactly what happened in the US's brief flirtation with death penalty abolition: because the majority of judges in *Furman* were not prepared to declare that capital punishment is *intrinsically* cruel and unusual (in the language of the US Constitution's Eighth Amendment), this left the door open in *Gregg* to say that relatively minor changes to the use and form of capital punishment meant that it was now compatible with US fundamental rights.[89] It was reified as *potentially acceptable* in *Furman*, which forced the discourse to consider the possibility that it could potentially continue. So the hard lines set by dignity concerns in punishment can have some distinctly fuzzy boundaries in practice, and their rhetorical force is not necessarily always in the direction of abandoning modes of punishment.[90]

The ability of rhetorical commitment to human dignity to support penal minimalism, in short, is limited at both an institutional and a discursive level. It can be a useful ally in the fight for penal minimalism, but it must be approached as a contingent one. At first glance it sets hard lines between permissible and impermissible punishments, but in difficult cases it offers little practical guidance on the fine details of acceptable sentencing, and it is itself an inevitably contingent

[87] See generally Deborah Drake and Andrew Henley, '"Victims" Versus "Offenders" in British Political Discourse: The Construction of a False Dichotomy' (2014) 53 *The Howard Journal of Crime and Justice* 141; Richard Jones, 'Populist Leniency, Crime Control and Due Process' (2010) 14 *Theoretical Criminology* 331.

[88] Recall van Zyl Smit and Ashworth, n 81.

[89] See *Furman v Georgia* 408 US 238 (1972); *Gregg v Georgia* 428 US 153 (1976); and see generally Garland, *Peculiar Institution*, above n 70, especially ch 8.

[90] Compare, eg, RA Duff, *Punishment, Communication, and Community* (2001, Oxford University Press), pp 152–155.

concept. This does not mean that dignity is a worthless concept, for a penal minimalist, or in general. It is *limited*, not defunct, and we do not need to disregard it, so long as we keep its limitations in mind.[91]

E. Solidarity: Conservative and Radical Commonality

The rhetorical and normative pursuit of respect for human dignity assumes a fairly objective basis for respecting and defending the interests of penal subjects. It asks us only to *respect* one another; we do not have to actually like each other! In that respect, it is straightforwardly liberal, preferring mere toleration to the pursuit of strong ties of affection and agreement as such.[92] *Solidarity*, by contrast, provides a subjective rationale for minimal intervention, based upon acceptance of the offender as someone worth caring about, in spite of their crime. As a concept, solidarity is rather nebulous, but at a minimum it refers to the tendency of something (a social group, community, or organisation) to remain cohesive and coherent. It implies a sense of unity, of fellow-feeling with other members of a grouping. Although it is therefore associated with communitarian and social-democratic movements in general, and with policies around the alleviation of social injustice in particular,[93] solidarity is an essentially apolitical aspect of any effective human community, which is reflected by the essentially (small-c) conservative role it plays in Durkheim's penology. We discussed Durkheim's conception of solidarity in Chapter 1, but for clarity's sake a brief restatement may be useful here. Durkheim distinguishes between *mechanical* and *organic* solidarity. The former arises out of ties of direct commonality to fellow group-members, reflecting shared values produced by relatively proximate social conditions, and reproduced by rituals, traditions, and relatively straightforward communal norms. The latter is the result of interdependence *between* different socioeconomic groups, and reflects a tendency to rely upon different communities in more complex societies, without the necessary shared ties of common values, rituals, or socio-cultural proximity. Although it is therefore more fragile, it is capable of achieving more complex and productive social relationships overall.[94]

Understood in this sense, solidarity calls for punishment, which on Durkheim's accounts serves to reflect, reiterate, and reinforce socially agreed values.[95]

[91] See Tarunabh Khaitan, 'Dignity as an Expressive Norm: Neither Vacuous nor a Panacea' (2012) 32 *OJLS* 1; Jukka Varelius, 'Two Challenges for Dignity as an Expressive Norm' (2012) 6 *Criminal Law and Philosophy* 327.

[92] See generally John Gray, *Two Faces of Liberalism* (2001, Oxford University Press); compare Henrique Carvalho, 'Liberty and Insecurity in the Criminal Law: Lessons from Thomas Hobbes' (2017) 11 *Criminal Law and Philosophy* 249.

[93] See, eg, Tim Horton and James Gregory, *The Solidarity Society: Why We Can Afford to End Poverty, and How to Do It with Public Support* (2009, Fabian Society).

[94] See generally Émile Durkheim, *The Division of Labor within Society* (1984, WD Halls (trans), Macmillan), pp 31–87.

[95] Ibid; see also Émile Durkheim; TA Jones and Andrew Scull (trans), 'Two Laws of Penal Evolution' (1973) 2 *Economy and Society* 285.

However, for this reason it provides a poor justification for the full range of crimes that currently exist in jurisdictions like England and Wales, especially purely regulatory offences that do not obviously breach socially-shared values. A commitment to social solidarity also implies procedural safeguards. To feel a sense of solidarity, one must feel that one's interests are respected and upheld by the criminal justice process, both as a victim or fellow-citizen, and as a potential defendant. This requires a commitment to due process and Rule of Law values, notably fair labelling and legal certainty, which limit the interpretation of criminal law and therefore impose some (broad) limits on the size of the penal State.[96] Moreover, as societies develop more organic solidarity, and so become more complex, the need for explicit, formalistic and ritualised punishment to shore up social solidarity decreases, reducing the demand for brutal, gory, or spectacular punishments. Thus, the development of greater and more complex connections has tended historically to reduce the excessiveness expected of the criminal justice system overall, and therefore played a role in limiting the penal State.[97]

However, despite setting some normative limits around the proper uses of the criminal law, Durkheim's solidarity has less to say about the most appropriate amount of punishment; indeed, his model tends to imply that those who commit crimes are effectively outsiders to the community, who cannot by definition be rehabilitated into it.[98] Although it is possible to reconcile Durkheim with some sort of rehabilitation (especially approaches that target the penal subject's moral attitudes) there must be some sort of castigation and harsh treatment of the offender involved.[99] As a result, Durkheim's conception of solidarity is vulnerable to punitive rhetoric, and has a tendency towards social exclusion and the entrenchment of social differences, tensions, and prejudices. It places some minimal limits on the size of the penal State but has little to say about imbalances of shape, and indeed can actively encourage the blooming of the penal State's shadow over already-marginalised groups.[100] Solidarity cannot therefore play a major part in any programme of radical penal reduction, if only because Durkheim's conception of social solidarity is a description of the processes by which the (excessive) status quo preserves itself!

[96] See generally Victor Tadros, 'Fair Labelling and Social Solidarity', in: Lucia Zedner and Julian Roberts (eds), *Principles and Values in Criminal Law and Criminal Justice: Essays in Honour of Andrew Ashworth* (2012, Oxford University Press).

[97] See also Fergus McNeill and Matt Dawson, 'Social Solidarity, Penal Evolution, and Probation' (2014) 54 *British Journal of Criminology* 892.

[98] See David Garland, 'Punishment and Social Solidarity', in Jonathan Simon and Richard Sparks (eds), *The SAGE Handbook of Punishment and Society* (2013, SAGE), pp 28–30.

[99] See ibid, p 31, at fn 21 (p 37) and accompanying text. See also McNeill and Dawson, above n 97; David Garland, *Punishment and Modern Society: A Study in Social Theory* (1990, Clarendon Press), chs 2–3; and Ashley Aubuchon-Rubin, 'Rehabilitating Durkheim: Social Solidarity and Rehabilitation in Eastern State Penitentiary, 1829–1850' (2009) 5 *International Journal of Punishment and Sentencing* 12.

[100] See, eg, Ruth Levitas, 'The Concept of Social Exclusion and the New Durkheimian Hegemony' (1996) 16 *Critical Social Policy* 5; Henrique Carvalho and Anastasia Chamberlen, 'Why Punishment Pleases: Punitive Feelings in a World of Hostile Solidarity' (2018) 20(2) *Punishment & Society* 217–234. Compare John Pratt, *Penal Populism* (2007, Routledge), ch 2.

But Durkheim's is not the only vision of solidarity. The concept is also part of a far more radical tradition of revolutionary politics, in which 'solidarity' is deployed rhetorically to describe the commonality of all humankind, and the implication of a need for revolutionary overturning of hierarchical and exploitative social orders. Thus solidarity is a key rhetorical plank of nineteenth- and twentieth-century communist ideology and political theory (from whence it has become endemic in the language of trade unions), although it is also deployed by conservative and Christian-democratic voices on the centre-right.[101] Solidarity, on this communist-flavoured account, is vital to the pursuit of a fair and just society. It is, for instance, the foundation of Peter Kropotkin's 'mutual aid', a recognition of the shared challenges and experiences that typify human life, which encourages altruism even towards relative strangers.[102] Such a sense of fellow-feeling for all humankind implies a minimum level of socio-political and – economic equality, which Kropotkin treats as the underpinning of any truly just society.[103] While Kropotkin's version of solidarity is one of many in the diverse field of radical political philosophy, it illustrates the extent of a more universal approach to solidarity, from which we can draw lessons as to how we might limit criminal justice within our existing (Statist, capitalist) order – notwithstanding that Kropotkin would reject that order (and its claim to do justice) out of hand![104]

Any such universal account of solidarity would face significant challenges in the context of anything like the contemporary penal system. After all, at least in normative theory, a crime is, in and of itself, an act of non-solidarity with its victims, which inevitably tends to bring moral opprobrium onto its perpetrator in a solidarian society. Especially in the case of more serious offences, criminality inherently symbolises the rejection of the rules of society, and it is very hard to feel solidarity with one who has so explicitly rejected your own values. However contemptible the status quo, however much we might wish to change it, it exists by the tacit or explicit acceptance (however passive and ignorant) of the majority. This does not make the status quo normatively justifiable or even morally good – but it does make a (serious) symbolic rejection of that status quo something that is liable to attract moral reprobation *from that majority*. That response cannot simply be shut off, because it is emotional as well as logical, irrational as well as rational.[105] As a result, labelling criminal offenders as such is liable to attract moral condemnation to them, which gets in the way of building solidarity on a universal basis.[106]

[101] See generally Steinar Stjernø, *Solidarity in Europe: The History of an Idea* (2009, Cambridge University Press).

[102] Peter Kropotkin, *Mutual Aid: A Factor of Evolution*, Third edn (2009, Freedom Press).

[103] See generally Peter Kropotkin, *Ethics: Origin and Development* (1924, Louis Friedland and Joseph Piroshnikoff (trans), Prism Press).

[104] See especially Peter Kropotkin, 'Law and Authority' and Peter Kropotkin, 'Prisons and their Moral Influence on Prisoners', both in: Peter Kropotkin; Roger Baldwin (ed), *Anarchism: A Collection of Revolutionary Writings*, Second edn (2002, Dover Press).

[105] See Rob Canton, 'Crime, Punishment, and the Moral Emotions: Righteous Minds and their Attitudes towards Punishment' (2015) 17 *Punishment & Society* 54; Carvalho and Chamberlen, above n 100.

[106] Compare Michelle Brown, 'Empathy and Punishment' (2012) 14 *Punishment & Society* 383.

However, this is not to say that nothing can be done to encourage greater solidarity within our criminal justice system. As discussed above, there is a conceptual difference between treating offenders as *responsible* and *blaming* them. After all, even if blaming is a natural human response to acts that discourage fellow-feeling, it is not a natural *institutional* response.[107] While I rejected Lacey and Pickard's paternalistic and reifying overtones above, they do raise a forceful broader point: that nothing about the state of the State is inevitable.

One essential feature of contemporary criminal justice that a focus on (penal-minimalist) solidarity could particularly address is its *mass* scale, and the *objective* way in which it represents and characterises criminal offenders. Simply put, modern criminal justice treats offenders as abstract actors shorn of their individual foibles and social context. This is intentional, and aims to ensure fair treatment of individuals and prevent corruption and discrimination, while also ensuring fidelity with wider values such as equality and respect for dignity.[108] However, the result of narrowing down that context and shearing away that individuality is a loss of a basis to recognise human commonality with the offender, and to recognise the longer-term social impact of their punishment on them and those around them.[109] It also risks mischaracterising at least some crimes. Consider the following two homely examples of the closeness of small Norwegian communities, provided by Nils Christie: a man exposes himself in front of some children, but the residents know him well enough to know that he is just an eccentric prone to embarrassing but harmless public urination, and does not pose any risk to the children.[110] A local sheriff recovers a cache of stolen guns that were taken by a local drunk to irritate his father, and treats the whole event as an eruption of a private, family quarrel into public life, rather than a serious risk to community (much less national) security.[111] In these examples, what seem like objectively serious offences (exposure of one's genitals to children; theft of military-grade weapons) are contextualised, but also trivialised, by contact with the local knowledge of the neighbourhood and the community, which provides important mitigating information – in these examples, to the extent that the wrong is not even treated as a crime. Christie's argument is that by knowing more about the context of the offender and the offence, we learn important information about the seriousness of the crime.[112] It can also help to highlight the distended shape of the penal State, reinforcing the regularity with which the already-downtrodden become the targets of criminal justice, and providing normative ammunition for policies pursuing non-penal solutions to social-welfare problems.[113] But this has an impact on our

[107] See Lacey and Pickard, 'To Blame or to Forgive', above n 49, pp 684–688.
[108] See generally William Lucy, *Law's Judgment* (2017, Hart).
[109] See generally Brown, above n 106; Hudson, *Penal Policy and Social Justice*, above n 54.
[110] Nils Christie, *A Suitable Amount of Crime* (2004, Routledge), pp 4–6.
[111] Nils Christie, *Limits to Pain*, above n 63, p 74.
[112] Compare Nils Christie, 'Conflicts as Property' (1977) 17 *British Journal of Criminology* 1.
[113] Nils Christie, 'Afterword: Justice in Modernity', in: Stephen Farrall et al (eds), *Justice and Penal Reform: Re-Shaping the Penal Landscape* (2015, Routledge).

capacity for solidarity, too. If the sex offender is not a conniving sociopath hell-bent on abusing children, but a person with deviant sexual desires over which they may not have any subjective sense of control, we still might not forgive their abuses, but at least we could begin to *understand* them. An explanation is neither a justification nor an excuse, but it can help to identify the human context of both the crime and the punishment, and provide reasons to build fellow-feeling, even with those who have committed awful crimes.[114]

It is important not to overstate this effect. The recognition of humanising contextual factors will not and should not always encourage sympathy with the offender, and will not defeat the sense of moral outrage that (especially the most serious) crimes prompt. Suppose that you discover that yesterday, a loved one sexually molested a young child, in conditions that make it clear that they did not care one jot for that child's consent or wellbeing. It might be possible to understand that crime as a human action, but it would be remarkably hard. More likely your conception of the loved one would change, rather than your understanding of the crime. There are limits to solidarity, especially in the face of atrocity. But then again, most crimes are not atrocities, notwithstanding that they are serious publicly-agreed wrongs. Putting a crime in its social context, and in the light of local knowledge, will not always tend to reduce the amount of blame that attaches to the crime, in other words, but there is reason to believe that it would have that general tendency.[115] Seeing the offender as a socially-situated individual provides a reason for us to treat them as one of 'us', to see their crime as an aberrant act that does not necessarily reveal an abhorrent individual. It enables us to recast the crime as something that we – the offender and the wider community alike – are better than, that we aim to go beyond. In doing so, we would necessarily bind our own hands in punishment – we cannot demonstrate a desire for a better calibre of social activity, after all, if we respond to crime by stooping to its level – for instance, by hurting simply for the sake of hurting someone who has hurt another.

Perhaps you will dismiss this position as morally simplistic, and politically naïve. It presupposes a society that aspires to a certain set of shared moral values and principles. In a society as fundamentally unequal as ours, where greed and selfishness are all but treated as virtues of the new hyper-individualism, it can be hard to find the basis for a shared understanding of what behaviour we are, in my words, 'better than'.[116] Moreover, the allure of 'local knowledge' presupposes that the old community order exists in a state capable of providing that knowledge, at precisely the time when old community ties enabling intimate knowledge of

[114] Compare Barbara Hudson, 'Victims and Offenders', in: Andrew von Hirsch et al (eds), *Restorative Justice and Criminal Justice: Competing or Reconcilable Paradigms?* (2003, Hart).

[115] Compare Vincenzo Ruggiero, *Penal Abolitionism* (2010, Oxford University Press), ch 2.

[116] Compare Jock Young, *The Vertigo of Late Modernity* (2007, SAGE).

one's neighbours are breaking down.[117] In that sense, Christie's localism agenda is more of an argument for why penal minimalists should pursue solidarity than it is for why solidarians should pursue penal minimalism. However, this conception of solidarity does suggest a broad, normative and populist agenda for modifying penal institutions so as to maximise the subjectivity of sentencing decision-making. Doing so would encourage cognitive processes that are alive to, and so capable of taking account of, social contexts liable to encourage empathy, and even sympathy. This is unlikely to substantially change sentencing processes in and of itself, but indirectly the rhetorical and normative impact would be significant, providing a strong political case against penal excess.

II. Conclusion: A 'First Among Equals' Approach to Proportionality?

What emerges from this overview of these principles aiming to limit penal severity is that there are no magic bullets. No one approach guarantees a moderate, let alone a minimal penal State, in theory or in practice. All remain vulnerable to wider socio-political pressures that can encourage penal excess, although each is stronger and weaker than the others in the face of different policy imperatives. It follows that penal minimalists must be realistic about the potential for any one limiting factor to secure the minimal penal State. We must look beyond the abstract realm of intended policy effects, and take account of social context and political culture. Any penal policy perspective must entail a wider vision of what society is, and what it is for. This remains as true for penal minimalists as it does for anyone else.

However, that each limiting factor has strengths and weaknesses does not mean that each is as good as the other. In this section, drawing the discussion above together, I argue that, while proportionality remains inherently limited in its own right, it provides a useful framework for the development of a theoretical approach that at least increases the odds of effectively pursuing penal minimalism in practice. To ensure that those odds are maximised, however, will require engaging with the other limiting factors we have discussed, to varying degrees. In other words, proportionality must be viewed not as being a superior and self-sufficient principle, or as a magic bullet for instant penal minimalism, but rather as a *first among equals* that provides distinctive advantages only when combined with other approaches. To do this, I will explore four key bases of comparison between our five theories, summarised below, in Table Three.

[117] See generally Simon Green, *Crime, Community and Morality* (2014, Routledge); Nicola Lacey and Lucia Zedner, 'Discourses of Community in Criminal Justice' (1995) 22 *Journal of Law and Society* 301.

Table Three Overview of Relative Strengths and Weaknesses of Limiting Factors

	Internal/ External	**Micro/ Macro**	**Fixity & Exactitude**	**Resilience to Punitiveness/ Managerialism**
Proportionality	Internal to specific penal theories	Micro-level only	Fixed but inexact	Moderate/Strong
Parsimony	External	Micro- and macro-level	Fixed but inexact	Strong/Weak
Mercy	External	Micro-level only	Unfixed and inexact	Moderate/Weak
Human Dignity	External	Macro-level only	Unfixed but exact	Moderate
(Radical) Solidarity	External	Macro-level only	Unfixed and inexact	Strong (if pre-existing)

The first basis for comparison is whether the limiting factor in question is *internal* or *external* to the reasoning of the penal theories it forms a component of. As discussed above, only proportionality is an internal principle, and then only to retributive and reparative approaches. The significance of internal limitation is that the limit forms part of the cognitive process of deploying one's penal theory in individual sentencing decisions, whereas an external limit is imposed in conscious opposition to that deployment. While this does not mean that internal limiting principles are always superior, or are somehow immune to overriding factors,[118] internality is an advantage where it is available because it makes the imposition of limits on sentencing decision-making more automatic. As noted above, one cannot be a retributivist without speaking the language of proportionality in sentencing, but one can pursue rehabilitation without equivalent regard for parsimony. Indeed, externalised constraints can actually reify and encourage the intervention that they seek to limit, by providing a normative thin end of the wedge to justify further interventions going forward.[119] Since the justification is external, it is easier to rhetorically sidestep, or do away with entirely, without undermining the intervention's overall aims. As we saw in Chapter 3, there are numerous practical challenges to overcome for internal limiting factors like proportionality, but they at least exert a (weak but substantial) *theoretical* advantage over external constraints.

However, proportionality can only speak to micro-level decisions made in individual sentencing decisions. As a result, it struggles to engage with macro-level

[118] Recall, eg, Padfield, 'Time to Bury the Custody "Threshold"?' n 7.

[119] See generally Carol Steiker, 'Proportionality as a Limit on Preventive Justice', in: Andrew Ashworth, Lucia Zedner, and Patrick Tomlin, *Prevention and the Limits of the Criminal Law* (2013, Oxford University Press), pp 207–213, in a context where proportionality is itself an external limiting factor.

questions affecting the aggregate size and shape of the penal State, particularly where one's model of retributivism calls for every detected guilty person to be punished.[120] Both the big and small pictures are needed in any account that pursues a penal minimalist agenda. We need guiding principles that will discourage unfair or undue treatment of the individual penal subject, *whilst simultaneously* countermanding punitiveness, managerialism, and other policy-level drivers of penal excess in wider policy debates. In this regard, parsimony is the best-placed of our five guiding principles, in that the metaphor of the least necessary intervention works for both the objectives of individual sentences in particular cases, *and* of the overall disposition and makeup of the penal system. However, as we saw, the advantages of parsimony are best pursued only if it is used in conjunction with a (comparatively flexible interpretation of) the proportionality principle, in that it can be hard to pin down precisely what the 'least necessary' intervention is, especially when pursuing prospective goals through the sentence.[121]

Moreover, respect for human dignity and solidarity both reinforce the potential impact of parsimony at the policy level. They have comparatively little guidance in their core content as regards the disposition of individual sentences, but are much more rhetorically and normatively rich as *political* justifications for penal minimalism, in precisely that arena where penal theories have tended to remain quiet, but which is so crucial to the effectiveness of proportionality and parsimony in practice.[122] As a corollary, and as a basic ethical commitment in any penal system claiming to be humane, some room must also be made for mercy (and executive clemency), if only in micro-level judicial personal mitigation. So while parsimony and proportionality can be combined to address the macro- and micro-levels simultaneously, they are further enriched by the other three limiting factors – albeit indirectly and, in the case of mercy, only occasionally.

The third basis for distinction in Table Three concerns two related characteristics that I have called *fixity* and *exactitude*. These describe the level of prescriptiveness that a particular principle has, at the sentencing and the policy levels, respectively. A limiting factor will produce 'fixed' sentences if that factor has clear implications for the severity of sentences in individual cases, and will be 'exact' if it imposes clear limits on the *overall* severity of sentences available to the penal State. So defined, none of our five limiting factors produces sentences that are both fixed and exact. Proportionality faces the problem of 'anchoring' the penal tariff: while it can impose strict limits on whether a sentence is proportionate (or at least, not disproportionate), the question of what the most and least severe sentence available should be is not something that any proportionality principle can determine.[123] For a penal minimalist, therefore, proportionality is limited in that it cannot, of itself, provide a justification for a more moderate (let alone minimal)

[120] Recall Chiao, n 8. Compare Hudson, *Justice through Punishment*, above n 54, pp 162–170.
[121] Recall Lippke, 'Retributive Parsimony', n 23; compare Steiker, above n 119, pp 207–208.
[122] Recall Lacey and Pickard, 'The Chimera of Proportionality', n 19.
[123] Recall von Hirsch, *Censure and Sanctions*, n 10.

anchoring point for the retributive tariff as a whole.[124] Parsimony faces similar problems, insofar as it struggles to internally define what the 'least necessary intervention' is in any consistent, or consistently convincing, way. Human dignity, by contrast, is exact but cannot produce fixed sentences. It imposes (relatively) hard limits on the range of available sentences, which will tend to push the overall range of available sentences down towards less intrusive, harmful and painful penal outcomes. However, dignity has relatively little to say as a principle informing decisions about how much punishment is enough in individual cases.

Finally, both mercy and solidarity are both unfixed and inexact in their effect on sentences. They provide general reasons for leniency and reduction of overall penal severity, but in the case of mercy, the effect only arises in cases where there is a compelling reason *for* mercy to be extended, and in the case of solidarity, there is no inherent guidance in the sense of empathy for and fellow-feeling with penal subjects to say *how much* we should restrain the hand of vengeance. Were we to rely on these principles alone, judges would have good reasons to hold back from excessive punishment, but precious little guidance about how to do so in a consistent or principled way. The questions of fixity and exactitude, then, produce good reasons to embrace some mixture of proportionality, parsimony, and respect for human dignity, but shed little light by themselves about which of these three are best placed to produce the strongest case for penal minimalism.

However, the fourth basis for comparison in Table Three further supports engaging with solidarity concerns. It concerns the susceptibility of a limiting factor to penal policy imperatives that argue in favour of penal excess, and in particular, to punitiveness and penal managerialism. At the end of Chapter 3 I concluded that the desert model's conception of proportionality failed politically because of its vulnerability to wider policy imperatives, in part because of its focus on retrospective acts. This narrowing of the scope of judicial attention enabled other policy imperatives to undermine proportionality as an overall principle in sentencing in English penal policy.[125] However, it remains the case that in individual cases it provides at least some principled defence against managerial aims, insofar as it encourages restraint of preventive and controlling dispositions. Parsimony, again, is weaker as a defence against managerialism, because of its externality and indeterminacy: the 'least necessary' intervention must accept that the rationale of protection *is* necessary in at least some cases, which opens the door as to a 'how much' question that cannot be answered without resorting to political debate. However, parsimony is a stronger argument against punitiveness, insofar as it focuses attention away from punishing what has been done, and towards achieving prospective aims going forward. By speaking in its 'utilitarian and humanitarian' terms,[126] it discourages a merely retaliatory attitude in sentencing authorities and

[124] Recall Honderich, n 10.
[125] See generally Andrew Ashworth, 'Prisons, Proportionality, and Recent Penal History' (2017) 80 *MLR* 473.
[126] Recall Morris, *The Future of Imprisonment*, n 20, p 61.

policy-makers, and so might be expected, when robustly applied in practice, to discourage merely punitive decision-making.

The appeal to mercy can act as a spur against punitiveness but only to an extent, in that not every case will demand mercy. Indeed, a punitive political climate will discourage us from responding to crime with mercy in the first place. The general tendency to see offenders as moral enemies who deserve to suffer disproportionately for their crimes that characterises mere punitiveness can be moderated by conditions that call for mercy, but those conditions will not arise in every case. Moreover, the fewer cases where there are reasons to exhibit mercy, the easier it will be for punitive attitudes towards offenders to harden, with the result that fewer and fewer conditions that encourage mercy are likely to be recognised in the first place.[127] So mercy needs additional support to ensure resilience against punitive attitudes over the longer term, given the tendency of punitiveness to reproduce and aggravate existing tensions between the mainstream and the marginalised.[128] It is also rather weaker in the face of managerialism, which tends towards a dehumanising concern with risk, on the one hand, and to speak in paternalistic terms of the offender's own good, on the other. Mercy, after all, is holding back from the penalty that is deserved in the situation; it is rather harder to speak of being merciful as holding back from delivering what the subject (or society) needs.[129]

Respect for human dignity provides a moderate rhetorical defence against both punitive and managerial rationales in penal policy. However, it is not proof against them, in and of itself, given the susceptibility of the norms it implies to being defined by the specific political pressures of space and time.[130] After all, the modern problems of penal managerialism and punitiveness have emerged over precisely the same period that international human rights law has entered its most expansionist period. Of course, this correlation in no way implies causation (although it may be indicative of trends that are at least partly a backlash *against* human rights jurisprudence).[131] In addition, because of their very (claimed) objectivity, human rights are necessarily abstract, and therefore tend to have relatively unclear implications in the face of necessary public imperatives such as public security and the reduction of risk. That level of abstraction potentially masks the individual challenges faced by offenders, and can obscure the potential difficulties that a penal sanction will create.

This is where solidarity becomes particularly useful. Its primary focus is subjective and individual, producing reasons for empathy and sympathy.

[127] Compare Nicola Lacey, *The Prisoners' Dilemma: Political Economy and Punishment in Contemporary Democracies* (2008, Cambridge University Press), pp 173–185; Jock Young, *The Exclusive Society: Social Exclusion, Crime and Difference in Late Modernity* (1999, SAGE).

[128] Compare Carvalho and Chamberlen, above n 100.

[129] See also Judah Schept, *Progressive Punishment: Job Loss, Jail Growth, and the Neoliberal Logic of Carceral Expansion* (2015, New York University Press).

[130] Recall discussion at nn 88–91 and accompanying text.

[131] See Philip Alston, 'The Populist Challenge to Human Rights' (2017) 9 *Journal of Human Rights Practice* 1.

Under conditions where there is a strong sense of universal solidarity, the punitive urge is blunted by the recognition that there are essential commonalities between the general public and even very serious offenders, which might hold us back from revenge. Moreover, managerialism is also strongly rejected, insofar as a solidarian understanding of criminal offenders creates a more nuanced understanding of the extent to which individuals actually pose a risk, and on what basis. However merely arguing that we *should* recognise our mutual common ground is not enough to force it to be so. Indeed, the sort of universal solidarity imagined by Christian democrats, anarchists, and socialists may only be possible in radically different socio-political and – economic contexts, which is why radical solidarity is usually associated with revolutionary (or at least strongly reformist) politics.[132] It may be that we cannot reach conditions of social solidarity capable of robustly resisting punitiveness and managerialism without profound change in the fabric of our society, economy, and politics. We might well aim to encourage greater solidarity in future, a mission with potentially utopian aims but with realistic short-term prospects.[133] In criminal justice, for example, we might adopt procedures and attitudes that emphasise local knowledge and so increase the possibility of solidarity in individual cases. To the extent that greater social solidarity *did* exist, though, there is reason to believe that it would encourage resilience to the policy drivers of penal excess. This might, for instance, help to explain the much-vaunted 'Scandinavian exceptionalism' – the trend of Nordic countries towards more lenient penal policies (at least for native-born penal subjects).[134]

More generally, the five limiting factors discussed in this chapter can complement each other's weaknesses and maximise each other's strengths. A normative commitment to universal solidarity and to respect for human dignity helps to highlight (albeit not resolve) the challenge of doing 'just deserts in an unjust world', upon which proportionality generally turns its back.[135] Moreover, they help to clarify the aggregate implications of proportionality-based sentencing, to ensure a focus on macro-level concerns in penal policy, and to provide rhetorical and normative grounds for attempting to defend the minimal penal State from expansionist policy imperatives. Binding parsimony to a retributive tariff ensures that the principle with the most restrictive implications in a particular case will always win out, while simultaneously resolving some of the challenges of indeterminacy about what the 'least necessary' (and indeed, 'most fitting') sentence is by imposing

[132] Recall Stjernø, above n 101, ch 2. Compare Simon Critchley, *Infinitely Demanding: Ethics of Commitment, Politics of Resistance* (2012, Verso).

[133] See generally Rutger Bregman, *Utopia for Realists: And How We Can Get There* (2016, Elizabeth Manton (trans), Bloomsbury).

[134] See, eg, John Pratt, 'Scandinavian Exceptionalism in an Era of Penal Excess, Part I: The Nature and Roots of Scandinavian Exceptionalism' (2008) 48 *British Journal of Criminology* 119; Thomas Ugelvik and Jane Dullum (eds), *Penal Exceptionalism? Nordic Penal Policy and Practice* (2012, Routledge).

[135] Recall Michael Tonry, 'Can Deserts Be Just in an Unjust World?', in: AP Simester, Antje du Bois-Pedain, and Ulfrid Neumann (eds), *Liberal Criminal Theory: Essays for Andreas von Hirsch* (2014, Hart); Hudson, *Justice through Punishment* n 54.

two relatively inexact criteria rather than only one. The mercy imperative, by itself relatively unclear and infrequent, provides an important reminder of macro-level humanitarian concerns at the micro-level, and allows us to step back further from penal severity in cases where it does arise as a sentencing factor.

However, while each principle is adding something, it is proportionality that provides the central plank – it clarifies the approach to individual cases, contextualises dignity and solidarity concerns, and prevents parsimony from being carried to extremes by particularly strong instrumental imperatives. The argument for balance and forethought in action implied by the proportionality principle may be politically vulnerable, and it may lack strong meaning without support from surrounding socio-political institutions, but that is not to say that it has *no* effect at the theoretical level as a device for guiding judicial reasoning, independently or in concert with other limiting factors. Treating proportionality as a first among equals, providing essential features but being by itself insufficient to achieve our aim of penal restraint, is therefore the best way forwards for the pursuit of penal minimalism. To return to a metaphor from Chapter 3, if proportionality is a chimera that we have by the tail, then we ought to keep hold of it.

PART III

Confronting Penal Excess

6

Groundwork for a Late Retributivism

In exploring retributivism's troubled pursuit of penal minimalism, I have focussed in detail on the conceptual, empirical, or theoretical context that retributivism commonly skims past, precisely because those oversights undermined the ability of retributive proportionality to confront penal excess. Retributivism's political failings as a vehicle for pursuing penal minimalism arose out of its focus on a narrow range of (sentencing-stage) factors, and its concomitant denial of the importance of social and political issues for the determination of what conduct is classed as criminal and how individuals are brought into the criminal justice system. Any retributive theory that avoids those failures, such as the one I sketch in Chapter 7, will therefore have to be alive to those factors. This implies certain things about the *content* of that theory, which I will explore in Chapter 7. However, implications also arise for the wider *approach* and *structure* of that theory, which we must discuss before laying out that content.

In this chapter, I therefore lay the groundwork for a new, 'late' retributivism, by answering three questions: firstly, what *sort* of a theory am I proposing; secondly, what makes that theory 'late'; and thirdly, why is that theory retributive at all? Having answered these three questions, we will be in a position to distinguish late retributivism from the desert model and other branches of traditional retributive thought, and to identify how those differences will actually make a difference to the pursuit of penal minimalism.

I. What Sort of a Theory?

Retributive penal theory tends to develop either *normative systems* for punishment, or *rational reconstructions* of pre-existing penal institutions. Desert theory is an example of the former: a system of normative defences for the imposition of deserved punishments to express censure.[1] Duff's model falls into the latter camp: it attempts to take seriously the commitments that liberal communities claim to pursue, in order to better understand what those commitments entail.[2]

[1] See especially Andrew von Hirsch, *Censure and Sanctions* (1993, Clarendon Press).

[2] See generally RA Duff, *Punishment, Communication, and Community* (2001, Oxford University Press).

Both approaches take a fundamentally abstract, counterfactual approach to penal theory. They focus on identifying what punishment *should* be, not what it *is*, and on providing justifications for punishment in a hypothetical society, rather than actually existing penal institutions. This is not to say that all penal theory lacks situation. After all, von Hirsch's desert theory is notable for drawing upon the particular problems facing the US penal system during the 1970s and 1980s.[3] Neither is it to say that abstract normative explanations or rational reconstructions are somehow invalid. Abstract theory teaches us to challenge our intuitions and critically re-examine the status quo. It expands the range of questions we can ask about the contemporary penal phenomena, and of the perspectives we can take on them.[4] Nevertheless, abstract theories of criminal justice tend to pay insufficient attention to the realities of the situation in which we actually find ourselves – the circumstances into which the existentialist Martin Heidegger would say we are *thrown*.[5]

Despite the complexity of Heidegger's ontological theory (not to mention his ethical legacy as a seemingly enthusiastic Nazi),[6] 'thrownness' can be explained with a relatively simple, albeit unlikely, metaphor. Imagine that you go to the park, and throw a ball. If that ball then suddenly became self-aware, there would be things it could not change about its existence: it is in motion, receding from a certain point, and facing the inevitability of a final descent back to earth, at speed. For Heidegger, human existence is very much like that of the self-aware ball: we come into awareness of ourselves as finite beings whilst already in motion, with a trajectory determined by the conditions of our childhood before we came into awareness of ourselves *as* ourselves, and indeed, by events before our birth. We cannot change this past, and while the future is partly within our control, to the fullest of our understanding, life only ever ends one way. This means that human existence is inevitably characterised by a 'being-towards-death': an existential challenge of living authentically as a spatially and temporally finite consciousness – a way of being in which one is confronted with the unalterable fact that one day, one will no longer be.[7]

Heidegger used 'thrownness' to explore the challenge of life for individual human beings. But societies and their institutions – including penal institutions – are also thrown. We do not know how human society will end, and – unlike the individual – the end of society is not necessarily inevitable, at least over next few millennia. We might kill our entire species tomorrow, in a nuclear Armageddon,

[3] Andrew von Hirsch, *Doing Justice: The Choice of Punishments* (1976, Hill & Wang).

[4] Compare RA Duff and Stuart Green (eds), 'Introduction: Searching for Foundations', in: RA Duff and Stuart Green (eds), *Philosophical Foundations of Criminal Law* (2011, Oxford University Press).

[5] Martin Heidegger, *Being and Time*, Revised Translation (2010, Joan Stambaugh (trans), Dennis Schmidt (ed), State University of New York Press), pp 131–132, 265–266.

[6] On Heidegger's political context, see generally Richard Wolin, *The Politics of Being: The Political Thought of Martin Heidegger* (1990, Columbia University Press); Rudiger Safranski, *Martin Heidegger: Between Good and Evil* (1998, Ewald Osers (trans), Harvard University Press); Harry Hunt, '"Triumph of the Will": Heidegger's Nazism as Spiritual Pathology' (1998) 19(4) *Journal of Mind and Behavior* 379.

[7] Heidegger, *Being and Time*, above n 5, pp 237–239.

or in the next 100 or 1,000 years through environmental degradation. We might be wiped off the face of the universe by a stray lump of interstellar rock, or by a pandemic virus. *But we might not*. We might reach out into the stars and escape even the consumption of the Earth by the expansion of the Sun. And all of these possibilities are quite beyond the scale of human comprehension. Even if we are dimly aware of the threat of annihilation, it is hard to reconcile that threat with the immediate issues of everyday life – a fact the campaign to limit human-made climate change has been forced to struggle with.[8] Unlike individuals, human societies lack a being-towards-death – and it may end up killing us all.[9]

However, human society *is* thrown in the sense that it has a fixed historical origin, which partly determines its future. While it is true that society only became the way it is through the interaction of specific powerful interests at particular historical moments,[10] rather than out of some inevitable destiny, it is equally true that *it still* is *the way it is*. We are the inheritors of a long history of human struggle, against one another and against a frequently hostile environment. That struggle has shaped our self-image as rational but selfish actors, who are capable of great things but who cannot be trusted without oversight.[11] This view of our essential nature is shaped by conditions of scarcity and competition that have confronted human societies throughout their long history – but it assumes that that untrustworthiness is endemic to human nature, and not *caused* by that struggle for survival, and by the ethics of tribalism and selfishness that it inculcates. The possibility that human nature might be malleable, or at least reactive to profound changes in social and environmental conditions, is the preserve of only the most utopian theories, and is for that reason dismissed as mere wishful thinking.[12] We assume that human rapacity and selfishness are baked into our chromosomes and could not be unlearned in social conditions where competition for scarce resources was not necessary for our individual and collective survival.[13]

Partly in consequence of the assumption that human beings will always need to be governed because they *have* always been governed, and partly because of the real need for governance to preserve minimal social order under conditions of economic scarcity, we are the inheritors of a range of social institutions that are, in and of themselves, troublingly coercive. The history of political reform has generally been one of accommodating, rejecting and replacing, or palliating these troublesome institutions. However, this process is not automatic, not least

[8] See, eg, Naomi Klein, *This Changes Everything: Capitalism vs the Climate* (2014, Simon & Schuster).

[9] See also John Gray, *Straw Dogs: Thoughts on Humans and Other Animals* (2002, Granta Books).

[10] See generally Michel Foucault, *The Order of Things: An Archaeology of the Human Sciences* (1970, Tavistock/Routledge (trans), Routledge); Michel Foucault, *The Archaeology of Knowledge* (1972, AM Sheridan Smith (trans), Routledge).

[11] Thomas Hobbes, *Leviathan*, (1996, JCA Gaskin (trans), Oxford University Press); but compare Peter Kropotkin, *Mutual Aid: A Factor of Evolution*, Third edn (2009, Freedom Press).

[12] See generally Ruth Levitas, *Utopia as Method: The Imaginary Reconstitution of Society*, (2013, Palgrave Macmillan).

[13] See generally Murray Bookchin, *Post-Scarcity Anarchism*, Third edn (2004, AK Press).

because we are used to those institutions in our day-to-day lives, having grown up with them, and because they do actually contribute to social order, and therefore provide some social benefit (despite their social costs). Reform is therefore a constant *agonistic* struggle between those seeking to make principled or pragmatic changes, and those who prefer the old ways.[14]

As a result, penal theorists can engage with the problem of punishment on several levels. They can speak to the problem of punishing *at all*, as a means of securing particular ends under the value system of a particular sort of society (say, a liberal democracy). But they can also examine the problem of punishment *as it is done, today*. It is in this latter spirit that this chapter confronts contemporary English punishment – with a theory not of eternal philosophical justification, but one of political *action*, in the moment we find ourselves in. For this reason, I must reject Duff's project of rational reconstruction, for all its uses. A penal theorist today is confronted by a system that routinely inflicts pains (and harms) upon offenders and formally innocent third parties, including the victims of crime. Those pains and harms are partly by design and partly unintentional, but even the unintentional harms stem from the thrownness of the penal system. We have inherited a ragtag patchwork of institutions, processes, and presuppositions that are rooted in a history that looks, from the contemporary perspective of good-faith liberal democracy,[15] oppressive, exploitative, and inhumane. We have attempted to rehabilitate those institutions, but we have only succeeded in part.

There is no *a priori* reason why a liberal democracy must punish criminal offences: at all, or through the specific modes of punishment deployed in contemporary England and Wales. Had we started a liberal-democratic society from some Rawlsian 'original position',[16] we might well have been able to design institutions that genuinely reflect liberal and democratic values. But the 'original position' is not (and should not be read as) a literal historical event – it is a thought experiment to help one make sense of the uneasy compromise between old authoritarianism and gradualist reform that modern society represents.[17] Arguments can be made for why a liberal or a democrat *might support* criminal punishment, which is the task of rational reconstructions of criminal justice. But there is no reason to treat punishment as being uniquely politically necessary, socially useful, or morally

[14] See, eg, Philip Goodman, Joshua Page, and Michelle Phelps, *Breaking the Pendulum: The Long Struggle over Criminal Justice* (2017, Oxford University Press); Nicola Lacey, *In Search of Criminal Responsibility: Ideas, Interests, Institutions* (2016, Oxford University Press).

[15] To avoid any doubt, I do not mean this to refer to any particular political party or movement in the contemporary UK – or anywhere else, for that matter!.

[16] John Rawls, *A Theory of Justice*, Revised edn (1999, Oxford University Press). Compare the common liberal rhetoric of the 'social contract', eg in Hobbes, above n 11, Part Two; John Locke, 'An Essay Concerning the True, Original, Extent, and End of Civil-Government'; in John Locke; Mark Goldie (ed), *Second Treatise of Government and A Letter Concerning Toleration* (2016, Oxford University Press); Jean-Jacques Rousseau, *The Social Contract* (1994, Christopher Betts (trans), Oxford University Press).

[17] See generally Matt Matravers, 'Political Theory and the Criminal Law', in: RA Duff and Stuart Green (eds), *Philosophical Foundations of Criminal Law* (2011, Oxford University Press).

good. Yet still we punish, and in ways that create tensions with liberal principles of individual autonomy and minimal interference, and with democratic notions of equality and solidarity (as we saw in empirical terms in Chapter 2). *That* is the context forming the starting point for a thrown theory of criminal justice. We are individually and collectively confronted with a series of embedded criminal justice systems that are historical accidents, not absolute necessities, and that engage in processes that propagate harm, pain, and inequality on a massive (and expanding) scale. We are not responsible for justifying this unasked-for inheritance, but we must reckon with it in constructing a political theory of where to go next.

II. Why 'Late' Retributivism?

From this perspective, we can at least reject criminal justice as an *inherently necessary* means of securing social order, communicating censure for wrongdoing, or achieving wider social goods. However, it currently serves all three purposes, and there are currently no alternative models for achieving those ends that are at once theoretically robust and politically palatable in the short- or medium-term. Both restorative justice and penal abolitionism offer the *promise* of radical alternatives, but only in the longer-term, and only with wider (small-r) revolutionary change in the political, social, cultural and economic institutions that underpin criminal justice. There has to be a better way – but, for the time being, there isn't. So what are we to do while we come up with one? Can, and should, we attempt to make amendments to the penal system, given that those reforms tend to shore up the validity of the status quo against radical change?[18]

It is the response to these questions that makes 'late' retributivism late. I adopt the modifier in conscious pastiche of the endemic social-science concepts of 'late modernity' and 'late capitalism'. These theories treat 'lateness' as a sign of imminent (but incomplete) passage from one system into another: from the dry, rationalised certainties and grand theory of modernity to the dynamic fluidity and plurality of meaning in postmodern thought;[19] or from the hierarchical inequality of capitalism to a (presumed) more equal and just distribution of goods. In both cases collapse is imminent as a result of the withering away of the old system's normative foundations, and yet the institutions and systems that those foundations supported persist.[20]

The problem with both theories is that rumours of the deaths of both modernity and capitalism have been greatly exaggerated. Consumerist capitalism

[18] See especially Thomas Mathiesen, 'The Politics of Abolition', in: Thomas Mathiesen (ed), *The Politics of Abolition Revisited* (2015, Routledge), pp 47–61.

[19] See, eg, Steven Winter, 'What Makes Modernity Late?' (2005) 1 *International Journal of Law in Context* 61; Jock Young, *The Vertigo of Late Modernity* (2007, SAGE).

[20] See, eg, Frederick Jameson, *Postmodernism: Or, the Cultural Logic of Late Capitalism* (1991, Duke University Press).

has proven to be a remarkably resilient economic system, capable of surviving serious shocks and of neutralising critiques of itself with impressive success during its 250-year history.[21] Late-modernity also describes a surprisingly drawn-out passage from the modern into the postmodern, and there is no reason to assume that the process is inevitable, or has even begun.[22] That said, we need not quibble about how long either modernist ways of thinking or capitalist modes of production are likely to endure. The point is that both 'late' theories discuss the shift from one paradigm to another, the death spasms of an old way of being as it changes, slowly and gradually but definitely, into a new order. Late retributivism echoes this way of looking at penal theory, one that incorporates a being-towards-death into its theory by actively contemplating the penal system's abolition (and therefore, its own obsolescence). Late retributivism, as we shall see, is characterised by its aiming for a time when it, and the penal system it applies to, will be utterly irrelevant. Unlike late modernity or late capitalism, late retributivism is the use of retributive concepts and systems regarding criminal punishment to pursue penal minimalism in the period until such a time when criminal punishment is unnecessary. It maintains the current system, in a way that attempts to support its eventual termination, and to inform the nature of its replacement. While success could never be inevitable, that aim will inform some of the policies that a committed late-retributivist ought to adopt.

III. Why Retributivism at All?

I contend that we can use retributivism to pursue penal minimalism within the criminal justice system, while making space for and presupposing the inevitability of the overall abolition of the present criminal justice status quo. But this raises the question – if our goal is the replacement of criminal justice with a radically different set of institutions, less harmful, painful, and socially damaging – why rely on any sort of retributivism at all? Granted, if I am right so far, we can reject the more partial forms of restorative justice and penal abolitionism (from a penal-minimalist perspective), since their compromise with existing criminal justice institutions does not meaningfully improve the capacity of the criminal justice system to hold itself in check. But, recall, we still need to discuss whether and why a retributive approach to proportionality would be superior to a reparative one. It seems to me that there are two reasons to prefer the retributive approach: that retributivism does some *good* in justifying criminal punishment that a purely reparative rationale would not; and that retributive theory is *ugly*.

Firstly, retributive accounts of proportionality do better at representing a system of criminal punishment than reparative ones, because of their focus

[21] Compare Thomas Kemple, 'Spirits of Late Capitalism' (2007) 24 *Theory, Culture & Society* 147.
[22] See, eg, Johan Fornas, *Cultural Theory and Late Modernity* (1995, SAGE), pp 32–38.

(especially since the desert model) on the *censure* of public wrongs. There is a descriptive and a normative version of this claim. The descriptive version argues that a purely reparative vision of proportionate punishment, focussed on repairing harms rather than on censuring wrongs, is simply an expanded tort law.[23] This is not necessarily to say that the replacement of State-prosecuted criminal law with a system of privately (or collectively) enforced torts would be a bad thing.[24] However, if we are adopting a penal theory that treats the existing criminal justice system as thrown – that is, as a given starting point for further change – then it does not describe a system predominantly characterised by deprivation for its own sake, especially one reliant upon imprisonment, non-reparative community penalties, and fines (which, as distinct from compensation orders, no longer directly pay for victim compensation in England and Wales).[25] Any attempt to transmute that system into a reparative one would therefore require substantial institutional and procedural realignment. This would include, at least, the abolition of imprisonment as a site of punishment for most or perhaps even all offences, since it is difficult to imagine any reparative work that can be done in prison that could not also be done in the community (and thus without the pains, harms, and costs that imprisonment imposes on the penal subject, their community, and the penal State itself). I can think of exceptions. For instance, a drug addict or gang member may find it difficult to make effective reparations in the community, and may be better placed in a secure facility where gang reprisals and easy access to drugs are not available – which would be functionally identical to the *purpose* of the modern prison. However, the prevalence of drugs and gang violence in our current prison estate mean that even in those cases where imprisonment remained necessary, the regimes, purposes, and processes of those prisons would need to change drastically.[26] This could not be done overnight – and if we are aiming for mere reparative reform, why not aim for a more ambitious programme of (strong) restorative justice at the same time?

But there is another, normative, reason to prefer the censure-based retributive approach to a harms-based reparative one. Put simply, there is some good in the delivery of deserved censure – of expressing (and indeed, communicating) that what has been done was not merely harmful, but also *wrongful*.[27] This is quite a common retributive argument, and one which is central to the core retributivist knowledge that punishment is in some sense *deserved*. In a recent and thoughtful analysis of deservedness, Leo Zaibert argues that prior wrongdoing makes the

[23] See generally Matthew Dyson, 'The State's Obligation to Provide a Coherent System of Remedies Across Crime and Tort', in: Antje du Bois-Pedain, Magnus Ülvang, and Petter Asp (eds), *Criminal Law and the Authority of the State* (2017, Hart), pp 173–175.

[24] See, eg, Gary Chartier, *Anarchy and Legal Order* (2013, Cambridge University Press).

[25] See, eg, Andrew Ashworth, *Sentencing and Criminal Justice*, Sixth edn (2015, Cambridge University Press), pp 340–357.

[26] See generally HM Chief Inspector for Prisons for England and Wales, *Annual Report 2017/18* (HM Inspectorate of Prisons), HC 1245, 11 July 2018.

[27] See generally Joel Feinberg, 'The Expressive Function of Punishment' (1965) 49 *The Monist* 397; RA Duff, *Punishment, Communication, Community* (2001, Oxford University Press), pp 79–82.

imposition of deserved suffering *valuable* (but, importantly, not necessary, and therefore capable of giving way to other values, such as forgiveness).[28] On Zaibert's argument, punishment is good because of the *ordering* it imposes on a sequence of pains: if *D* commits a crime against *V*, which causes them *X* amount of suffering, and in response, the State imposes *Y* amount of suffering on *D*, then that is a better outcome than if *D* suffered *Y* after the fact due to an unrelated mishap, or indeed, had *Y* imposed upon them before the crime was committed. The existence of *X* + *Y* suffering is bad in the abstract, but their ordering in a particular (punishment-oriented way) makes them valuable.[29] This analysis is useful, especially insofar as it shifts retributive thinking about punishment away from *deontology* ('we *must* punish because it is *always* good to punish') and towards *axiology* ('we *should generally* punish because it achieves *one kind of value* to punish').[30] It compels any penal theorist to think about the complexity and plurality of values that the criminal justice system currently pursues, and therefore helps to recognise that *the way things are might not be the best way to achieve those values*, even while embracing the idea that *punishment can achieve some value*. However, Zaibert's approach falls foul of a long-standing objection to the idea that one deserves *punishment*, especially as expressed by Ted Honderich.

It may be, Honderich argues, that we can say that the punishment of wrongdoing is good because it is deserved, but it does not follow that *a specific amount of a particular sort of punishment* is deserved.[31] Five years' imprisonment may be fitting in one system for one offence, but that sense of fittingness is entirely determined by the socio-political values and expectations underlying the system, and a theory of desert cannot give any definitive guidance as to when an amount of punishment will or will not 'fit' the crime. The question is only ever determined politically, and cannot therefore tell us that any actual punishment is good.[32] As a result, Honderich concludes that we ought to abandon retributivism, and focus instead on what makes a society 'ideal' more generally – pre-empting the Lacey-Pickard critique.[33]

Indeed, this is a major problem with censure-based models of retributivism that defend existing penal institutions.[34] Even if there are some wrongs that are so heinous that we cannot adequately communicate censure with words alone, it is not clear why we must accept that: (a) all crimes that are currently punished are so heinous as to require more than verbal censure; (b) that even if they are, their

[28] Leo Zaibert, *Rethinking Punishment* (2016, Cambridge University Press).

[29] See generally ibid, ch 2.

[30] Ibid, chs 1, 7–8, and Appendix.

[31] See especially Ted Honderich, *Punishment: The Supposed Justifications Revisited* (2005, Polity Press), pp 30–32, 38–41, 193–194.

[32] Ibid, pp 40–41, 193–194.

[33] See ibid, pp 201–210; Nicola Lacey and Hanna Pickard, 'The Chimera of Proportionality: Institutionalising Limits on Punishment in Contemporary Social and Political Systems' (2015) 78 *MLR* 216.

[34] See, eg, Joshua Glasgow, 'The Expressive Theory of Punishment Defended' (2015) 34 *Law and Philosophy* 601.

existing punishments communicate meaningful censure at all;[35] and (c) that even if censure is communicated, a proportionate amount of censure is expressed by the punishment.[36] A normative argument for what punishment *should* communicate can survive points (a) and (b) by arguing that we *ought* to reconsider what we criminalise, and that they are not committed to defending a particular set of penal circumstances, which may well punish too harshly and sporadically to effectively express censure.[37] But to the extent that they retreat into a more abstract and normative realm, these theories inevitably fall foul of point (c), because the precise degree of censure communicated by a particular length of a given mode of punishment is constituted by the values, expectations, and politics of the society on whose behalf they are imposed, *including* the particular institutions and processes that embody the censure.[38] If we only speak of punishment in an ideal society, then we cannot actually imagine a better means of communicating deserved censure than the present (flawed) system. The ideal penal system is distanced from (or outright presupposes, and therefore bakes into itself) the very sources of sociocultural value that determine how much censure is communicated by particular treatment. All punishment is situated, in other words; Lacey and Pickard's chimera rears its heads again.

This is ultimately a reason to embrace the lateness of late retributivism: we are trapped in a losing game and ought to think about alternatives. Nevertheless, there is a residuum of value in retributive theory. Retributive proportionality at least captures the *idea* of censuring wrongs in a way that reparative justice does not. It may be difficult to say precisely how much of what sort of hard treatment adequately expresses the censure that a murder deserves, but that does not mean that there is never any value in censuring murder.[39] Committing to a late *retributive* approach therefore recognises that one reason for the persistence of State punishment is that it satisfies the deeply-ingrained desire for wrongdoing to be confronted – an urge with which any longer-term replacement for current criminal justice will have to contend.[40] But more than that, it achieves at least some value in the communication of moral disapprobation where words alone would struggle to communicate the tenor of societal outrage. Expressing the values of one's society in the face of wrongdoing communicates that we, as a society, aim to be better than a society in which those acts are merely permitted. It is therefore a form of good faith with the values we claim to hold. So retributivism does

[35] See, eg, Marguerite Schinkel, 'Punishment as Moral Communication: The Experience of Long-Term Prisoners' (2015) 16 *Punishment & Society* 578.

[36] See, eg, John Kleinig, 'What Does Wrongdoing Deserve?' in: Michael Tonry (ed), *Retributivism Has a Past: Has It a Future?* (2011, Oxford University Press).

[37] See, eg, RA Duff, 'Penance, Punishment, and the Limits of Community' (2003) 5 *Punishment & Society* 295, p 304.

[38] Compare Honderich, above n 31, pp 192–194, 201–204.

[39] RA Duff, 'Punishment, Communication and Community', in Matt Matravers (ed), *Punishment and Political Theory* (1998, Hart), p 50.

[40] See generally Rob Canton, 'Crime, Punishment and the Moral Emotions: Righteous Minds and their Attitudes towards Punishment' (2015) 17(1) *Punishment & Society* 54–72.

some – highly attenuated – good. Its logic possesses a moral value, although that is undermined by the ways that retributive justice is actually done.

At the same time, retributivism is superior to reparative justice as a response to the thrownness of criminal justice because it is simply *uglier*. Aesthetically, a purely retributive theory of justice leaves a bitter taste in the mouth of the humane and benevolent observer because it looks so much like authoritarian revenge. This disgust can be expressed in *utilitarian* or *civilised* terms. In both cases, the sense is that retributivism revels in all that is worst about punishment, and feeds a part of our baser selves that we would rather restrain – at least in the administration of State institutions and processes.

The utilitarian perspective on the ugliness of retributivism has a long heritage, dating back at least as far as Jeremy Bentham's theory of government. For Bentham, punishment was a permissible part of the State's functioning in order to maximise 'utility' – happiness, satisfaction, pleasure, or however you want to define it.[41] However, punishment was at an immediate disadvantage because it (definitionally) involves suffering, which amounts to a fundamental *disutility*. It can only therefore be worth the painful 'cost' of punishment if the benefits – to the penal subject or to society as a whole – outweigh that cost, and produce a net gain for the public good.[42] So the objection here is that punishment is inevitably bad, because it causes suffering. From a utilitarian perspective, retributivism, with all its focus on moral desert, therefore seems to take impermissible glee in the infliction of suffering, for purposes that are at best frivolous and metaphysical. Who, after all, can say precisely how much one person deserves?

We dismissed this claim above as a rather inaccurate picture of the desert model, and of the various other expressive and communicative forms of retributivism that have followed. The point is not that *suffering* is deserved, but rather *censure* – and if that censure could be pursued by non-punitive means, then one ought to do so.[43] In that sense, modern retributivism is itself consequentialist about the pains of punishment: they only matter insofar as they adequately communicate to the relevant audience that what has been done is wrong and worthy of rebuke. This can amount to an attempt to define away the pains of punishment – to deny that they have any necessary relationship between experienced unpleasantness and punishment at all.[44] A thrown theory of retributive justice does not have this option: we

[41] See generally Jeremy Bentham, 'An Introduction to the Principles and Morals of Legislation', ch I.III, excerpted in: Michael Tonry (ed), *Why Punish? How Much? A Reader on Punishment* (2011, Oxford University Press), p 52.

[42] Ibid, ch XIII.II, p 57.

[43] Recall von Hirsch, *Censure and Sanctions*, n 1; Duff, 'Punishment, Communication and Community' n 39; Kleinig, n 36.

[44] See especially Dan Markel and Chad Flanders, 'Bentham on Stilts: The Bare Relevance of Subjectivity to Retributive Justice' (2010) 98 *California Law Review* 907, pp 945–947. For critique, see: John Bronsteen, Christopher Buccafusco, and Jonathan Masur, 'Retribution and the Experience of Punishment' (2010) 98 *California Law Review* 1463, pp 1469–1473; Michael Tonry, 'Can Deserts Be Just in an Unjust World?', in: AP Simester, Antje du Bois-Pedain, and Ulfrid Neumann (eds), *Liberal Criminal Theory: Essays for Andreas von Hirsch* (2013, Hart), pp 164–165.

must accept the current institutions of justice as our starting point, warts and all. In this case, the warts here are a long history of quite abominable cruelty, mediated over time but still making up the historical and cultural preconceptions about what punishment *is* – to wit, a form of imposed suffering.

That process of mediation brings us to the second, *civilised* take on the ugliness of retributivism. This account relies on a historical grand narrative of general progress, and is associated with the thinking of such luminary sociologists as Émile Durkheim and Norbert Elias. On their accounts, punishment is initially brutal and spectacular in form because of its need to shore up a system built around the exercise of militaristic power. However, as exploitative power hierarchies are replaced by more consensual political systems, and societies become more complex, interconnected, and mutualistic, these explicitly cruel bodily punishments are gradually replaced by less barbaric and ineffective penal options that do not inflict such obviously severe pains.[45] This is, of course, a very simplistic model, masking both the continuing exercise of political power and the continued presence of pain in the contemporary system.[46] It also steamrolls the political give-and-take between competing viewpoints beneath a vision of history as a constant procession towards the light of perfection.[47] But I am not interested in the relative merits of this account, so much as in what it says about the aesthetics of retributivism – a penal theory it presents as downright archaic, and even Palaeolithic. The central notion of retributive proportionality has ties to ancient practices in the Code of Hammurabi, imported by the Mosaic *lex talionis*: 'eye for eye, tooth for tooth'.[48] Although virtually no contemporary retributivist relies upon the idea of mere retaliation as the basis for proportionate punishment,[49] the connection is hard to break. This cultural connection can make retributivism seem like a hangover from a cruel time of State-sanctioned revenge on the body of the perpetrator, unfit for an age in which we have come to realise that 'an eye for an eye leaves the whole world blind'.[50] Weighing out a calibrated, 'fit' amount of punishment seems like something society ought to have moved beyond, on this account: it flirts with

[45] See especially Émile Durkheim, TA Jones and Andrew Scull (trans), 'Two Laws of Penal Evolution' (1973) 2 *Economy and Society* 285; Norbert Elias, *The Civilizing Process, Volume One: The History of Manners* (1969, Blackwell); Norbert Elias, *The Civilizing Process, Volume Two: State Formation and Civilization* (1982, Blackwell); and see generally John Pratt, 'Punishment and the "Civilizing Process"', in: Jonathan Simon and Richard Sparks (eds), *The SAGE Handbook of Punishment and Society* (2013, SAGE).

[46] See, eg, Michel Foucault, *Discipline and Punish: The Birth of the Prison* (1977, Alan Sheridan-Smith (trans), Penguin); Michael Ignatieff, *A Just Measure of Pain: The Penitentiary in the Industrial Revolution, 1750–1850* (1978, Penguin); and compare Louise Brangan, 'Civilizing Imprisonment: The Limits of Scottish Penal Exceptionalism' (2019) *British Journal of Criminology*, forthcoming.

[47] Recall Goodman, Page, and Phelps, n 14.

[48] Leviticus 24: 19–21. See generally Michael Fish, 'An Eye for an Eye: Proportionality as a Moral Principle in Punishment' (2008) 28 *OJLS* 57; David Wright, *Inventing God's Law: How the Covenant Code of the Bible Used and Revised the Laws of Hammurabi* (2009, Oxford University Press).

[49] See, eg, David Hayes, 'Penal Impact: Towards a More Intersubjective Measurement of Penal Severity' (2016) 36 *OJLS* 724, pp 726–731 for an overview of different metrics.

[50] Martin Luther King, Jr; Coretta Scott King (ed), *The Words of Martin Luther King, Jr* (1987, Newmarket Press), p 73.

the baser parts of human nature, scratching a psychological itch that has negative effects for the cohesion and solidarity of society as a result.[51]

While both forms of aesthetic unease with retributivism are laid out here in the context of particular theorists' positions, each critique has taken on a life of its own. One does not need to be a utilitarian in order to adopt the utilitarian critique of the ugliness of retribution, for instance: indeed, Cullen and Gilbert (who are certainly consequentialists but not necessarily utilitarians) embrace both flavours of this concern when they reject the desert model in favour of a return to the rehabilitative ideal.[52] Both are subtly different, however, in their point of rejection: the utilitarian version attacks the inherent value of suffering; the civilised version rejects proportionality as a valid means of determining punishment. They are separate sources of objections that a theory of retribution must overcome in some way.

These accounts are aesthetic rather than ethical, for three reasons. Firstly, as I have already noted, they both address the common cultural conception of retributivism, especially as extracted from the Old Testament, rather than the censure-based accounts that actually abound today. Secondly, they shade into concerns about what retributive justice implies for public discourse, for instance in the context of the desert-severity hypothesis.[53] But thirdly, and most importantly, because they are concerned not so much with what is done in the name of punishment, but for what reason. While historically, proponents of the progressive civilisation model have opposed specific forms of punishment that had been accepted within retributive theories of the day, such as the death penalty and corporal punishment, in practice both utilitarians and humanitarians are quite comfortable with the modes of punishment in England and Wales. The pains of a sentence of two years' imprisonment, imposed for rehabilitative or reparative ends are worth indulging in a way that the pains of a sentence of two years' imprisonment imposed as a means of communicating deserved censure are not. This is not to say that there is no ethical component to this claim at all – the ethical reasons why we should send someone to prison for two years differ between the rehabilitative, reparative, and retributive accounts. But there are aesthetic considerations at play too: how a particular penal policy *looks*, and how that image rebounds upon and influences wider policy decision-making. The point I am drawing out here is that retributivism might be something one argues it is worth doing, but that does not prevent one from nevertheless agreeing that it is ugly.

Indeed, that ugliness is a central attraction of retributive theory as a counterbalance to the prevalence of euphemism and invisibility within the criminal justice system. The ugliness of retributive justice helps to remind us that even in our modern, 'civilised' society, we routinely harm other citizens in the name of liberal and democratic values, even (and especially) where we seek positive outcomes

[51] Recall, eg, Nicola Lacey and Hanna Pickard, 'To Blame or to Forgive? Reconciling Punishment and Forgiveness in Criminal Justice' (2015) 35 *OJLS* 665.

[52] See Francis Cullen and Karen Gilbert, *Re-Affirming Rehabilitation*, Second edn (2013, Anderson Publishing).

[53] Recall Andrew Ashworth, 'Prisons, Proportionality, and Recent Penal History' (2017) 80 *MLR* 473.

such as desistance from crime or reparation between victims, offenders, and wider communities. A retributive theory that embraces its own ugliness is likely to be unattractive to many, but counters the tendency to clothe coercive interventions in benevolent or technical language. It also gives reason to be concerned with what goes on outside of prisons at the level of penal theory – to also consider the much less studied and publicly considered arena of community sanctions and measures (and indeed, other non-custodial sentences), for instance,[54] and the collateral consequences of punishment.[55] It takes us closer to an 'absolute' theory of punishment,[56] where pain delivery is undertaken for its own sake, without any reference to wider ends. It does not take us that far, again, because it still speaks to the value of the communication of censure, rather than of pain as such. But an ugly theory of criminal justice still resists penal quietism: it reminds us that when we punish, it must always be in bad conscience.[57]

Most retributive theories attempt to skirt between the ugliness of retributivism and the goodness of censure, in order to justify why effective expression of social outrage requires the hard treatment of penal subjects. However, as a thrown theory of political action under imperfect conditions, late retributivism is perfectly capable of embracing the good and the ugly together. Retributive criminal justice is simultaneously an endeavour that pursues an essentially good aim – holding individuals to account for the wrongful acts they are found to have committed – but does so in a way that is ugly and messy, harming and inflicting subjective suffering on penal subjects, their dependents, the victims of crime, and other third parties. Late retributivism's goals are therefore bounded: to highlight the ugliness of retributivism as a means of reminding us that it is an unsustainable long-term social project in a genuinely liberal, egalitarian and solidarian society, and as a rationale for relying upon it only as a last resort, while still upholding the value of communicating the wrongness of criminal conduct according to shared public values. In that sense, late retributivism is a means to the end of expressing censure, but also of penal minimalism.

IV. Conclusion: Late Retributivism and Orthodox Retributivism

From here, I can begin to lay out the bones of the model for a late retributive theory, against the specific backdrop of contemporary England and Wales. Firstly,

[54] See generally Gwen Robinson, 'The Cinderella Complex: Punishment, Society and Community Sanctions' (2016) 18 *Punishment & Society* 95; Fergus McNeill, *Pervasive Punishment: Making Sense of Mass Incarceration* (2019, Emerald Publishing).

[55] See, eg, Christopher Bennett, 'Invisible Punishment is Wrong – But Why? The Normative Basis of Criticism of Collateral Consequences of Criminal Conviction' (2017) 56 *The Howard Journal of Crime and Justice* 480.

[56] See Nils Christie, *Limits to Pain: The Role of Punishment in Penal Policy* (1982, Martin Robinson), pp 100–101.

[57] Willem de Haan, 'Abolition and the Politics of "Bad Conscience"' (1987) 26 *The Howard Journal of Crime and Justice* 15.

however, I should clarify exactly which features of orthodox retributivism are retained in my approach, to highlight where the key differences will emerge in the rest of the book. In fact, in many respects, a late-retributivist is committed to many of the same basic propositions as more established accounts.

Firstly, contemporary retributivism is correct insofar as it argues that wrongdoing – breaching a publicly agreed wrong – deserves censure (that is, a calling to account in which the wrongdoing is labelled *as* wrongdoing). This is a feature of living within a (hierarchical) liberal democracy, which conceives of itself as being committed to individual autonomy, dignity, pluralism, mutual toleration, equality, and solidarity. So long as those are values that the State even purports to uphold, it ought to call those who violate those values to account, because otherwise it is not acting in good faith, either with its claimed values, or with the very basis for its existence as the guarantor of minimal socioeconomic order.

Secondly, I am willing to recognise as a socio-cultural fact that presently, certain wrongs cannot be adequately censured without something else than just a very strong verbal rebuke. If only by historical accident, existing penal institutions such as prisons and probation offices are places where symbolic castigation is performed through the imposition of hard treatment as a sort of extension of the vocabulary available to the State, as an agent of society. *However*: (a) this is a descriptive fact, not (necessarily) a normatively good thing; and (b) evidence suggests that the current communicative potential of criminal sanctions is mixed, at best.[58] Even if deserved censure *is* a good thing, it does not follow that the current institutions of criminal justice are particularly effective at communicating that censure *to the penal subject* – to say nothing of wider audiences. So I accept that contemporary retributive justice *pursues a basically good idea, but badly*. It can be improved by increasing the focus of criminal punishments upon communication, by engaging in socio-cultural activism to encourage an evolving discourse about what punishments mean in their modes and durations, and by challenging the assumption that punishment is the only way to communicate all the censure that a particular wrong deserves. These are essentially the ethical questions to be answered by a late-retributivist in the context of existing criminal justice institutions. To the extent that punishments can be 'fixed' – made to adequately communicate enough censure, then those institutions serve a public good. To the extent they cannot, they should be abolished and replaced with alternative means of better communicating censure.

Thirdly, I agree that proportionality has a key role to play in internally limiting the size and shape of the penal State – subject to my conclusion in Chapter 5 that it is only a first principle among equals. To the extent that this limits the criminal justice system to a relatively narrow range of social functions, social order and cohesion will need to be preserved by other means, whether by other actions of State or by private actors, individually or collectively, commercially or voluntarily.

[58] Recall Schinkel, n 35.

This is a feature, and not a bug, of retributive theorising, and a key component of retributivism's previous (failed) attempts to limit the penal State. As a result of the liberal-democratic penal minimalism it pursues, late retributivism must be concerned with critically reviewing the extent to which human conduct is criminalised, exploring decriminalisation and diversion as options for reducing the reach of the State in wrongs requiring a relatively low level of public censure, and shifting down the maximum level of censure to be deployed across society, to the lowest possible anchoring point. All of this will require a metric of sentence severity capable of gauging how much censure is likely to be communicated by a given sentence. To the extent that this gauging is impossible, criminal justice cannot achieve theoretical perfection as a means of properly censuring wrongdoing, and late retributivism ought to make discursive space for the consideration of sufficiently complex replacement systems, institutions, and processes – provided that they would suit the needs of a mass society and take seriously the value of censuring wrongdoing.

Within these confines, however, late retributivism represents a radical departure from orthodox forms of retributivism. It is more explicitly concerned with pursuing penal minimalism as an end in itself, and less committed to the necessity of particular forms of punishment (or, indeed, of punishment at all), as a means of expressing proportionate censure. Given its thrown perspective, late retributivism offers a more critical and open-minded means of reconstructing criminal justice to confront penal excess, because it is not committed to justifying the whole kit and caboodle of the penal State as an edifice. Retaining what is good and valuable in the censuring of wrongdoing, it recognises that we may not be able to change everything that is unjust about our system overnight, but it is willing to try to make things *less unjust* in the first analysis. This general outlook invests a late retributive position with four key elements – and it is to exploring these and their implications for penal policy and practice that I turn in Chapter 7.

7

Elements of a Late Retributivism

We are now, at last, in a position to discuss late retributivism as a theoretical response to the problem of punishment in detail, and as a pragmatic attempt to get beyond the theoretical vulnerabilities that led desert-model retributivism to fail to safeguard penal minimalism. To do so, this chapter explores four characteristics of the late retributive approach, which distinguish it from other retributive theories in practice. Specifically, this chapter will argue that late retributivism must demonstrate (in turn): *social awareness*; *political outspokenness*; commitment to some sort of *intersubjectivity* in the measurement of penal severity; and *self-deprecation* regarding the short- and long-term primacy of retributive considerations in penal decision-making. These four elements are closely interrelated, and their implications for specific late-retributive policy positions overlap. Accordingly, the discussion of each characteristic will become more involved (and lengthier) than the last. By the end of the chapter, however, we will have a clear and layered understanding of what a late retributivism consists of, what the theory's priorities are for penal policy and practice, and how it can relate to other penal theories in practice.

I. Social Awareness: Thinking Beyond the Penal State

A central question for the legitimacy of the desert model, is how to do 'just deserts in an unjust world'.[1] The problem is that the desert model is predicated on the assumption that social justice concerns are not so foundational that they undermine the assumptions about society that a liberal model of criminal justice makes: principally that each individual is equally well-placed to obey the law. Since a liberal theory of criminal justice typically assumes some sort of social contract, sufficient social injustice will place the State in breach of that contract, and might even, in certain circumstances, justify, excuse, or offer mitigation for the disadvantaged offender for certain sorts of crimes.[2] But more generally, to the extent that

[1] See especially Andrew von Hirsch, *Doing Justice: The Choice of Punishments* (1976, Hill & Wang), pp 149–150; Michael Tonry, 'Can Deserts Be Just in an Unjust World?', in: AP Simester, Antje du Bois-Pedain, and Ulfrid Neumann (eds), *Liberal Criminal Theory: Essays for Andreas von Hirsch* (2013, Hart). Compare Barbara Hudson, *Penal Policy and Social Justice* (1993, Macmillan Press).

[2] See generally John Kleinig and William Heffernan (eds), *Poverty and the Administration of Criminal Law* (2000, Oxford University Press).

social injustice is endemic within society, and to the extent that this social injustice places the already marginalised within easier reach of the criminal justice system, retributivism has no internal means of avoiding their over-inclusion, and will not be able to help perpetuating and exacerbating that over-representation within penal populations. This worsens (or at least maintains) the excessively distended shape of the penal State, and therefore frustrates the pursuit of penal minimalism. I have argued above that the penal minimalist should respond to this challenge by robustly insisting on a minimal level of State support to prevent and reverse social injustices prior to any penal interventions, rather than viewing criminal justice as just another tool at the State's disposal for maximising social order, cohesion, and justice. However, that requires the good-faith retributivist *to actually commit* to advocating for non-penal solutions to social order problems, something that the bulk of retributive policy influencers have tended to downplay or ignore entirely as a moral imperative in penal policy-making and sentencing practice. Even von Hirsch and Ashworth retreated from an active pursuit of the *Sozialstaat* to the much more circumspect claim that desert works better in States like Sweden, for a variety of reasons *including* the presence of a more robust welfare State. From a thrown perspective, that is not enough to justify desert or any other retributivism, because we find ourselves in England and Wales, with its own specific socio-cultural, -political, and -economic contexts. Whether we might want to *become* Swedish enough for the desert model to 'work' is an open question – but one of goals, not strategy.

Social awareness means keeping in mind the conditions within wider society when applying one's theoretical ambitions to the policy arena of the day. This means reflecting upon the shape of the present penal population, but also the wider underlying social, economic, and political causes of that shape. It means thinking critically (because one is *self-deprecating*) about whether a penal equivalent of affirmative action is needed to redress systemic imbalances. Perhaps we might support a poverty defence for some crimes in the meantime, until something can be done to close the income gap to the point where social inequality no longer intrudes upon the validity of choice-based theories of responsibility. This is an abstract question, of course, and it is hard to judge the limits. But it offers a means of taking the social into account when mediating one's beliefs about censure into an imperfect and failing system. Social awareness can also allow one to distinguish between particular interventions that might be available in particular cases – to emphasise rehabilitative programmes focussing on particular criminogenic needs, or to develop strategies for effective reparation and community-building.

Of the four criteria I highlight in this chapter, social awareness is the most preliminary and nebulous, and accordingly, I have the least to say about it in its own right. We shall discover more about the content of this characteristic better by engaging directly with the other three discussed in this chapter, and particularly, with the next two: *political outspokenness*, and *inter-subjectivity.*

II. Political Outspokenness: Towards Substantive Democracy

The failure of desert theory to take the problem of 'just deserts in an unjust world' seriously was one of action, not intention. The message that criminal justice could not exist without social justice, and therefore that justifiable punishment depends in at least some sense upon the existence of a minimally effective *Sozialstaat*, became in effect a dismissal of the wider issue. In effect, it becomes very easy to say: 'criminal justice depends upon social justice, but we are not talking about social welfare for the moment, so let us put that question to one side for now.' *But it did not have to.* The problem is that desert theory became so successful in Anglo-American penal policy without (and without its academic and political champions *insisting on*) any concomitant welfare investment, and at precisely the same time that commitment to State welfarism collapsed in the Anglophone world as a result of Thatcherism-Reaganism. That correlation does not imply causation, but it undoubtedly contributed to the desert model's political failure. I am unsure whether desert-model retributivism could or could not have resisted the pursuit of a neoliberal night-watchman State, but the simple fact of the matter was that it *did not.*

But late retributivism does not have the option of kicking the social justice question into the weeds of political science and sociology. Since it requires *social awareness*, it must confront the criminal justice system as only one emanation of the State, and as only one method of social control – albeit one with a uniquely censorious and stigmatising role, and with unique negative effects.[3] If one is going to argue that such a system is a terrible place to attempt social reform, because of the high costs of criminal convictions for offenders, the State, and wider society,[4] then one had better actually make that argument, in public, and in a way so as to maximise your chances of influencing policy! To faithfully follow their values, late retributivists would have to understand their scholarship as political activity, insofar as it is inherently influenced by political considerations, concerns inherently political processes, and has ramifications for political decision-making and practice. The criminal justice system is thrown into a particular, inherently political context, and the late-retributivist is then thrown into that thrownness.

It is one thing to criticise a figure like von Hirsch for failing to defend his ambitions on the political stage, given his considerable policy influence, at least in the US.[5] But what, exactly, is an academic (especially, say, an early-career researcher

[3] Compare Hudson, *Penal Policy and Social Justice*, above n 1.

[4] See, eg, Andrew von Hirsch, *Censure and Sanctions* (1993, Clarendon Press), pp 97–99.

[5] *Doing Justice* (above n 1) was, after all, a report of the Committee for the Study of Incarceration. For details of this Committee and its pedigree, see, eg, Stephen Schiller, 'Book Review – *Doing Justice: The Choice of Punishments*' (1976) 67 *Journal of Criminal Law and Criminology* 356.

with no substantial policy-maker contacts) to do to speak meaningfully and politically? Below, I discuss the prospects of effective late-retributive (penal) politics in general, and the politics of criminalisation and of sentencing in particular, but for now, suffice it to note that a late retributivist would need to commit to at least some sort of *public criminology*. This rather nebulous term has several inter-related meanings and decidedly fuzzy boundaries, but at its heart is the idea that academic research should contribute to public discourses to which it is relevant.[6] This covers a cluster of university-sector buzzwords, including 'public engagement' (talking directly to lay audiences, for instance through newspaper articles, documentary television, public lectures, and advisory roles in entertainment media productions – but commonly through blogging)[7] and 'research impact' (especially insofar as it relates to influencing and advising governmental policy). But generally, it calls for any engagement with public life to advocate for specific policies and use rhetorical and normative arguments to bring one's research agenda to political parties', civil society's, and the general public's attention. This might involve engagement with activist organisations like the Howard League for Penal Reform, publishing open-access research outputs that are genuinely accessible to a lay audience, and using social media and other radically democratic public forums to raise awareness of issues in criminal justice policy.

This is not to justify politically biased research. Academic impartiality is an important feature of the research process. However, when one is engaged with a subject that is inherently political, and one's research is inherently related to policy decision-making, one cannot pretend that an 'objective', 'scientific' detachment is possible or helpful.[8] This is particularly so given the purely formal approach to democratic processes in the modern UK, and the general level of invisibility and ignorance that blankets the operation of the criminal justice system.[9] So long as your political activism stems from and is supported by your research, you are not undermining your scientific credentials. Rather, you are taking them seriously, and following through on their implications. In the process, you become a 'democratic under-labourer'– supporting a more effective exercise of (substantive) democratic choice by the electorate through the provision of information, advice, and critique of the comfortable orthodoxies that have long characterised the debate between the major parties over criminal justice in England and Wales.[10]

After all, if the problem is that the public are ignorant of criminal justice issues and fail to grasp the complex, technical ramifications of their representatives'

[6] See Ian Loader and Richard Sparks, *Public Criminology?* (2011, Routledge), 1–9.

[7] See, eg, Martina Feilzer, 'Criminologists Making News? Providing Factual Information on Crime and Criminal Justice through a Weekly Newspaper Column' (2007) 3 *Crime Media Culture* 285.

[8] See, eg, Stanley Cohen, *Against Criminology* (1988, Transaction), pp 8–32.

[9] Se, eg, Alana Barton and Howard Davies (eds), *Ignorance, Power and Harm: Agnotology and the Criminological Imagination* (2018, Palgrave Macmillan).

[10] Loader and Sparks, above n 6, ch 5, and compare chs 3–4. See also Nicola Lacey, *The Prisoners' Dilemma: Political Economy and Punishment in Contemporary Democracies* (2008, Cambridge University Press), ch 4.

decisions, then the answer in a democratic society cannot be to simply exclude the masses from criminal justice decision-making in favour of a council of technocratic elders. That would be paternalism to the point of authoritarianism; to abandon the possibility of engaging the democratic voice *behind* a programme of penal minimalism. This perspective effectively concludes that the electorate is inevitably and always the enemy of effective criminal justice in the service of liberal-democratic ideals. Not only is that empirically unfair to the nuanced views of the public (which tend to be misrepresented by and filtered through political party manifestoes, and never adequately represented in their own right),[11] it is downright contradictory of democratic principles of government.[12] By all means let us be pragmatic and realistic about the way in which 'populist punitiveness' corrupts and undermines genuine public debate. But there is a great deal of common-ground between this anti-democratic authoritarianism and complaints about the absence of 'evidence-led' policy that deny the inherently political nature of crime. If one accepts that crime is political, then in a democracy, crime-related policies must be subject to democratic controls, however imperfect or inefficient. For the late retributivist, particularly one who values penal minimalism on liberal-democratic grounds, this is not a risk worth running. One must, therefore, speak out in public about the consequences of one's research agenda.

III. Inter-Subjectivity: Sentencing, for Humans

The third characteristic of late retributivism is an *intersubjective* understanding of social reality. In practice, this means approaching proportionality via a middle path between the formal fairness and equality provided by an objective account (the same rights are deprived by sentence *X*, regardless of who one is), and the substantial accuracy and clarity of a subjective one (the same treatment of penal subjects *A* and *B* can have radically different impacts upon them and their wider contexts). Consider the following example: say that you and I both keep a beloved dog in our respective homes. Suppose, one day, that our dogs both die of the same cause. You and I will both suffer the same loss objectively, but our *subjectively experienced* grief could take radically different forms.[13] You, for instance, might have a large family and an active social life, while I am a social recluse for whom the dog

[11] Ibid; see also Roger Matthews, 'The Myth of Punitiveness' (2005) 9 *Theoretical Criminology* 175; Lisa Miller, *The Myth of Mob Rule: Violent Crime and Democratic Politics* (2016, Oxford University Press).

[12] See generally Russell Hogg, 'Punishment and "The People": Rescuing Populism from its Critics', in: Kerry Carrington, Matthew Ball, Erin O'Brien, and Juan Tauri (eds), *Crime, Justice and Social Democracy: International Perspectives* (2013, Palgrave Macmillan); Ernesto Laclau, *On Populist Reason* (2005, Verso); Jacques Rancière, *Hatred of Democracy* (2006, Steve Corcoran (trans), Verso).

[13] Recall Kolber's 'truncation': Adam Kolber, 'The Subjective Experience of Punishment' (2009) 109 *Columbia Law Review* 182, pp 188–189.

was my only close companion. Perhaps you have kept dogs previously and are at least somewhat inured to the pain of losing a pet, whereas I have never faced the death of a companion animal, and so on. The trouble with pure subjectivism is that it becomes almost impossible to compare like with like, because the idea of two equal cases becomes impossible.[14] Moreover, there are difficulties in knowing that one is consistently *describing* the same experience in a way that allows for effective comparison between cases (and therefore, in the penal context, fair and equal treatment during sentencing). If you and I were asked to rank the pain caused to us by the death of our respective dogs on a scale of '1' to '10', for instance, then even if we had exactly the same (subjective) experience of that loss, we would run into measurement problems: your '3' might be my '7', or vice versa, due to factors connected to our previous histories, cultural preconceptions, and emotional awareness of ourselves.

With that said, attempts to measure phenomena inter-subjectively are by no means doomed. For instance, one might ask penal subjects to weight the respective pains of punishment from most to least severe, and from this draw trends about which are the most and least significant contributors to the pains of punishment. While this would not tell you *how punitive* a particular punishment is, it might suggest, say, that liberty deprivations are a comparatively minor component of the pains of probation supervision, and accordingly, that measuring penal severity purely in terms of liberty deprivation will tend to undervalue those sentences as proportionate punishments.[15] This would allow a more robust theory of what makes sentences severe to be developed, which, in turn, would produce a better basis for retributive sentencing policies.

A. Late-Retributive Theory and Empirical Data: A Research Agenda

Two points should be drawn from this example. Firstly, late retributivism requires inter-subjectivity, because of its commitments to *social awareness*, equality, dignity, and proportionality. This has procedural as well as epistemological ramifications, since it requires an engagement with meaningful information about the subject ahead of their sentencing, a task made more difficult by recent reforms to the delivery of pre-sentence reports.[16] Secondly, inter-subjectivity compels an *empirical* as well as a theoretical account. Since this empirical data must support the commitment to being *politically outspoken*, late retributivists must engage with a range of quantitative and qualitative data. So far, exploratory, small-scale qualitative studies

[14] Nils Christie, *Limits to Pain: The Role of Punishment in Penal Policy* (1982, Martin Robinson), p 9.

[15] See, eg, David Hayes, 'The Impact of Supervision on the Pains of Community Penalties in England and Wales: An Exploratory Study' (2015) 8 *European Journal of Probation* 85.

[16] See Gwen Robinson, 'Stand-Down and Deliver: Pre-Sentence Reports, Quality, and the New Culture of Speed' (2017) 64 *Probation Journal* 337.

have been the norm in the study of subjective experiences of punishment,[17] but these studies tend to remain unpersuasive in the modern policy context, since they are not usually generalisable in the statistical sense. For that, one generally needs quantitative data, but the trade-off is that the data one can generate are typically flatter and less detailed about the subjective experiences that an inter-subjective account must engage with. As such, a mixed-methods programme of research is needed. A first programme of qualitative research exploring the range of pains of punishment (say – and I defend such an approach below) will identify a rough schema of pains associated with a particular penalty.[18] This would enable an instrument and a rough schedule of pains, and their respective severity, to be deployed as a quantitative survey instrument, which could be used to develop a more generalisable set of data about those pains. Inevitably, of course, there would be some differences between the qualitative and quantitative data sets, and those inconsistencies would need to be considered by fresh qualitative data – say, in the form of focus groups with particular survey participants – which might well point to the need for another round of quantitative data, and so on.

All of this would need to be undertaken in the context of every penalty on the sentencing tariff before one could truly comment upon the proportionality of punishment in terms of pain. While the pains arising from different studies and different contexts could never be directly comparable, they could point to common sources of pains, give a rough account of their impacts, and add these into the range of sentencing factors for the judge to consider. In other words, at the very least one could *update* the definition of that which is 'normally considered unpleasant', and on what basis, in the light of the more sophisticated research designs available in the twenty-first century. Of course, this would be hugely work-intensive. But if one is committed to developing sentencing policies that recognise the complex consequences of conviction and punishment it is the only path that is left open. More research, if you like, is needed – from an ethical standpoint as much as from an epistemological one.

B. The Pains of Punishment: An Intersubjective Metric for an Ugly Theory

Equipped with these data, we could move towards an account of proportionality using the full range of the pains of punishment for our metric. In my previous

[17] Although see Randy Gainey and Brian Payne, 'Understanding the Experience of House Arrest with Electronic Monitoring: An Analysis of Quantitative and Qualitative Data' (2000) 44 *International Journal of Offender Therapy and Comparative Criminology* 84; Ellen Raaijmakers et al, 'Changes in the Subjectively Experienced Severity of Detention: Exploring Individual Differences' (2017) 97 *The Prison Journal* 644; Ioan Durnescu et al, 'Experiencing Offender Supervision in Europe: The Eurobarometer – Lessons from the Study' (2018) 65 *Probation Journal* 7.

[18] Eg, Hayes, 'The Impact of Supervision', above n 15, although the massive organisational change in the recent history of the Probation Service has rendered these data somewhat outdated.

work, I have argued in defence of aspects of this broad claim, and so I will not rehearse those points again here.[19] However, since I am committing to a normative defence of inter-subjectivity in general and of the pains of punishment as a metric of punishment in particular, there are two points I need to defend against here. The first concerns the *ethical* implications of using the pains of punishment as an intentional essence of punishment, rather than its unfortunate by-product, in a society that prides itself on (at least the profession of) civility and benevolence. The second relates to *political* arguments that pure objectivity is required in order to ensure equal treatment before the law.

(i) The Ethics of Pain Infliction: 'Dangerously Approaching Sadism'?[20]

The first question to answer is why we *should* use the infliction of pain as a metric for calibrating proportionate sentences. Even assuming that we use the pains of punishment to measure sentence severity inter-subjectively, by building up and comparing portfolios of pain and the circumstances in which they arise out of the imposition of a certain sentence, there remain important ethical considerations. Should we be comfortable with describing punishment in terms of intentionally imposed suffering? Dan Markel and Chad Flanders, in particular, are concerned with the idea that criminal justice exists for the infliction of pain, measure for measure, as an exercise in sadism – mere revenge rather than retribution, which can only serve to frustrate the pursuit of genuine liberal values underpinning their (naïve) conception of expressive retributive justice. They argue that to insist on a certain amount of subjective pain is to demand that the judge hover over the subject and impose a satisfactory amount, potentially leading to the imposition of longer sentences or harsher conditions in order to satisfy the pain threshold set by the original sentence.[21] This commitment also has potential political ramifications: in a punitive environment, does not speaking in terms of pain infliction feed the punitive desire to see suffering, and encourage a gnawing desire for more pain? Might it not encourage penal excess by showing that we can be tougher (in an explicitly sadistic sense) on crime?

These are reasonable concerns, and because of them, I do not think that a normative defence of retributive justice measured in terms of pain infliction could survive. But late retributivism is a thrown theory of punishment in an imperfect, inherited context, rather than a defence of punishment in a perfect moral abstract. We speak in terms of pain only because pain is already such an ingrained

[19] See David Hayes, 'Penal Impact: Towards a More Intersubjective Measurement of Penal Severity' (2016) 36 *OJLS* 724; Esther van Ginneken and David Hayes, '"Just" Punishment? Offenders' Perspectives on the Meaning and Severity of Punishment' (2017) 17 *Criminology & Criminal Justice* 62; David Hayes, 'Proximity, Pain, and State Punishment' (2018) 20 *Punishment & Society* 235.

[20] Dan Markel and Chad Flanders, 'Bentham on Stilts: The Bare Relevance of Subjectivity to Retributive Justice' (2010) 98 *California Law Review* 907, p 915.

[21] Ibid, pp 982–984.

and expected component of punishment – because we think it is better to try to minimise the pain built into the system than to pretend it does not exist. Indeed, approaching proportionality in terms of pain offers a range of advantages from a penal-minimalist perspective. Conceptually, pain is an extraordinarily broad concept, encapsulating not just physical but also psychological and emotional suffering.[22] This is a subjective, unpleasant experience – as distinct from an objective, short- or long-term *harm* in the sense of a setback to one's interests.[23] Something can be painful but not harmful on this definition (and, for that matter, harmful but not painful): for instance, effective rehabilitation may cause me to feel shame at my previous actions, and to re-evaluate and alter my life in ways that I find difficult and even unpleasant, but will also help me to live more effectively within society. One ramification of this definition is that *virtually everything can be painful*, not just penal State interventions. This creates a certain degree of indeterminacy that must be accounted for: when can a pain be said to 'arise' from a punishment? When is a 'pain of punishment' distinct from everyday life?[24]

But this blurring of boundaries creates opportunities, too. Firstly, by divorcing our definition of pain from any objectivising metric, we allow for the cross-comparison of different modes of punishment. Pain is, after all, the only constant across imprisonment, community sanctions, and fines, modes of punishment that are radically different in their effects and implications. Cross-comparisons are not necessarily impossible across different units of duration and 'bite',[25] but they are necessarily artificial, especially compared to a single, cross-cutting metric. Recognising competing clusters of pains makes it easier to take non-custodial penalties seriously as penalties, without creating a rhetorical basis to argue that we should 'toughen' them up.[26] Importantly, this includes the pains in rehabilitative or otherwise benevolent processes, which can also restrain or frustrate their subjects, especially in the short-term.[27] So, in practice, a pains analysis allows us to break down the old assumption that there is an inherent tension between pain and healing, retribution and rehabilitation.[28] In other words, the pains of punishment are not necessarily counterbalanced (and certainly not erased) by any gains of punishment, for the purpose of calculating penal severity.[29] We can therefore

[22] See, eg, Christie, *Limits to Pain*, above n 14, pp 9–11; Hayes, 'Proximity, Pain and State Punishment', above n 19, p 239.

[23] See, eg, Joel Feinberg, *Harm to Others: The Moral Limits of the Criminal Law, Volume One* (1984, Oxford University Press), ch 2; Andrew von Hirsch and Nils Jareborg, 'Gauging Criminal Harm: A Living Standard Analysis' (1991) 11 *OJLS* 1.

[24] See Jesper Ryberg, 'Punishment and the Measurement of Severity', in: Jesper Ryberg and Angelo Corlett (eds), *Punishment and Ethics: New Perspectives* (2010, Palgrave Macmillan), pp 82–87.

[25] Against Dan Kahan, 'Punishment Incommensurability' (1998) 1 *Buffalo Criminal Law Review* 691.

[26] A point I argue in Hayes, 'Penal Impact', above n 19, pp 749–750; Hayes, 'Proximity, Pain and State Punishment', above n 19, pp 248–250.

[27] Compare Hayes, 'The Impact of Supervision', above n 15, pp 91–93; Briege Nugent and Marguerite Schinkel, 'The Pains of Desistance' (2016) 16 *Criminology & Criminal Justice* 568.

[28] See also Fergus McNeill, 'Probation, Credibility and Justice' (2009) 58 *Probation Journal* 9.

[29] See also David Hayes, 'Experiencing Penal Supervision: A Literature Review' (2018) 65 *Probation Journal* 387, pp 389–390.

justify rehabilitative interventions *as part of punishment*, while also gain a fuller, more accurate picture of what punishment can look like, and under which circumstances an intervention is more or less painful.

A second upshot of understanding penal severity in terms of pain is that we can recognise its *permeability* with wider society. Again, an expansive understanding of punishment as pain infliction exposes the blurriness of the borders of punishment as a category. In the first instance, pre-punishment criminal justice processes are inevitably painful, and carry a penal 'weight' that might be relevant to the overall determination of a sentence's severity.[30] But more widely, punishment has a range of painful impacts on (formally innocent) third parties to it,[31] and a range of unintended 'collateral consequences' for the subject themselves, particularly arising out of community and societal responses *to* the stigma of conviction and punishment.[32] The State is generally committed to eradicating these insofar as it claims a monopoly on the use of legitimate force, and upholds the presumption of innocence as a barrier to punishment. Therefore, an account that recognises and engages with these issues challenges the ethical success of the penal State on both grounds, requiring either that the State intervene to prevent effects that overstep the boundaries of its own principles, or that it accepts that its claimed monopoly over punishment is impossible in practice. Given that every punishment has a range of social effects and involves the censuring and stigmatisation of individual penal subjects, the latter is inevitable to at least some extent: every punishment will provoke at least some social response, and on a pains of punishment account it is difficult to meaningfully separate these from the punishment. However, one can reduce these impacts (for instance, by strictly restricting the availability of criminal background checks to limit the impact of criminal record on future employability). At the end of the day, understanding those third-party pains of punishment that *cannot* be avoided or minimised should encourage the State to reduce its own infliction of punishment, accordingly.

Overall, then, the pains of punishment enable a better understanding of the existing injustices of the system. Targeted sadism, if you like, is at least marginally better than reckless action taken in wilful ignorance. But moreover, and thirdly, the very ugliness of this system should discourage the formation of any system demanding that judges sadistically monitor penal subjects to ensure that they suffer 'enough'. It should bring home to theorists that using 'hard treatment' and 'liberty deprivation' to communicate censure inevitably exposes their subjects to pains, harms, and costs. That would encourage us to be less circumspect about

[30] See Malcolm Feeley, *The Process is the Punishment: Handling Cases in a Lower Criminal Court* (1972, Russell Sage Foundation); Hayes, 'The Impact of Supervision', above n 15, pp 96–98. Compare Adam Kolber, 'Against Proportional Punishment' (2013) 66 *Vanderbilt Law Review* 1141.

[31] See eg Richard Lippke, 'Punishment Drift: The Spread of Penal Harm and What We Should Do about It' (2017) 11 *Criminal Law and Philosophy* 645.

[32] Recall, eg, Christopher Bennett, 'Invisible Punishment is Wrong – But Why? The Normative Basis of Criticism of Collateral Consequences of Criminal Conviction' (2017) 56 *The Howard Journal of Crime and Justice* 480.

those consequences, and provide an incentive for policy-makers to attempt to find less painful alternatives to criminal punishment, in a way that more abstract metrics of penal severity do not.

I am therefore sceptical of the claim that speaking in terms of pain infliction *inevitably* encourages punitiveness. After all, it is one thing to say that *X* deserves to lose certain liberties because of what they did, or that they deserve five years' imprisonment. It is quite another to say that he deserves to be in pain, at all or in a certain degree.[33] Insofar as they are currently undervalued, a fuller recognition of the pains of non-custodial penalties is liable to make them more appealing to a punitive public, *as alternative punishments to imprisonment*. But by the same token, a more graphic and vivid confrontation with the likely consequences of punishments as against one another will give us pause for thought, because they are generally easier to empathise with than abstract political deprivations (not all of us have been to prison, but every one of us has suffered hardship), and because they are more explicit about the unpleasantness of that which is to be imposed. To the extent that a punitive demagogue did call for greater and greater penal excess in terms of pain, they would be forced to demand an explicit increase in the amount of suffering rather than a change in the restrictiveness of present conditions. They would be forced to explain why the current amount of pain is not enough, and how their proposals would fill that shortfall. They would have to confront and explain their punitiveness, and that reflection should be fatal to merely punitive theories in societies that are genuinely civilised and humane.[34] At the very least, a system built around calibrating the pains of punishment would be no less inevitably punitive than our current system, and would bring with it the advantage of encouraging a more open and honest dialogue about what punishment actually is.

Most importantly, however, the ugliness of pain-based retributivism should be a reminder of the need for radical alternatives – a stripping away of the mask of benevolent euphemism that disguises routine and substantial pain delivery.[35] To discuss punishment as pain delivery is to foreground its ethical tensions, and emphasise the need to find better, more justifiable systems for retaining social order. Importantly, those systems can never be free of pain, insofar as late retributivism posits that it *is* good to censure wrongdoing, since censure involves the infliction of pain.[36] But to the extent that they can do a better job of delivering the proper censure by inflicting less pain, they will be better systems than the ones we have now.[37] Thus, measuring penal severity in terms of the pains of punishment provides a rhetorical basis on which to confront and reduce reliance on the penal State, *precisely by highlighting what is ugliest about it*.

[33] See, eg, John Kleinig, 'What Does Wrongdoing Deserve?' in: Michael Tonry (ed), *Retributivism Has a Past: Has It a Future?* (2011, Oxford University Press).

[34] See, eg, Christie, *Limits to Pain*, above n 14, pp 100–101.

[35] Ibid, pp 13–19.

[36] Recall Joel Feinberg, 'The Expressive Function of Punishment' (1965) 49 *The Monist* 397.

[37] See also Amartya Sen, *The Idea of Justice* (2010, Penguin), pp 8–19.

(ii) The Politics of Pain Infliction: Fairness, Equality, and Sentencing (for) Humans

In short, there are reasons to believe that pain infliction is at least as ethically defensible a metric of proportionality as its objective alternatives. However, another defence of penal objectivity is *political*: the claim that punishment must be objective in order to preserve Rule-of-Law values such as equality, fairness, and dignity.[38] The argument essentially runs that we must treat individuals as abstract rights-bearers in a liberal democracy in order to avoid possible forms of positive or negative bias towards particular groups. Where two like cases have occurred, in which *A* and *B* both inflict the same amount of harm to their respective victims, in exactly the same ways, it is impermissible in a proportionate system to treat them differently, and so they should be punished equally. I am not convinced that this argument makes sense, at least not in a criminal justice context, because of how reductive objective approaches are about what it means to treat like cases alike when engaging in the punishment of human beings.

The penal objectivist's[39] insistence upon a fundamentally reductive account of what equality and fairness look like as a result of focussing on equality of *treatment* rather than of *outcome*. This is a reasonable stance to take in sentencing. After all, a sentencing judge cannot (and will never be able to) accurately predict how a particular penal subject will experience their sentence and its wider effects, but they can at least predict how they should be treated by the State agents responsible for their punishment. By standardising the sentence in terms of intended treatment, we prevent unjustifiable factors from taking root – such as explicit bias on the grounds of race, or preferential treatment of the wealthy on the basis that the same deprivations will damage their life of comfortable luxury more than the impact on a poorer person.[40] However, this blinds one to the very different results that emerge from that equal treatment – information that can be made available to the judge in at least some form. It is nothing short of misrepresentative to say that an outcome is unpredictable just because it is not *perfectly* predictable. We know that a vast range of negative consequences attend upon criminal conviction and upon particular modes of punishment. To the extent that the State does not ameliorate or eradicate them, it is obliged to take account of them as part of its punishment, because the only other alternatives are either to propagate their already-uneven (and unfair) impact upon society, or not to punish at all.[41]

English penal law already makes this sort of judgement with regard to the apportionment of fines. In England and Wales, fines are calculated in sentencing

[38] See generally William Lucy, *Law's Judgement* (2017, Hart).

[39] For the sake of clarity, this is purely shorthand for those advocating an objective metric for penal severity. No association with Ayn Rand's pseudo-philosophy is intended.

[40] See generally Kolber, 'The Subjective Experience of Punishment', above n 13, pp 230–235.

[41] See generally Hayes, 'Proximity, Pain and State Punishment', above n 19, for a fuller argument.

guidelines with respect to the weekly earnings of the subject, rather than in absolute amounts.[42] The justification of this approach is that a subject in financial penury will be practically incapable of paying a fixed fine that might scarcely be noticed by the wealthy person. By scaling the sum of the fine against the recipient's ability to pay it, one attempts to produce some modicum of equality in terms of the impact of the sentence. So at least getting closer to equality of impact is not as beyond our reach as pure penal objectivism tends to insist.[43] Moreover, if that logic applies to financial penalties, it is not at all clear why it ought not to apply in some form to the duration and requirements imposed by a community sanction, or to the length of a prison sentence. Given its commitment to *social awareness*, late retributivism must engage with these complexities, and confront them as a relevant question in the attribution of punishment. That means talking about subjective experience, to the fullest extent possible, and subject to policy-makers' attempts to ameliorate those consequences elsewhere. To the extent that we do not, we are committed to ignoring differences in impact, which undermines the very basics of the liberal (and democratic) conception of equality: one is treating different cases as though they are alike, and therefore failing to properly do justice to difference. Barbara Hudson is right that law does not have any value independently of its relevance to the social world, and therefore that criminal justice policy is a species of social policy insofar as it must keep society in view when it punishes.[44] Put simply, sentencing is not just a ritual involving the defence of abstract principles and symbolically important values. It targets human beings and affects human beings. Any system targeting penal minimalism must engage with those subjects *as* human beings, which means recognising as much of their subjective differences as one can.[45] Since we are not seeking to defend a normative vision of a perfect system, but rather to respond to a thrown collection of institutional and procedural compromises between normative visions, fine talk of equality and fairness in our deeply unequal and unfair society looks, frankly, grotesque. As a consequence, criminal justice must mediate its ambitions and seek rather to limit the unfairness of the system, by recognising the subjects of State impositions for what they are. First and foremost, that means sentencing them as human beings, and therefore as embodied, imperfectly rational actors characterised by innately subjective experiences. The objective defence is at least somewhat internally consistent, but it is simply not good enough for an account aiming to confront penal excess within the present system.

[42] See Criminal Justice Act, ss 164(1)-(4); Sentencing Council, 'Approach to the Assessment of Fines', available online at: www.sentencingcouncil.org.uk/explanatory-material/magistrates-court/item/fines-and-financial-orders/approach-to-the-assessment-of-fines-2/.

[43] See, eg, Markel and Flanders, 'Bentham on Stilts', above n 20, pp 977–982.

[44] See especially Hudson, *Penal Policy and Social Justice*, above n 1.

[45] Lori Sexton, 'Penal Subjectivities: Developing a Theoretical Framework for Penal Consciousness' (2015) 17 *Punishment & Society* 114, p 115.

C. Pain, Proportionality, and Other Limiting Principles in Sentencing

The question now becomes more concrete: how can an intersubjective notion of proportionality actually work as a limiting principle in practice? As we discussed in Chapter 5, proportionate punishment is unlikely, by itself, to effectively resist penal excess, regardless of the metric upon which it is based. It requires combination with the principles of parsimony, mercy, human dignity, and solidarity to even begin to pursue penal minimalism. These limiting principles have a range of interacting and intersecting effects, at two different levels: the *big-picture normative debate* around sentencing policies and practice, and the *recalibration of sentencing* in individual cases.

(i) Big-Picture Normative Debate: Dignity, Parsimony, and Solidarity

A proportionate sentencing system must at least engage with macro-social (or *big picture*) values and debates, if it is to avoid the myopic focus on sentencing that enabled desert-based retributivism to be undercut by punitive and managerial tendencies in the penal policy context. In Chapter 5 we mentioned three principles with an effect at this level: parsimony, solidarity, and respect for human dignity. Each provides normative and rhetorical reasons to use criminal justice exclusively as a weapon of last resort: parsimony because it implies the least interventionist system necessary overall; solidarity because it encourages us to see one another as fellow human beings who are harder to demonise because they are recognisably individual and human; and human dignity because it insists on a core collection of rights that the State must not interfere with (unnecessarily or at all).

All three of these principles are capable of interacting with a pain-based measurement of proportionality, in a way that will provide rhetorical and normative force in favour of penal minimalism. Respect for human dignity can have the most obvious effect – because, historically, it already has had, given its role in justifying the limitation (and indeed, abolition) of excessively severe and grossly disproportionate punishments.[46] By measuring penal severity explicitly in terms of pain, one strengthens the hand of the argument for minimalism from human dignity in two ways. Firstly, one increases the visibility of the punitive dimensions of non-custodial sentences, making it easier to suggest that a penalty is excessively severe and inconsistent with respect for human dignity. This argument also works from the perspective of parsimony – if non-custodial options are recognised as being more painful (and therefore punishing) than we have tended to credit them with, then they are more likely to be the least *necessary* punishment. Secondly, one draws

[46] Recall Dirk van Zyl Smit and Andrew Ashworth, 'Disproportionate Sentences as Human Rights Violations' (2004) 67 *MLR* 541; Dirk van Zyl Smit, 'Punishment and Human Rights', in: Jonathan Simon and Richard Sparks (eds), *The SAGE Handbook of Punishment and Society* (2013, SAGE).

greater attention to the uglier aspects of punishments, preventing benevolent (or coldly calculating, managerial) intentions from masking the inherent interference with human wellbeing that pains (of punishment) represent. In neither case is the claim that dignity is threatened by the infliction of pain an indefeasible barrier to punishment – rather, it draws greater attention to what must be justified, by reference to core liberal principles, not to mention State obligations under international human rights law.

From a solidarity standpoint, likewise, one can provide normative force to penal minimalist policies by pointing to the pains of punishment. It is far harder to demand the infliction of pain on someone one recognises commonality with – which is reflected in the relative ease with which we forgive close friends and family members of misdeeds that we would begrudge strangers for. Solidarity faces a harder struggle, because of the (generally very serious) public wrongs that crimes represent (at least in the cultural consciousness, but often in truth; I am not sure how readily I could forgive even my brother for a rape or a murder, for instance), and because England and Wales is a society predicated on the pursuit of passive liberal toleration, rather than active solidarity. Nevertheless, since I argue that solidarity *ought* to form a part of substantive democratic penal politics, then speaking about punishment in terms of pain infliction must give us pause when deciding who to punish and how much. It is harder to justify the ugliness of pain infliction against those we recognise commonality with, and that provides rhetorical force to the overall limitation of the penal State. Again, this mirrors the humanitarian aspects of the parsimony principle, making it easier to argue that more severe pain inflictions go farther than necessary.

I engage more fully with penal policy issues in the last section of this chapter, and so I defer broader discussion of the big-picture debates around pain-based proportionality until then. But it is worth remembering from the outset that proportionality judgments at a sentencing level cannot be divorced from wider concern with the normative and rhetorical underpinnings of that process as a (legitimate) State activity. This brief overview suggests that an intersubjective metric using the pains of punishment could encourage greater circumspection about the rush to punish. However, the impact of that circumspection is likely to be limited without attention to the facts of individual cases – and therefore to individual sentencing decisions.

(ii) Recalibrating Sentencing: Proportionality, Parsimony, and Mercy in Practice

An intersubjective measurement of punishment, based upon the necessarily rather nebulous pains of punishment, would frustrate any attempt to ensure mathematical 'fit' between offence seriousness and sentence severity. Only a looser, more negative conception of proportionality can be possible when comparing subjective experiences. However, recall that this approach to proportionality pairs neatly with the principle of parsimony, mandating that the sentence is either: the least severe sentence that is appropriate to use to punish an offence of that seriousness; or the highest proportionate sentence that comes closest to being parsimonious in terms of punishment's prospective aims – whichever is lower.[47]

This could be achieved through relatively modest amendments to current Anglo-Welsh sentencing guidelines. Under the existing Sentencing Council's regime for sentencing, harm and culpability are judged by an exhaustive list of factors relating to the particular offence, which are used to classify both criteria as either relatively 'high' or 'low'. That creates three categories: high harm and high culpability ('high-high'); high-low or low-high; and low-low. For each of these, a sentencing range is prescribed around a starting point, from which one can aggravate or mitigate the sentence on the basis of a non-exhaustive list of factors to do with the quality of the offence, its wider context, and characteristics of the offender (so-called 'personal mitigation').[48] One could introduce pains analysis into this model with the relatively anodyne expansion of factors concerned with personal mitigation – for instance, particular susceptibility to certain types of pains; the likelihood that one will lose one's job; and so forth. However, if pain is the metric of punishment, then from a symbolic and cognitive perspective, it makes no sense to define the range of available punishments and only then consider which pains are likely to arise from a given penalty. If pain is the point then it ought to come earlier in the thought process.

For this reason I advocate altering the starting ranges on the basis of the pains expected to arise (certainly, as a virtual certainty, and possibly where the pain is only highly likely).[49] Given the completion of the research agenda outlined above, we would be able to say at least: that certain pains are more likely to arise from the characteristics of a particular penal subject or order; and to be aggravated, ameliorated, or even avoided in particular circumstances. Thereby, we could form some idea of the relative severity of different kinds of pain as a result of the quantitative comparison of relative subjective weightings. This would not tell us what pains *will arise* in particular cases, or how they definitely will be experienced should they arise. However, they would give the judge greater certainty about which negative consequences are likely. One cannot assign numerical value to pain with any degree of meaning, and the risk is that doing so results in an overly mechanical and unreflective imposition of particular sentences – just look at the US sentencing grids.[50] However, if one is ranking pains from most to least severe, then one might as well attach a number score to those. One could then calculate additive ranges of all the pains likely to be experienced – although further research would be needed to refine these abstractions, since there is no reason to think that pains interact in such a straightforward manner. For instance, serious pains may 'blot out' the

[47] See generally Richard Lippke, 'Retributive Parsimony' (2009) 15 *Res Publica* 377.

[48] See generally Andrew Ashworth and Julian Roberts (eds), *Sentencing Guidelines: Exploring the English Model* (2013, Oxford University Press).

[49] On these concepts of certainty, see Hayes, 'Proximity, Pain and State Punishment', above n 19.

[50] For an overview, see Mandeep Dhami, Ian Belton, and Jane Goodman-Delahunty, 'Quasirational Models of Sentencing' (2015) 4 *Journal of Applied Research in Memory and Cognition* 239, pp 242–243.

experience of less significant pains, which are scarcely noticeable as a result, or, conversely, they may lead to the experiencing of every pain as a serious violation.[51] However, the arbitrariness of attaching numerical scores to pains is reduced by the adoption of a *negative* standard of proportionality, because one is aiming for only rough approximations of equivalence rather than exact mathematical parity. Within this approximate range of 'proportionate enough' sentencing options, judges must pick the most parsimonious sentence that best achieves the subsidiary aims of the sentence (such as rehabilitation and reparation), assuming that the parsimonious sentence falls within this range.

There are several corollaries to this approach that will tend to reduce penal excess in practice, compared to current Anglo-Welsh sentencing. Firstly, a pains analysis indicates that 'process pains' associated with being brought to trial and of being publicly (or even privately) declared guilty and judged to have done wrong are a significant component of any penal experience.[52] It follows that there is no such thing as a painless punishment, or a punishment without severity – the mere communication of censure to the subject is punishing, whether or not the subject accepts that censure as valid![53] This ought to encourage us to think critically about the decriminalisation of conduct typically dealt with at the very bottom of the penal tariff. If we currently think of an absolute discharge as containing no punishment at all, then we must think again, on a pain-based metric.

Secondly, we must consider the diminishing rate of returns in terms of pain delivery over time. There is empirical evidence that pain tends to lessen the longer one is subject to a negative experience, and so longer sentences will tend to add progressively less and less to the overall severity they purport to communicate.[54] They are very harmful, in other words, without being as painful. As a result, they become progressively less useful means of fixing a proportionate sentence. A pains analysis therefore enables us to get beyond the fetishisation of duration as a means of straightforwardly increasing penal severity.[55] It therefore tends to discourage longer sentences where the same level of pain can be acquired from more intensive but shorter sentences – given the principle of parsimony, which demands that if pain is our object, we should achieve a proportionate amount of pain with the least necessary infliction of harm.

Thirdly, and relatedly, one would expect to see greater commensurability between the modes of punishment. In other words, a sentence of imprisonment would not always or axiomatically be treated as being more serious than a community penalty, and nor would a fine always be less severe than both. One would *typically* expect subjects to experience them in that way, but not necessarily

[51] See, eg, van Ginneken and Hayes, '"Just" Punishment', above n 19; Sexton, 'Penal Subjectivities', above n 45.

[52] Recall n 30 and accompanying text.

[53] Recall Feinberg, 'The Expressive Function of Punishment', above n 36.

[54] See, eg, John Bronsteen, Christopher Buccafusco, and Jonathan Masur, 'Happiness and Punishment' (2009) 76 *University of Chicago Law Review* 1037.

[55] Recall Kolber, 'The Subjective Experience of Punishment', n 13.

in every case. In particular, a late-retributivist should expect short sentences of imprisonment to be wholly replaced by community sanctions and measures. That would require a substantial reinvestment in probation services, whether or not the current part-privatisation of the Probation Service was maintained or not. High probation caseloads reduce the ability of the supervisor to make effective interventions, lower the ability to deliver effective public protection, and increase the likelihood of the subject's breaching their order,[56] and so it is sensible to consider the institutional and fiscal ramifications of policy change before undertaking it. For this reason one must also be prepared to down-tariff offences towards the bottom of the community sentencing range, punishing them instead with fines or other non-custodial options.

Fourthly, sentencing authorities will also have an increased workload at the sentencing stage, having to abandon the cosy but ineffective shorthand that duration and mode of punishment currently represent and craft sentences more carefully. They will also have to engage closely with sources of local social and communal knowledge about the penal subject and their circumstances. This will require expertise and training, and will necessitate a lower caseload in the criminal courts overall – an aim that can only be achieved by decriminalisation or diversion of certain groups from the earlier stages of the criminal justice system. At the same time, since sentencing authorities are now being asked explicitly to consider the pain that they wish to inflict on penal subjects, there may well be recruitment and turnover issues within the judiciary and magistracy. This is unavoidable, and from a certain perspective, desirable. It is and should be a challenge of conscience to impose punishment, as a balance to the intuitive satisfaction of censuring wrongdoers. If sentencing authorities are not prepared to punish in bad conscience, then they ought not to be punishing in the first place. Their reticence would also be a spur towards thinking seriously and in good faith about the radical alternatives offered by (at least, weaker) restorative justice and penal abolitionism.

Finally, it is worth remembering the subsidiary role of mercy, as a principled factor of personal mitigation and as a more case-specific exercise of executive clemency. The role of mercy is comparatively minor but ought not to be ignored in a humane system. Moreover, to the extent that sentencing authorities do struggle with the ethical challenge of intentionally inflicting pain on penal subjects, it may well become easier to recognise reasons to be merciful during mitigation, or to call for executive clemency where further mercy is desirable but unlawful. The upshot, again, would be in favour of penal reduction, albeit in a very minor and rather attenuated way.

Notably, while all of these aspects provide forceful arguments for pursuing penal minimalism, they speak mainly to the size rather than the shape of the penal State. Confronting the over-representation of marginalised communities

[56] See, eg, John Deering and Martina Feilzer, *Privatising Probation: Is* Transforming Rehabilitation *the End of the Probation Ideal?* (2015, Policy Press); Jane Dominey, 'Fragmenting Probation: Recommendations from Research' (2016) 63 *Probation Journal* 136.

will require a more root-and-branch interrogation of the exercise of discretion in the criminal process, and with social patterns of criminalising, policing, and prosecution more generally. In this regard, dignity and solidarity are important (but ultimately nebulous) rhetorical principles, and the broader politics of the late-retributive model must be considered. Ultimately, however, the unevenness of contemporary criminal punishment needs a wider set of challenges than late retributivism can provide by itself. In this sense, late retributivism must know its own limits. It must, in a word, *self-deprecate*.

IV. Self-Deprecation: Towards a Finite Retributivism

Late retributivism is self-deprecating in two senses. Firstly, they must be *pluralist* in terms of recognising the limits of retributivism as a description of criminal justice's wider aims; and secondly, they must embrace an inherently *bounded* rationale of criminal justice in a 'meantime' period involving the refinement of alternatives, rather than as a permanent solution to current socio-political problems. Both senses oblige the late retributivist to be passionate in the defence of their retributivism, but realistic about its reach and scope in both the bigger and smaller pictures, across both the short and longer terms.

A. Pluralism, Hybrid Theories and Doing Good through Criminal Justice

One consequence of the interaction discussed above between proportionality and parsimony is that it affords room for the pursuit of other penal aims (such as rehabilitation and reparation), as well as other social functions of criminal justice (such as the perceived maintenance of social order), within the limits imposed by the overall commitment to imposing a proportionate overall amount of pain. This is true of all retributivism, after a fashion – after all, if proportionality is about balancing the two baskets of a weighing scale, the retributivist ought not to care much about what goes into the penal basket, so long as it 'weighs' enough. But what should the precise relationship between retributivist and other penal aims be, in politics or in day-to-day sentencing? The theories covered in Chapters 3 and 4 were generally *monistic* – that is, they offer only one justification for criminal punishment. While penal philosophers argue the best means (if any) of justifying criminal punishment, in practice most policy and sentencing practice adopts a *pluralistic* model aimed at pursuing several of these monistic penal aims and their social benefits at once. We can distinguish two types of pluralistic penal policy: *hybrids* and *hydras*.

'Hydra' policies pursue multiple penal aims that are functionally disconnected from one another, without attempting to properly align those aims in the same political or pragmatic direction. Like Heracles' mythical enemy, a hydra has one tail but many heads. For example, the sentencing regime of the Criminal Justice Act 2003, however much it emphasises retributive proportionality, offers five discrete and potentially contradictory objectives for the sentencing judge: punishment; deterrence; rehabilitation; public protection; and reparation.[57] It attempts to get the best of all five worlds by letting judges choose between these aims, with very little structuring guidance (notwithstanding the role of the Sentencing Council), on a case-by-case basis. The pluralism involved occurs only at the level of practice, with no attempt to justify the pursuit of multiple penal aims in any concerted way. Hydras essentially fudge the question of what, if anything, makes punishment *just*, in order to take advantage of what makes punishment socio-politically *useful* in particular circumstances.[58]

A 'hybrid' penal policy, by contrast, involves a theoretical entwining of disparate penal aims, whether in the service of an instrumental purpose that connects otherwise opposed penal justifications (as with the limiting models of Hart and Morris),[59] or as part of an attempt to restructure penal aims within a wider coherent theory of punishment as political action.[60] The aim here is to provide a *consistent* means of doing what hydras do by brute force: to maximise the benefits of different penal aims while minimising their drawbacks. Thus, in Morris's 'limiting retributivism', public protection and rehabilitation are placed within the limits of retributive proportionality. This ensures that the criminal justice system is able to pursue good ends, while still avoiding outright excess (at least in theory) because the overall punishment of any one individual is always tied to offence seriousness. Retributivism is ideologically secondary to the good done by the prospective ends of punishment, but it prevents those goods from being pursued at too high a cost.[61] By contrast, Duff's hybrid is more focused, because it is underpinned by a single theory of liberal community. Its pluralistic pursuit of retribution, rehabilitation, and reparation stems from a monistic conception of the ideal liberal community. As a result, the linkages between disparate penal theories are informed by a consistent vision of what a good society should do when it punishes, who it should punish, in what ways, and how much. In both cases, however, diverse penal aims are united in a concerted and fairly uniform way, with the aim of providing

[57] See ss 142–142A of the Criminal Justice Act 2003; Gavin Dingwall, 'Deserting Desert? Locating the Present Role of Retributivism in the Sentencing of Adult Offenders' (2008) 47 *The Howard Journal of Crime and Justice* 400–410.

[58] See also Andrew von Hirsch and Julian Roberts, 'Legislating Sentencing Principles: The Provisions of the Criminal Justice Act 2003 Relating to Sentencing Purposes and the Role of Previous Convictions' [2004] *Crim LR* 639.

[59] See HLA Hart, 'Prolegomenon to the Principles of Punishment', in: HLA Hart (ed), *Punishment and Responsibility: Essays in the Philosophy of Punishment*, Second edn (2007, Oxford University Press), pp 8–13; Norval Morris, *The Future of Imprisonment* (1974, University of Chicago Press).

[60] Recall Duff's 'liberal-communitarian' model: RA Duff, *Punishment, Communication, and Community* (2001, Oxford University Press).

[61] Recall Richard Frase, 'Limiting Retributivism', in Michael Tonry (ed), *The Future of Imprisonment* (2004, Oxford University Press).

structure to the exercise of judicial discretion during sentencing, while still allowing a number of different ends to be pursued at once.

While hybrids are at least superior to hydras, we ought to avoid them both. Hydras are theoretically uninformed and often blissfully ignorant of the challenges of simultaneously pursuing disparate penal ends. Although some of the aims of punishment (notably retributivism and rehabilitation) are not as mutually exclusive as they are sometimes assumed to be,[62] a lack of *any* structuration is likely to lead to a confused and inconsistent mess as judges respond to individual cases in isolation from one another, and thereby enable the pursuit of managerial and punitive agendas that tend to ratchet up the level of penal excess. The trouble with hybrids, by contrast, is that they are too *static*. In order to try to square the circle between 'doing good and doing justice',[63] both the Morris/Hart and Duff types of hybrid fix the relationships between different penal theories from the word 'go', creating a system that is workable only insofar as those relationships remain tenable. The more fixed and absolute the plan for trying to reform the criminal justice system, the more that plan can only work within the surrounding structures, processes and policies that surrounded the formulation of that plan.[64] Moreover, the more fixed and absolute the plan, the more vulnerable it is to unexpected shocks and changes (such as the rise of managerial and punitive excesses over the last three decades that we charted in Part I).

To resolve this impasse between the usefulness of pluralism and the weaknesses of hybrids and hydras, late retributivism pursues a more *dynamic* and *political* approach. Before I discuss what I mean by this, I should note two broad points affecting practice on the micro- and macro-social scale. Firstly, as we have noted, the *intersubjective* measurement of retributive penal severity using the pains of punishment allows much greater accommodation to be made for the pains of rehabilitation, and therefore for rehabilitative interventions (whether successful or not) to contribute to making an intervention more punishing for retributive purposes.[65] This makes it far easier to embrace opportunities to pursue good in individual cases – without forgetting that one is also causing pain. Pains analysis enables one to move past the binary between wholly benevolent-rehabilitative and wholly vengeful-retributive interventions, and to recognise the essentially conflicted role of the penal social worker engaged in rehabilitation *within an inherently harmful penal system*. So a late-retributivist should not be afraid to embrace rehabilitative interventions for individual penal subjects, where they are practicable within the overall limits imposed by retributive proportionality, parsimony, and mercy.

Secondly, and crucially, a late-retributivist must recognise the limits of their own theoretical model. A theoretical model is essentially a perspective on a phenomenon

[62] See, eg, McNeill, 'Probation, Credibility and Justice', above n 28.

[63] See Stanley Cohen, *Visions of Social Control: Crime, Punishment and Classification* (1985, Polity), pp 245–254.

[64] Recall Ted Honderich, *Punishment: The Supposed Justifications Revisited* (2005, Polity Press), pp 192–194, 201–204.

[65] Recall n 27 and accompanying text.

(here, the criminal justice system), and every perspective is limited. Any theoretical approach will necessary privilege certain aspects of the phenomena it examines, and downplay others. Again, a central limitation of the desert model's practical impact was its more-or-less total focus on sentencing in response to offence seriousness, and tendency to neglect or downplay systemic factors such as patterns of discretion in policing, prosecution, and criminalisation. The incorporation of the other limiting principles discussed above helps to resist that monomania, at least somewhat. But there must also be room to recognise the situational value of other penal aims, even in a 'late' system operating under the shadow of its own replacement. Adopting a retributive approach that emphasises the pains of punishment and downplays its gains encourages theorists and sentencing authorities to think in a much richer, more nuanced, and better-faith way about the challenge of doing justice in a complex, imperfect society. Since one is *politically outspoken* and committed to the lateness of retributive justice, the late retributivist will need to stick to their guns in insisting on the limitations and the ugliness of punishment. But that is not to say that they should stand in the way of intervening for individual or collective good, where possible, so long as one keeps one's long-term conception of the better alternative firmly in mind at all times. The challenge lies in recognising that the gains of punishment exist when one's vocabulary speaks only in terms of its pains, *whilst still highlighting and thinking carefully about those pains.*

With this in mind, let us turn to the correlates of a *dynamic, political* approach to criminal justice policy-making. This is really a question of how late retributivism should interact with other dominant strands in contemporary penal policy-making. Firstly, we should discuss the relationship between an outspoken-but-deprecating retributivism and *punitiveness*, which will enable the relationship between rehabilitative and late-retributive policy agendas to be further clarified. Secondly, we must engage with issues in *penal managerialism* and the relationship between public protection, social order, and liberal-democratic criminal justice. This will leave us in a position to consider the relationship between late retributivism and penal abolitionism, which will also enable us to move on to the second sense in which a late retributivist should be self-deprecating.

B. Dynamic Penal Politics, Desistance-Friendly Retribution, and Punitiveness

The first driver of penal excess that we have discussed in this book is *punitiveness* – the emotional desire for unconstrained punishment, for its own sake. Concerns about punitiveness have traditionally preoccupied penal theorists mapping the relationship between rehabilitation and retributivism; between humane benevolence and censure of wrongdoing. In previous chapters, I have broadly rejected the claim that retribution *directly encourages* punitiveness, and suggested that late retributivism leaves space for rehabilitative considerations at the sentencing level. However, it is less clear how much room there is for collaboration between rehabilitative and late-retributive agendas on the policy level, particularly in opposition to punitive policy-making.

Let us start from three basic propositions concerning the late-retributive attitude towards rehabilitation as a penal objective. Firstly, rehabilitation can work wonders. Penal subjects' lives can be changed for the better by giving them new skills, improving their ability to live alongside their loved ones and members of their community, and empowering them to achieve their own autonomous desires within society more fully. Third parties, including penal subjects' dependents and the victims of crime can also benefit from an offender's rehabilitation, whether in socioeconomic terms, through the reduction of crime rates, or the improvement of the subject's capacity to interact successfully with that third party. Rehabilitation, when it succeeds, can return husbands to wives, mothers to daughters, and children to parents.

However, secondly, just because rehabilitation *can* be effective does not mean that it always will be, and does not mean that its benefits will always outweigh (much less override) the pains of rehabilitation. We know that rehabilitation hurts, whether or not the intervention succeeds in encouraging reform or desistance from crime.[66] Good intentions or outcomes do not erase those pains, and neither do they erase the wider pains (and harms) associated with criminal trial, conviction, and punishment. If our aim is to provide a minimum 'safety net' below which fellow-citizens should not fall, then advocates of a rehabilitative penal State bear a burden of proof to show why it is necessary to provide re-habilitation through (coercive and harmful) criminal justice, instead of pursuing the 'habilitation' of potential offenders with less stigmatising and painful alternatives in the wider State and/or within civil society more broadly.[67]

With that said, thirdly, one must always be aware that any human system – including systems of criminal or social justice – will be prone to error, oversight, and failure, especially where it operates on the mass scale of an industrialised society.[68] As a result, the possibility of greater social welfare provision by the State and civil society does not entirely undermine rehabilitation as a rationale of penal action. After all, people are always going to slip through the cracks, especially of more-or-less monolithic State welfare institutions (which we should not assume, moreover, will themselves be painless or harmless in their impact on their subjects). So we should not assume that rehabilitation will become unnecessary with a sufficiently advanced social welfare system. The upshot is that late retributivism should not dismiss the very idea of rehabilitation outright, because the penal State *will* sometimes be in a position to deliver rehabilitative interventions, which *will* sometimes have the capacity to improve the world.

[66] See, eg, David Hayes, 'The Impact of Supervision on the Pains of Community Penalties in England and Wales: An Exploratory Study' (2015) 7 *European Journal of Probation* 85, pp 91–93.

[67] See generally Pat Carlen, 'Against Rehabilitation, For Reparative Justice', in: Kerry Carrington et al (eds), *Crime, Justice and Social Democracy: International Perspectives* (2013, Palgrave Macmillan).

[68] Compare RA Duff, *Punishment, Communication, and Community* (2001, Oxford University Press), pp xii–xiii.

In short, late retributivists should see themselves as *critical friends* of rehabilitative accounts of punishment (and hopefully, vice versa). We must critique and oppose simplistic accounts of rehabilitation as automatically humanitarian and benevolent – liable as they are to subversion by managerialism and authoritarianism – but we should also support rehabilitative agendas where we can, by recognising the pains involved in rehabilitation pursued for its own sake, as well as the genuine value of using the penal system for reform where it serves the interests of both subject and community. The terms of this critical friendship would be heavily dependent upon the nature of the particular rehabilitative agenda in question, and the wider penal-political context around it. However, two particular points should be made: firstly, that late-retributive penal policy can make particular room for *humanitarian* models of rehabilitation; and secondly, that any interaction between retributive and rehabilitative policy agendas would need to be *dynamic* to properly resist penal excess.

We have previously distinguished between rehabilitation as a principle of the distribution of punishment, and rehabilitation as an operational imperative in individual cases. I argued that none of the several approaches to rehabilitation discussed above can be relied upon by penal minimalists as a distributive principle, but that there is room for rehabilitation in the latter. Late-retributivists ought to be alive to the particular opportunities for collaboration with approaches to rehabilitation that focus less on reducing reoffending as a proxy for effectiveness, and instead concern their subjects' agency within (and/or their right to) rehabilitative interventions.[69] Paradoxically, the justification of rehabilitation *as a public good in its own right* opens up when it is subordinated to the broader aims of proportionate pain calibration, while simultaneously resisting the tendency of rehabilitation to give way to managerial and euphemistic impulses. That subordination frees rehabilitation to be justified on a case-by-case basis, and with regard to the overarching aims of our penal system and wider society – goals that must include respect for human dignity and the promotion of mutual solidarity. Both are imperatives that drive the justification of rehabilitation away from a percentage rate of reoffending and towards a more *humanitarian* assumption that improving people's lives ought to be a good in itself.

In particular, late retributivism should be particularly positive about Rotman's theory of rehabilitation as a right following from the depredations of punishment (and potentially, pre-crime marginalisation),[70] and about *desistance theory*. We discussed the latter only in passing above, in the context of the rather modest reforms proposed by the Good Lives Model. The outlook of desistance, as a theory of personal withdrawal from criminal behaviour, is particularly appealing to the

[69] Recall, respectively: Fergus McNeill, 'A Desistance Paradigm for Offender Management' (2006) 6 *Criminology & Criminal Justice* 39; and Egardo Rotman, *Beyond Punishment: A New View of the Rehabilitation of Criminal Offenders* (1990, Greenwood Press).

[70] See Edgardo Rotman, 'Do Criminal Offenders Have a Constitutional Right to Rehabilitation?' (1987) 77 *Journal of Criminal Law and Criminology* 1023; compare Insa Koch, 'Moving Beyond Punitivism: Punishment, State Failure, and Democracy at the Margins' (2017) 19 *Punishment & Society* 203.

agency- and autonomy-focussed liberal values underpinning late retributivism. It frames rehabilitation as a choice, but also as a process, which may involve back-sliding, failures, or the substitution of less-harmful wrongs instead of immediate cessation of criminality.[71] It invokes 'redemption scripts' that provide motivation for new ways of acting and behaving, while also front-lining the role of the offender themselves in the construction of that narrative.[72] In short, a desistance-based account of rehabilitation emphasises the agency and involvement of the offender in their own reform, and focuses attention onto the individual challenges and difficulties facing subjects in their rehabilitation.

In and of themselves, I have argued that neither a desistance paradigm nor a rights paradigm can pursue the minimal penal State. But they do provide compelling and interesting accounts about what the penal State should do within the limits of penal minimalism, which interface well with liberal and democratic values like equality, respect for human dignity, and solidarity. What matters is that, at the policy level, humanitarian defences of rehabilitation provide useful allies in pursuit of shared political values. The humanitarian rehabilitative theory's invocation of fellow-feeling, proactive and constructive intervention, and engagement with the offender as a human being are all valuable additions to an anti-punitive dialogue, while the focus on the penal subject's agency meshes well with a retributive approach built around moral autonomy as the basis for penal censure. Indeed, by engaging self-deprecatingly with humanitarian rehabilitation, the late retributivist can better recognise that crime is very rarely caused *only* by the individual offender's choices, but that, by the same token, it very rarely happens without *any* choice on the offender's part, for which they ought to be responsible.[73] I have argued for retributivism because I consider censuring wrongdoing at a formal, symbolic level to be a genuine public good. But that does not mean that we can afford to ignore the wider array of causal factors that feed into every action, including criminal activity. In emphasising the role of choice in constrained circumstances, humanitarian accounts of rehabilitation provide a strong anti-punitive and pro-solidarity rhetoric that is compatible with penal minimalist values and reflects the complexities with which contemporary penal systems must wrestle.

However, this relationship must remain *dynamic*, and somewhat ambiguous. It is the rare model of rehabilitation that accepts unconditionally the notion that offenders deserve censure for their actions, but still rarer the one who accepts that pain calibration is a necessary and meaningful part of that enterprise. Neither side of the (often exaggerated, but undoubtedly real) tension between retributive and rehabilitative penal theories can, or should, wholly reconcile with one another

[71] See generally Anton Ashcroft, 'Cycle of Change', in: Rob Canton and David Hancock (eds), *Dictionary of Probation and Offender Management* (2007, Willan), 83–84; Fergus McNeill, 'A Desistance Paradigm for Offender Management' (2006) 6 *Criminology & Criminal Justice* 39, pp 45–57.

[72] See generally Shadd Maruna, *Making Good: How Ex-Convicts Reform and Rebuild their Lives* (2001, American Psychological Association).

[73] See generally Christopher Bennett, 'Punishment and Rehabilitation', in: Jesper Ryberg and JA Corlett (eds), *Punishment and Ethics: New Perspectives* (2010, Palgrave Macmillan).

because they *are* different visions of what the penal State is, and what it should be. The point is that the principles underpinning these different visions overlap, but incompletely. Those principles can be debated, and one can be convinced (as I am convinced) that one of those sets of arguments is more persuasive than the other. But, as we discussed above, we cannot simply smash the overlapping portions of the two theories together into a hybrid, and therefore we must engage with questions about how different penal theories interact.

The only solution in-line with the democratic values underpinning our conception of penal minimalism is a *political* one – one that necessarily involves the hurly-burly of debate. By all means let the advocates of humanitarian rehabilitation (or indeed, another approach) try to explain the weaknesses of my account, and convert me to their own conception of the penal State. I shall try to do the same. Firstly, however, we must engage with one another as we are, in good faith; and secondly, we must not allow the debate over tensions between our guiding *political philosophies* distract us from *policy*-level issues that both sides of the argument agree about. The common core between (especially humanitarian) rehabilitation and late retributivism is a strong repudiation of penal excess in general, and of punitiveness in particular, because both accounts are predicated on a social awareness of the causes of crime and on seeing the offender as a situated human actor. Whatever we may think of the broader principles underpinning each other's accounts, we should be able to agree that punitiveness is dangerous and counterproductive, condemn it as such, and unite behind policy options that tend to resist it.

Doing this effectively requires a minimum level of *discursive solidarity* – a willingness to see the strengths and limitations of all sides of an argument, without necessarily conceding one's own position. The other side cannot simply be dismissed, when its arguments are in good faith, as ignorant and misguided, but engaged with according to their own logic – at least to the extent that some common engagement is actually possible. In a substantive democracy, that discursive solidarity must be developed in public discourse, between political parties and ordinary voters in everyday discussions. But critically, academia has a part to play in encouraging that solidarity by practising it itself, and far too often academic penal theory simply has not. This is partly a disciplinary problem, since there tend to be comparatively few advocates of rehabilitation in jurisprudence and political philosophy, and virtually no retributivists at all in the more empirically focussed 'wing' of criminology – to the detriment of both sets of penal theories.[74] To fix it will require a greening of interdisciplinarity in penal-theoretical research. But it will also require a general improvement of the *rigour* of discourse between researchers and disciplines, too. Too often, a retributive theory starts from the general proposition that rehabilitation is always indistinguishable from authoritarian brainwashing.[75] But to at least

[74] For now this remains an anecdotal observation. I intend to explore this phenomenon in future research.

[75] Fergus McNeill, 'Four Forms of "Offender" Rehabilitation: Towards an Interdisciplinary Perspective' (2012) 17 *Legal and Criminological Psychology* 18; Rob Canton, 'Probation and the Philosophy of Punishment' (2018) 65 *Probation Journal* 252.

the same extent, advocates of rehabilitation too often conflate retributivism and punitiveness, proportionate censure and mere revenge. By reducing each other to lazy stereotypes, the two sides of the debate continue to exaggerate the extent to which their theories are mutually exclusive, while also simultaneously encouraging poorer standards of debate around penal theory outside the Academy. Not only can better-faith debate encourage higher standards in public discourse more generally, but it will necessarily improve the quality and outcomes of those debates, highlighting the anti-punitive agenda behind both sides of the traditional retributive/rehabilitative divide and encouraging further refinement of each account in the light of its critical friends' counter-arguments.

C. Dynamic Politics, Public Protection, and the Management of Risk

One of the features of the unnecessary antagonism between rehabilitative and retributive theorists has been the tendency to conflate penal managerialism and punitiveness into the same agenda, with the effect that retributivism tends to be stereotyped into punitive revenge, and thereby, into managerial authoritarianism. The overlap between punitiveness (driven by outrage and by fear of the criminal 'other') and penal managerialism (driven by risk-aversion and the perception of insecurity) cannot be denied, but they are separate policy imperatives and come from very different perspectives. We have seen, for instance, that some versions of rehabilitation are far more likely to encourage penal managerialism (and thereby, penal excess) than a purely retributive policy.[76] We need to be alive to the weaknesses of competing penal theories in the policy arena, and to compensate for them with aggressive insistence on essential values.

Much of what I have said regarding the relationship between late retributivism, (humanitarian) rehabilitation, and punitiveness can be transplanted into a discussion of the relationship between public protection and penal managerialism. But I should say something specific about the proper scope of protective and preventive interventions, because I have side-lined the issue so much in the analysis above, and dealt so summarily with deterrence and incapacitation as particular penal aims. I can foresee my critics dismissing my refusal to engage with prevention as undermining the ability of my theory to engage with the real world, and with the incredibly risk-suffused policy environment of present-day England and Wales. This concern deserves a response: what role *can* and *should* public protection play in a late-retributive vision of criminal justice?

Public protection is undeniably a central purpose of the criminal justice system. The most influential theories of criminalisation focus on the *prevention*

[76] Recall Robinson, 'Late-Modern Rehabilitation: The Evolution of a Penal Strategy' (2008) 10 *Punishment & Society* 429; Judah Schept, *Progressive Punishment: Job Loss, Jail Growth, and the Neoliberal Logic of Carceral Expansion* (2015, New York University Press).

of harm (and offence) as key justifications for prohibition,[77] while deterrence and incapacitation have been influential justifications for the punishment of those crimes for centuries.[78] To pretend otherwise would be an act of conscious bad faith that would, at the very least, fail to account for the politics of the contemporary period that late retributivism must contend with. At worst, it would deny that public protection has a logic, and thereby fall foul of the very stereotyping I have just condemned! So it will not do to pretend that public protection has no role in the justification of punishment in a polity guided by liberal-democratic values. It is an inherent component of the ambiguous construction of freedom under liberal accounts, as something to be simultaneously safeguarded and protected against.[79]

Moreover, it would be naïve to assume that the genie of risk-management could be put back into the bottle at the policy level, at least in the short-term. Penal managerialism differs from punitiveness precisely because it provides a *soothing* response to fear. Fear of crime encourages punitiveness because the criminal is conceived as a dangerous outsider, an aggressive Other who is not to be trusted and who must be expelled and made an example of.[80] Managerialism, by contrast, responds to the fear of crime by pursuing a rational solution to an irrational emotional need. Where punitive penal policies satiate the emotional response to the challenge to social order that crime represents, managerial policies displace and repress them behind a technocratic faith in the power of (social) science to control that risk.[81] Provided that we accept the capacity of the State to control criminality, we can shore up our faith in the security of our everyday lives, and accept that crime is a freak occurrence rather than an imminent threat. This is, in part, a feature of the mass scale of criminal justice, which largely takes place out of sight of the public eye, and which is such a complex and byzantine structure that specialist institutional knowledge is needed to make sense of it.[82] Especially in a purely formal democracy, such as the UK, penal politics is left at a remove, the preserve of experts who preserve institutional control over the specialist knowledge that grants them the power of their expertise,[83] and of political elites who handle the distasteful and difficult work of criminal justice. This is work, in the last analysis, which the electorate may well be only too happy to palm off to others,

[77] See, eg, Joel Feinberg, *Harm to Others: The Moral Limits of the Criminal Law, Volume One* (1984, Oxford University Press), pp 26–27; Andrew Ashworth and Lucia Zedner, *Preventive Justice* (2014, Oxford University Press).

[78] See, eg, James Stephen, *A History of the Criminal Law of England, Volume Two* (1883, Macmillan), p 83.

[79] See Henrique Carvalho, *The Preventive Turn in Criminal Law* (2017, Oxford University Press).

[80] See generally John Pratt et al (eds), *The New Punitiveness: Trends, Theories, Perspectives* (2005, Willan).

[81] See generally Rob Canton, 'Crime, Punishment and the Moral Emotions: Righteous Minds and their Attitudes towards Punishment' (2015) 17 *Punishment & Society* 54; Barbara Hudson, *Justice in the Risk Society* (2003, SAGE), ch 2.

[82] See David Garland, *The Culture of Control: Crime and Social Order in Contemporary Society* (2001, Oxford University Press), pp 127–131; see also Fergus McNeill, *Pervasive Punishment: Making Sense of Mass Supervision* (2018, Emerald Publishing), especially ch 1.

[83] Recall Peter Berger and Thomas Luckmann, *The Social Construction of Reality* (1966, Penguin).

even if it means a loss of democratic or autonomous self-control.[84] So public protection is an appealing policy directive, even to the extent that it masks a more general managerial tendency towards penal excess, by reframing ever more issues as risks to be controlled by the penal State. Again, this is not a problem in and of itself. A particular offender may well continue to pose a risk of harm to others, and protecting others from known risks should be one of the concerns of the criminal justice system. The two key questions are *when* and *how* to accommodate those concerns.

One persistent problem of public protection rhetoric is that it tends to homogenise and demonise offenders, which counteracts attempts to understand their individual contexts. If we accept that *some* offenders pose a risk of reoffending (or of serious harm if they do reoffend), then it is a relatively easy elision to presume that *all* offenders are as risky as the worst offenders, such as serial murderers, rapists, and burglars.[85] Confronting that elision at the level of policy-making requires a robust set of responses to the demand for control. Greater emphasis on solidarity and respect for dignity as policy imperatives in their own right, combined with firm proportionality- and parsimony-based limits, can help to provide that restraint – which is precisely what the model laid out over the last two chapters offers. So public protection, like rehabilitation, can be engaged with by late retributivists … but only up to a point. Which *is* the point – to curb the impulse to turn to the criminal law first, to insist (in fidelity with liberal and democratic values) that less harmful alternatives to criminal justice are taken seriously and used wherever possible.[86]

Another point we tend to gloss over is *how* to manage risk. 'Public protection' is by no means synonymous with 'lengthy incarceration'. Risk is routinely managed in the community, even in cases involving serious offences.[87] In this sense, genuine public protection concerns can be better accommodated in some cases by late retributivism's willingness to substitute between different modes of punishment. If an offence: is serious enough to presently deserve imprisonment; but relates to risks that would be better dealt with in the community (for example, because there are better prospects of long-term reform there, without sacrificing short-term avoidance of reoffending); and would be adequately painful to communicate an appropriate amount of censure, subject to parsimony and proportionality concerns; then the community penalty would be better, all else being equal. If we accept that at least some cases will satisfy these criteria, then late retributivism is actually better at handling risk than the current system, in that it does not insist on flat seriousness-based custody and community thresholds in sentencing. Again,

[84] Recall Erich Fromm, *The Fear of Freedom* (1940, Routledge).

[85] See, eg, Erin Donohue and Dawn Moore, 'When is an Offender Not an Offender? Power, the Client, and Shifting Penal Subjectivities' (2009) 11 *Punishment & Society* 319, especially pp 320–321.

[86] See, eg, Feinberg, *Harm to Others*, above n 77, pp 22–26; AP Simester and Andreas von Hirsch, *Crimes, Harms, and Wrongs: On the Principles of Criminalisation* (2013, Hart), chs 11–12.

[87] See, eg, Bill Hebenton and Toby Seddon, 'From Dangerousness to Precaution: Managing Sexual and Violent Offenders in an Insecure and Uncertain Age' (2009) 49 *British Journal of Criminology* 343.

public protection can be pursued within clear limits set by liberal-democratic principles, without the empirically vacuous assertion that only prison can protect 'the public'.

As with rehabilitation, the pursuit of social order through preventive criminal justice bears a burden of proof that no less harmful (and painful) means of achieving a minimally secure State exist. A genuine engagement with the socio-economic and -political factors behind the (often but not always highly constrained) choices to offend would force us to confront public protection on a case-by-case basis, which would require in-depth information about each penal subject's unique situation and the implications they present for preventing reoffending. That is unlikely in a system of mass risk-averse 'offender management', and requires considerable investment in criminal justice and its alternatives, in and outside of the State. As a result, while late retributivism has some room to accommodate the protection of individuals and communities from the risk of crime through criminal justice, it places hard limits around them. Protection is an important purpose of criminal justice, sometimes – but we ought not to put the cart before the horse and treat it as the *only* purpose of penal interventions. To do so, ultimately, threatens to replace less painful (or at least less harmful) alternatives with an ever-expanding penal State.[88]

D. But Criminal Law is Not a Solution: Retributivism in the Master's House

The second sense in which late retributivism is self-deprecating is that its long-term vision involves a better criminal justice system than the thrown starting-point it responds to – one which imagines radical reform, and perhaps replacement, of the very retributive system it espouses. Technically, a firm commitment to penal minimalism need not mean a willingness to abolish the criminal justice system altogether – which is what separates abolitionism from minimalism as a socio-political strategy.[89] However, we have seen that none of retributivism's competitors offer a convincingly better way to meaningfully restrain penal excess in the short-term. At the same time, the most radical proposals of abolitionism and restorative justice require widespread social change, and therefore (assuming a rejection of vanguardist revolutionary politics) time. Seen from this angle, late retributivism is a counsel of despair, a realisation that penal theory cannot (perfectly or perhaps even adequately) satisfy the requirements of penal minimalism.

This conclusion leaves us with three options. Firstly, we might simply abandon penal theory altogether, and speak of punishment only in terms of wider social,

[88] See also Seth Prins and Adam Reich, 'Can We Avoid Reductionism in Risk Reduction?' (2018) 22 *Theoretical Criminology* 258.

[89] Although see Johannes Feest, 'Abolitionism: Some Answers to Frequently Answered Questions' (2015) 7 *Sortuz: Oñati Journal of Emergent Socio-Legal Studies* 141, p 144.

political and cultural values. We might move the question of penal minimalism wholly out of the realm of whether punishment is morally justifiable, in other words. But it seems odd to say that punishment *should* be pursued minimally, as a last resort, without normative ethics entering into the equation at all. Secondly, we might abandon traditional theory (and the orthodox criminal justice system) altogether, delving into radical restorative justice, penal abolitionism, or indeed, still other novel approaches to the problem of punishment. But the danger here is that we think too much about the utopian future and not enough about how to get there from the imperfect present. In the meantime, things may well get worse, and our failure to engage may actually end up allowing our utopia to drift further away. For fear of both of these options, I prefer, thirdly, a *rejection* of the current tranche of traditional penal theory and a celebration of the ideals of the radical critique of orthodox criminal justice, which nevertheless recognises that criminal justice, for all its flaws, serves *some* purposes. This is essentially an attempt to create a liminal space for radical alternatives to be developed within, without abandoning the short-term cause of minimising harm. There is some good in what we do, but not enough to justify our current approach. Late retributivism takes the conditions in which we operate as a starting point for political action, but repudiates their moral foundations.

However, this is easier said than done. One is simultaneously committed to defending retributive criminal justice as a means of pursuing shorter-term penal minimalism, and rejecting retributive justice as a flawed means, at best, of censuring wrongdoing in the long run. It will not always be clear when the self-deprecating retributivist should defend retributive principles, and when they should recognise the flaws of the penal system. The risk is that these two aims become confused, with the end result that radical change is ultimately frustrated. Indeed, I can foresee an immediate objection to this approach, and to its appropriation of the abolitionist concept of 'The Unfinished', based along the same lines of Audre Lorde's famous observation that 'the master's tools will never dismantle the master's house. They may allow us temporarily to beat him at his own game, but they will never enable us to bring about genuine change'.[90] Lorde's claim is that institutions of domination and exploitation cannot be repurposed for the construction of egalitarian and constructive social orders. Fundamentally, there must be a stronger, more revolutionary overhaul before we can create a truly better world, because the old institutions compel us to think along the same (unjust) lines that led us to reject the old order – in Lorde's case, the presence of homophobia and racism within an academic feminism dominated by straight, white, middle-class voices.

At first blush, Lorde's example might look like a poor choice of metaphor: after all, the master's hammer in the freeperson's hands can make as well as destroy. But this is to miss the point. The slave's hammer is not the master's tool – it is the master's *property*, much like the slave themselves. The whole point of

[90] Audre Lorde, 'The Master's Tools Will Never Dismantle the Master's House', in: Audre Lorde (ed), *Sister Outsider: Essays and Speeches* (1984, The Crossing Press), p 112.

slavery is that one does not *have* to hammer in one's own nails. The trouble with these tools is that one acquires a taste for using them, and it is hard to build anything but a new tyranny with them. In a slavery-based society, the master's tools are the whip and the bridle, the police officer and the court of law. If we are committed to confronting the injustices of the current criminal justice system, then it seems odd that theories of justice that ultimately endorse an orthodox criminal justice system should be used as a tool of penal abolitionism – of rebellion against the mastery of the penal State. If late retributivism aims to minimise the harms and pains of punishment, then that potentially serves to entrench the validity of the current (from an abolitionist perspective, fundamentally invalid) penal order.[91]

Although there is some strength in this argument, it seems to me that we can at least *qualify* it. Although late retributivism is a theory of criminal justice – an archetypal tool of the masters, from the time of Hammurabi – it is driven by a desire to *minimise* penal harm within a thrown system, not to justify it ab initio. This distinction between the justification of immediate political action and of an abstract, timeless ideal is an important one for The Unfinished. The problem, on that account, is that reform tends to be incapable of really challenging existing values and practices because it is imagined from within existing institutional and epistemological spaces. Reform also makes it easier to dismiss the problem of punishment, because it suggests that things are (gradually) getting better, that the harms of criminal justice are getting ameliorated.[92] But I do not think that the harm-reducing aims of late retributivism fall foul of that objection. Late retributivism pursues harm reduction not to produce a stable, defensible system, but for its own sake, *because* of the inexorable imperfections of orthodox criminal justice. The aim is to reduce harm *without hiding the ugliness of pain infliction*, to minimise reliance on the penal State *precisely because* of its negative features. In that sense, late retributivism gives succour to penal abolitionism, by exposing and highlighting the human and other costs of the present penal State.

Whether late retributivism is *sufficiently* self-deprecating for the purposes of penal abolitionists remains an open question. However, late retributivism *is* at least self-deprecating in the sense that it rejects the long-term necessity of criminal justice as a means of expressing and communicating censure, of protecting social order, and of securing effective rehabilitation and reparation. While it remains agnostic about the long-term aim of strong penal abolitionism, it is cautiously open to the possibility (forgive an old cliché) that another criminal justice system is possible. One particular way in which late retributivism leaves space for penal abolitionists within the policy discourse is in its implications for debates around *criminalisation*.

[91] See, eg, Thomas Mathiesen, 'The Politics of Abolition', in Thomas Mathiesen (ed), *The Politics of Abolition Revisited* (2015, Routledge), pp 58–61.

[92] Ibid, pp 51–56.

E. Criminalisation, Censure, and Community

A point I have reiterated several times throughout this book is that a comprehensive account of the criminal process is needed if we are to meaningfully confront the causes of penal excess.[93] In particular, one ought to pay careful attention to questions about how the criminalisation of conduct increases the size of the penal State in its own right, and enables discretionary expansion of the size and shape of the penal State throughout the criminal process.[94] There are a few points to make about late retributivism's attitude towards proper criminalisation, which arise from my essentially *legal-moralist* stance on the definition of crime.

Above, I argued for an essentially *moralist* definition of crime, characterising crime as something that we ought to be better than, according to collectively agreed moral values in the polity in question. This account has some intrinsic appeal – it captures the serious wrongdoing that the word 'crime' typically evokes. However, it is a poor description of criminal law as it actually exists, failing in particular to cover so-called '*mala prohibita*' – offences that are prohibited not because they are inherently wrong ('*mala in se*') but because their criminalisation serves a convenient purpose – such as enforcing the amoral but practically important rule that we all drive on one side of the road.[95] *Mala prohibita* can potentially include very serious offences, depending upon where the boundaries are drawn. For instance, the concept of individual property rights is a legal construct, which supports a particular set of institutional arrangements of (capitalist) political economy, and is not an intrinsic feature of human society. It therefore follows that property crimes are *mala prohibita*, because they defend a right (to individual property) that it serves a useful purpose, rather than protecting an unambiguous and inarguable moral good,[96] but that is not to say that thefts can never be serious offences. Theft is a regulatory offence, supporting the social practice of using individual property rights to regulate the distribution of scarce resources. So it is not possible to say that *all* regulatory crimes can simply be swept off into alternative forms of order-keeping regime; they constitute a substantial part of the range of offences we think about when we think about the concept of 'crime'.[97]

There are two limits to this critique of legal moralism. The first is that it is only trivially true in many cases. There is, in fact, quite a large range of regulatory crimes that *could* be dealt with elsewhere. Traffic and parking offences are a good example. The major purpose of traffic offences (especially those involving no direct harms) is simply to provide a legal basis for police officers to intervene

[93] Recall, eg, Barbara Hudson, *Justice through Punishment: A Critique of the 'Justice' Model of Corrections* (1987, Macmillan), pp 113–114, 125–129, and 162–170.

[94] See particularly Simester and von Hirsch, *Crimes, Harms and Wrongs*, above n 86; Ashworth and Zedner, *Preventive Justice*, above n 77.

[95] See, eg, RA Duff, 'Crime, Prohibition and Punishment' (2002) 19 *Journal of Applied Philosophy* 97.

[96] See, eg, Wade Mansell, *A Critical Introduction to Law*, Fourth edn (2015, Routledge), ch 4.

[97] See generally Malcolm Thorburn, 'Criminal Law as Public Law', in: RA Duff and Stuart Green (eds), *Philosophical Foundations of Criminal Law* (2011, Oxford University Press).

to prevent risks from becoming actual harms. They create a footing for the State to intervene to ensure that the rules of the road are respected and that minimum standards of road safety are maintained. But that is not the only means of doing so. One could, for instance, use administrative regulations to empower police officers to intervene without the related inherent deprivations of criminal law, as in the German system of *Ordnungswidrigkeiten*.[98] So the reclassification of minor regulatory offences into other regimes is entirely possible, and can reduce the harms (if not necessarily the pains) of police and penal interventions. Moreover, we can identify ranges of crimes where other, non-legal methods of social control may be preferable to criminalisation, as in the recent discussion of 'public health' approaches to offences of bodily harm where partners transmit sexually transmitted diseases, or where consenting partners engage in extreme BDSM.[99] Finally, the use of an essentially moralising tone to identify a core subject-matter of crime can highlight areas where fully-fledged decriminalisation is possible, such as in possession of drugs for personal use, or sex work. These examples are up for debate, but the broader point is not: if some regulatory crimes seem to fit into the core of what criminal law should respond to, there is also much that does not. We should not let the grey area between regulatory and moral offences distract us from the task of challenging the criminalisation of those that clearly fall beyond criminal law's censuring purpose.[100] All else is distraction, at least from the perspective of reducing the scope of the criminal law in the name of confronting penal excess.

The second limitation to the anti-moralist argument concerning regulatory crimes is that the distinction relies upon a limiting construction of the sources of moral wrong, which is an inherent feature of the arbitrary nature of the division between *mala in se* and *mala prohibita* categories. This seemingly tidy distinction collapses into confusion upon close attention.[101] In the first instance, even if a crime is criminalised because it is wrongful in general, circumstances may render it not (inherently) wrongful in particular cases. Consider the famous European Court of Human Rights case of *Stübing v Germany*,[102] which involved consensual incest between a brother and sister. By the time of his European appeal Stübing had undergone a vasectomy, preventing him from endangering the health of his offspring through inbreeding. Moreover, there were no allegations of sexual abuse

[98] See, eg, John Langbein, 'Controlling Prosecutial Discretion in Germany' (1974) 41 *University of Chicago Law Review* 439, pp 451–455; Daniel Ohana, 'Administrative Penalties in the *Rechtsstaat*: On the Emergence of the *Ordnungswidrigkeit* Sanctioning System in Post-War Germany' (2014) 64 *University of Toronto Law Journal* 243.

[99] See, eg, Chris Ashford, 'Barebacking and the "Cult of Violence": Queering the Criminal Law' (2010) 74 *Journal of Criminal Law* 339; George Mawhinney, 'To Be Ill or to Kill: The Criminality of Contagion' (2013) 77 *Journal of Criminal Law* 202.

[100] See RA Duff, *Answering for Crime: Responsibility and Liability in the Criminal Law* (2008, Hart), pp 166–174.

[101] See generally Naomi Wolfe, '*Mala in Se*: A Disappearing Distinction?' (1981) 19 *Criminology* 131; Richard Gray, 'Eliminating the (Absurd) Distinction between *Malum in Se* and *Malum Prohibitum* Crimes' (1995) 73 *Washington University Law Quarterly* 1369.

[102] Application No 43547/08 *Stübing v Germany*, 12 April 2012, [2012] ECHR 656.

or coercion by Stübing against his sister. In other words, neither of the (secular) objections to incest applied in Stübing's case. Nevertheless, the European Court held that Germany was entitled to criminalise Stübing's conduct, even after his vasectomy.[103] My point is not (necessarily) that the European Court decided correctly in *Stübing*, so much as it is to note the thought process going on in the case: incest is usually a *malum in se*, for clear moral reasons; in *Stübing*, those reasons did not obviously arise; and nevertheless, the crime continued to be treated as criminal, even in an individual case where it involves no wrong. Incest – one of the last taboo subjects in an era of Western sexual revolution – effectively became a *malum prohibitum*.[104]

Moreover, while most *mala in se* are generally accepted to be morally wrongful, the basis of the moral wrong is up for debate. Anyone with a working conscience should acknowledge that rape is morally wrongful, for example, but the *basis* of that wrongness has proven surprisingly susceptible to change throughout history, partly because the definition of rape as an offence has changed significantly over the centuries.[105] However, notwithstanding this conceptual confusion, we can see various changing conceptions of the nature of the wrongness of rape throughout English legal history: from a pseudo-property crime where the victim is the husband of a wife, or father of an unwed daughter; to an offence involving violent force against the reproductive potential of the female victim; to one involving the violation of one's consent, and therefore, one's autonomous control over one's own body.[106] The possibility of multiple different justifications for criminalisation is hardly a cause for concern, but it does raise the further question (with apologies to Alasdair MacIntyre) of *whose justifications* and *which morality*?[107] The particular basis for moral wrongness depends upon the terms of the moral code considered relevant for justifying criminalisation, which, in a democratic society, should derive in some sense from the shared morality of the electorate. This is usually a point against legal moralism, because it is vulnerable to the broader threat of moral authoritarianism posed by the tyranny of the majority.[108]

In this regard, my earlier reference to theft as a *malum prohibitum* was consciously controversial, since most traditional accounts class thefts as *mala in se* – as inherently wrongful according to relevant moral criteria. The idea that it is not,

[103] Ibid, [46]–[50], [58]–[65]. See generally Peter Bowsher, 'Should Incest between Consenting Adults Be Legalised?' [2015] *Crim LR* 208.

[104] Compare Duff, 'Crime, Prohibition and Punishment', above n 95, p 102, for a more general (and hypothetical) example.

[105] See generally Susan Brownmiller, *Against Our Will: Rape, Women, and Men* (1975, Fawcett Columbine).

[106] See especially Nicola Lacey, 'Unspeakable Subjects, Impossible Rights: Sexuality, Integrity and Criminal Law', in: Nicola Lacey (ed.), *Unspeakable Subjects: Feminist Essays in Legal and Social Theory* (1998, Hart), pp 117–124.; John Gardner and Stephen Shute, 'The Wrongness of Rape', collected in: John Gardner (ed.), *Offences and Defences: Essays in the Philosophy of Criminal Law* (2007, Oxford University Press); and Michelle Madden Dempsey and Jonathan Herring, 'Why Sexual Penetration Requires Justification' (2007) 27 *OJLS* 467.

[107] See Alasdair MacIntyre, *Whose Justice? Which Rationality?* (1988, Duckworth Press).

[108] See, eg, Thorburn, 'Criminal Law as Public Law', above n 97, pp 29–30.

or not straightforwardly, has recently been taken up by Stuart Green.[109] Critically, Green argues that whether the source of a crime's purported wrongness is innate or as a result of prohibition must be considered *relatively* rather than in a *binary* 'either-or' manner. We might say that there is nothing inherently immoral about driving the wrong way down a one-way street, unless and until it is formally and lawfully labelled *as* a one-way street.[110] We might also say that there is nothing inherently immoral about taking an object in someone's possession, unless and until that possession is formally and lawfully labelled as the subject's property – all else being equal. In a polity like that in England and Wales today, however, the regulatory institution of property ownership is rather more foundational to everyday life than the institution of one-way streets is. We could reverse the direction of all one-way streets in the country tomorrow, but the havoc caused by doing so would be much less than that which would arise from the abolition of all property rights. Property is a higher order of social structuring, a more essential basis of the liberal-democratic-capitalist order, than one-way traffic systems are. It follows that the disruption of property rights is much closer to a *malum in se*, even if property is an artificial concept. From such a perspective, a legal moralist position should require a certain *level* of moral significance to be reached in order to justify criminalisation, rather than insisting on some metaphysical pre-existing principle establishing moral wrongfulness.

Importantly, I make this claim descriptively rather than normatively. I am not arguing that we *should* invest property institutions with a moral backing; only that England and Wales *has* done so as a polity, and will continue to do so in a way that could not easily be overcome. In other words, this account of crime as conduct that we, as a community, ought to be better than, is yet another part of the context into which the late-retributivist finds themselves thrown. It replicates what I take to be a 'common-sense' folk definition of crime, the sort that proliferates in our public discussions about crime, and which therefore influences our policy decision-making about crime, criminal justice, and punishment.

The point, however, is that this definition is inherently moralistic, and that provides rhetorical force for pursuing the decriminalisation and diversion of offence types (and individual offenders) to whom that folk definition does not apply. Just as we should abide by liberal-democratic values to the extent that we claim to be a liberal democracy, so too ought we to act in good faith with our conception of what crime is and why it is of public interest. That can, and should, be used as the foundation of a politics of aggressive critique of existing criminalisation, especially where it involves increasingly remote risks of harm (as in 'pre-inchoate' offences),[111] the absence of meaningful mens rea components that provide the basis of why the penal subject deserves censure,[112] and of crimes

[109] Stuart Green, 'The Conceptual Utility of *Malum Prohibitum*' (2016) 55 *Dialogue* 33, p 41.

[110] Duff, *Answering for Crime*, above n 100, pp 90–91.

[111] Recall Ramsay, n 79.

[112] See generally AP Simester (ed), *Appraising Strict Liability* (2005, Oxford University Press); Winnie Chan and AP Simester, 'Four Functions of Mens Rea' (2011) 70 *CLJ* 381. See also Findlay Stark, *Culpable*

whose moral dubiousness in the public sphere has become murky (such as drug possession for personal use). To the extent that we view wrongness as a continuum between 'prohibited' and 'intuitively wrong' wrongs, we must try to find (collectively as a polity, through open and honest debate) the point at which there is too little inherent wrongness to justify criminal prohibition, compared with the alternatives. In this, the self-deprecation of the late retributivist will provide a voice that calls for greater coherence with principle, and greater recognition between the phenomena of unconstrained recourse to the criminal law as a knee-jerk solution to social problems, and of penal excess.

V. Conclusion: The Core of Late Retributivism

Although this chapter has covered a great deal of ground rather quickly, it at least lays out the bones of a new and innovative approach to retributivism. It presents a penal theory fundamentally targeted at limiting the size and shape of the penal State, which conceives of the problem of punishment not in the abstract, but rather in specific historical, political and cultural contexts. The institutions of punishment are ultimately understood as repurposed relics of a hierarchical past antithetical to liberal-democratic ideals, and as a system of compromises that have formed complex cultural and normative justifications.

Late retributivism responds to this ragtag patchwork by recognising the validity of communicating censure of public wrongs as a moral and political aim, but also by noting the flaws of the present system as a means of doing so. To pursue penal minimalism, we must supplement proportionality with a range of other limiting factors (principally, at the level of sentencing, parsimony and mercy), and reconceive of penal severity in terms of the pains of punishment – the subjective experience of unpleasantness that is the only thing that unites all punishments *as* punishments. This pains-based analysis allows for more dynamic sentencing models that enable greater substitution between modes of punishments, allowing the pursuit of prospective penal aims insofar as they are capable of contributing to the pains of punishment. However, the model's fundamental refusal to disguise the fact that pain calibration is the ultimate end of this process draws the 'justice' of the criminal justice system into question, consistently and stridently, as a means of supporting a broader shift away from relying on the penal State to produce social order.

The late retributivist must also be outspoken in bridging the connection between academic scholarship, on the one hand, and the public discourse around criminal justice, on the other. They must recognise the value of other penal aims,

Carelessness: Recklessness and Negligence in the Criminal Law (2016, Cambridge University Press). But compare RA Duff, *Answering for Crime: Responsibility and Liability in the Criminal Law* (2007, Hart), pp 232–260, complicating the picture.

where they can be accommodated, without ceding the importance of pursuing penal minimalism overall, or denying the critiques offered by more radical opponents of the penal State, as it currently stands. While not a realist theory by any stretch of the imagination (the dream of penal minimalism is a fundamentally utopian goal, after all),[113] late retributivism must confront penal excess in a contested policy ecosystem of different theories, vested interests, objectives, and presumptions – and to do that, it must know what other bodies of thought occupy its various discursive neighbourhoods. This self-deprecation should be bounded by a firm and thorough-going commitment to the end of penal minimalism, on the one hand, and a fundamental belief that another, better means of communicating censure within a liberal democracy can be found, on the other.

I have focussed in this chapter (and indeed, throughout this book) upon the situation in contemporary England and Wales. However, the essential lessons of this inquiry – about the social and political context of penal theory, and the need for good-faith debate and substantive democracy in penal policy-making – are more generally applicable. The thrown approach to penal theory as a site for conceiving of imperfect political action instead of (or as well as) perfect philosophical justification is also one that is potentially relevant elsewhere. The twin challenges underpinning English penal excess – punitiveness and penal managerialism – are also hardly unique to this jurisdiction, and so the overall challenge of confronting penal excess is also one that theorists and scholars outside of England and Wales ought to contend with. The specific challenges facing England and Wales, and so the specific form of late retributivism that I advocate here, will not be meaningful in other jurisdictions' penal systems. However, the general challenge that late retributivism represents – to conventional accounts of retributive justice and to their detractors – is more general, and applicable wherever States claim to do criminal justice in pursuit of liberal-democratic goods. The late-retributive perspective must be situated within its local context – but that should not mean that its scope can be parochial. Taking penal minimalism seriously, and considering theories of political action for attaining it, ought to be part of future penal theory's agenda more generally.

[113] Compare Cohen, *Visions of Social Control*, above n 63, pp 127–130.

8

Conclusion: Confronting Penal Excess

In a sense, the thesis of this book is simple: from the perspective of a penal minimalist, contemporary penal politics is badly flawed. Despite its ostensible commitment to proportionality, penal excess is everywhere in English criminal justice, and things are only getting worse. These flaws are at least attributable to the political failure of retributivism in general, and of the desert model in particular, to resist the twin tides of punitiveness and penal managerialism. With that being said, however, retributivism is hardly alone in this situation, and better placed than any of its traditional rivals (particularly rehabilitative theories) to resist managerial excess in particular. More radical alternatives offer an attractive picture of a systematic approach to criminal justice that deals with the problems represented by crime in a less harmful manner. However, weaker versions of these models tend to lack an alternative mechanism for limiting punishment in what remains in a restoratively-focussed or partially abolished criminal justice system. By contrast, stronger versions of radical penal approaches require a wider revolution in our social, political, economic, and/or cultural institutions before they could be achieved. I leave open the question of whether that is desirable, but even to the extent that it is, it will not happen tomorrow – and penal excess is a problem now.

Excessive reliance of the penal State harms offenders, and causes them subjective pain. It harms third parties, including dependents of the offender, and it harms victims. Moreover, it harms the general interests of society, because an expansionist criminal justice State necessarily impinges upon the available choices and actual behaviour of all citizens. So too, of course, does crime, but the role of punishment in regulating behaviour is increasing, at a time when the threat of crime is not getting obviously worse. Different penal theorists identify different causes for this increasing reliance upon the penal State, and its differentiated coverage across various indices of social marginalisation. Seeing this state of affairs as the starting point, to be responded to rather than justified, I have developed an approach to retributivism that recognises what is appealing and valuable about its approach to criminal justice (namely, its ability to satisfy the demand that wrongdoing be *censured*) while also front-lining its grotesque and ambiguous nature in the context of a liberal-democratic value system. This 'late' retributivism is explicitly committed to penal minimalism as the end goal of its penal policies. It relies upon a range of interacting principles intended to limit the penal State, both at the level of individual sentencing and at the level of big-picture penal policy, within which proportionality is the principal but not sole limiting principle. To secure penal restraint, late retributivists will have to be politically outspoken and shrewd, recognising their shared ground with (certain conceptions of) rehabilitation, public protection, and penal abolitionism, without fixing that arrangement into a static 'new normal' that proves vulnerable to tomorrow's policy imperatives.

Indeed, the very 'lateness' of late retributivism accepts that there may be no meaningful way of successfully justifying punishment as an institution within a purported liberal democracy. Ultimately, late retributivism offers a modest and somewhat pessimistic, bounded vision of the political penal theorist's task – to impose constraints on the systematic, institutional, and policy imperatives that encourage excess in the size and shape of the penal State, while the actual solution to the problem of punishment is hashed out by other theorists. It is hardly a counsel of hope. But two things. Firstly, radical theories of alternative criminal justice are still relatively untested and at least somewhat light on detail, especially when dealing with the complexities and hard cases of everyday criminal justice in a mass-scale, post-industrialised society. Inevitably they must always be a little abstracted, unless and until the supporting infrastructural and institutional changes happen to make it possible to put them seriously to the test. Until that time, which may never come, we need an alternative to respond to the serious consequences of penal excess, without compromising the call *for* such an alternative.

Secondly, it may be the case that there simply *is* no alternative that provides a better answer for the problem of punishment. In other words, it may be the case that not only criminal justice but also justice more generally is as impossible in human societies that do without criminal justice systems as it is in those that retain them. If that were the case, we would have to concede that human beings are incapable of living together harmoniously (on a mass scale or possibly at all) without cruelty, suffering, and injustice. Even in such a shabbily Hobbesian world, the late retributivist can at least speak for *less* pain, and *better targeted harm*. Maybe that is all that late retributivism should aim for: to provide a robust voice in penal politics for the concept of justice in a free society, even if justice and freedom are ultimately impossible dreams. That is not to discredit the pursuit of more intrinsic accounts of justice and freedom – utopia is worth chasing after *precisely because* it is impossible to ever reach it.[1] But the interlocking crises of our politics, culture and society, of which penal excess is a symptom, demand that we choose our utopias carefully. While we work that out, an account that recognises that criminal justice is fundamentally *about* pain (as a presumed means of communicating effective censure to penal subjects) but that argues that pain should be limited, where possible, is a good start.

Again, the primary question is what to do in the particular circumstances in which we find ourselves. Under those circumstances, the best we can be depends

[1] See generally Simon Critchley, *Infinitely Demanding: Ethics of Commitment, Politics of Resistance* (2007, Verso); Ruth Levitas, *Utopia as Method: The Imaginary Reconstitution of Society* (2013, Palgrave Macmillan).

upon a commitment to rebuilding and developing new penal politics to better support the architecture of a minimalist penal order. Our vision must not be limited to penal policy, or even to the State's policy as a whole, but also upon the institutions and systems through which that policy is created and maintained. Lacey and Pickard are entirely right in that respect: any attempt to secure minimal State intervention, in the penal system or elsewhere, must look both behind and beyond that system, to get a full picture of what is causing the excess, and to have any idea of what is causing it.[2] Desert-based and other existing approaches to retributivism have failed to prevent penal excess in part because they sought to justify punishment as inherently good, and therefore failed to provide a principled defence of penal minimalism in its own right. But rehabilitative and preventative thinking has proven equally incapable of valuing penal minimalism as a good in its own right, and radical rejections of the current penal order offer too little advice about how to deal with penal excess today. Any route out of dystopia, regardless of where we want to head, must engage more fully with the socio-political backdrops before which punishment is performed. That means valuing penal minimalism as an end in itself.

That proportionality is limited does not render it a mere chimera, an utterly dependent symptom of underlying attitudes, structures, and orders. Rather, the limits of proportionality as a means of guaranteeing penal minimalism require us to shift our perspective on the role of proportionality as a limiting factor, and on its place within a constellation of wider socio-political values concerning the penal State. Importantly, if retributive proportionality is to serve as an effective limiting principle, it must look beyond the sentencing judge, and indeed, beyond criminal justice. It cannot justify itself politically as a relatively limited approach to criminal punishment unless it does so, and it fails to defend the political-philosophical precepts that underpin its ethical justification, too. So on the one hand, opponents of retributivism like Lacey and Pickard are incorrect to cast proportionality aside, however attenuated its effects, and however much it should be supplemented by other limiting factors. But on the other, their critique undercuts contemporary retributive theories, which have tended to see penal minimalism as a merely desirable side-benefit of proportionate sentencing, rather than as a public value in its own right. To the extent that other orthodox retributive accounts fail to engage with social context, to embrace intersubjectivity, and to recognise the limits of their own doctrine, they are not and cannot be justified. In brief, to be a just retributivist, one must actually confront penal excess.

Confronting penal excess means engaging with the challenge of being an academic social scientist in an imperfect liberal democracy, and the role academics play in perpetuating and informing policy agendas. It means rejecting criminal law and justice as solutions to problems where other less harmful, painful, and constraining alternatives exist. It means taking the values that guide one's own

[2] Recall Nicola Lacey and Hanna Pickard, 'The Chimera of Proportionality: Institutionalising Limits on Punishment in Contemporary Social and Political Systems' (2015) 78 *MLR* 216.

theory seriously, while recognising the strengths of other positions, and the limitations of one's own viewpoint. It means being better academics, as well as more substantive democrats. We need to be courageous in bringing academic ideas into the political realm, and defending them, once there, against subversion. Let us better explore the political implications of the criminology, law and philosophy of punishment, without losing track of the empirical data, overarching principles, and guiding precepts that underpin our research.

We inhabit an imperfect system, dogged by social injustice and the ossification of imbalanced political power across society. Nevertheless, it may ultimately be that another criminal justice system is possible. At least until such time as that system is *practicable*, however, another retributivism – one that is committed to principle, politically dynamic, and contemplative of its own eventual redundancy – is necessary. The task of building this system of criminal justice theory and practice will be long-winded and demanding, both in terms of building up the empirical research base on which to intersubjectively compare the pains of punishment, and in terms of developing and maintaining democratic support for the late-retributive conception of the minimal penal State. However, if we want to seek a meaningful and robust answer to the problem of punishment – and the wider problem of (criminal) justice in a liberal-democratic society that it forms a part of – then that work is unavoidable. If there is one lesson of the last three decades of criminal justice theory and policy, it is that there are no easy answers in the pursuit of (criminal) justice.

BIBLIOGRAPHY

Aebi, M, Delgrande, N, and Magruet, Y, 'Have Community Sanctions and Measures Widened the Net of the European Criminal Justice Systems?' (2015) 17 *Punishment & Society* 575.

Alexander, M, *The New Jim Crow: Mass Imprisonment in an Age of Colorblindness* (2010, The New Press).

Aliverti, A, *Crimes of Mobility: Criminal Law and the Regulation of Mobility* (2013, Routledge).

Allen, F, *The Decline of the Rehabilitative Ideal: Penal Policy and Social Purpose* (1981, Yale University Press).

Alston, P, 'The Populist Challenge to Human Rights' (2017) 9 *Journal of Human Rights Practice* 1.

American Friends Service Committee, *Struggle for Justice* (1971, Hill and Wang).

Anderson, E, 'Democracy: Instrumental vs. Non-Instrumental Value', in: T Christiano and J Christman (eds), *Contemporary Debates in Political Philosophy* (2009, Wiley-Blackwell).

Andrews, DA, Bonta, J, and Wormith, JS, 'The Risk-Need-Responsivity (RNR) Model: Does Adding the Good Lives Model Contribute to Effective Crime Prevention?' (2011) 38 *Criminal Justice and Behavior* 735.

Aristotle (attrib.), *The Athenian Constitution* (1984, PJ Rhodes (trans), Penguin).

Aristotle, *The Nicomachean Ethics* (2009, D Ross, trans, L Brown, ed, Oxford University Press).

Aristotle, *Politics* (1995, E Baker (trans), RF Stalley (ed), Oxford University Press).

Arneson, R, 'Human Flourishing Versus Desire Satisfaction' (1999) 16 *Social Policy and Philosophy* 113.

Ashcroft, A, 'Cycle of Change', in: Rob Canton and David Hancock (eds), *Dictionary of Probation and Offender Management* (2007, Willan), 83–84.

Ashford, C, 'Barebacking and the "Cult of Violence": Queering the Criminal Law' (2010) 74 *Journal of Criminal Law* 339.

Ashworth, A, 'A Decade of Human Rights in Criminal Justice' [2014] *Criminal Law Review* 325.

Ashworth, A, 'Is the Criminal Law a Lost Cause?' (2000) 116 *Law Quarterly Review* 225.

Ashworth, A, 'Prisons, Proportionality, and Recent Penal History' (2017) 80 *Modern Law Review* 473.

Ashworth, A, 'Responsibilities, Rights, and Restorative Justice' (2002) 42(3) *British Journal of Criminology* 578.

Ashworth, A, *Sentencing and Criminal Justice*, Sixth Edition (2015, Cambridge University Press).

Ashworth, A, 'Social Control and "Anti-Social Behaviour": The Subversion of Human Rights?' (2004) 120 *Law Quarterly Review* 263.

Ashworth, A, and Redmayne, M, *The Criminal Process*, Fourth Edition (2010, Oxford University Press).

Ashworth, A, and Roberts, JV, (eds), *Sentencing Guidelines: Exploring the English Model* (2013, Oxford University Press).

Ashworth, A, and Zedner, L, 'Defending the Criminal Law: Reflections on the Changing Character of Crime, Procedure, and Sanctions' (2008) 2 *Criminal Law and Philosophy* 21.

Ashworth, A, and Zedner, L, *Preventive Justice* (2014, Oxford University Press).

Ashworth, A, and Zedner, L, 'Preventive Orders: A Problem of Undercriminalization?' in: RA Duff, L Farmer, SE Marshall, M Renzo, and V Tadros (eds), *The Boundaries of the Criminal Law* (2014, Oxford University Press), 59–87.

Ashworth, A, Zedner, L, and Tomlin, P (eds), *Prevention and the Limits of the Criminal Law* (2013, Oxford University Press).

Aubuchon-Rubin, A, 'Rehabilitating Durkheim: Social Solidarity and Rehabilitation in Eastern State Penitentiary, 1829–1850' (2009) 5 *International Journal of Punishment and Sentencing* 12.

Bailkin, J, 'Leaving Home: The Politics of Deportation in Postwar Britain' (2008) 47 *Journal of British Studies* 852.
Baldwin, C, 'The Vetting Epidemic in England and Wales' (2017) 81 *Journal of Criminal Law* 478.
Barton, A, and Davies, H (eds), *Ignorance, Power and Harm: Agnotology and the Criminological Imagination* (2018, Palgrave Macmillan).
Bazyler, MJ, 'The Role of the Soviet Union in the International Military Tribunal at Nuremberg', in: HR Reginbogin and CJM Safferling, with WR Hippel (eds) *The Nuremberg Trials: International Criminal Law Since 1945: 60th Anniversary International Conference* (2006, KG Saur), 45–52.
Bell, D, 'What is Liberalism?' (2014) 42(6) *Political Theory* 682–715.
Bennett, C, *The Apology Ritual: A Philosophical Theory of Punishment* (2008, Cambridge University Press).
Bennett, C, 'Invisible Punishment is Wrong – But Why? The Normative Basis of Criticism of Collateral Consequences of Criminal Conviction' (2017) 56 *The Howard Journal of Crime and Justice* 480.
Bennett, C, 'Punishment and Rehabilitation', in J Ryberg and JA Corlett (eds), *Punishment and Ethics: New Perspectives* (2010, Palgrave Macmillan), 52–71.
Bennett, C, 'Taking the Sincerity Out of Saying Sorry' (2006) 23 *Journal of Applied Philosophy* 127.
Bentham, J, 'An Introduction to the Principles and Morals of Legislation', excerpted in: M Tonry (ed), *Why Punish? How Much? A Reader on Punishment* (2011, Oxford University Press), 51–70.
Berger, P, and Luckmann, T, *The Social Construction of Reality: A Treatise in the Sociology of Knowledge* (1966, Penguin).
Bingham, T, *The Rule of Law* (2010, Penguin).
Bloch, M, *Feudal Society, vol. 2: Social Classes and Political Organisation* (1964, Routledge).
Bobbio, N, *Liberalism and Democracy* (1990, M Ryle and K Soper (trans), Verso).
Bobbio, N, *Left and Right: The Significance of a Political Distinction* (1996, A Cameron (trans), Polity Press).
Bolívar, D, Vanfraechem, I, and Aertsen, I, 'General Introduction', in I Vanfraechem, D Bolívar, and I Aertsen (eds), *Victims and Restorative Justice* (2015, Routledge).
Bookchin, M, *The Ecology of Freedom: The Emergence and Dissolution of Social Hierarchy*, Third Edition (2005, AK Press).
Bookchin, M, *Post-Scarcity Anarchism*, Third Edition (2004, AK Press).
Boonin, D, *The Problem of Punishment: A Critical Introduction* (2008, Cambridge University Press).
Borges, JL, and Guerrero, M, *The Book of Imaginary Beings* (1974, JL Borges and N di Giovanni (trans), Vintage).
Bosworth, M, 'Introduction: Reinventing Penal Parsimony' (2010) 14 *Theoretical Criminology* 251.
Bosworth, M, and Turnbull, S, 'Immigration, Detention, and the Expansion of Penal Power in the United Kingdom', in K Reiter and Al Koenig (eds), *Extreme Punishment: Comparative Studies in Detention, Incarceration, and Solitary Confinement* (2015, Palgrave Macmillan), 50–67.
Bottoms, AE, 'An Introduction to "The Coming Crisis"', in: AE Bottoms and RH Preston (eds), *The Coming Penal Crisis: A Criminological and Theological Exploration* (1980, Scottish Academic Press), 1–24.
Bottoms, AE, 'The Philosophy and Politics of Punishment and Sentencing', in C Clarkson and R Morgan (eds), *The Politics of Sentencing* (1995, Clarendon Press).
Bottoms, AE, and McWilliams, W, 'A Non-Treatment Paradigm for Probation Practice' (1979) 9 *British Journal of Social Work* 160.
Bottoms, A, and von Hirsch, A, 'The Crime-Preventive Impact of Penal Sanctions', in P Cane and H Kritzer (eds), *The Oxford Handbook of Empirical Legal Research* (2010, Oxford University Press), 96–124.
Bowsher, P, 'Should Incest between Consenting Adults Be Legalised?' [2015] *Criminal Law Review* 208.
Box, S, *Power, Crime, and Mystification* (1983, Routledge).
Braithwaite, J, and Pettit, P, *Not Just Deserts: A Republican Theory of Justice* (1990, Oxford University Press).
Brangan, L, 'Civilizing Imprisonment: The Limits of Scottish Penal Exceptionalism' (2019) *British Journal of Criminology*, forthcoming.

Bregman, R, *Utopia for Realists: And How We Can Get There* (2016, Elizabeth Manton (trans), Bloomsbury).
Bronsteen, J, Buccafusco, C, and Masur, J, 'Happiness and Punishment' (2009) 76 *University of Chicago Law Review* 1037.
Bronsteen, J Buccafusco, C, and Masur, J, 'Retribution and the Experience of Punishment' (2010) 98 *California Law Review* 1463.
Brooker, C, 'Healthcare and Probation: The Impact of Government Reforms' (2015) 62 *Probation Journal* 268.
Brown, E, and Smith, A, 'Challenging Mass Incarceration in the City of Care: Punishment, Community, and Residential Placement' (2018) 22 *Theoretical Criminology* 4.
Brown, M, 'Empathy and Punishment' (2012) 14 *Punishment & Society* 383.
Brownmiller, S, *Against Our Will: Rape, Women, and Men* (1975, Fawcett Columbine).
Burke, L, and Collett, S, '*Transforming Rehabilitation*: Organisational Bifurcation and the End of Probation as We Knew It?' (2016) 63 *Probation Journal* 120.
Burney, E, *Making People Behave: Anti-Social Behaviour, Politics and Policy* (2005, Willan).
Caldwell, B, 'Banished for Life: Deportation of Juvenile Offenders as Cruel and Unusual Punishment' (2013) 34 *Cardozo Law Review* 2261.
Canton, R, 'Crime, Punishment and the Moral Emotions: Righteous Minds and their Attitudes towards Punishment' (2015) 17 *Punishment and Society* 54.
Canton, R, 'Probation and the Philosophy of Punishment' (2018) 65 *Probation Journal* 252.
Canton, R, 'Probation and the Tragedy of Punishment' (2007) 46 *The Howard Journal of Crime and Justice* 236.
Canton, R, *Why Punish?* (2017, Palgrave).
Canton, R, and Dominey, J, *Probation: Working with Offenders*, Second Edition (2018, Routledge).
Carlen, P, 'Against Rehabilitation; For Reparative Justice', in: K Carrington, M Ball, E O'Brien, and J Tauri (eds), *Crime, Justice and Social Democracy: International Perspectives* (2013, Palgrave Macmillan), 89–104.
Carlen, P, *Alternatives to Women's Imprisonment* (1990, Open University Press).
Carlen, P, 'Crime, Inequality, and Sentencing', in P Carlen and D Cook (eds), *Paying for Crime* (1989, Open University Press), 8–28.
Cartwright, P, 'Crime, Punishment, and Consumer Protection' (2007) 30 *Journal of Consumer Policy* 1.
Carvalho, H, 'Liberty and Insecurity in the Criminal Law: Lessons from Thomas Hobbes' (2017) 11 *Criminal Law and Philosophy* 249.
Carvalho, H, *The Preventive Turn in Criminal Law* (2017, Oxford University Press).
Carvalho, H, and Chamberlen, A, 'Why Punishment Pleases: Punitive Feelings in a World of Hostile Solidarity' (2018) 20(2) *Punishment & Society* 217–234.
Cate, S, and HoSang, D, '"The Better Way to Fight Crime": Why Fiscal Arguments Do Not Constrain the Carceral State' (2018) 22 *Theoretical Criminology* 169.
Cavadino, M, Dignan, J, and Mair, G, *The Penal System: An Introduction*, Fifth Edition (2013, SAGE).
Charles, P, 'Restoring "Life, Liberty, and the Pursuit of Happiness" in Our Constitutional Jurisprudence: An Exercise in Legal History' (2011) 20 *William and Mary Bill of Rights Journal* 457.
James Chalmers, '"Frenzied Law-Making": Overcriminalisation by Numbers' (2014) 67 *Current Legal Problems* 483.
Chalmers, J, and Leverick, F, 'Criminal Law in the Shadows: Creating Offences in Delegated Legislation' (2018) 38 *Legal Studies* 221.
Chalmers, J, and Leverick, F, 'Tracking the Creation of Criminal Offences' [2013] *Criminal Law Review* 543.
Chalmers, J, Leverick, F, and Shaw, A, 'Is Formal Criminalisation Really on the Rise? Evidence from the 1950s' [2015] *Criminal Law Review* 177.
Chan, W, and Simester, AP, 'Four Functions of Mens Rea' (2011) 70 *Cambridge Law Journal* 381.
Chartier, G, *Anarchy and Legal Order: Law and Politics for a Stateless Society* (2013, Cambridge University Press).
Chau, P, 'Bennett's Expressive Justification of Punishment' (2017) 11 *Criminal Law and Philosophy* 661.

Cheeseman, N, *Democracy in Africa: Successes, Failures and the Struggle for Political Reform* (2015, Cambridge University Press).
Chiao, V, 'Mass Incarceration and the Theory of Punishment' (2017) 11 *Criminal Law and Philosophy* 431.
Christie, N, 'Afterword: Justice in Modernity', in: S Farrall, B Goldson, I Loader, and A Dockley (eds), *Justice and Penal Reform: Re-Shaping the Penal Landscape* (2015, Routledge), 198–204.
Christie, N, 'Conflicts as Property' (1977) 17 *British Journal of Criminology* 1.
Christie, N, *Limits to Pain: The Role of Punishment in Penal Policy* (1982, Martin Robinson).
Christie, N, *A Suitable Amount of Crime* (2004, Routledge).
Cohen, SA, '"The Quality of Mercy": Law, Equity, and Ideology in *The Merchant of Venice*' (1994) 27 *Mosaic* 35.
Cohen, S, *Against Criminology* (1988, Transaction).
Cohen, S, 'The Punitive City: Notes on the Dispersal of Social Control' (1979) 3 *Contemporary Crises* 339.
Cohen, S, *Visions of Social Control: Crime, Punishment, and Classification* (1985, Polity).
Collett, S, 'Riots, Revolution and Rehabilitation: The Future of Probation' (2013) 52 *The Howard Journal of Crime and Justice* 163.
Cook, D, *Poverty, Crime and Punishment* (1997, Child Poverty Action Group).
Cracknall, M, 'Post-Release Reform to Short Prison Sentences: Re-Legitimising and Widening the Net of Punishment' (2018) 65 *Probation Journal* 302.
Critchley, S, *The Faith of the Faithless: Experiments in Political Theology* (2012, Verso).
Critchley, S, *Infinitely Demanding: Ethics of Commitment, Politics of Resistance* (2012, Verso).
Cullen, F, and Gilbert, K, *Re-Affirming Rehabilitation*, Second Edition (2013, Anderson Publishing).
Cunneen, C, 'Reviving Restorative Justice Traditions', in: Gerry Johnstone and Daniel van Ness (eds), *Handbook of Restorative Justice* (2007, Willan), 113–131.
Dagger, R Republicanism and the Foundations of Criminal Law', in RA Duff and SP Green (eds), *Theoretical Foundations of Criminal Law* (2011, Oxford University Press), 44–66.
Daly, K, 'The Punishment Debate in Restorative Justice', in: Jonathan Simon and Richard Sparks (eds), *The SAGE Handbook of Punishment and Society* (2013, SAGE), 356–374.
Davis, L, 'The Dynamic and Revolutionary Utopia of Ursula K Le Guin', in: L Davis and P Stillman (eds), *The New Utopian Politics of Ursula K Le Guin's* The Dispossessed (2005, Lexington Books), 3–36.
de Giorgi, A, *Rethinking the Political Economy of Punishment: Perspectives on Post-Fordism and Penal Politics* (2006, Ashgate).
de Haan, W, 'Abolition and the Politics of "Bad Conscience"' (1987) 26 *The Howard Journal of Crime and Justice* 15.
de Tocqueville, A, *Democracy in America, Volume One*, Third American Edition (1889, H Reeve (trans), J Spencer (ed), George Adlard).
De Vos, H, and Gilbert, E, 'Freedom, So Close But Yet So Far: The Impact of the Ongoing Confrontation with Freedom on the Perceived Severity of Punishment' (2017) 9 *European Journal of Probation* 132.
Deering, J, 'Attitudes and Beliefs of Trainee Probation Officers: A "New Breed"?' (2010) 57 *Probation Journal* 9.
Deering, J, and Feilzer, M, *Privatising Probation: Is* Transforming Rehabilitation *the End of the Probation Ideal?* (2015, Policy Press).
Dhami, M, Belton, I and Goodman-Delahunty, J, 'Quasirational Models of Sentencing' (2015) 4 *Journal of Applied Research in Memory and Cognition* 239.
Dhami, M, Mantle, G, and Fox, D, 'Restorative Justice in Prisons' (2009) 12 *Contemporary Justice Review* 433.
Dickens, C, *American Notes for General Circulation, Volume One* (1842, Cambridge University Press).
Dickens, C, 'Mr Charles Dickens and the Execution of the Mannings,' *The Times*, 13th November, collected in: G Hogarth and M Dickens (eds), *Letters of Charles Dickens, Book II: 1843–1857* (1893, Cambridge University Press).

Dignan, J, 'Restorative Justice: Towards a Systemic Model of Restorative Justice: Reflections on the Concept, its Context, and the Need for Clear Constraints', in: A von Hirsch, AE Bottoms, K Roach, J Roberts, and M Schiff (eds), *Restorative Justice or Criminal Justice: Competing or Reconcilable Programmes?* (2003, Hart), 135–156.

Dingwall, G, 'Deserting Desert? Locating the Present Role of Retributivism in the Role of Sentencing Adult Offenders' (2008) 47 *The Howard Journal of Criminal Justice* 400.

Dominey, J, 'Fragmenting Probation: Recommendations from Research' (2016) 63 *Probation Journal* 136.

Donohue, E, and Moore, D, 'When is an Offender Not an Offender? Power, the Client, and Shifting Penal Subjectivities' (2009) 11 *Punishment & Society* 319.

Donohue, J, and Wolfers, J, 'The Uses and Abuses of Empirical Evidence in the Death Penalty Debate' (2006) 58 *Stanford Law Review* 791.

Drake, D, and Henley, A, '"Victims" Versus "Offenders" in British Political Discourse: The Construction of a False Dichotomy' (2014) 53 *The Howard Journal of Crime and Justice* 141.

Drumbl, M, 'Collective Violence and Individual Punishment: The Criminality of Mass Atrocity' (2005) 99 *Northwestern University Law Review* 539.

du Bois-Pedain, A, 'Punishment as an Inclusionary Practice: Sentencing in a Liberal Constitutional State', in A du Bois-Pedain, M Ulväng, and P Asp (eds), *Criminal Law and the Authority of the State* (2017, Hart), 199–228.

Duff, RA, *Answering for Crime: Responsibility and Liability in the Criminal Law* (2007, Hart).

Duff, RA, 'Crime, Prohibition and Punishment' (2002) 19 *Journal of Applied Philosophy* 97.

Duff, RA, 'A Criminal Law for Citizens' (2010) 14 *Theoretical Criminology* 293.

Duff, RA, 'In Defence of One Kind of Retributivism: A Reply to Bagaric and Amarasekara' (2000) 24 *Melbourne University Law Review* 411.

Duff, RA, 'Penance, Punishment, and the Limits of Community' (2003) 5 *Punishment & Society* 295.

Duff, RA, 'Probation, Punishment and Restorative Justice: Should Al Truism Be Engaged in Punishment?' (2003) 42 *Howard Journal of Crime and Justice* 181.

Duff, RA, *Punishment, Communication, and Community* (2001, Oxford University Press).

Duff, RA, 'Punishment, Communication and Community', in: M Matravers (ed), *Punishment and Political Theory* (1998, Hart), 48–68.

Duff, RA, and Green, SP, 'Introduction: Searching for Foundations', in: RA Duff and SP Green (eds), *Philosophical Foundations of Criminal Law* (2011, Oxford University Press), 1–18.

Durkheim, É, *The Division of Labor within Society* (1984, WD Halls (trans), Macmillan), pp 31–87.

Durkheim, É; Jones, TA, and Scull, A (trans), 'Two Laws of Penal Evolution' (1973) 2 *Economy and Society* 285.

Durnescu, I, 'Pains of Probation: Effective Practice and Human Rights' (2011) 55 *International Journal of Offender Therapy and Comparative Criminology* 530.

Durnescu, I, Kennefick, L, Sucic, I, and Glavak Tkalic, R, 'Experiencing Offender Supervision in Europe: The Eurobarometer – Lessons from the Study' (2018) 65 *Probation Journal* 7.

Dyson, M, 'The State's Obligation to Provide a Coherent System of Remedies across Crime and Tort', in: A du Bois-Pedain, M Ülvang, and P Asp (eds), *Criminal Law and the Authority of the State* (2017, Hart), 171–198.

Dzur, A, *Punishment, Participatory Democracy, and Juries* (2012, Oxford University Press).

Edwards, JR, and Simester, AP, 'Prevention with a Moral Voice', in AP Simester, Antje du Bois-Pedain, and Ulfrid Neumann (eds), *Liberal Criminal Theory: Essays for Andreas von Hirsch* (2013, Hart), 43–65.

Elias, N, *The Civilizing Process, Volume One: The History of Manners* (1969, Blackwell).

Elias, N, *The Civilizing Process, Volume Two: State Formation and Civilization* (1982, Blackwell).

Farrant, F, 'Knowledge Production and the Punishment Ethic: The Demise of the Probation Service' (2006) 53 *Probation Journal* 317.

Farrington, D, 'Age and Crime' (1986) 7 *Crime and Justice* 189.

Faucher, L, 'Revisionism and Moral Responsibility for Implicit Attitudes', in M Brownstein and J Saul (eds), *Implicit Bias and Philosophy, Volume Two: Moral Responsibility, Structural Injustice, and Ethics* (2016, Oxford University Press), 115–144.

Feeley, M, *The Process is the Punishment: Handling Cases in a Lower Criminal Court* (1979, Russell Sage Foundation).

Feeley, M, and Simon, J, 'The New Penology: Notes on the Emerging Strategy of Corrections and its Implications' (1992) 30 *Criminology* 449.

Feest, J, 'Abolitionism: Some Answers to Frequently Answered Questions' (2015) 7 *Sortuz: Oñati Journal of Emergent Socio-Legal Studies* 141.

Feilzer, MY 'Criminologists Making News? Providing Factual Information on Crime and Criminal Justice through a Weekly Newspaper Column' (2007) 3 *Crime Media Culture* 285.

Feinberg, J, 'The Expressive Function of Punishment' (1965) 49 *The Monist* 397.

Feinberg, J, *Harm to Others: The Moral Limits of the Criminal Law, Volume One* (1984, Oxford University Press).

Feinberg, J, *Offense to Others: The Moral Limits of the Criminal Law, Volume Two* (1985, Oxford University Press).

Feinberg, J, *Harms to Self: The Moral Limits of the Criminal Law, Volume Three* (1986, Oxford University Press).

Feinberg, J, *Harmless Wrongdoing: The Moral Limits of the Criminal Law, Volume Four* (1988, Oxford University Press).

Ferns, C, 'Future Conditional or Future Perfect? *The Dispossessed* and Permanent Revolution', in: L Davis and P Stillman (eds), *The New Utopian Politics of Ursula K Le Guin's* The Dispossessed (2005, Lexington Books), 249–262.

Fish, M, 'An Eye for an Eye? Proportionality as a Moral Principle of Punishment' (2008) 28 *Oxford Journal of Legal Studies* 57.

Fish, MS, *Democracy Derailed in Russia: The Failure of Open Politics* (2012, Cambridge University Press).

Fornas, J, *Cultural Theory and Late Modernity* (1995, SAGE).

Foster, J, Newburn, T, and Souhami, A, *Assessing the Impact of the Stephen Lawrence Enquiry*, Home Office Research Study 294 (Home Office, October 2005).

Foster, M, and Lambert, H, 'Statelessness as a Human Rights Issue: A Concept Whose Time Has Come' (2016) 28 *International Journal of Refugee Law* 564.

Foucault, M, *Abnormal: Lectures at the* Collège de France, *1974–1975* (2003, G Burchell (trans), V Marchetti and A Salomoni (eds), Verso).

Foucault, M, *The Archaeology of Knowledge* (1972, AM Sheridan Smith (trans), Routledge).

Foucault, M, *Discipline and Punish: The Birth of the Prison* (1977, A Sheridan (trans), Penguin).

Foucault, M, *The Order of Things: An Archaeology of the Human Sciences* (1970, Tavistock/Routledge (trans), Routledge).

Fox, R, 'Someone to Watch Over Us: Back to the Panopticon?' (2001) 1 *Criminology and Criminal Justice* 251.

Frank, D, 'Abandoned: Abolishing Female Imprisonment to Prevent Sexual Abuse and Herald an End to Incarceration' (2014) 29 *Berkeley Journal of Gender, Law and Justice* 1.

Frase, R, *Just Sentencing: Principles and Procedures for a Workable System* (2013, Oxford University Press).

Frase, R, 'Limiting Retributivism', in: M Tonry (ed), *The Future of Imprisonment* (2004, Oxford University Press), 143–205.

Frase, R, 'Sentencing Principles in Theory and Practice' (1997) 22 *Crime & Justice* 363.

Frazer, L, Drinkwater, N, Mullen, J, Hayes, C, O'Donoghue, K, and Cumbo, E, 'Rehabilitation: What Does "Good" Look Like Anyway?' (2014) 6 *European Journal of Probation* 92.

Fromm, E, *The Fear of Freedom* (1942, Routledge and Kegan Paul).

Fuller, LL, 'The Case of the Speluncean Explorers' (1949) 62 *Harvard Law Review* 616.

Gainey, R, and Payne, B, 'Understanding the Experience of House Arrest with Electronic Monitoring: An Analysis of Quantitative and Qualitative Data' (2000) 44 *International Journal of Offender Therapy and Comparative Criminology* 84.

Gardner, J, 'Crime: In Proportion and in Perspective', in: A Ashworth and M Wasik (eds), *Fundamentals of Sentencing Theory: Essays in Honour of Andrew von Hirsch* (1998, The Clarendon Press), 31–52.
Gardner, J, and Shute, S, 'The Wrongness of Rape', collected in: J Gardner (ed), *Offences and Defences: Essays in the Philosophy of Criminal Law* (2007, Oxford University Press), 1–32.
Garland, D, *The Culture of Control: Crime and Social Order in Contemporary Society* (2001, Oxford University Press).
Garland, D, 'Introduction: The Meaning of Mass Imprisonment' (2001) 3 *Punishment and Society* 4.
Garland, D, *Peculiar Institution: America's Death Penalty in an Age of Abolition* (2011, Harvard University Press).
Garland, D, 'Penality and the Penal State' (2013) 51 *Criminology* 475.
Garland, D, *Punishment and Modern Society: A Study in Social Theory* (1990, Clarendon Press).
Garland, D, 'Punishment and Social Solidarity', in J Simon and R Sparks (eds), *The SAGE Handbook of Punishment and Society* (2013, SAGE), 23–39.
Garland, D, *Punishment and Welfare: A History of Penal Strategies* (1985, Ashgate).
Gelsthorpe, L, and Rex, S, 'Community Service as Reparation: Exploring the Potential', in: G Mair (ed), *What Matters in Probation* (2004, Willan), 229–254.
Giddens, A, *Beyond Left and Right: The Future of Radical Politics* (1994, Polity Press).
Glasgow, J, 'The Expressivist Theory of Punishment Defended' (2015) 34 *Law and Philosophy* 601.
Gleason, A, *Totalitarianism: The Inner History of the Cold War* (1995, Oxford University Press).
Goffman, E, *Asylums: Essays on the Social Situation of Mental Patients and Other Inmates* (1961, Anchor Books).
Goodman, P, Page, J, and Phelps, M, *Breaking the Pendulum: The Long Struggle over Criminal Justice* (2017, Oxford University Press).
Goold, B, Loader, I, and Thumala, A, 'The Banality of Security: The Curious Case of Surveillance Cameras' (2013) 53 *British Journal of Criminology* 977.
Grapes, T, 'Offender Management', in: R Canton and D Hancock (eds), *Dictionary of Probation and Offender Management* (2007, Willan), 188–191.
Gray, J, 'On Negative and Positive Liberty', in Gray (ed), *Liberalisms: Essays in Political Philosophy* (1989, Routledge), 45–68.
Gray, J, *Straw Dogs: Thoughts on Humans and Other Animals* (2002, Granta Books).
Gray, J, *Two Faces of Liberalism* (2001, Oxford University Press).
Gray, R, 'Eliminating the (Absurd) Distinction between *Malum in Se* and *Malum Prohibitum* Crimes' (1995) 73 *Washington University Law Quarterly* 1369.
Green, S, *Crime, Community and Morality* (2014, Routledge).
Green, S, 'The Victims' Movement and Restorative Justice', in: G Johnstone and D van Ness (eds), *Handbook of Restorative Justice* (2007, Willan), 171–191.
Green, SP, 'The Conceptual Utility of *Malum Prohibitum*' (2016) 55 *Dialogue* 33.
Gregory, M, 'Practical Wisdom and the Ethic of Care in Probation Practice' (2011) 3 *European Journal of Probation* 60.
Gross, H, *Crime and Punishment: A Concise Moral Critique* (2013, Oxford University Press).
Gur-Ayre, M, 'Human Dignity of "Offenders": A Limitation on Substantive Criminal Law' (2012) 6 *Criminal Law and Philosophy* 187.
Habermas, J, 'The Concept of Human Dignity and the Realistic Utopia of Human Rights' (2010) 41 *Metaphilosophy* 464.
Habermas, J, *Moral Consciousness and Communicative Action* (1990, C Lenhardt and S Nicholson (trans), Polity Press).
Hagemann, O, 'Restorative Justice in Prison?' in: L Walgrave (ed), *Repositioning Restorative Justice* (2003, Willan), 221–235.
Hallsworth, S, and Lea, J, 'Reconstructing Leviathan: Emerging Contours of the Security State' (2011) 15 *Theoretical Criminology* 141.
Hart, HLA, 'Prolegomenon to the Principles of Punishment', in HLA Hart (ed), *Punishment and Responsibility: Essays in the Philosophy of Punishment*, Second Edition (2007, Oxford University Press), 1–27.

Hannah-Moffatt, K, 'Punishment and Risk', in Jonathan Simon and Richard Sparks (eds), *The SAGE Handbook of Punishment and Society* (2013, SAGE), 129–151.
Hay, D, 'Property, Authority and the Criminal Law', in D Hay, P Linebaugh, J Rule, EP Thompson, and C Winslow (eds), *Albion's Fatal Tree: Crime and Society in Eighteenth-Century England*, Revised Edition (2011, Verso).
Hayek, FA, *The Constitution of Liberty* (1960, Routledge).
Hayes, D, 'Experiencing Penal Supervision: A Literature Review' (2019) *Probation Journal*, (2018) 65 *Probation Journal* 387.
Hayes, D, 'The Impact of Supervision on the Pains of Community Penalties in England and Wales: An Exploratory Study' (2015) 7 *European Journal of Probation* 82.
Hayes, DJ, 'Penal Impact: Towards a More Intersubjective Measurement of Penal Severity' (2016) 36 *Oxford Journal of Legal Studies* 724.
Hayes, D, 'Proximity, Pain and State Punishment' (2018) 20 *Punishment & Society* 235.
Hebenton, B, and Seddon, T, 'From Dangerousness to Precaution: Managing Sexual and Violent Offenders in an Insecure and Uncertain Age' (2009) 49 *British Journal of Criminology* 343.
Heffernan, WC, and Kleinig, J (eds), *From Social Justice to Criminal Justice: Poverty and the Administration of Criminal Law* (2000, Oxford University Press).
Hegel, GWF, *Elements of the Philosophy of Right* (1991, HB Nisbet (trans), Allen Wood (ed), Cambridge University Press).
Heidegger, M, *Being and Time*, Revised Translation (2010, J Stambaugh (trans), D Schmidt (ed), State University of New York Press).
Herzog-Evans, M, 'Consent and Probation: An Analogy with Contract Law' (2015) 7 *European Journal of Probation* 143.
Hillner, J, Ulrich, J, and Jakob Engberg (eds), *Clerical Exile in Late Antiquity* (2016, Peter Lang).
HM Chief Inspector for Prisons for England and Wales, *Annual Report 2017/18* (HM Inspectorate of Prisons), HC 1245, 11 July 2018.
Hobbes, T, *Leviathan* (1996, JCA Gaskin (trans), Oxford University Press).
Hobhouse, LT, *Liberalism and Other Writings* (1994, James Meadowcroft (ed), Cambridge University Press).
Hoffman, S, and McDonald, S, 'Should ASBOs Be Civilised?' [2010] *Criminal Law Review* 457.
Hogg, R, 'Punishment and "The People": Rescuing Populism from its Critics', in: K Carrington, M Ball, E O'Brien, and J Tauri (eds), *Crime, Justice and Social Democracy: International Perspectives* (2013, Palgrave Macmillan), 105–119.
Home Office, *Crime, Justice and Protecting the Public: The Government's Proposals for Legislation* (1990, The Stationery Office, Cm 965).
Honderich, T, *Punishment: The Supposed Justifications Revisited*, revised edition (2006, Pluto Press).
Horder, J, *Ashworth's Principles of Criminal Law*, Eighth Edition (2016, Oxford University Press).
Hörnle, T, 'Criminalizing Behaviour to Protect Human Dignity' (2012) 6 *Criminal Law and Philosophy* 307.
Horton, T, and Gregory, J, *The Solidarity Society: Why We Can Afford to End Poverty, and How to Do It with Public Support* (2009, Fabian Society).
Hostettler, J, *A History of Criminal Justice in England and Wales* (2009, Waterside Press).
Howard, J, *The State of the Prisons in England and Wales: With Preliminary Observations and an Account of Some Foreign Prisons*, Second Edition (1784, Cambridge University Press).
Hudson, B 'Beyond Proportionate Punishment: Difficult Cases and the 1991 Criminal Justice Act' (1995) 22 *Crime, Law & Social Change* 59.
Hudson, B, *Justice in the Risk Society: Challenging and Re-Affirming Justice in Late Modernity* (2003, SAGE).
Hudson, B, *Justice through Punishment: A Critique of the 'Justice' Model of Corrections* (1987, Macmillan Education).
Hudson, BA, *Penal Policy and Social Justice* (1993, Macmillan).
Hudson, B, 'Punishing the Poor: A Critique of the Dominance of Legal Reasoning in Penal Policy and Practice', in RA Duff, SE Marshall, R Emerson-Dobash, and R Dobash (eds), *Penal Theory and Practice: Tradition and Innovation in Criminal Justice* (1994, Manchester University Press), 292–305.

Hudson, B, 'Punishing the Poor: Dilemmas of Justice and Difference', in WC Heffernan and J Kleinig (eds), *From Social Justice to Criminal Justice: Poverty and the Administration of Criminal Law* (2000, Oxford University Press), 189–216.

Hudson, B, 'Victims and Offenders', in: A von Hirsch, AE Bottoms, K Roach, J Roberts, and M Schiff (eds), *Restorative Justice or Criminal Justice: Competing or Reconcilable Programmes?* (2003, Hart), 177–194.

Hunt, H, '"Triumph of the Will": Heidegger's Nazism as Spiritual Pathology' (1998) 19(4) *Journal of Mind and Behavior* 379.

Husak, D, '"Already Punished Enough"' (1990) 18 *Philosophical Topics* 79.

Husak, D, *Overcriminalization: The Limits of the Criminal Law* (2008, Oxford University Press).

Ignatieff, M, *A Just Measure of Pain: The Penitentiary in the Industrial Revolution, 1750–1850* (1978, Peregrine).

Ignatieff, M, 'State, Civil Society, and Total Institutions: A Critique of Recent Social Histories of Punishment' (1981) 3 *Crime & Justice* 153.

Jacobson, J, and Hough, M, 'Personal Mitigation: An Empirical Analysis in England and Wales', in: JV Roberts (ed), *Mitigation and Aggravation at Sentencing* (2011, Cambridge University Press), 146–167.

Jacobson, J, and Hough, M, *Unjust Deserts: Imprisonment for Public Protection* (2010, Prison Reform Trust).

Jameson, F, *Postmodernism: Or, the Cultural Logic of Late Capitalism* (1991, Duke University Press).

Jennings, W, Farrall, S, Gray, E, and Hay, C, 'Penal Populism and the Public Thermostat: Crime, Public Punitiveness, and Public Policy' (2017) 30 *Governance* 463.

Johnstone, G, and van Ness, D, 'The Meaning of Restorative Justice', in: G Johnstone and D van Ness (eds), *Handbook of Restorative Justice* (2007, Willan), 5–23.

Johnstone, R, and Pattie, C, 'Models of Voting', in: R Johnstone and C Pattie (eds), *Putting Voters in their Place: Geography and Elections in Great Britain* (2006, Oxford University Press), 1–39.

Jones, R, 'Populist Leniency, Crime Control and Due Process' (2010) 14 *Theoretical Criminology* 331.

JUSTICE, *Mental Health and Fair Trial* (2017, JUSTICE).

Kafka, F, 'In the Penal Colony', in: F Kafka; J Crick (ed, trans), The Metamorphosis *and Other Stories* (2009, Oxford University Press), 75–99.

Kahan, D, *Punishment Incommensurability* (1998) 1 *Buffalo Criminal Law Review* 691.

Kant, I, *Groundwork on the Metaphysics of Morals*, revised translation (2012, M Gregor and J Timmerman (trans); J Timmerman (ed), Cambridge University Press).

Kemple, T, 'Spirits of Late Capitalism' (2007) 24 *Theory, Culture & Society* 147.

Kendall, K, 'Dangerous Thinking: A Critical History of Correctional Behaviourism', in: George Mair (ed), *What Matters in Probation* (2004, Willan), 53–89.

Khaitan, T, 'Dignity as an Expressive Norm: Neither Vacuous nor a Panacea' (2012) 32 *Oxford Journal of Legal Studies* 1.

King, ML Jr; Scott King, C (ed), *The Words of Martin Luther King, Jr* (1987, Newmarket Press).

Klein, N, *This Changes Everything: Capitalism vs the Climate* (2014, Simon & Schuster).

Kleinig, J, 'Paternalism and Human Dignity' (2017) 11 *Criminal Law and Philosophy* 19.

Kleinig, J, 'What Does Wrongdoing Deserve?', in M Tonry (ed), *Retributivism Has a Past: Has It a Future?* (2011, Oxford University Press), 46–62.

Koch, I, 'Moving Beyond Punitivism: Punishment, State Failure, and Democracy at the Margins' (2017) 19 *Punishment & Society* 203.

Kolber, A, 'Against Proportional Punishment' (2013) 66 *Vanderbilt Law Review* 1141.

Kolber, A, 'The Subjective Experience of Punishment' (2009) 109 *Columbia Law Review* 182.

Kropotkin, P, *Ethics: Origin and Development* (1924, L Friedland and J Piroshnikoff (trans), Prism Press).

Kropotkin, P, 'Law and Authority', in: P Kropotkin; R Baldwin (ed), *Anarchism: A Collection of Revolutionary Writings* (2002, Dover), 195–218.

Kropotkin, P, *Mutual Aid: A Factor of Evolution*, Third Edition (2009, Freedom Press).

Kropotkin, P, 'Prisons and their Moral Influence on Prisoners', in: P Kropotkin; R Baldwin (ed), *Anarchism: A Collection of Revolutionary Writings*, Second Edition (2002, Dover Press), 219–235.

Lacey, N, 'Historicising Criminalisation: Conceptual and Empirical Issues' (2009) 72 *Modern Law Review* 936.
Lacey, N, 'The Metaphor of Proportionality' (2016) 43 *Journal of Law and Society* 27.
Lacey, N, *The Prisoners' Dilemma: Political Economy and Punishment in Contemporary Democracies* (2008, Cambridge University Press).
Lacey, N, 'Punishment, (Neo)Liberalism, and Social Democracy', in J Simon and R Sparks (eds), *The SAGE Handbook of Punishment and Society* (2013, SAGE), 260–280.
Lacey, N, *In Search of Criminal Responsibility: Ideas, Interests, and Institutions* (2016, Oxford University Press).
Lacey, N, 'Unspeakable Subjects, Impossible Rights: Sexuality, Integrity and Criminal Law', in: N Lacey (ed.), *Unspeakable Subjects: Feminist Essays in Legal and Social Theory* (1998, Hart), 98–124.
Lacey, N, and Pickard, H, 'To Blame or to Forgive? Reconciling Punishment and Forgiveness in Criminal Justice' (2015) 35 *Oxford Journal of Legal Studies* 665.
Lacey, N, and Pickard, H, 'The Chimera of Proportionality: Institutionalising Limits on Punishment in Contemporary Social and Political Systems' (2015) 78 *Modern Law Review* 216.
Lacey, N, and Pickard, H, 'From the Consulting Room to the Court Room? Taking the Clinical Model of Responsibility without Blame into the Legal Realm' (2013) 33 *Oxford Journal of Legal Studies* 1.
Lacey, N, and Zedner, L, 'Criminalization: Historical, Legal, and Criminological Perspectives', in: A Liebling, S Maruna, and L McAra (eds), *The Oxford Handbook of Criminology*, Sixth Edition (2017, Oxford University Press), 57–76.
Lacey, N, and Zedner, L, 'Discourses of Community in Criminal Justice' (1995) 22 *Journal of Law and Society* 301.
Laclau, E, *On Populist Reason* (2005, Verso).
Langbein, J, 'Controlling Prosecutial Discretion in Germany' (1974) 41 *University of Chicago Law Review* 439.
Lavi, S, 'Revocation of Citizenship as Punishment: On the Modern Duties of Citizens and their Criminal Breach' (2011) 61 *University of Toronto Law Review* 783.
Le Guin, UK, *Always Coming Home* (1985, Gollancz).
Le Guin, UK, *The Dispossessed: An Ambiguous Utopia* (1976, Gollancz).
Lee, A, 'Public Wrongs and the Criminal Law' (2015) 9 *Criminal Law and Philosophy* 155.
Lee, Y, 'Repeat Offenders and the Question of Desert', in JV Roberts and A von Hirsch, *Previous Convictions at Sentencing: Theoretical and Applied Perspective* (2010, Hart), 49–72.
Levi, M, and Lord, N, 'White-Collar and Corporate Crime', in A Liebling, S Maruna, and L McAra (eds), *The Oxford Handbook of Criminology*, Sixth Edition (2017, Oxford University Press), 722–743.
Levitas, R, 'The Concept of Social Exclusion and the New Durkheimian Hegemony' (1996) 16 *Critical Social Policy* 5.
Levitas, R, *Utopia as Method: The Imaginary Reconstitution of Society* (2013, Palgrave Macmillan).
Lippke, RL, 'Parsimony and the Sentencing of Multiple Offenders', in: J Ryberg, JV Roberts, and JW de Keijser (eds), *Sentencing Multiple Crimes* (2017, Oxford University Press), 95–111.
Lippke, R, 'Punishment Drift: The Spread of Penal Harm and What We Should Do About It' (2017) 11 *Criminal Law and Philosophy* 645.
Lippke, R, 'Retributive Parsimony' (2009) 15 *Res Publica* 377.
Lister, S, and Rowe, M, 'Electing Police and Crime Commissioners for England and Wales: Prospecting for the Democratisation of Policing' (2015) 25 *Policing and Society* 358.
Loader, I, 'The Fall of the "Platonic Guardians": Liberalism, Criminology and Political Responses to Crime in England and Wales' (2006) 46 *British Journal of Criminology* 561.
Loader, I, 'For Penal Moderation: Notes towards a Public Philosophy of Punishment' (2010) 14 *Theoretical Criminology* 349.
Loader, I, and Sparks, R, *Public Criminology?* (2011, Routledge).
Locke, J, 'An Essay Concerning the True, Original, Extent, and End of Civil-Government'; in J Locke; M Goldie (ed), *Second Treatise of Government and A Letter Concerning Toleration* (2016, Oxford University Press).

Lorde, A, 'The Master's Tools Will Never Dismantle the Master's House', in: A Lorde (ed), *Sister Outsider: Essays and Speeches* (1984, The Crossing Press), 110–113.

Lovegrove, A, 'Sanctions and Severity: To the Demise of Von Hirsch and Wasik's Sanction Hierarchy' (2001) 40 *The Howard Journal of Criminal Justice* 126.

Lucy, W, *Law's Judgement* (2017, Hart).

Lynch, M, 'Mass Incarceration, Legal Change, and Locale: Understanding and Remediating American Penal Overindulgence' (2011) 10 *Criminology & Public Policy* 673.

Lynch, M, 'Waste Managers? The New Penology, Crime Fighting, and Parole Agent Identity' (1998) 32 *Law & Society Review* 839.

MacIntyre, A, *After Virtue: A Study in Moral Theory*, Third Edition (2007, University of Notre Dame Press).

McIvor, G, 'Paying Back: 30 Years of Unpaid Work by Offenders in Scotland' (2010) 2 *European Journal of Probation* 41.

McKnight, J, 'Standing Up for Probation' (2009) 48 *The Howard Journal of Crime and Justice* 327.

McNeill, F, 'A Desistance Paradigm for Offender Management' (2006) 6 *Criminology and Criminal Justice* 39.

McNeill, F, 'Four Forms of "Offender" Rehabilitation: Towards an Interdisciplinary Perspective' (2012) 17 *Legal and Criminological Psychology* 18.

McNeill, F, 'Mass Supervision, Misrecognition, and the "Malopticon"' (2018) *Punishment and Society*, forthcoming.

McNeill, F, *Pervasive Punishment: Making Sense of 'Mass Supervision'* (2018, Emerald Publishing).

McNeill, F, 'Probation, Credibility and Justice' (2009) 58 *Probation Journal* 9.

McNeill, F, and Beyens, K, 'Introduction: Studying Mass Supervision', in F McNeill and K Beyens (eds), *Offender Supervision in Europe* (2013, Palgrave Macmillan), 1–18.

McNeill, F, and Dawson, M, 'Social Solidarity, Penal Evolution, and Probation' (2014) 54 *British Journal of Criminology* 892.

Macpherson, W, Cook, T, Sentamu, J, and Stone, R, *The Stephen Lawrence Inquiry*, Cm 4262, 24 February 1999.

Madden Dempsey, M, and Herring, J, 'Why Sexual Penetration Requires Justification' (2007) 27 *Oxford Journal of Legal Studies* 467.

Maglione, G, 'The Political Rationality of Restorative Justice' (2018), *Theoretical Criminology*, forthcoming.

Maguire, M, and McVie, S, 'Crime Data and Crime Statistics: A Critical Reflection', in: A Liebling, S Maruna, and L McAra (eds), *The Oxford Handbook of Criminology*, Sixth Edition (2017, Oxford University Press), 163–189.

Mair, G, 'Community Penalties in England and Wales' (1998) 10 *Federal Sentencing Reporter* 263.

Mair, G, 'The Origins of What Works in England and Wales: A House Built on Sand?', in G Mair (ed), *What Matters in Probation?* (2004, Willan), 12–33.

Mair, G, 'Research on Community Penalties', in: R King and E Wincup (eds), *Doing Research on Crime and Justice*, Second Edition (2007, Oxford University Press), 399–429.

Mair, G, (ed), *What Matters in Probation* (2004, Willan).

Mansell, W, *A Critical Introduction to Law*, Fourth Edition (2015, Routledge).

Mantle, G, 'Counterblast: Probation: Dead, Dying or Poorly?' (2006) 45 *The Howard Journal of Crime and Justice* 321.

Mantu, S, '"Terrorist" Citizens and the Human Right to Nationality' (2018) 26 *Journal of Contemporary European Studies* 28.

Margetts, H, 'Electoral Reform', in: J Fisher, D Denver, and J Benyon (eds), *Central Debates in British Politics* (2003, Routledge), 64–82.

Markel, D, 'Are Shaming Punishments Beautifully Retributive? Retributivism and the Implications for the Alternative Sanctions Debate' (2001) 54 Vanderbilt Law Review 2157.

Markel, D, and Flanders, C, 'Bentham on Stilts: On the Bare Relevance of Subjectivity to Retributive Justice' (2010) 98 *California Law Review* 907.

Marshall, S, *Demanding the Impossible: A History of Anarchism*, Third Edition (2008, Harper Perennial).
Maruna, S, *Making Good: How Ex-Convicts Reform and Rebuild their Lives* (2001, American Psychological Association).
Maruna, S, and King, A, 'Public Opinion and Community Penalties', in A Bottoms, S Rex, and G Robinson (eds), *Alternatives to Prison: Options for an Insecure Society* (2004, Willan).
Maslen, H, *Remorse, Penal Theory and Sentencing* (2015, Hart).
Mathiesen, T, 'The Future of Control Systems – The Case of Norway' (1980) 8 *International Journal of the Sociology of Law* 149.
Mathiesen, T, 'The Politics of Abolition', in: T Mathiesen (ed), *The Politics of Abolition Revisited* (2015, Routledge), 43–246.
Mathiesen, T (ed), *The Politics of Abolition Revisited* (2015, Routledge).
Matravers, M, 'Political Theory and the Criminal Law', in RA Duff and Stuart Green (eds), *Philosophical Foundations of Criminal Law* (2011, Oxford University Press), 67–82.
Matravers, M, 'Punishment, Suffering and Justice' in: Stephen Farrall et al (eds), *Justice and Penal Reform: Re-Shaping the Penal Landscape* (2016, Routledge), 27–46.
Matthews, R, 'The Myth of Punitiveness' (2005) 9 *Theoretical Criminology* 175.
Mauer, M, 'Addressing the Political Environment Affecting Mass Imprisonment' (2011) 10 *Criminology & Public Policy* 699.
Maurutto, P, and Hannah-Moffatt, K, 'Assembling Risk and the Restructuring of Penal Control' (2006) 46 *British Journal of Criminology* 438.
Mawhinney, G, 'To Be Ill or to Kill: The Criminality of Contagion' (2013) 77 *Journal of Criminal Law* 202.
Mill, JS, 'On Liberty', in JS Mill, *On Liberty, Utilitarianism and Other Essays*, New Edition (2015, M Philp and F Rosen (eds), Oxford University Press).
Miller, L, *The Myth of Mob Rule: Violent Crime and Democratic Politics* (2016, Oxford University Press).
Mills, H, *Community Sentences: A Solution to Penal Excess?* (Centre for Crime and Justice Studies, July 2011).
Minear, R, *Victor's Justice: Tokyo War Crimes Trial* (1971, Princeton University Press).
Ministry of Justice, *Deaths of Offenders in the Community, England and Wales, 2017/18* (Ministry of Justice, 25 October 2018).
Ministry of Justice, *National Offender Management Service Annual Offender Equalities Report, 2016/17* (Ministry of Justice, 30 November 2017).
Ministry of Justice, *Offender Management Statistics Quarterly: October to December 2017 and Annual 2017* (Ministry of Justice, 26 April 2018).
Ministry of Justice, *Safety in Custody Statistics, England and Wales: Deaths in Prison Custody to September 2018, Assaults and Self-Harm to June 2018* (Ministry of Justice, 25 October 2018).
Ministry of Justice, *Statistics on Race and the Criminal Justice System 2016* (Ministry of Justice, 30 November 2017).
Moore, MS, *Placing Blame: A General Theory of Criminal Law* (1997, Oxford University Press).
Morgan, R, 'Austerity, Subsidiarity and Parsimony: Offending Behaviour and Criminalisation', in A Silvestri (ed), *Lessons for the Coalition: An End of Term Report on New Labour and Criminal Justice* (Centre for Crime and Justice Studies, January 2011), 18–21.
Morris, N, *The Future of Imprisonment* (1974, University of Chicago Press).
Morris, N, *Madness and the Criminal Law* (1982, University of Chicago Press).
Morris, N, and Tonry, M, *Between Prison and Probation: Intermediate Punishments in a Rational Sentencing System* (1990, Oxford University Press).
Mustafa, N, Kingston, P and Beeston, D, 'An Exploration of the Historical Background of Criminal Record Checking in the United Kingdom: From the Eighteenth to the Twenty-First Century' (2013) 19 *European Journal on Criminal Policy and Research* 15.
Nagin, D, and Peppers, J (eds), *Deterrence and the Death Penalty* (2012, National Academies Press).
Nash, M, 'Probation, PSRs and Public Protection: Has a "Critical Point" Been Reached?' (2011) 11 *Criminology & Criminal Justice* 471.

National Offender Management Service, *Probation Statistics: Quarterly Brief: October to December 2004, England and Wales* (Home Office, nd, archived 4 December 2007).
Nef, J, and Reiter, B, *The Democratic Challenge: Rethinking Democracy and Democratization* (2009, Palgrave Macmillan).
Nelken, D, *Comparative Criminal Justice: Making Sense of Difference* (2010, SAGE).
Nellis, M, 'Understanding the Electronic Monitoring of Offenders in Europe: Expansion, Regulation and Prospects' (2014) 62 *Crime, Law and Social Change* 489.
Newburn, T, '"Tough on Crime": Penal Policy in England and Wales' (2007) 36 *Crime and Justice* 425.
Novak, A, *Comparative Executive Clemency: The Constitutional Pardon Power and the Prerogative of Mercy in Global Perspective* (2016, Routledge).
Oakley, A, 'Crime, Justice and "The Man Question"', in: S Farrall, B Goldson, I Loader, and A Dockley (eds), *Justice and Penal Reform: Re-Shaping the Penal Landscape* (2016, Routledge), 99–115.
O'Donnell, I, *Prisoners, Solitude, and Time* (2014, Oxford University Press).
Office for National Statistics, *Statistical Bulletin: 2011 Census: Population Estimates for the United Kingdom, March 2011* (Office for National Statistics, 17 December 2012).
Ohana, D, 'Administrative Penalties in the *Rechtsstaat*: On the Emergence of the *Ordnungswidrigkeit* Sanctioning System in Post-War Germany' (2014) 64 *University of Toronto Law Journal* 243.
O'Malley, P, *Risk, Uncertainty, Government* (2004, Glasshouse Press).
O'Sullivan, E, and O'Donnell, I, 'Introduction: Setting the Scene', in: E O'Sullivan and I O'Donnell (eds), *Coercive Confinement in Ireland: Patients, Prisoners and Penitents* (2012, Manchester University Press), 1–41.
O'Sullivan, J, 'Introduction' (1837) 1 *The United States Magazine and Democratic Review* 1.
Packer, H, 'Two Models of the Criminal Process' (1964) 113 *University of Pennsylvania Law Review* 1.
Padfield, N, 'Intoxication as a Sentencing Factor: Mitigation or Aggravation?', in: JV Roberts (ed), *Mitigation and Aggravation at Sentencing* (2011, Cambridge University Press), 81–101.
Padfield, N, 'Judicial Rehabilitation? The View from England' (2011) 3 *European Journal of Probation* 36.
Padfield, N, 'Time To Bury the Custody "Threshold"?' [2011] *Criminal Law Review* 593.
Paine, T, *Rights of Man, Common Sense, and Other Political Writings* (1995, Philp, M (ed), Oxford University Press).
Pamment, N, and Ellis, T, 'A Retrograde Step: The Potential Impact of High Visibility Uniforms within Youth Justice Reparation' (2010) 49 *The Howard Journal of Crime and Justice* 18.
Peay, J, *Mental Health and Crime* (2010, Routledge).
Peay, J, 'Mental Health, Mental Disabilities, and Crime', in: A Liebling, S Maruna, and L McAra (eds), *The Oxford Handbook of Criminology*, Sixth Edition (2017, Oxford University Press), 639–662.
Pettit, P, and Braithwaite, J, 'Not Just Deserts, Not Even in Sentencing' (1993) 4 *Current Issues in Criminal Justice* 222.
Phelps, M, 'The Paradox of Probation: Community Supervision in an Age of Mass Incarceration' (2013) 35 *Law & Policy* 51.
Phillips, C, and Bowling, B, 'Ethnicities, Racism, Crime, and Criminal Justice', in: A Liebling, S Maruna, and L McAra (eds), *The Oxford Handbook of Criminology*, Sixth Edition (2016, Oxford University Press), 190–212.
Phillips, J, Gelsthorpe, L, and Padfield, N, 'Non-Custodial Deaths: Missing, Ignored, or Unimportant?' (2017) *Criminology and Criminal Justice*, forthcoming.
Plutarch; Philip Stadter (ed), *Greek Lives: A Selection of Nine Greek Lives* (1998, Robin Waterfield (trans), Oxford University Press).
Pranis, K, 'Restorative Values', in: G Johnstone and D van Ness (eds), *Handbook of Restorative Justice* (2007, Willan), 59–74.
Pratt, J, 'Scandinavian Exceptionalism in an Era of Penal Excess, Part I: The Nature and Roots of Scandinavian Exceptionalism' (2008) 48 *British Journal of Criminology* 119.
Pratt, J, *Penal Populism* (2007, Routledge).
Pratt, J, 'Punishment and "The Civilizing Process"', in: J Simon and R Sparks (eds), *The SAGE Handbook of Punishment and Society* (2013, SAGE), 90–113.

Pratt, J, Brown, D, Brown, M, and Hallsworth, S (eds), *The New Punitiveness: Trends, Theories, Perspectives* (2005, Willan).
Prins, S, and Reich, A, 'Can We Avoid Reductionism in Risk Reduction?' (2018) 22 *Theoretical Criminology* 258.
Prison Reform Trust, *Bromley Briefings Prison Factfile: Autumn 2018* (2018, Prison Reform Trust).
Proctor, R, and Schiebinger, L, (eds), *Agnotology: The Making and Unmaking of Ignorance* (2008, Stanford University Press).
Raaijmakers, E, de Keijser, JW, Nieuwbeerta, P, and Dirkzwager, AJE, 'Changes in the Subjectively Experienced Severity of Detention: Exploring Individual Differences' (2017) 97 *The Prison Journal* 644.
Ramsay, P, 'Democratic Limits to Preventive Criminal Law', in: A Ashworth, L Zedner, and P Tolmin (eds), *Prevention and the Limits of the Criminal Law* (2013, Oxford University Press), 214–234.
Ramsay, P, *The Insecurity State: Vulnerable Autonomy and the Right to Security in Criminal Law* (2012, Oxford University Press).
Ramsay, P, 'Overcriminalization as Vulnerable Citizenship' (2010) 13 *New Criminal Law Review* 262.
Ramsay, P, 'Substantially Uncivilised ASBOs' [2010] *Criminal Law Review* 761.
Rancière, J, *Hatred of Democracy* (2006, Steve Corcoran (trans), Verso).
Rawls, J, *A Theory of Justice*, Revised Edition (1999, Oxford University Press).
Raynor, P, 'Is Probation Still Possible?' (2012) 41 *The Howard Journal of Crime and Justice* 173.
Raynor, P, and Vanstone, M, 'Towards a Correctional Service', in L Gelsthorpe and R Morgan (eds), *Handbook on Probation* (2007, Willan), 59–89.
Raz, J, *The Morality of Freedom* (1986, Oxford University Press).
Reiman, J, and Leighton, P, *The Rich Get Richer and the Poor Get Prison*, Eleventh Edition (2017, Routledge).
Reiner, R, 'Political Economy, Crime, and Criminal Justice', in Alison Liebling, Shadd Maruna, and Lesley McAra (eds), *The Oxford Handbook of Criminology*, Sixth Edition (2017, Oxford University Press), 116–137.
Renwick, C, *Bread for All: The Origins of the British Welfare State* (2017, Penguin).
Ristroph, A, 'Proportionality as a Principle of Limited Government' (2005) 55 *Duke Law Journal* 263.
Roach, K, *The 9/11 Effect: Comparative Counter-Terrorism* (2011, Cambridge University Press).
Roberts, C, Hudson, B, and Cullen, R, *The Supervision of Mentally Disordered Offenders: The Work of Probation Officers and their Relationship with Psychiatrists in England and Wales* (1995) 5 *Criminal Behaviour and Mental Health* 75.
Roberts, JV (ed), *Mitigation and Aggravation at Sentencing* (2011, Cambridge University Press).
Roberts, JV, 'Punishing, More or Less: Exploring Aggravation and Mitigation at Sentencing', in JV Roberts (ed), *Mitigation and Aggravation at Sentencing* (2011, Cambridge University Press), 1–20.
Roberts, JV, Stalans, L, Indermauer, D, and Hough, M, *Penal Populism and Public Opinion: Lessons from Five Countries* (2003, Oxford University Press).
Roberts, P, 'Criminal Law Theory and the Limits of Liberalism', in AP Simester, A du Bois-Pedain, and U Neumann (eds), *Liberal Criminal Theory: Essays for Andreas von Hirsch* (2014, Hart), 327–360.
Roberts, R, and Garside, R, 'Punishment before Justice? Understanding Penalty Notices for Disorder' (Crime and Society Foundation Briefing #1, March 2005).
Robinson, G, 'The Cinderella Complex: Punishment, Society, and Community Sanctions' (2016) 18 *Punishment & Society* 95.
Robinson, G, 'Late-Modern Rehabilitation: The Evolution of a Penal Strategy' (2008) 10 *Punishment and Society* 429.
Robinson, G, 'Power, Knowledge, and "What Works" in Probation' (2001) 40 *The Howard Journal of Crime and Justice* 235.
Robinson, G, 'Stand Down and Deliver: Pre-Sentence Reports, Quality and the New Culture of Speed' (2017) 64 *Probation Journal* 337.
Robinson, G, 'Three Narratives and a Funeral: Community Punishment in England and Wales', in G Robinson and F McNeill (eds), *Community Punishment: European Perspectives* (2016, Routledge), 30–50.

Robinson, G, and Shapland, J, 'Reducing Recidivism: A Task for Restorative Justice?' (2008) 48 *British Journal of Criminology* 337.
Robinson, G, and Ugwudike, P, 'Investing in "Toughness": Probation, Enforcement, and Legitimacy' (2012) 51 *The Howard Journal of Criminal Justice* 300.
Robinson, P, *Intuitions of Justice and the Utility of Desert* (2013, Oxford University Press).
Roche, D, 'Retribution and Restorative Justice', in: G Johnstone and D van Ness (eds), *Handbook of Restorative Justice* (2007, Willan), 75–90.
Rotman, E, *Beyond Punishment: A New View of the Rehabilitation of Criminal Offenders* (1990, Greenwood Press).
Rotman, E, 'Do Criminals Offenders Have a Constitutional Right to Rehabilitation?' (1987) 77(4) *Journal of Criminal Law and Criminology* 1023.
Rousseau, J-J, *The Social Contract* (1994, Christopher Betts (trans), Oxford University Press).
Ruggiero, V, 'An Abolitionist View of Restorative Justice' (2011) 39 *International Journal of Law, Crime and Justice* 100.
Ruggiero, V, 'Crime and Punishment in Classical and Libertarian Utopias' (2013) 52 *Howard Journal of Crime and Justice* 414.
Ruggiero, V, *Penal Abolitionism* (2010, Oxford University Press).
Russell-Brown, K, 'Making Implicit Bias Explicit: Black Men and the Police', in A Davis (ed), *Policing the Black Man: Arrest, Prosecution, and Imprisonment* (2017, Pantheon Books), 135–160.
Ryan, M, and Ward, T, 'Prison Abolitionism in the UK: They Dare Not Speak its Name?' (2015) 41 *Social Justice* 107.
Ryberg, J, 'Punishment and the Measurement of Severity', in J Ryberg and JA Corlett (eds), *Punishment and Ethics: New Perspectives* (2010, Palgrave Macmillan), 72–91.
Safranski, R, *Martin Heidegger: Between Good and Evil* (1998, Ewald Osers (trans), Harvard University Press).
Sanders, A, and Young, R, 'From Suspect to Trial', in M Maguire, R Morgan and R Reiner (eds), *The Oxford Handbook of Criminology*, Fifth Edition (2012, Oxford University Press), 838–865.
Sanders, A, Young, R, and Burton, M, *Criminal Justice*, Fourth Edition (2010, Oxford University Press).
Schabas, W, *The Abolition of the Death Penalty in International Law*, Third Edition (2002, Cambridge University Press).
Schauer, F, 'The Ubiquity of Prevention', in A Ashworth, L Zedner, and P Tomlin (eds), *Prevention and the Limits of Criminal Law* (2013, Oxford University Press), 10–22.
Schept, J, *Progressive Punishment: Job Loss, Jail Growth, and the Neoliberal Logic of Carceral Expansion* (2015, New York University Press).
Schiff, M, 'Gauging the Intensity of Criminal Sanctions: Developing the Criminal Punishment Severity Scale (CPSS)' (1997) 22 *Criminal Justice Review* 175.
Schiller, S, 'Book Review – *Doing Justice: The Choice of Punishments*' (1976) 67 *Journal of Criminal Law and Criminology* 356.
Schinkel, M, 'Punishment as Moral Communication: The Experience of Long-Term Prisoners' (2014) 16 *Punishment and Society* 578.
Schur, E, *Radical Non-Intervention: Rethinking the Delinquency Problem* (1973, Prentice-Hall).
Sen, A, *Development as Freedom* (1999, Oxford University Press).
Sen, A, *The Idea of Justice* (2009, Penguin).
Sexton, L, 'Penal Subjectivities: Developing a Theoretical Framework for Penal Consciousness' (2015) 17 *Punishment and Society* 114.
Shapland, J, 'Forgiveness and Restorative Justice: Is it Necessary? Is it Helpful?' (2016) 5 *Oxford Journal of Law & Religion* 94.
Shapland, J, Atkinson, A, Atkinson, H, Colledge, E, Dignan J, Howes, M, Johnstone, J, Robinson, G, and Sorsby, A, 'Situating Restorative Justice within Criminal Justice' (2006) 10 *Theoretical Criminology* 505.
Sharp, C, and Budd, T, *Minority Ethnic Groups and Crime: Findings from the Offending, Crime and Justice Survey*, Second Edition, Online Report 33/05 (2005, Home Office).
Sim, J, *Prisons and Punishment: Power and the Carceral State* (2009, SAGE).

Simester, AP, (ed), *Appraising Strict Liability* (2005, Oxford University Press).
Simester, AP, and von Hirsch, A, *Crimes, Harms, and Wrongs: On the Principles of Criminalisation* (2014, Hart).
Simon, J, 'Do These Prisons Make Me Look Fat? Moderating the US's Consumption of Punishment' (2010) 14 *Theoretical Criminology* 257.
Simon, J, *Governing through Crime: How the War on Crime Transformed American Democracy and Created a Culture of Fear* (2007, Oxford University Press).
Simpson, AWB, *Cannibalism and the Common Law* (1984, University of Chicago Press).
Simpson, AWB, *Human Rights and the End of Empire: Britain and the Genesis of the European Convention* (2001, Oxford University Press).
Singleton, N, Meltzer, H, and Gatward, R, with Coid, J, and Deasy, D, *Psychiatric Morbidity among Prisoners in England and Wales* (1998, Office for National Statistics).
Snacken, S, 'Punishment, Legitimacy, and the Role of the State: Reimagining More Moderate Penal Policies', in: S Farrall, B Goldson, I Loader, and A Dockley (eds), *Justice and Penal Reform: Re-Inventing the Penal Landscape* (2016, Routledge), 47–68.
Snacken, S, 'Punishment, Legitimate Policies and Values: Penal Moderation, Dignity, and Human Rights' (2015) 17 *Punishment & Society* 397.
Snacken, S, 'Resisting Punitiveness in Europe?' (2010) 14 *Theoretical Criminology* 273.
Social Exclusion Unit, *Reducing Reoffending by Ex-Prisoners* (2002, Social Exclusion Unit).
Soothill, K, and Francis, B, 'When Do Ex-Offenders Become Like Non-Offenders?' (2009) 48 *The Howard Journal of Crime and Justice* 373.
Stark, F, *Culpable Carelessness: Recklessness and Negligence in the Criminal Law* (2016, Cambridge University Press).
Steiker, C, 'Proportionality as a Limit on Preventive Justice', in: A Ashworth, L Zedner, and P Tomlin, *Prevention and the Limits of the Criminal Law* (2013, Oxford University Press), 194–213.
Stephen, J, *A History of the Criminal Law of England*, Volume Two (1883, Macmillan).
Stevenson, K, and Harris, C, 'Breaking the Thrall of Ambiguity: Simplification (of the Criminal Law) as an Emerging Human Rights Imperative' (2010) 74 *Journal of Criminal Law* 516.
Stiglitz, J, *The Price of Inequality* (2012, Penguin).
Stjernø, S, *Solidarity in Europe: The History of an Idea* (2009, Cambridge University Press).
Sykes, GM, *The Society of Captives: A Study of a Maximum Security Prison* (1958, Princeton University Press).
Tadros, V, 'Fair Labelling and Social Solidarity', in: L Zedner and JV Roberts (eds), *Principles and Values in Criminal Law and Criminal Justice: Essays in Honour of Andrew Ashworth* (2012, Oxford University Press), 67–80.
Tadros, V, *The Ends of Harm: The Moral Foundations of Criminal Law* (2011, Oxford University Press).
Thomas, T, and Hebenton, B, 'Dilemmas and Consequences of Prior Criminal Record: A Criminological Perspective from England and Wales' (2013) 26 *Criminal Justice Studies* 228.
Thompson, EP, *Whigs and Hunters: The Origins of the Black Act* (1976, Penguin).
Thorburn, M, 'Criminal Law as Public Law', in: RA Duff and Stuart Green (eds), *Philosophical Foundations of Criminal Law* (2011, Oxford University Press), 22–43.
Tifft, L, and Sullivan, D, *The Struggle to Be Human: Crime, Criminology, and Anarchism* (1980, Cienfuegos Press).
Tonry, M, 'Can Deserts Be Just in an Unjust World?', in AP Simester, Antje du Bois-Pedain, and Ulfrid Neumann (eds), *Liberal Criminal Theory: Essays for Andreas von Hirsch* (2014, Hart), 141–165.
Tonry, M, 'Can Twenty-First Century Punishment Policies Be Justified in Practice?' in Michael Tonry (ed), *Retributivism has a Past: Has it a Future?* (2011, Oxford University Press), 3–29.
Tonry, M, *Malign Neglect: Race, Crime, and Punishment in America* (1995, Oxford University Press).
Tonry, M, 'Proportionality, Parsimony, and the Interchangeability of Punishments', in: RA Duff, S Marshall, R Dobash, and R Dobash (eds), *Penal Theory and Practice: Tradition and Innovation in Criminal Justice* (1994, Manchester University Press), 59–83.
Tonry, M, and Lynch, M, 'Intermediate Sanctions' (1996) 20 *Crime and Justice* 99.

Tremblay, RE, and Nagin, DS, 'The Developmental Origins of Aggression in Humans', in: R Tremblay, W Hartup, and J Archer (eds), *Developmental Origins of Aggression* (2005, The Guildford Press), 83–106.

Trotter, C, 'Reducing Recidivism through Probation Supervision: What We Know and Don't Know from Four Decades of Research' (2013) 77 *Federal Probation* 43.

Tulkens, F, 'The Paradoxical Relationship between Criminal Law and Human Rights' (2011) 9 *Journal of International Criminal Justice* 577.

Ugelvik, T, and Dullum, J (eds), *Penal Exceptionalism? Nordic Penal Policy and Practice* (2012, Routledge).

United Nations, *Basic Principles for the Use of Restorative Justice Programmes in Criminal Matters*, UN Doc E/2000/INF/2/Add.2.

van Dijk, G, 'The Ordered Apology' (2017) 37 *Oxford Journal of Legal Studies* 562.

van Ginneken, E, and Hayes, D, '"Just" Punishment? Offenders' Views on the Meaning and Severity of Punishment' (2017) 17 *Criminology and Criminal Justice* 62.

van Zyl Smit, D, *Handbook of Basic Principles and Promising Practices on Alternatives to Imprisonment* (2007, UN Office on Drugs and Crime).

van Zyl Smit, D, 'Punishment and Human Rights', in: J Simon and R Sparks (eds), *The SAGE Handbook of Punishment and Society* (2013, SAGE), 395–415.

van Zyl Smit, D, 'Outlawing Irreducible Life Sentences: Europe on the Brink?' (2010) 23 *Federal Sentencing Reporter* 39.

van Zyl Smit, D, 'Prison Law', in MD Dubber and T Hörnle (eds), *The Oxford Handbook of Criminal Law* (2014, Oxford University Press), 988–1011.

van Zyl Smit, D, and Appleton, C, *Life Imprisonment: A Global Rights Analysis* (2019, Harvard University Press).

van Zyl Smit, D, and Appleton, C, (eds), *Life Imprisonment and Human Rights* (2016, Hart).

van Zyl Smit, D, and Ashworth, A, 'Disproportionate Sentences as Human Rights Violations' (2004) 67 *Modern Law Review* 541.

van Zyl Smit, D, and Snacken, S, *Principles of European Prison Law and Policy: Penology and Human Rights* (2009, Oxford University Press).

Vanfraechem, I, and Bolívar, D, 'Restorative Justice and Victims of Crime', in: I Vanfraechem, D Bolívar, and I Aertsen (eds), *Victims and Restorative Justice* (2015, Routledge), 48–75.

Vanfraechem, I, Bolívar, D, and Aertsen, I (eds), *Victims and Restorative Justice* (2015, Routledge).

Vannucci, D, and Singer, R, *Come Hell or High Water: A Handbook on Collective Process Gone Awry* (2010, AK Press).

Varelius, J, 'Two Challenges for Dignity as an Expressive Norm' (2012) 6 *Criminal Law and Philosophy* 327.

Vaughan, B, 'Punishment and Conditional Citizenship' (2000) 2 *Punishment & Society* 23.

von Hirsch, A, 'Equality, "Anisonomy", and Justice: A Review of *Madness and the Criminal Law*' (1984) 82 *Michigan Law Review* 1093.

von Hirsch, A, *Censure and Sanctions* (1993, Clarendon Press).

von Hirsch, A, *Deserved Criminal Sentences* (2017, Hart).

von Hirsch, A, *Doing Justice: The Choice of Punishments* (1976, Hill and Wang).

von Hirsch, A, *Past or Future Crimes: Deservedness and Dangerousness in the Sentencing of Criminals* (1986, Manchester University Press).

von Hirsch, A, 'Proportionality and the Progressive Loss of Mitigation: Some Further Reflections', in JV Roberts and A von Hirsch, *Previous Convictions at Sentencing: Theoretical and Applied Perspectives* (2010, Hart), 1–16.

von Hirsch, A, and Ashworth, A, *Proportionate Sentencing: Exploring the Principles* (2005, Oxford University Press).

von Hirsch, A, and Jareborg, N, 'Gauging Criminal Harm: A Living Standard Analysis' (1991) 11 *Oxford Journal of Legal Studies* 1.

von Hirsch, A, and Roberts, JV, 'Legislating Sentencing Principles: The Provisions of the Criminal Justice Act 2003 Relating to Sentencing Purposes and the Role of Previous Convictions' [2004] *Criminal Law Review* 639.

von Hirsch, A, Roberts, JV, Bottoms, AE, Roach, K, and Schiff, M, (eds), *Restorative Justice and Criminal Justice: Competing or Reconcilable Paradigms?* (2003, Hart).
von Hirsch, A, and Wasik, M, 'Civil Disqualifications Attending Conviction: A Suggested Conceptual Framework' (1997) 56 *Cambridge Law Journal* 599.
Vonnegut, K, Jr, *Mother Night: A Novel* (1961, Random House).
Wacquant, L, 'Class, Race, and Hyperincarceration in Revanchist America' (2010) 139 *Daedelus* 74.
Wacquant, L, *Punishing the Poor: The Neoliberal Government of Social Insecurity* (2009, Duke University Press).
Walgrave, L, 'Imposing Restoration Instead of Inflicting Pain', in: A von Hirsch, AE Bottoms, K Roach, J Roberts, and M Schiff (eds), *Restorative Justice or Criminal Justice: Competing or Reconcilable Programmes?* (2003, Hart).
Walgrave, L, 'Integrating Criminal Justice and Restorative Justice', in: Gerry Johnstone and Daniel van Ness (eds), *Handbook of Restorative Justice* (2007, Willan), 559–579.
Walker, N, *Why Punish?* (1991, Oxford University Press).
Ward, T, 'Dignity and Human Rights in Correctional Practice' (2009) 1 *European Journal of Probation* 110.
Ward, T, and Fortune, C, 'The Good Lives Model: Aligning Risk Reduction with Promoting Offenders' Personal Goals' (2013) 5 *European Journal of Probation* 29.
Ward, T, Melser, J, and Yates, P, 'Reconstructing the Risk-Need-Responsivity Model: A Theoretical Elaboration and Evaluation' (2007) 12 *Aggression and Violent Behavior* 208.
Ward, T, Yates, P, and Willis, G, 'The Good Lives Model and the Risk Needs Responsivity Model: A Response to Andrews, Bonta and Wormith (2011)' (2012) 39 *Criminal Justice and Behavior* 94.
Western, B, *Punishment and Inequality in America* (2006, Russell Sage Foundation).
Wilson, M, *Rules without Rulers: The Possibilities and Limits of Anarchism* (2014, Zero Books).
Winter, S, 'What Makes Modernity Late?' (2005) 1 *International Journal of Law in Context* 61.
Wolfe, N, '*Mala in Se*: A Disappearing Distinction?' (1981) 19 *Criminology* 131.
Wolin, R, *The Politics of Being: The Political Thought of Martin Heidegger* (1990, Columbia University Press).
Wood, P, and Grasmick, H, 'Toward the Development of Punishment Equivalencies: Male and Female Inmates Rate the Severity of Alternative Sanctions Compared to Prison' (1999) 16 *Justice Quarterly* 19.
Wormald, P, *The Making of English Law: King Alfred to the Twelfth Century, volume 1: Legislation and its Limits* (1999, Blackwell).
Wright, D, *Inventing God's Law: How the Covenant Code of the Bible Used and Revised the Laws of Hammurabi* (2009, Oxford University Press).
Yonglin, J (trans), *The Great Ming Code: Da Ming Lü* (2005, University of Washington Press).
Young, J, *The Exclusive Society: Social Exclusion, Crime and Difference in Late Modernity* (1999, SAGE).
Young, J, *The Vertigo of Late Modernity* (2007, SAGE).
Zaibert, L, *Rethinking Punishment* (2016, Oxford University Press).
Zedner, L, 'Reparation and Retribution: Are They Reconcilable?' (1994) 57 *Modern Law Review* 228.
Zedner, L, 'Terrorizing Criminal Law' (2014) 8 *Criminal Law and Philosophy* 99.
Zehr, H, *Changing Lenses: A New Focus for Crime and Justice* (1990, Herald Press).

INDEX

Milton Keynes UK
Ingram Content Group UK Ltd.
UKHW022127230424
441539UK00004B/53